D0917373

The
United States Response
to
Turkish Nationalism
and
Reform
1914–1939

Published with assistance
from the Roger E. Joseph Memorial Fund
for greater understanding
of public affairs, a cause in which
Roger Joseph believed

The
United States Response
to
Turkish Nationalism
and
Reform
1914–1939

ROGER R. TRASK

The University of Minnesota Press
Minneapolis

Published in Great Britain and India by the Oxford University
Press, London and Bombay, and in Canada
by the Copp Clark Publishing Co. Limited, Toronto

Library of Congress Catalog Card Number: 74-153505
ISBN 0-8166-0613-7

Part of the fourth chapter, "America Faces Turkey," appeared in modified form as "The 'Terrible Turk' and Turkish-American Relations in
the Interwar Period" in *The Historian*, XXXIII
(November, 1970), 40–53. Part of the sixth
chapter appeared in modified form as "The
United States and Turkish Nationalism: Investments and Technical Aid During the Atatürk
Era" in *The Business History Review*, XXXVIII
(Spring, 1964), 58–77. Part of the seventh
chapter appeared in modified form as " 'Unnamed Christianity' in Turkey During the Atatürk Era" in *The Muslim World*, LV (January,
1965), 66–76 (Pt. I), 101–111 (Pt. II). The
map on page 17 has been reproduced from John
A. DeNovo's *American Interests and Policies in
the Middle East, 1900–1939* (Minneapolis:
University of Minnesota Press, 1963), p. 231;
© 1963 by the University of Minnesota. The papers of Joseph C. Grew and of the American
Board of Commissioners for Foreign Missions
have been quoted herein by permission of the
Harvard College Library.

For
John A. DeNovo

⚅ Preface

THIS study, as the title suggests, surveys the history of Turkish-American relations from the beginning of World War I to the beginning of World War II. It was conceived as a work in diplomatic history, in the broad sense. My concern here is not just formal diplomacy, although that is not ignored; I have paid attention to other important aspects of United States–Turkish relations — political, economic, social, cultural, philanthropic, and so on. The title suggests also the basic theme of the book: how the United States responded, during a period when the isolationist impulse was at its peak, to one nationalistic people's efforts at reform and modernization.

Simply stated, knowledge and understanding of past events are necessary as we face the problems of the present and plan for the future. This truism can be aptly applied to the history of Turkish-American relations between 1914 and 1939. I cannot argue that the problems of the relationship between the two countries in that period were critical from the point of view of the United States government, but they were important within the context of total American foreign policy. The United States *was* concerned about Turkey in the interwar era, even though some scholars and other writers often bill the period as one of isolation. Knowledge of what happened during these years is important background for an understanding of Turkish-American relations after World War II.

Except for the still useful work by Leland J. Gordon published in 1932, historians generally ignored the history of Turk-

Preface

ish-American relations until the events of World War II and the Cold War thrust republican Turkey into a critical Middle Eastern and international position. Now we have, in addition to some chapters in John A. DeNovo's comprehensive volume on the United States and the Middle East, 1900–1939, specialized studies by Robert Daniel, Laurence Evans, James A. Field, James B. Gidney, Joseph L. Grabill, and Harry N. Howard. Several other historians are laboring on additional topics, and their work will appear over the next several years. There is no book which covers in detail the history of Turkish-American relations in the interwar period after 1923. Although I have dealt in the initial chapters with the period up to 1924, I believe that the most original contribution of this book is the detailed treatment of events as they occurred after 1923.

I wish to thank Macalester College for two grants from its Faculty Research Fund in support of my work on this book. A grant from the Penrose Fund of the American Philosophical Society made possible some of the research. Mrs. Willadene Stickel typed the manuscript with a critical eye and great expertise. The University of Minnesota Press did perceptive and efficient editorial work. John A. DeNovo of the University of Wisconsin has advised and assisted me constantly since this project was conceived more than a dozen years ago. The dedication which appears elsewhere in this book suggests the depth of my gratitude to him. Finally, I wish to thank my wife, Dorothy, for her support and encouragement.

Roger R. Trask

Saint Paul, Minnesota
August 1, 1970

☸ Table of Contents

The Highlights of Turkish-American Relations
    to 1914 3

World War I to Lausanne, 1914–1923 16

Rejection of the Lausanne Treaty and Resumption
    of Diplomatic Relations, 1923–1927 37

America Faces Turkey: The Framework of Turkish-
    American Relations in the Interwar Period 65

The Economic Dimension: Commercial Relations
    Between the Wars 94

The Economic Dimension: Investments and
    Technical Aid 127

"Unnamed Christianity": The American Educational
    Effort 147

The Expansion of Friendship: Social, Cultural,
    and Philanthropic Activities 170

The Status of Citizens: Problems and Solutions 188

The United States, Turkey, and International
    Politics, 1923–1939 217

Conclusions 240

Bibliography 249

Index 271

The
United States Response
to
Turkish Nationalism
and
Reform
1914–1939

🏵 The Highlights of Turkish-American Relations to 1914

AN APPRECIATION of Turkish-American relations in the twentieth century requires understanding of interaction extending back to the late eighteenth century. Associations between the two nations before World War I were at least formally cordial, although neither could look to the other as a close friend or as an important diplomatic or commercial partner.[1]

Early Relations and the Treaty of 1830

During the American colonial period traders were the first Americans attracted to the Ottoman Empire, particularly to the port of Izmir.[2] United States newspapers advertised figs and other Turkish goods as early as the

---

[1] For useful surveys of early Turkish-American relations, see James A. Field, Jr., *America and the Mediterranean World, 1776–1882* (Princeton, 1969); Leland James Gordon, *American Relations with Turkey, 1830–1930: An Economic Interpretation* (Philadelphia, 1932), *passim*; John A. DeNovo, *American Interests and Policies in the Middle East, 1900–1939* (Minneapolis, 1963), pp. 3–26; Sydney N. Fisher, "Two Centuries of American Interest in Turkey," in David H. Pinkney and Theodore Ropp, eds., *A Festschrift for Frederick B. Artz* (Durham, N.C., 1964), pp. 113–138; L. Lucile Morse, "Relations Between the United States and the Ottoman Empire," (Ph.D. thesis, Clark University, 1924), pp. 1–263; and Walter L. Wright, Jr., "American Relations with Turkey to 1831," (Ph.D. thesis, Princeton University, 1928).

[2] Nasim Sousa, *The Capitulatory Régime of Turkey: Its History, Origin, and Nature* (Baltimore, 1933), p. 128; David H. Finnie, *Pioneers East: The Early American Experience in the Middle East* (Cambridge, Mass., 1967), pp. 24–25. Izmir was known as Smyrna before 1930. In that year the Grand National Assembly passed a law requiring the use of old Turkish names for many communities long known in the West by other names. Constantinople became Istanbul, Angora became Ankara. A 1934 law required Turks to take surnames. Mustapha Kemal Pasha became Kemal Atatürk, Prime Minister Ismet Pasha became Ismet Inönü. The modern surnames

3

1780s. Philadelphia interests established the mercantile firm of Woodmas and Offley as the first American commercial house at Izmir in 1811; three others opened by 1827. David Offley, a partner in Woodmas and Offley, succeeded in securing informal trade privileges with the Ottoman government soon after his arrival in 1811, but until the establishment of formal treaty arrangements in 1830 American traders normally used the facilities of the English Levant Company. As trade increased in volume and importance, the Department of State recognized the need for a commercial treaty and for consular representation in Turkey. Although the United States designated a Philadelphia merchant, William Stewart, as consul in Izmir as early as 1802, the Ottoman government did not recognize him, and no American vessels called at Izmir while he was there in 1803. Offley received an appointment from the United States government in 1823 as a "consular commercial agent," but without formal treaty relations his authority was limited.[3]

Following the traders to the Ottoman Empire were American missionaries. The Reverends Pliny Fisk and Levi Parsons, sent by the American Board of Commissioners for Foreign Missions, an agency of the Congregational Church and other denominations, arrived at Izmir on January 5, 1820. These two religious pioneers launched an effort soon to become an important American tie with Turkey and a frequent source of diplomatic friction.[4] The American Board directed Fisk and Parsons to "survey with earnest attention the various tribes and classes . . ." and to ask themselves constantly, "What good can be done?" and "By what means?" After this modest start the mission board gradually expanded its force and established stations in various parts of the Ottoman Empire.[5]

will be used for those individuals who span the entire chronological period of this study, except where the old names appear in direct quotation. The old names will be used for those persons who appear only before 1934, the modern names for those who appear only after 1934.

[3] Gordon, *American Relations with Turkey*, p. 41; Finnie, *Pioneers East*, pp. 25–30; Lewis Heck, "Sidelights on Past Relations Between the United States and Turkey," *American Foreign Service Journal*, XVII (February, 1940), 63.

[4] William E. Strong, *The Story of the American Board* (Boston, 1910), pp. 80–82; Sousa, *Capitulatory Régime*, p. 140; Edward Mead Earle, "American Missions in the Near East," *Foreign Affairs*, VII (April, 1929), 400; Albert Howe Lybyer, "America's Missionary Record in Turkey," *Current History*, XIX (February, 1924), 802. See Fred Field Goodsell, *You Shall Be My Witnesses* (Boston, 1959), pp. 5–12, for a brief history of the founding and early years of the American Board of Commissioners for Foreign Missions. Finnie, in *Pioneers East*, discusses mission activities up to 1850. For information about Parsons and Fisk, see Finnie, pp. 149–152.

[5] Quoted in James L. Barton, *Daybreak in Turkey* (Boston, 1908), pp. 119–120.

4

The developing interests and problems of missionaries and traders in the Empire prompted the United States government to initiate efforts to formalize the relations of the two countries. In 1800 Commodore William Bainbridge of the *George Washington* delivered the annual American tribute to the Barbary state of Algeria. The Dey of Algiers, using a threat of force, persuaded Bainbridge to sail his vessel to Constantinople to deliver the Algerian tribute to the Ottoman government. Bainbridge's vessel, the first from a country unknown to most Turks, created great interest when it arrived in Constantinople harbor. When a Turkish official suggested to Bainbridge that the United States and Turkey establish formal relations, Bainbridge informed him that in 1799 President John Adams had appointed a commission headed by William L. Smith, Minister to Portugal, to negotiate a Turkish-American treaty of amity and commerce. However, Smith never received official instructions from the State Department and his proposed mission did not materialize. Later efforts to arrange a treaty in 1820, 1823, and 1828 also failed.[6]

In 1829, President Andrew Jackson designated Charles Rhind, David Offley, and Commodore James Biddle to try again. Their efforts culminated successfully on May 7, 1830, when Rhind signed a treaty destined to provide the framework of Turkish-American relations for a century. The nine-article agreement emphasized most-favored-nation treatment for commerce; American traders would benefit from all privileges extended by Turkey to other countries. The treaty also provided for mutual recognition of consular representatives.[7] The heart of the new treaty, Article IV, extended to the United States the privileges known as the "capitu-

See also Sousa, *Capitulatory Régime*, pp. 140–141; Strong, *Story of the American Board*, pp. 80–107; and Field, *America and the Mediterranean World*, pp. 92–98.

[6] Gordon, *American Relations with Turkey*, pp. 7–10; G. Bie Ravndal, *Turkey: A Commercial and Industrial Handbook* (Washington, 1926), p. 228; Finnie, *Pioneers East*, pp. 46–57; Wright, "American Relations with Turkey to 1831," pp. 10–43; Field, *America and the Mediterranean World*, pp. 113–120, 133–148.

[7] Sousa, *Capitulatory Régime*, pp. 130–133; Gordon, *American Relations with Turkey*, pp. 10–12; Ravndal, *Turkey: A Commercial and Industrial Handbook*, p. 228; Finnie, *Pioneers East*, pp. 57–63. The proclaimed text of the treaty, several other versions and translations, and extensive commentary on the negotiations and other matters can be found in Hunter Miller, ed., *Treaties and Other International Acts of the United States of America* (6 vols., Washington, 1931–1942), III, 541–598. The treaty text also is in J. C. Hurewitz, ed., *Diplomacy in the Near and Middle East: A Documentary Record, 1535–1956* (2 vols., Princeton, 1956), I, 102–105. Rhind was a New York merchant and Biddle was commander-in-chief of the United States Mediterranean Squadron. Most of Wright, "American Relations with Turkey to 1831," deals in detail with the negotiation and ratification of this treaty.

lations." Described by one writer as "a code of legal reconciliation founded upon the immiscibility of Christianity and Islam," the capitulatory system began in 1535 with a treaty between Francis I of France and Sultan Suleiman. The system eventually developed into comprehensive personal, economic, and judicial privileges which practically eliminated Ottoman control over foreigners within the Empire. France, Austria, England, Holland, Sweden, Denmark, Prussia, Bavaria, Spain, Russia, and parts of Italy had secured these rights before the United States, and several other countries joined the roster later. Nationals of countries having capitulations not only enjoyed freedom of residence, travel, and religion, and exemption from all taxes except those pertaining to commerce, but also virtual freedom of control by Ottoman courts.[8]

Article IV restrained Ottoman judicial bodies from considering cases between Turkish and American citizens without the presence of a dragoman, a Turkish interpreter. Local authorities were enjoined from arresting and trying American citizens even if a crime had obviously been committed. Arrest was the exclusive privilege of United States diplomatic and consular officials. A long and unresolved dispute beginning in the late 1860s ensued over this part of the treaty because of differences between the two nations over translation of the official Turkish text. The Turks refused to admit that American citizens were immune from arrest by local officials or that they were to be tried by their own diplomatic representatives.[9]

There was a curious secret article in the 1830 treaty, added by the American negotiators in an effort to compensate the Sultan for the concessions he had agreed to make to the United States. The secret provision stated that, whenever the Ottoman government wished to contract for the

---

[8] Lucius E. Thayer, "The Capitulations of the Ottoman Empire and the Question of Their Abrogation as It Affects the United States," *American Journal of International Law*, XVII (April, 1923), 207–217; James B. Angell, "The Turkish Capitulations," *American Historical Review*, VI (January, 1901), 254–259; Sousa, *Capitulatory Régime*, pp. 53–66. See also G. Bie Ravndal (Consul General, Istanbul) to William Jennings Bryan, June 22, 1915, with report, "Origin of the Capitulations and of the Consular Institution and Incidentally a Historical Sketch of the Early Commerce of the Countries Around the Mediterranean," in file 711.673/65, Department of State Archives (Record Group 59, National Archives, Washington). State Department records hereafter cited as DS followed by file number.

[9] Miller, *Treaties and Other International Acts*, III, 598; John Bassett Moore, *A Digest of International Law* (8 vols., Washington, 1906), II, 662–714; Sousa, *Capitulatory Régime*, pp. 131–132; Thayer, "Capitulations of the Ottoman Empire," pp. 218–220; Oscar S. Straus, *Under Four Administrations: From Cleveland to Taft* (Boston & New York, 1922), pp. 87–89.

6

construction of naval vessels in the United States, Turk officials could consult with the United States minister in Constantinople regarding the terms of the contract and other details of the sale, including the stipulation that the price of such vessels would be no higher than that paid by the United States government. Technically, the article did not guarantee the construction and sale of naval vessels for the Turks, but rather was only a promise that the minister resident in Constantinople would discuss the "manner of making a contract." President Jackson submitted the secret article to the Senate along with the full treaty in December, 1830; when the Senate approved the treaty on February 1, 1831, by a vote of forty-two to one, it rejected the provision because of objections to its secrecy and substance. This was one of the rare occasions when a President has asked the Senate to approve secret arrangements with a foreign country.[10]

Turkish disappointment on this matter was somewhat alleviated by the private activities of Henry Eckford, an accomplished naval architect and shipbuilder. With assistance from the United States government, Eckford arrived in Constantinople in August, 1831, aboard his corvette *United States*, which he had designed and built in New York. After successfully negotiating the sale of the vessel to the Ottoman government for $150,000, Eckford took over direction of the Turkish naval shipyard and supervised the construction of other craft for the Ottoman navy. After Eckford's death in Constantinople late in 1832, his assistant, Foster Rhodes of New York, succeeded to his position and remained in Turkey until 1839. During this period he built several more ships for the Turks and supplied them with an impressive and modern naval force.[11]

The Commercial Treaty of 1862

Even though its interpretation and application were subject to considerable dispute, the treaty of 1830 was the only durable basis for Turkish-American relations for almost a century. In 1862 a supplementary treaty of amity and commerce continued most-favored-nation treatment and Turkish import duties for United States goods at 8 per cent ad valorem, the level which had prevailed since 1830. The treaty also sanctioned an

---

[10] Miller, *Treaties and Other International Acts*, III, 570–581; Field, *America and the Mediterranean World*, pp. 150–151.

[11] Finnie, *Pioneers East*, pp. 63–81; Merle E. Curti and Kendall Birr, *Prelude to Point Four: American Technical Missions Overseas, 1838–1938* (Madison, Wis., 1954), pp. 22–24; Field, *America and the Mediterranean World*, pp. 152–153, 166–167, 169–171.

annual reduction in Turkish export duties on American purchases from the existing 8 per cent to 1 per cent ad valorem. Other clauses in the treaty included reduction in the land transit duty within the Empire, the establishment of a joint tariff commission to develop a schedule of values as a basis for the ad valorem duties, and a privilege granted to the signatories to propose tariff revisions to take effect at the end of each seven-year period. In 1874 and 1883, in an effort to increase government revenues, the Turks proposed to raise import duties to 20 per cent ad valorem. The United States agreed to the earlier proposal, but it was not confirmed because several European countries to which the new rates were to apply rejected them. In 1883 the Turks considered applying a 20 per cent rate to United States products but not to those of European nations protected against such increases by existing treaties. The United States government rejected this discriminatory plan. The Ottoman government, using its option to terminate the 1862 agreement at the end of twenty-one years, declared that it was no longer valid. This left the 1830 pact as the formal foundation for Turkish-American trade.[12]

Turkey and the Civil War

An indication of benevolent Turkish attitudes toward the United States after three decades of formal relations came during the Civil War, when the Ottoman government exhibited sincere sympathy for the Union cause. After an initial audience with the Sultan following his appointment as Minister to Turkey in 1861, Edward Joy Morris reported to Secretary of State William E. Seward:

. . . [The Sultan] expressed his sympathy with the government of the United States for the troubles in which it is involved, and the hope that the war would soon terminate with the maintenance of the American Union in all its original power and integrity, and with the restoration of peace and concord among the American people.

I am happy in thus being able to report to you that the United States has a true and loyal friend in the sovereign of this great empire.

In April, 1862, the Turkish Grand Vizier gave tangible support to the

[12] *Papers Relating to the Foreign Relations of the United States* [1876] (Washington, 1876), pp. 591–593; *Papers Relating to the Foreign Relations of the United States* [1883] (Washington, 1884), pp. 836–837, 841–842; Moore, *Digest of International Law*, V, 795–801; Gordon, *American Relations with Turkey*, pp. 45, 162–164; Thayer, "Capitulations of the Ottoman Empire," p. 221; Sousa, *Capitulatory Régime*, pp. 134–135.

Union position by issuing a decree interdicting entrance into Ottoman waters and ports of privateers operating against United States shipping. In 1865, in separate despatches, Minister Morris commented on the joyful excitement created in Turkey by General Ulysses S. Grant's victories at Petersburg and Richmond and the sadness following President Abraham Lincoln's assassination. Morris informed Seward that, "lest there should be some apprehension relative to the qualifications of President Johnson to high office," he had published a biographical sketch of the new chief executive in Constantinople newspapers.[13]

Expansion of Missionary and Trade Activities to 1914

The tempo of Turco-American relations, based on commercial relations and missionary work, increased throughout the nineteenth and early twentieth centuries. Trade between the two countries never reached high levels before 1914 but, as the table on page 10 indicates, the total value of exchanged goods increased by more than forty times between 1830 and 1914. The tariff policies of both nations and the reliance of United States commercial interests on English carriers until the start of the twentieth century discouraged any large increase in the exchange of goods. American businessmen did not see a need to organize the American Chamber of Commerce for Turkey until 1911. The most important United States exports to Turkey in the latter part of the nineteenth century were cotton manufactures, mineral oils, distilled spirits, and iron and steel manufactures. Wool, fruits and nuts, licorice root, rugs and carpets, opium, and hides and skins were the most desired Turkish products imported by Americans.[14]

The work of American missionaries was the more important of the two major activities before World War I. By 1914 the American Board of Commissioners for Foreign Missions had 174 missionaries in what later

[13] Morris to Seward, *Papers Relating to Foreign Affairs* [1862] (Washington, 1862), p. 787 (source of the first quotation); Morris to Seward, May 6, 1862, *ibid.*, p. 788; Morris to Seward, April 19, 1865, *Papers Relating to Foreign Affairs* [1865] (Washington, 1866), p. 284; Morris to Seward, May 1, 1865, *ibid.*, p. 288 (source of the second quotation).

[14] Gordon, *American Relations with Turkey*, pp. 49, 51, 119–127, 155–157, 161–167, 181–187. The group later was renamed the American Chamber of Commerce for the Levant. American exports dropped to a low point in 1890 because the openings of Russian and Rumanian oil wells cut the demand for United States mineral oils. Also, the establishment of an English shipping monopoly in the Levant raised prices to a level which closed Ottoman markets to many American goods. See *ibid.*, p. 48.

Turkish-American Trade, 1831–1914

Year	United States Exports to Turkey	Turkish Exports to the United States	Total Trade Value
1831	$ 38,503	$ 521,598	$ 560,101
1840	119,745	563,476	683,221
1850	204,397	801,023	1,005,420
1860	783,081	1,379,860	2,162,941
1870	2,565,289	2,196,524	4,761,813
1880	1,607,229	3,528,917	5,136,146
1890	44,894	3,863,657	3,908,551
1900	567,012	7,754,237	8,321,249
1910	2,340,160	16,353,901	18,694,061
1914	3,328,519	20,843,077	24,171,596

SOURCE: Gordon, *American Relations with Turkey*, pp. 46–47, 60.

became the territory of the Turkish Republic. The Board maintained 17 principal mission stations and 9 hospitals, and either operated directly or supervised 426 schools with twenty-five thousand pupils.[15] During the nineteenth century the missionaries worked almost exclusively with Christian minorities, mainly Armenians. Their effort was not designed to win converts among Muslims, a practice forbidden by Ottoman law, but rather to develop the Christian churches in the Empire. Although the American Board was the most active Christian group in the Ottoman Empire, other foreign and United States missionaries entered the field, most of them in Istanbul and Asia Minor. The division in 1870 of the Near East mission field between the American Board and the Presbyterian Board of Missions left the former the only important American group in what is now the Turkish Republic.[16]

American Board missionaries in Turkey emphasized educational work. They felt this was the best method of achieving their objectives in view of Turkish hostility toward direct proselytizing. Robert College, the most important American educational enterprise in Turkey, was founded in 1863 by a former missionary, Cyrus Hamlin, under the auspices of Christopher R. Robert, a rich New York merchant who had business interests in Tur-

[15] Heck, "Sidelights on Past Relations Between the United States and Turkey," p. 110.
[16] *The One Hundred and Twentieth Annual Report of the American Board of Commissioners for Foreign Missions* [1930], (Boston, n.d.), pp. 163–164; Barton, *Daybreak in Turkey*, pp. 144–146; Kenneth Scott Latourette, *A History of the Expansion of Christianity* (7 vols., New York & London, 1937–1945), VI, 49, 52–53; Samuel S. Cox, *Diversions of a Diplomat in Turkey* (New York, 1887), pp. 295–296.

10

key. Although it never had formal ties with the church, Robert College catered to Christian minorities in Turkey. Istanbul Woman's College, which severed its connections with the American Board in 1908, developed from a mission school for girls.[17]

Not until the reign of Sultan Abdul Hamid II (1876–1909) did American missionaries encounter really serious opposition, and then mainly because of their identification with the Armenians. The first genuine crisis in Turkish-American relations occurred from 1894 to 1896 when the Sultan's forces brutally repressed the Armenian revolutionary movement. "From American missionaries and mission schools," one writer has pointed out, "Armenians learned anew to cherish their language and historical traditions; became acquainted with western ideals of political, social, and economic progress; acquired more active discontent with their lot and developed an acute sense of superiority to their Moslem peasant neighbors." [18] In the United States the Armenian crisis provoked a public outcry. A New York lawyer, Everett D. Wheeler, speaking before the American Board at Toledo in October, 1896, suggested a radical demonstration by the American government: "In the position in which Turkey has placed us, is there any course consistent with honor or duty but to support our demands by an adequate force? The American government should send a powerful fleet to the Mediterranean, accompanied by a sufficient number of regular troops, and should demand at the cannon's mouth what has been refused to milder requests. In no other way can either redress or security be obtained. Unless we do this we expose our citizens to further

[17] Field, *America and the Mediterranean World*, pp. 262–301, 345–359; Gordon, *American Relations with Turkey*, pp. 225–226; Latourette, *A History of the Expansion of Christianity*, VI, 51; Earle, "American Missions in the Near East," p. 402; Goodsell, *You Shall Be My Witnesses*, pp. 54–55; Fred Field Goodsell, *They Lived Their Faith: An Almanac of Faith, Hope and Love* (Boston, 1961), pp. 322–323; and Merle E. Curti, *American Philanthropy Abroad: A History* (New Brunswick, N.J., 1963), pp. 148–154. For information on Istanbul Woman's College, see Mary Mills Patrick, *A Bosporus Adventure: Istanbul (Constantinople) Woman's College, 1871–1924* (Stanford, Calif., & London, 1934), pp. 29–31.

[18] The quotation is from Earle, "American Missions in the Near East," pp. 403–404; see also Gordon, *American Relations with Turkey*, pp. 23–26. For a detailed treatment of the Armenian problem and United States involvement in it, see Rosaline de Gregorio Edwards, "Relations Between the United States and Turkey, 1893–1897" (Ph.D. thesis, Fordham University, 1952), *passim*. See also Curti, *American Philanthropy Abroad*, pp. 119–133; W. M. Ramsay, *Impressions of Turkey During Twelve Years' Wanderings* (New York, 1897), pp. 220–239; and Leon Arpee, *A History of Armenian Christianity from the Beginning to Our Own Time* (New York, 1946), pp. 274–278, 293–299.

11

outrages and their property to destruction." [19] Cooler heads prevailed in the State Department; the United States did not intervene directly, although Congress twice directed the President to submit information on the Armenian struggle. The Turkish government in 1901 met American Board demands for an indemnity for damages suffered during the Armenian uprising. An important by-product of these disturbances was the immigration of a large number of Armenians to the United States, probably more than sixty thousand by 1914.[20] Propaganda related to the events of 1894–1896 and the presence eventually of an Armenian group in the United States helped mold the "Terrible Turk" stereotype and a pro-Armenian attitude, both destined to be important forces affecting Turkish-American relations in the years after 1914.

Diplomatic and Consular Representation in Turkey

The steady expansion of United States diplomatic and consular representation in Turkey during the nineteenth and early twentieth centuries illustrated the growing importance of that country to the United States. Commodore David D. Porter was the first American diplomat to serve in Turkey on the basis of the 1830 treaty. Porter received his commission as chargé d'affaires in Istanbul on April 15, 1831, was promoted to the rank of minister in March, 1839, and remained in Turkey until his death in 1843.[21] In 1906 the American legation in Istanbul became an embassy, thirteen years after Congress authorized that rank for United States diplomatic establishments. The elevation of the Istanbul mission facilitated the transaction of business since its head then had easier direct access to the Sultan. John G. A. Leishman was the first United States ambassador under the new arrangement.[22]

[19] Everett D. Wheeler, *The Duty of the United States of America to American Citizens in Turkey* (New York, Chicago, & Toronto, 1896), pp. 20–21.
[20] Strong, *Story of the American Board*, pp. 392–398, discusses the Armenian massacres and Board problems. See also Gordon, *American Relations with Turkey*, pp. 24–27; Straus, *Under Four Administrations*, pp. 141–142; Ralph E. Cook, "The United States and the Armenian Question, 1884–1924" (Ph.D. thesis, Fletcher School of Law and Diplomacy, 1957); and DeNovo, *American Interests and Policies*, pp. 42–43.
[21] David Dixon Porter, *Memoir of Commodore David Porter of the United States Navy* (Albany, N.Y., 1875), pp. 394–399, 413, 421; Finnie, *Pioneers East*, pp. 82–98. See Gordon, *American Relations with Turkey*, pp. 369–370, for a list of top United States diplomats in Turkey from 1830 to 1930.
[22] Gordon, *American Relations with Turkey*, p. 57; Alfred L. P. Dennis, *Adventures in American Diplomacy, 1896–1906* (New York, 1928), p. 465; Americus,

By 1893 American consular officials in the Ottoman Empire totaled thirty-four, including eleven in the territory of present-day Turkey. In 1914 there were forty-eight, of whom six were at Istanbul, two at Harput, two at Mersin, one at Sivas, four at Izmir, three at Trebizond, and one at Samsun. The consuls' main task was to care for missionary and commercial interests. The Ottoman government appointed a consul in the United States in 1856 but waited until 1867 to send Blacque Bey as the first Turkish envoy extraordinary and minister plenipotentiary. By 1914 the Ottoman government had consular offices in San Francisco, Chicago, Boston, New York, and Manila in the Philippine Islands.[23]

The Eastern Question, the Young Turks, and the Chester Concession

A significant aspect of the Turkish policy of the United States before World War I was abstention from involvement in Turkish domestic politics and the confused "Eastern Question," the problem of the future of the Ottoman Empire. The Monroe Doctrine, a cornerstone of American foreign policy, following the concept of the "two spheres," not only discouraged European intervention in the Western Hemisphere but also held that the United States would not meddle in European political affairs. While European nations alternately plotted or delayed the demise of the "sick man of Europe," the United States generally remained aloof.

The year of the "Young Turk" revolution, 1908, marked a notable turning point in the history of the Eastern Question. Weary of both the despotism of Sultan Abdul Hamid II and extensive foreign control and intervention, the Young Turk leaders of the revolutionary Committee of Union and Progress (CUP) forced the Sultan to make effective a constitution formulated in 1876 and to call a parliamentary election. After successfully withstanding a counterrevolution in April, 1909, the Young Turks deposed Abdul Hamid and proclaimed Mehmed V as his successor. Until 1918 the CUP controlled the government of the Ottoman Empire. The Eastern Question boiled over during this period, confronting the CUP with a series of disasters — the Austrian annexation of Bosnia and Herze-

"Some Phases of the Issues Between the United States and Turkey," *North American Review*, CLXXXLI (May, 1906), 690–691; Straus, *Under Four Administrations*, pp. 135–136.

[23] *Register of the Department of State Corrected to July 1, 1893* (Washington, 1893), p. 45; *Register of the Department of State, November 18, 1914* (Washington, 1914), pp. 51–52, 192; Heck, "Sidelights on Past Relations Between the United States and Turkey," p. 63; Sousa, *Capitulatory Régime*, p. 130, n. 10.

govina in 1908, a war with Italy in 1911–1912, the Balkan Wars of 1912–1913, and finally, World War I.[24]

The only pre–World War I deviation of the United States from its traditional policy in the Ottoman Empire occurred between 1909 and 1911 when President William Howard Taft and Secretary of State Philander C. Knox, advocates of "dollar diplomacy," actively supported a group of Americans interested in railroad and mineral concessions. Admiral Colby M. Chester was attracted to economic opportunities in Turkey in 1900 when, as captain of the U.S.S. *Kentucky,* he went there to demand compensation for American claims arising from the Armenian massacres of 1894–1896. In 1909 Admiral Chester and several others organized the Ottoman-American Development Company. During the next two years the company tried repeatedly to get its projects approved by the Turkish government and parliament, but domestic red tape and the opposition of influential German interests delayed the parliament's final decision. By late 1911, when some of the company's backers withdrew their investments, the possibility of securing the Chester concession seemed remote. The Chester group's collapse proved extremely embarrassing to the State Department which, through Ambassador Oscar S. Straus and other representatives in Turkey, had strongly backed the concession hunters. The result was a return to the traditional policy of political noninvolvement in the Ottoman Empire. Efforts of another Chester company in 1912 and 1913 to get State Department support proved futile and the proposed Turkish project remained dormant until after World War I.[25] The protection of trade and missionary enterprises once again became the main concern of American diplomats in Turkey.

[24] For information on the Eastern Question and the Young Turk movement, see J. A. R. Marriott, *The Eastern Question: An Historical Study in European Diplomacy* (Oxford, 4th ed., 1940); William Miller, *The Ottoman Empire and Its Successors, 1801–1927, with an Appendix, 1927–1936* (Cambridge, 4th ed., 1936); M. S. Anderson, *The Eastern Question 1774–1923: A Study in International Relations* (London, Melbourne, Toronto, & New York, 1966); Ernest E. Ramsaur, Jr., *The Young Turks: Prelude to the Revolution of 1908* (Princeton, 1957); Altemur Kilic, *Turkey and the World* (Washington, 1959), pp. 15–26; and Bernard Lewis, *The Emergence of Modern Turkey* (London, 1961), pp. 171–233.
[25] John A. DeNovo, "A Railroad for Turkey: The Chester Project, 1908–1913," *Business History Review,* XXXIII (Autumn, 1959), pp. 300–329; DeNovo, *American Interests and Policies,* pp. 58–87. See also Naomi W. Cohen, "Ambassador Straus in Turkey, 1909–1910: A Note on Dollar Diplomacy," *Mississippi Valley Historical Review,* XLV (March, 1959), 632–642. The Chester project was approved by the Turkish government in 1923, only to be canceled seven months later. See below, p. 130.

Highlights of Turkish-American Relations to 1914

With the outbreak of World War I in 1914, these diplomats and other American interests in Turkey faced a difficult and sometimes dangerous situation. The war forced the United States temporarily to play a more active role in the Middle East than it had in the previous century. The decade beginning in 1914 brought momentous change to Turkey and consequent problems and transformations in Turkish-American relations.

⚜ World War I to Lausanne, 1914–1923

EUROPE'S eruption into war in late July and early August, 1914, seriously complicated relations between the United States and Turkey. The Ottoman Empire's assessment of its national interest ultimately dictated association with the German Empire. The Turks had reason to identify with Germany, in part because the Kaiser's government opposed two countries, Russia and Great Britain, against which Turkey had special grievances. The Ottoman government, still controlled by the Young Turks, feared that Russia, if victorious in the struggle, would attempt to satisfy its historic ambition to dominate the Straits area. Russia's ally, Great Britain, had not sympathized with the Turkish cause during the disastrous Balkan Wars. England, in fact, had sacrificed its traditional role as protector of the "sick man of Europe" by entering into an entente with Russia in 1907. The Turkish leaders also were incensed when, at the beginning of hostilities, the British government pressed into its own service two warships being built for the Turks by private English shipbuilders.[1]

[1] Ulrich Trumpener, in a series of articles (*Journal of Modern History*, XXXII [June, 1960], 145–149; *ibid.*, XXXIV [December, 1962], 369–380; and *Journal of Contemporary History*, I [1966], 179–192) and in a book, *Germany and the Ottoman Empire, 1914–1918* (Princeton, 1968), has questioned the traditional interpretation of Turkish subservience to Germany during World War I. Y. T. Kurat, "How Turkey Drifted into World War I," in K. Bourne and D. C. Watt, eds., *Studies in International History* (Hamden, Conn., 1967), pp. 291–315, uses Turkish sources and places some emphasis on German influence. Kemal H. Karpat, *Turkey's Politics: The Transition to a Multi-Party System* (Princeton, 1959), p. 24, suggests that the Turks were influenced by Pan-Turkism. See also Arnold J. Toynbee and Kenneth P. Kirkwood, *Turkey* (London, 1926), pp. 54–55, and Edward R. Vere-Hodge, *Turkish Foreign Policy 1918–1948* (Ambilly-Annemasse, France, 1950), p. 13. See Djemal Pasha, *Memories of a Turkish Statesman, 1913–1919* (New York, 1922), pp. 90–97, 115–117, for comments by the Turkish Admiralty chief.

16

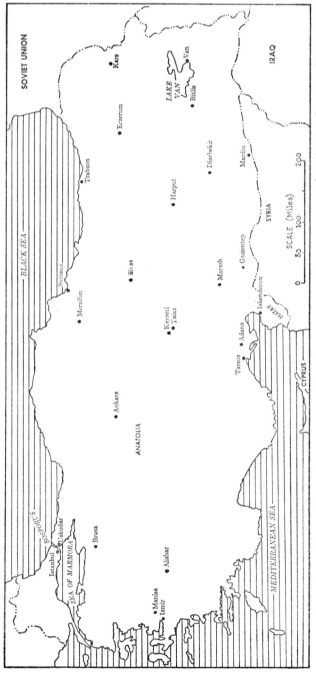

Atatürk's Turkey

from *American Interests and Policies in the
Middle East, 1909–1939*, by John A. DeNovo (Minnesota)

17

American Response to Turkish Nationalism and Reform

Even though Turkey and Germany entered into a secret alliance and a military convention early in August, 1914, the Turkish government at the start of the war declared its neutrality, describing the mobilization of its armed forces as a precautionary measure. On August 11, the Turkish government allowed the German battleships *Goeben* and *Breslau* to pass into the Dardanelles. The Turks rebuffed British protests with references to nondelivery of the two vessels ordered in England and a contention that the Turkish government had purchased the German ships. American Ambassador Henry Morgenthau in Istanbul reported to Secretary of State William Jennings Bryan that the arrival of the *Goeben* and *Breslau* "most likely will precipitate Turkish Government into participation of general war." [2] Noting the Turkish cabinet's indecision whether Turkey should enter the war, Morgenthau suggested that American interests would be "best served by the preservation of Turkey's neutrality," and that he might "urge Minister of War and Minister of Interior to remain neutral." The State Department denied Morgenthau permission to take this course but authorized him to express the opinion, if queried by Turkish officials, that the United States government, "solely in the interest of humanity and from no political consideration," would be pleased to see Turkey remain neutral.[3] There is no indication that Morgenthau ever found an opportunity to express these views. Weber Pasha, a German general in Turkish employ, closed the Dardanelles on September 27 and a month later the *Goeben* and *Breslau*, with units of the Turkish fleet, raided the Russian navy in the Black Sea harbor of Odessa. Russia declared war on Turkey on November 4 and within a few days Turkey officially entered the conflict.[4]

In the meantime, two events occurred to strain United States relations with Turkey. On September 8, 1914, the Washington *Evening Star* pub-

[2] George Lenczowski, *The Middle East in World Affairs* (3rd ed., Ithaca, N.Y., 1962), pp. 37–38; Leland James Gordon, *American Relations with Turkey, 1830–1930: An Economic Interpretation* (Philadelphia, 1932), p. 16; Henry Morgenthau to William Jennings Bryan, August 11, 1914, *Papers Relating to the Foreign Relations of the United States, 1914, Supplement, the World War* (Washington, 1928), p. 62 (hereafter cited as *FR 1914 Supplement*) (source of the quotation); Henry Morgenthau, *Ambassador Morgenthau's Story* (Garden City, N.Y., 1918), p. 72; Djemal Pasha, *Memories of a Turkish Statesman*, pp. 107–122. The Ottoman army had been trained by a group of German officers headed by General Liman von Sanders.

[3] Morgenthau to Bryan, undated, received August 25, 1914, *FR 1914 Supplement*, 75; Bryan to Morgenthau, August 26, 1914, *ibid.*, 77.

[4] Morgenthau to Bryan, September 27, 1914, *ibid.*, 113–114; Gordon, *American Relations with Turkey*, pp. 17–18; Djemal Pasha, *Memories of a Turkish Statesman*, pp. 127–133.

18

lished a statement by Turkish Ambassador Ahmed Rustem condemning the American press for its criticism of Turkey, particularly in regard to the treatment of Armenians. Rustem quite undiplomatically inquired what would happen to American Negroes if they conspired with the Japanese to invade the United States. "How many of them would be left alive to tell the tale?" he asked. After refusing a State Department request to withdraw his statement, Rustem returned to Turkey. This incident, occurring simultaneously with Turkey's unilateral abrogation of the capitulations, discouraged sympathy for the Turkish cause in the United States.[5]

Abrogation of the Capitulations and the Armenian Problem

The Turks took advantage of the outbreak of war to rid themselves of the capitulatory regime. In a note dated September 9, 1914, to the representatives of countries having capitulatory privileges, Minister for Foreign Affairs Said Halim contended that the capitulations were "in complete opposition to the juridical rules of the century and to the principle of national sovereignty" and were "an impediment to the progress and the development of the Ottoman Empire." The basis of Turkey's relations with all states, the note continued, would be the "general principles of international law" when the abrogation became effective on October 1, 1914. Ambassador Morgenthau informed the Turkish government even before receiving instruction that the United States would not recognize abrogation of the capitulations. They could be discarded, Morgenthau pointed out, only by agreement among all of the nations concerned.[6]

The United States did not alter this official capitulations policy until 1923 even though the Ottoman Foreign Ministry considered the capitulations dead and notified the American embassy in September, 1915, that further communications regarding them would be ignored. Robert Lansing, Bryan's successor as Secretary of State, instructed Morgenthau to reiterate the argument that provisions of a bilateral treaty like the Turkish-American treaty of 1830 could not be abrogated until both countries

---

[5] Rustem statement quoted in *Papers Relating to the Foreign Relations of the United States, the Lansing Papers, 1914–1920* (2 vols., Washington, 1939–1940), I, 70–71; Rustem to Bryan, September 12, 1914, *ibid.*, 68–69; Robert Lansing (Counselor of the State Department) to Bryan, September 14, 1914, *ibid.*, 73–74; Rustem to Lansing, September 20, 1914, *ibid.*, 74.

[6] Text of the note is in *Papers Relating to the Foreign Relations of the United States, 1914* (Washington, 1922), pp. 1092–1093 (hereafter cited as *FR 1914*); Morgenthau to Said Halim, September 10, 1914, *ibid.*, 1093; Bryan to Morgenthau, September 16, 1914, *ibid.*

19

agreed. The Turkish government, Lansing warned, would be held responsible for injuries to American citizens caused by interference with extraterritorial rights in the Ottoman Empire. Until the United States entered the war, there were only isolated incidents involving the capitulations. The Ottoman government supervised and taxed American schools and colleges but no serious diplomatic problems resulted. In April, 1916, Turkish provincial authorities received instructions "to avoid in all matters friction with Americans"; any disputes were to be referred directly to Istanbul for settlement.[7] At this point the Turks wished to avoid a direct confrontation with the United States on the capitulations question.

A new Ottoman effort to suppress the Armenians beginning in 1915 exacerbated anti-Turkish feeling in the United States. The Turks justified the massacre and forced migration of these people by claiming that their residence in strategic areas could cause serious harm to the Turkish war effort. The Armenians generally favored the Allied cause and many of them, in fact, were involved in treason and armed resistance against the Turkish government. As Professor Lewis V. Thomas has pointed out, "In the long run the Turks would have had no true alternatives except either to excise the non-Turks from Anatolia or themselves be excised therefrom." The Turks had understandable reasons for ending Armenian resistance activities, but the methods they employed were inhumane.[8]

Ambassador Morgenthau described the ruthless suppression of the Armenians as "the murder of a nation." The graphic descriptions of Turkish atrocities penned by Morgenthau and others stirred up anti-Turkish

[7] Morgenthau to Lansing, September 22, 1915, *Papers Relating to the Foreign Relations of the United States, 1915* (Washington, 1924), pp. 1304–1305 (contains text of Turkish note, September 4, 1915); Lansing to Morgenthau, November 4, 1915, *ibid.*, pp. 1305–1306; Gordon, *American Relations with Turkey*, p. 199; Hoffman Philip (Chargé d'Affaires, Istanbul) to Lansing, April 24, 1916, *Papers Relating to the Foreign Relations of the United States, 1916* (Washington, 1925), pp. 964–965.

[8] Bernard Lewis, *The Emergence of Modern Turkey* (London, 1961), p. 350; Lenczowski, *The Middle East in World Affairs*, pp. 48–49; Lewis V. Thomas, "The National and International Relations of Turkey," in T. Cuyler Young, ed., *Near Eastern Culture and Society: A Symposium on the Meeting of East and West* (Princeton, 1951), pp. 170–171; Roderic H. Davison, "The Armenian Crisis, 1912–1914," *American Historical Review*, LIII (April, 1948), 481–505. For a Turkish account, see Djemal Pasha, *Memories of a Turkish Statesman*, pp. 241–302. For historical background of the Armenian problem and a brief description of events in 1915, see James B. Gidney, *A Mandate for Armenia* (Kent, Ohio, 1967), pp. 1–59. A useful documentary collection is Viscount Bryce, *The Treatment of Armenians in the Ottoman Empire, 1915–1916: Documents Presented to Viscount Grey of Fallodon* (London, 1916).

opinion in the United States. The State Department protested to the Turkish government and even requested Germany to remonstrate against the treatment of the Armenian minority.[9] In response to pleas from Morgenthau and other Americans in Turkey, an Armenian Relief Committee was established in New York City in September, 1915, to raise funds for the suffering Armenians. James L. Barton of the American Board of Commissioners for Foreign Missions headed the organization, later renamed the American Committee for Armenian and Syrian Relief. Within a month of the original appeal the committee raised $100,000, and by the end of the war it had spent more than $11,000,000 for relief purposes in the Middle East.[10] The Armenian problem itself became an issue of paramount importance in Turco-American relations after World War I.

The Severance of Diplomatic Relations, 1917

When Germany and the United States broke diplomatic relations in February, 1917, the Turkish Minister of Foreign Affairs told Ambassador Abram I. Elkus, Morgenthau's successor, that there was no reason why the United States and Turkey could not remain friends. But the subsequent American declaration of war against Germany made inevitable the Turkish note of April 20, 1917, breaking diplomatic relations with the United States.[11] Logically, declarations of war might have followed but neither Turkey nor the United States chose to take this step. Turkey obviously had nothing to gain even though its German ally would have welcomed a Turkish-American conflict. Turkey would have been impelled into closer cooperation with Germany, and American military forces would have

[9] Gordon, *American Relations with Turkey*, p. 27; Morgenthau, *Ambassador Morgenthau's Story*, pp. 298–325; Fridtjof Nansen, "Rescuing Millions of War Victims from Disease and Starvation," *Current History*, XXX (July, 1929), 573–575; Robert L. Daniel, "The Armenian Question and American-Turkish Relations, 1914–1927," *Mississippi Valley Historical Review*, XLVI (September, 1959), 252–255. See also the emotional accounts of Herbert A. Gibbons, *The Blackest Page of Modern History: Events in Armenia in 1915* (New York & London, 1916), and Bertha S. Papazian, *The Tragedy of Armenia: A Brief Study and Interpretation* (Boston & Chicago, 1918).

[10] James L. Barton, *Story of Near East Relief (1915–1930): An Interpretation* (New York, 1930), pp. 4–15; A Committee of Trustees of Near East Relief, *Near East Relief Consummated — Near East Foundation Carries On* (n.p., 1944), pp. 3–5.

[11] Lansing to Abram I. Elkus, February 5, 1917, *Papers Relating to the Foreign Relations of the United States, 1917, Supplement I, The World War* (Washington, 1931), 113; Elkus to Lansing, February 8, 1917, *ibid.*, 148–149; Ahmed Nessimi (Turkish Minister of Foreign Affairs) to Elkus, April 20, 1917, *ibid.*, 603.

been required to fight over a wider area. When the Allies recognized the possible military advantage to Germany, they advised against an immediate American declaration of war against Turkey. It was clear also that, in the event of Turco-American hostilities, American relief work in the Middle East would be halted and American property probably would suffer heavy damage. President Wilson sympathized with American mission interests and obviously worried about what might happen to them in the event of a war with Turkey. His announced reason for not recommending war was that Turkey had committed no overt acts against the United States. Wilson held firm to his decision in the face of abortive moves in Congress to force a declaration of war against Turkey.[12]

Former Ambassador Henry Morgenthau may have been of some importance in forestalling a declaration of war. Morgenthau, who believed the Turks could be persuaded to agree to a separate peace, received State Department and presidential authorization to undertake a secret mission in May, 1917. Morgenthau's plans, however, conflicted with those of the British government and Zionist leaders, who combined to prevent their implementation. A planned British offensive in Palestine could not be undertaken if Turkey left the war at that moment, and Zionist hopes for a national homeland probably would be crushed if the Turks secured peace prematurely. With aid from the British Foreign Office, Chaim Weizmann, the Zionist leader, intercepted Morgenthau at Gibraltar and persuaded him to scrap his plans. Apparently, Weizmann convinced Morgenthau that the mission would fail, putting its originator in an embarrassing position, and made clear that the Zionist organization would oppose it.[13]

Weizmann's obviously biased account of his encounter with Morgenthau is not complimentary to the latter. Weizmann wrote:

. . . as the talks went on, it became embarrassingly apparent that he [Morgenthau] had merely had a vague notion that he could utilize his per-

---

[12] Gordon, *American Relations with Turkey*, p. 20; Laurence Evans, *United States Policy and the Partition of Turkey, 1914–1924* (Baltimore, 1965), pp. 32–33, 38–42; Daniel, "The Armenian Question and American-Turkish Relations, 1914–1927," 255–259. President Woodrow Wilson referred to Turkey in his war message to Congress on April 2, 1917. See *Congressional Record*, 65 Cong., 1 Sess., LV, pt. 1, 104.

[13] William Yale, "Ambassador Henry Morgenthau's Special Mission of 1917," *World Politics*, I (April, 1949), 308–320; Evans, *United States Policy and the Partition of Turkey*, pp. 43–45; Leonard Stein, *The Balfour Declaration* (London, 1961), pp. 352–358; Chaim Weizmann, *Trial and Error: The Autobiography of Chaim Weizmann* (New York, 1949), pp. 195–199; Frank Jewett, "Why We Did Not Declare War on Turkey," *Current History*, XIV (September, 1921), 989–991.

sonal connections in Turkey to some end or other; but on examining the question more closely, he was compelled to admit that he did not know the position of Turkey and was not justified in saying that the time had arrived for negotiations. Nor had he received any definite instructions from President Wilson. In short, he seemed not to have given the matter sufficiently serious consideration. . . . It was no job at all to persuade Mr. Morgenthau to drop the project. He simply persuaded himself, and before long announced his intention of going to Biarritz instead of Egypt.[14]

Thus, Morgenthau's scheme fell through, much to the chagrin of President Wilson and his adviser, Colonel Edward M. House. House noted in his diary on July 14, 1917, that "Morgenthau's trip had turned out to be a fiasco." Apparently, Morgenthau's later realization that he had been cleverly sidetracked by Weizmann conditioned his public opposition to the Zionist movement.[15]

The Swedish legation cared for United States interests in the Ottoman Empire after the severance of diplomatic relations. Many Americans left Turkey, and American philanthropic activity, exclusive of Near East Relief, was somewhat curtailed. But much of the educational and medical work continued even though the war period resulted in the elimination of much of the non-Turkish constituency of these American institutions. Although some Americans who remained in Turkey testified to the fair treatment they received from Ottoman authorities, a large group of claims against Turkey developed between 1914 and 1918.[16] This was only one of the problems to be considered after Turkey capitulated to the Allies at Mudros on October 30, 1918.[17] Even though the United States and Turkey were not declared enemies, the American delegation at the Versailles conference following the termination of World War I was vitally interested in the Turkish settlement.

The United States at Versailles: The Mandates Proposal

The fact that the United States had never declared war on Turkey complicated the situation after the conflict ended. Except for the Ver-

[14] Weizmann, *Trial and Error*, p. 198.

[15] Yale, "Ambassador Henry Morgenthau's Special Mission of 1917," p. 320; Weizmann, *Trial and Error*, p. 199; Stein, *Balfour Declaration*, pp. 357–358.

[16] Gordon, *American Relations with Turkey*, pp. 21, 200; James Thayer Addison, *The Christian Approach to the Moslem* (New York, 1942), p. 100; Caleb Frank Gates, *Not to Me Only* (Princeton, 1940), p. 249; Lynn A. Scipio, *My Thirty Years in Turkey* (Rindge, N.H., 1955), pp. 149–150.

[17] Gordon, *American Relations with Turkey*, p. 21. For text of the armistice of

sailles meetings, the United States could never participate in conferences dealing with Turkish questions on the same basis as nations earlier the enemies of Turkey. Nevertheless, President Wilson indicated his personal interest when he suggested on January 8, 1918, in the twelfth of his Fourteen Points that "the Turkish portions of the present Ottoman Empire should be assured a secure sovereignty . . . and the Dardanelles should be permanently opened as a free passage to the ships and commerce of all nations under international guarantees." [18] The Allied powers, in contrast, came to Versailles expecting to implement several secret agreements formulated during the war. The Constantinople Agreement (Great Britain, France, and Russia, March 18, 1915), the Treaty of London (Great Britain, France, Russia, and Italy, April 26, 1915), the Sykes-Picot Agreement (Great Britain, France, and Russia, May 16, 1916), and the St. Jean de Maurienne Agreement (Great Britain, France, and Italy, April 17, 1917), born of the desire of the powers to share in the dismemberment of the Ottoman Empire, were not consistent with Wilson's lenient plans.[19] Partly because of this situation, the conferees at Versailles were unable to agree on a peace treaty for Turkey.

Shortly after the Versailles meetings began, the Intelligence Section of the American delegation (popularly known as the "Inquiry") submitted recommendations to President Wilson on United States policy for the Middle East. The Inquiry report proposed that Istanbul and the Straits should be within an internationalized state under a mandatory power, with the Straits open to ships and commerce of all nations. The report also recommended the establishment of mandatory states in Turkish Anatolia, Armenia, Mesopotamia, Syria, and Palestine. The Allied powers, which could thus pay lip service to Wilson's program and still satisfy indirectly the aims of their secret agreements, reluctantly accepted the mandate idea.[20] The Allies suggested at Versailles that the United States accept

Mudros, see J. C. Hurewitz, ed., *Diplomacy in the Near and Middle East: A Documentary Record, 1535–1956* (2 vols., Princeton, 1956), II, 36–37.

[18] Ray Stannard Baker and William E. Dodd, eds., *The Public Papers of Woodrow Wilson* (6 vols., New York & London, 1925–1927), V, 160–161.

[19] The texts of these agreements and accompanying documents are in Hurewitz, *Diplomacy in the Near and Middle East*, II, 7–12, 18–25. See also Toynbee and Kirkwood, *Turkey*, pp. 68–71, and Evans, *United States Policy and the Partition of Turkey*, pp. 49–85.

[20] "Tentative Recommendations for President Wilson by the Intelligence Section of the American Delegation to the Peace Conference," January 21, 1919, in Hurewitz, *Diplomacy in the Near and Middle East*, II, 40–45.

mandates over the Istanbul-Straits area and Armenia. Before the conference convened, Wilson told the British Prime Minister, David Lloyd
George, that Americans "were extremely proud of their disinterested position . . ." in the war and thus would be reluctant to accept any mandates.
But by March, 1919, Wilson reversed himself and agreed to submit the
mandate proposals to the American people. Justifiably cautious, Wilson
on various occasions made it clear that the final decision would be up to
the American people speaking through their representatives in Washington. Wilson's idealism influenced his thinking on mandates, even though
Secretary of State Lansing opposed the plan. Lansing wrote later about the
"sustained propaganda" in the United States favoring the mandates, which
he predicted would be "a constant financial burden." The purpose of this
propaganda, Lansing observed, "was to take advantage of the unselfish-
ness of the American people and of the altruism and idealism of President
Wilson." [21]

Because of dissension among the Allies over the assignment of other
mandates in the Middle East, Wilson advocated the despatch of an international commission on mandates in Turkey to determine the wishes of
the people concerned. France refused to participate because Great Britain
had not withdrawn its troops from Syria and permitted their replacement
by the French army, and Lloyd George insisted that his country could not
join in the work of the commission unless the French cooperated.[22] Wilson
then sent out the United States section of the commission, composed of
President Henry C. King of Oberlin College and Charles R. Crane, a businessman. The King-Crane report, submitted on August 28, 1919, recommended a United States mandate over Syria, a proposal inimical to
French and British plans. The commission also proposed the establish-

[21] David Lloyd George, *Memoirs of the Peace Conference* (2 vols., New Haven,
1939), I, 117; Minutes of the Meeting of the Council of Four, March 20, 1919,
*Papers Relating to the Foreign Relations of the United States, 1919: The Paris Peace
Conference* (13 vols., Washington, 1942–1947), V, 10 (hereafter cited as *FR 1919
Peace Conference*); Minutes of the Meeting of the Council of Four, May 14, 1919,
ibid., 614; Minutes of the Meeting of the Council of Four, May 13, 1919, *ibid.*, 583;
Robert Lansing, *The Peace Negotiations, a Personal Narrative* (Boston & New York,
1921), pp. 149–150, 159; Gidney, *A Mandate for Armenia*, pp. 74–96; Evans,
United States Policy and the Partition of Turkey, pp. 89–107.
[22] Minutes of the Meeting of the Council of Four, May 21, 1919, *FR 1919
Peace Conference*, V, 760–761, 766; Minutes of the Meeting of the Council of Four,
May 31, 1919, *ibid.*, VI, 132; John A. DeNovo, *American Interests and Policies in
the Middle East, 1900–1939* (Minneapolis, 1963), pp. 119, 122, 124; Evans, *United
States Policy and the Partition of Turkey*, pp. 138–152.

ment of an Armenian state where, it was pointed out, the people favored an American mandate. Significantly, the report advised against a national home for the Jews in Palestine because of Arab and Christian opposition. Notwithstanding Wilson's interest in United States mandates in the Middle East, the King-Crane report went unpublished until 1922. Among reasons for the delay was the fact that its recommendations were hostile to English, French, and Zionist plans.[23]

Before King and Crane finished their work, the Versailles conference decided to postpone the Turkish settlement until the United States made clear its position on mandates.[24] In the meantime, in July, 1919, Colonel William N. Haskell had begun his duties as "Resident Commissioner for Relief in Armenia," where he was to represent United States, British, French, and Italian interests and direct relief activities for the area. To provide factual background for an American decision on the Armenian mandate proposal, a commission headed by Major General James G. Harbord traveled to Armenia in September, 1919. Harbord's report, dated October 16, 1919, after surveying the history and current status of Armenia, listed fourteen reasons for accepting the mandate, thirteen opposed to it. Harbord, in favoring the mandate, emphasized humanitarian motives but pointed out that the cost of the undertaking, estimated at $756,014,-000 for a five-year period, was a heavy factor against it.[25] Harbord's rec-

[23] Minutes of the Daily Meeting of the American Commissioners Plenipotentiary, March 27, 1919, *FR 1919 Peace Conference*, XI, 133 (about the King-Crane appointments); Charles R. Crane and Henry C. King, "Report of the American Section of the International Commission on Mandates in Turkey," August 28, 1919, *ibid.*, XII, 792–793, 796–797, 841–842. The entire text of the report covers pp. 751–863. See also Harry N. Howard, *The King-Crane Commission: An American Inquiry in the Middle East* (Beirut, 1963), and Evans, *United States Policy and the Partition of Turkey*, pp. 153–154. In note 38 on pp. 154–155, Evans discusses reasons for nonpublication of the report until 1922. In the Mark Lambert Bristol MSS (Manuscripts Division, Library of Congress, Washington), Box 9, there is a copy of *Editor and Publisher*, LV (December 2, 1922), containing the "First Publication of King-Crane Report on the Near East," described as "A Suppressed Official Document of the United States Government." For background, see Richard G. Hovannisian, *Armenia on the Road to Independence, 1918* (Berkeley & Los Angeles, 1967).

[24] Minutes of the Meeting of the Council of Four, June 27, 1919, *FR 1919 Peace Conference*, VI, 729; Notes of a Meeting of the Heads of Delegations of the Five Great Powers, July 18, 1919, *ibid.*, VII, 193.

[25] Commission to Negotiate Peace to Acting Secretary of State, July 11, 1919, *Papers Relating to the Foreign Relations of the United States, 1919* (2 vols., Washington, 1934), II, 827 (hereafter cited as *FR 1919*); James G. Harbord to Lansing, October 16, 1919, *ibid.*, 841–874 (text of the Harbord Report); Gordon, *American Relations with Turkey*, p. 31; Gidney, *A Mandate for Armenia*, pp. 168–191, describes the Harbord mission in detail.

ommendations, favoring the Armenian mandate for idealistic reasons but opposing it for realistic ones, came after the beginning of President Wilson's illness brought on by his vigorous fight in the United States for the League of Nations and the Treaty of Versailles. The Senate rejection of the treaty on November 19, 1919, contributed to American retrenchment in Europe and the Middle East. Thus the Allies, still waiting for an American decision on Armenia, had to consider plans for a Turkish treaty without provision for United States mandates.[26]

The Treaty of Sèvres and the Nationalist Movement

After preliminary discussions in London, the Allies met at San Remo in mid-April, 1920, to decide on the Turkish treaty. Robert U. Johnson, American Ambassador in Italy, represented the United States as an unofficial observer. The San Remo conference extended another invitation to the United States to accept a mandate over Armenia, which as an independent republic had been accorded de facto recognition by the United States on April 23, 1920. Congress soon turned down Wilson's request for permission to accept the mandate.[27] The possibility of American mandates in former Ottoman territory, very unlikely after rejection of the Versailles treaty, thus definitely was eliminated. The Allies at San Remo decided on the distribution of other mandates and preliminary terms for the Turkish treaty, later formally signed at Sèvres on August 10, 1920. The Treaty of Sèvres, a thorough humiliation for Turkey, detached a substantial part of its territory, limited its sovereignty, maintained the capitulations, and internationalized the Straits.[28] The treaty provided for arbitration of the disputed Turco-Armenian border by President Wilson, a task finally com-

[26] See Alexander L. George and Juliette L. George, *Woodrow Wilson and Colonel House: A Personality Study* (New York, 1956), pp. 292–303, for a brief account of Wilson's western trip, his collapse, and defeat of the treaty. See also Lloyd George, *Memoirs of the Peace Conference*, II, 818–819. Evans covers the peace conference in detail in his *United States Policy and the Partition of Turkey*, pp. 89–265.

[27] Bainbridge Colby (Secretary of State) to Robert U. Johnson, April 20, 1920, *Papers Relating to the Foreign Relations of the United States, 1920* (3 vols., Washington, 1935–1936), I, 2; *Congressional Record*, 66 Cong., 2 Sess., LIX, pt. 7, 7533–7534, 7549; *ibid.*, pt. 8, 8073; Gordon, *American Relations with Turkey*, pp. 30–32; Daniel, "The Armenian Question and American-Turkish Relations, 1914–1927," pp. 262–265. See also M. B. Giffen (Near East Division), "The Project for an American Mandate in Armenia, 1919–1920," May 27, 1937, in DS 860j.01/656. See also Gidney, *A Mandate for Armenia*, pp. 192–239, for a useful discussion of the Armenian mandate question.

[28] See Hurewitz, *Diplomacy in the Near and Middle East*, II, pp. 81–87, for political clauses of the Treaty of Sèvres.

pleted in November, 1920. About the same time the independent Armenian Republic of Erivan passed out of existence after being overrun and divided by Russian and Turkish Nationalist forces.[29]

During the period of indecision on the Turkish settlement, the United States and Turkey did not re-establish formal diplomatic relations. The Greeks, with permission and naval support from England, France, and the United States, had invaded Turkey through the port of Izmir on May 15, 1919. This act complicated the already confused Turkish political situation by stimulating a nationalist movement led by Kemal Atatürk, a World War I military hero. The ensuing conflict between the Greeks and Turkish nationalists contributed to the downfall of the Sultan's government in Istanbul and the scrapping of the Treaty of Sèvres. Atatürk rallied the people of the Anatolian interior to oppose the Greeks in a war ending in an armistice at Mudania on October 11, 1922, after the invaders had been expelled from Turkey through the port of Izmir.[30] The basis for the Kemalist political program was a "National Pact" adopted in 1919 by nationalist deputies at Ankara and confirmed by the Turkish parliament at Istanbul on January 28, 1920. The pact's program emphasized complete territorial, political, judicial, and economic independence for Turkey.[31]

United States Representation and Interests in Turkey

The first American to represent the United States in Turkey after the end of World War I was Lewis Heck, who arrived in Istanbul in December, 1918, with the rank of commissioner.[32] In the same month, the United States government appointed Rear Admiral Mark Lambert Bristol to be the senior American naval officer in Turkish waters. Thus began a mission

[29] R. W. Flournoy (Near East Division), "A Reconsideration of This Government's Position in the Matter of Its Recognition of Armenia," July 13, 1925, DS 860j.01/581.

[30] Lewis, *The Emergence of Modern Turkey*, pp. 234–256; Karpat, *Turkey's Politics*, pp. 32–39; M. S. Anderson, *The Eastern Question 1774–1923: A Study in International Relations* (London, Melbourne, Toronto, & New York, 1966), pp. 363–372; Toynbee and Kirkwood, *Turkey*, pp. 78–110. See *A Speech Delivered by Ghazi Mustapha Kemal, President of the Turkish Republic, October 1927* (Leipzig, 1929), pp. 9–572, for a detailed first-person narrative of the events of 1919–1922.

[31] Roderic H. Davison, "Turkish Diplomacy from Mudros to Lausanne," in Gordon A. Craig and Felix Gilbert, eds., *The Diplomats, 1919–1939* (Princeton, 1953), p. 180; Anderson, *Eastern Question*, pp. 366–367.

[32] Lansing to Pleasant A. Stovall (American Minister to Switzerland) (for Lewis Heck), November 30, 1918, *FR 1919*, II, 810; Frank L. Polk (Acting Secretary of State) to Heck, January 21, 1919, *ibid.*, 810–811.

which was to last until 1927. By mid-February, 1919, Bristol had moved into the United States embassy in Istanbul and had assumed broad duties, as he reported himself: "I have taken the responsibility of Senior U.S. Representative. . . . I am taking care of the relations so far as the armistice terms and all military and naval affairs are concerned. I hold myself responsible under any circumstances for the proper relations between the United States and the Turkish government and the representatives of all other countries." After only one month in Turkey he considered himself well enough acquainted with the local situation to state his opinion that the Turks were not capable of governing themselves and that one mandate should be established for the whole country.[33]

G. Bie Ravndal arrived in Turkey as Heck's successor in May, 1919. His instructions cautioned him to "bear in mind that the rupture of diplomatic relations between the Turkish Government and the United States still continues. . . . You will therefore avoid all acts which may convey the idea that your presence or that of other American officials in Turkey means a resumption of diplomatic relations." [34] Working relationships between Ravndal and Bristol were strained at times, a situation owing at least partly to the failure of the United States government to clarify the respective authority of naval and civilian officials in Turkey. Thus, Bristol's reaction in a letter to a friend to his appointment on August 12, 1919, as United States High Commissioner in Turkey: "It came as a clap of thunder out of a clear sky and it made me feel that all my hard work was well worth while. I might also tell you privately that it came just at the right time for things were getting pretty disagreeable and I made up my mind to get out." [35] Bristol's new appointment clearly established him as the chief United States representative in Turkey.

Although formal Turkish-American diplomatic relations had not been resumed, missionaries continued to work in Turkey, and commercial exchanges between the two nations revived significantly. After securing the

[33] Vice-Admiral William S. Sims to Bristol, December 17, 1918, Bristol MSS, Box 9; Bristol to Force Commander, February 14, 1919, *ibid.*, Box 16 (source of the quotation); War Diary, February 18, 1919, *ibid.*; Bristol to Sims, March 10, 1919, *ibid.*, Box 9.

[34] Polk to G. Bie Ravndal, May 3, 1919, *FR 1919*, II, 812.

[35] Lansing to Commission to Negotiate Peace, August 12, 1919, *FR 1919*, II, 812; Bristol to E. Vail Stebbins, September 5, 1919, Bristol MSS, Box 9 (source of the quotation); Henry P. Beers, *U.S. Naval Detachment in Turkish Waters, 1919–1924* ("Administrative Reference Service Report No. 2," Washington, 1943), pp. 5–6, 13; Robert A. Bachman, "The American Navy and the Turks," *The Outlook*, CXXXII (October 18, 1922), 288–289.

approval of the Allied Supreme Economic Council, the United States War Trade Board announced on February 15, 1919, that trade with Turkey could be resumed. Total trade expanded to $62,234,724 in 1919 and $82,014,734 in 1920, as contrasted with $527,596 in 1918. A large market in Turkey, the inability of European nations to compete, large expenditures by American philanthropists, and the availability of United States merchant vessels to carry the goods helped make the trade boom possible. A decline in volume beginning in 1921 brought trade within the next few years back to prewar levels.[36]

These trade relations and the continued residence of Americans in Turkey without formal treaty guarantees accentuated the need for a regularization of Turco-American relations. An invitation to an Allied-Turkish conference at Lausanne late in 1922 afforded United States diplomats an opportunity to arrange such a settlement.[37]

The Lausanne Conferences

The European powers convened the Lausanne conference to replace the Treaty of Sèvres, which Atatürk's Nationalists had effectively killed. The Allies recognized that they had to deal with a "new" Turkey. As Joseph C. Grew, United States Ambassador in Switzerland and an observer at Lausanne, put it, "The Turks are not just in the same position they were when the Treaty of Sèvres was drawn up; they are coming, not hat in hand, but with a victorious army behind them. That makes a lot of difference. . . ."[38] The key territorial and political questions at the conference dealt with the Straits, Thrace, Mosul, the Aegean Islands, the minorities, reparations from Greece, and the capitulations.[39] The first phase of the conference, from November 20, 1922, to February 4, 1923, broke up in an impasse, mainly because of disagreement on the capitulations.[40] The

[36] William Sharp (American Ambassador to France) to Polk, February 13, 1919, *FR 1919*, II, 814; Polk to Sharp, February 20, 1919, *ibid.*; Gordon, *American Relations with Turkey*, pp. 21, 59–61.
[37] British Embassy (Washington) to Department of State, October 27, 1922, *Papers Relating to the Foreign Relations of the United States, 1923* (2 vols., Washington, 1938), II, 889 (hereafter cited as *FR 1923*).
[38] Grew to Margaret Perry, November 13, 1922, in Joseph C. Grew, *Turbulent Era: A Diplomatic Record of Forty Years, 1904–1945*, ed. Walter Johnson (2 vols., Boston, 1952), I, 486.
[39] Editor's note, *ibid.*, 480.
[40] Diary, February 4, 1923, *ibid.*, 550–554; Special Mission at Lausanne to Charles Evans Hughes, February 4, 1923, *FR 1923*, II, 966. See "Notes on the Conference at Lausanne, 1922–1923," read to the American Men's Luncheon Club, Is-

second phase, from April 23, 1923, to July 24, 1923, ended with the signing of an Allied-Turkish treaty which recognized Atatürk's government, established boundaries, acknowledged the death of the capitulations, and regulated the general relations of the signatory nations. A convention dealing with the Straits was appended.[41]

Turkey alone of the defeated Central Powers had been able to discard a vindictive treaty imposed in 1920. Ambassador Grew described Turkish Prime Minister Ismet İnönü's work at Lausanne in superlative terms: "It was probably the greatest diplomatic victory in history and could hardly result otherwise if we stop to consider that Ismet held all of the cards in his hands from the very start." Ismet held "four aces," according to Grew — a recently victorious army, an army ready to fight again on short notice, the reluctance of the powers to fight against Turkey, and their inability to present a solid front at the conference.[42]

Besides Grew, the United States observers at the conference's first phase were Admiral Bristol and Ambassador to Italy Richard Washburn Child, who headed the mission. The State Department emphasized that Child, Grew, and Bristol were observers who would not play an official role in the Allied-Turkish negotiations or assume responsibility for any political and territorial adjustments, since a state of war between Turkey and the United States had never existed. As Ambassador Child told the conference delegates, the United States was present at Lausanne "to protect American interests, idealist or commercial, humane or financial, without discrimination. It is represented to protect . . . humanitarian interests regardless of their nationality. It is represented to serve in all appropriate ways the cause of peace." [43]

tanbul, January 30, 1930, in Joseph C. Grew MSS (Houghton Library, Harvard University, Cambridge, Mass.), 1930, vol. 3, for very interesting comments on the personalities and issues of the Lausanne conference.

[41] Davison, "Turkish Diplomacy from Mudros to Lausanne," in *The Diplomats, 1919–1939*, pp. 206–208.

[42] Informal talk, Grew to American consular officials gathered at Interlaken, Switzerland, September 2, 1923, *Turbulent Era*, I, 569–570. Grew's detailed and intimate account of the Lausanne conference is in *ibid.*, 485–585. Grew made his judgment of İnönü with full knowledge of the conference's results. During the first phase of the conference, after he and Mrs. Bristol had taken tea with Ismet, Bristol wrote in his diary: ". . . Ismet is human, has a sense of humor and is quite frank, but at the same time he hasn't a big brain. . . . Thus it does not seem strange if Ismet does not put his best foot forward in the Conference at Lausanne." See War Diary, January 26, 1923, Bristol MSS, Box 21.

[43] Editor's note, *Turbulent Era*, I, 484; diary, January 31, 1923, *ibid.*, 544. For Ambassador Child's account, see Richard Washburn Child, *A Diplomat Looks at Europe* (New York, 1925), pp. 79–124.

United States participation, nevertheless, was not completely disinterested politically and economically. The State Department suggested to the three observers that they should "state the American position if at any time it seems necessary. In view of our direct interests it would expose us to serious criticism were we to keep aloof from the sessions and very likely would put in jeopardy opportunity for complete observation and the use of appropriate influence." [44] In another document the State Department listed specific concerns: guarantees to replace the capitulations, claims for damages incurred between 1914 and 1922, freedom of the Straits, provision for archaeological work in Turkey, and protection of minorities, commercial interests, and educational, religious, and philanthropic institutions. At the same time, the State Department brought out a basic principle, traditional by this time in American foreign policy: "It [the United States] desires nothing which need conflict with the interests of other countries, if the principle of commercial opportunity for all nations is recognized at the outset. The United States has no intention of seeking for itself or its nationals a position of special privilege but it desires to protect its rights and to assure the Open Door." [45]

Working arrangements within the United States delegation at Lausanne were not completely happy, especially from Admiral Bristol's point of view. Bristol apparently thought the three United States delegates had equal rank, but that does not seem to have been the State Department's intention. When Secretary Hughes telegraphed Child of his appointment as an observer at Lausanne, he mentioned that Grew would be "associated" with him and that "Admiral Bristol will be requested to be present in Lausanne for such time as he can be appropriately spared from his post at Constantinople." [46] Bristol's assumption that he was better informed than his colleagues is apparent in his comments on his first meeting with them: "I was most favorably impressed with Mr. Child, as well as Mr. Grew. I am afraid both gathered the impression that I was throwing cold water on some of their enthusiasm and some facts that they believed were already established. However, this is generally necessary in dealing with Near Eastern questions." [47] On many occasions during his stay in Lausanne, Bristol reflected in his "War Diary" his feeling that he was not being con-

[44] Hughes to Child, November 15, 1922, *FR 1923*, II, 899.
[45] Hughes to Myron T. Herrick (Ambassador in France), October 27, 1922, *ibid.*, 884–885.
[46] Hughes to Child, October 28, 1922, *ibid.*, 889.
[47] War Diary, November 26, 1922, Bristol MSS, Box 21.

sulted properly, especially by Child, and that his talents were not being fully utilized. Illustrative is his entry for January 14, 1923: "I took occasion to tell Grew that I was not satisfied with the work we were accomplishing and I intended to bring up the subject and come to an agreement so that each one of us on the delegation should work to the maximum and as a team so that each one would do the work that he was best qualified for. I stated that unless we could combine in this way that I felt I was not accomplishing what was expected of me and that I was not giving my best effort to the Government." [48]

When the first phase of the conference broke up early in February, 1923, Child, Grew, and Bristol left Lausanne to return to their regular posts. In April, 1923, when it became apparent that the conference would resume, the State Department placed Grew at the head of the American delegation. Secretary Hughes explained to Child that he was not being sent back to Lausanne because the earlier heads of Allied delegations were not returning and that the initial work of the second phase would be technical. Although Hughes instructed Child to hold himself ready on short notice to travel to Lausanne, there is no evidence that the matter was given further consideration.[49] Admiral Bristol remained in Istanbul during this phase of the Lausanne conference.

Both the Turkish and United States governments hoped that a formal treaty between the two nations would result, at least indirectly, from a successful conference at Lausanne. Informal talks about such a settlement began as soon as the conference started in November, 1922. The initial assumption was that a United States–Turkish treaty would follow signature of an Allied-Turkish settlement and that it would depend somewhat on the latter.[50] But when the second Lausanne phase opened, Ismet Inönü immediately proposed negotiations with the United States. As Grew reported, "Ismet exhibits a strong desire to enter at once upon negotiations looking toward a treaty with the United States. He argues that an early settlement with the Allies would be promoted by a prior agreement with us." [51] Although Turkish and American experts began an exchange of

[48] War Diary, January 14, 1923, *ibid.* See also the entries for December 5, 13, and 28, 1922, *ibid.*, for further examples.
[49] Allen W. Dulles (Chief, Division of Near Eastern Affairs) to Hughes, April 4, 1923, *FR 1923*, II, 979–980; Hughes to Grew, April 7, 1923, *ibid.*, 980–981 (contains a copy of a State Department telegram to Child).
[50] Child and Grew to Hughes, November 22, 1922, *ibid.*, 901.
[51] Grew to Hughes, April 22, 1923, *ibid.*, 987.

views on major problems in May, 1923, and formal talks early in June, their final agreement came after the Turks had signed a treaty with the European allies.[52]

Significantly, the American most directly concerned with relations with Turkey, Admiral Bristol, felt that the proposed negotiations were premature. After a talk with a colleague in Istanbul, Bristol wrote in his diary:

We could see every possible disadvantage to us in following the new procedure of negotiating with the Turks while the Allies are negotiating. Under no circumstances can we hope by this means to get any more advantages . . . than the Allies got. . . . Further, it looks to us that if the Conference should break up we would be placed in an embarrassing position by practically not being able to refuse to go on with our negotiations. We cannot help but remember that America by virtue of never going to war with Turkey is in quite a different position from those countries that were at war with Turkey.[53]

And in a telegram to Grew, Bristol stated: "It is my firm conviction that the desire of the Turks to begin immediate negotiations with us springs from a wish to play us off against the Allies." [54] Notwithstanding Bristol's advice, the negotiations continued.

Grew, Ismet Inönü, and two other Turkish representatives signed a general treaty of amity and commerce and an extradition treaty on August 6, 1923, after two months of difficult negotiations. Article I provided for an exchange of diplomatic officials and Article II decreed complete abrogation of the capitulations. Articles III–VIII prescribed conditions for establishment and residence for individuals and businesses of each country in the other on the basis of reciprocal equality of treatment. Article IX guaranteed "freedom of commerce and navigation," based on the most-favored-nation principle, and subsequent articles (X–XVI) provided details related to taxes, import and export duties, and rights of United States vessels in the Straits area. Articles XVII–XXVII dealt with the rights and duties of consular officers. Article XXX was especially significant: "From the coming into force of the present Treaty the Treaties heretofore con-

---

[52] See Grew to Hughes, May 23, 1923, *ibid.*, 1067–1069, and Grew to Hughes, May 28, 1923, *ibid.*, 1070–1071.

[53] War Diary, May 6, 1923, Bristol MSS, Box 22.

[54] Grew to Hughes, May 13, 1923, *FR 1923*, II, 1059–1060 (includes text of Bristol's telegram to Grew, May 12, 1923).

cluded between the United States of America and the Ottoman Empire shall absolutely and finally cease to be effective. . . ." [55]

The Lausanne Treaty was not completely consistent with the United States position at the start of the negotiations. As Grew wrote to Secretary Hughes, the treaty "is far from what I should have wished it. It represents a considerably greater number of concessions on our part to meet the Turkish point of view than concessions on their part to meet ours." Grew particularly regretted the absence of provisions on naturalization, claims, and the minorities problem. But he believed "that more favorable terms could not have been obtained at this time and . . . it is at least open to doubt whether even equally favorable terms could be obtained later." [56] It should be noted that the United States gained at Lausanne certain guarantees that Turkey had accorded to the Allies. On August 4, 1923, Ismet Inönü sent to Grew copies of his July 24, 1923, declaration to the Allies containing guarantees on the administration of justice and the sanitary administration of Turkish frontiers. Inönü also guaranteed to United States institutions treatment equal to that promised to England, France, and Italy in a convention of establishment and residence signed at Lausanne on July 24, 1923. By this instrument the Turkish government recognized the existence of religious, educational, and medical institutions established before October 30, 1914, and promised to examine favorably the status of others founded after that date.[57] In effect, American institutions were given a new legal basis for existence in Turkey.

Shortly after the Lausanne conference, negotiations in Ankara between Bristol and the Turkish foreign minister resulted in establishment of procedures for future settlement of the claims issue. According to an exchange of notes dated December 24, 1923, a four-member joint claims commission would meet within six months of the exchange of ratifications of the Lausanne treaty. In the same period there were talks on the naturalization problem, but insoluble differences forced the State Department to suspend the negotiations.[58]

[55] The English text of the treaty is included in Grew to Hughes, January 29, 1924, *ibid.*, 1153–1166. See also Edgar W. Turlington, "The American Treaty of Lausanne," *World Peace Foundation Pamphlets*, VII, 593–595, quoted in *Turbulent Era*, I, 603–605.

[56] Grew to Hughes, August 6, 1923, *FR 1923*, II, 1148–1149.

[57] Ismet Inönü to Grew, August 4, 1923, *ibid.*, 1139–1141; Inönü to Grew, August 4, 1923, *ibid.*, 1141–1142.

[58] Bristol to Hughes, January 4, 1924, *ibid.*, 1189–1191. Documents related to the naturalization question are in *ibid.*, 1191–1198.

All things considered, and given the need to restore formal diplomatic relations as a means of protecting American interests in Turkey, the Treaty of Lausanne was very good. Certainly, its ratification by both nations would make it easier to resolve problems not settled by the treaty itself. The natural course for the State Department would have been immediate submission of the treaty to the Senate for advice and consent. However, President Calvin Coolidge did not send the treaty to the Senate until May 3, 1924.[59] The Senate delayed its decision until January, 1927, when it rejected the treaty. A strong anti-Turkish feeling in the United States, built up by certain missionary interests and Armenians and their supporters, intervened. Furthermore, the Lausanne Treaty became a political issue between the Democratic and Republican parties. In the meantime, Admiral Bristol continued as High Commissioner and Turkish-American relations remained in an official state of suspended animation.

The largest group of Americans affected by the lack of formal relations were the successors of Messrs. Parsons and Fisk, the Congregational pioneers who landed at Izmir in 1820. American commercial interests also felt the effects of inadequate guarantees. The task of the Department of State between 1923 and 1927 was to secure Senate approval of the Lausanne Treaty. Its rejection necessitated an alternate approach to the mechanics of restoring diplomatic relations.

[59] See *Congressional Record*, 69 Cong., 1 Sess., LXVII, pt. 6, 6250, for Coolidge's message submitting the treaty to the Senate.

Rejection of the Lausanne Treaty and Resumption of Diplomatic Relations, 1923–1927

ON JANUARY 18, 1927, the United States Senate rejected the Treaty of Lausanne by a vote of fifty to thirty-four, six short of the required two-thirds majority. Strong Armenian and church opposition and the injection of a partisan political struggle complicated the treaty's congressional history. The Senate vote almost three years after President Calvin Coolidge submitted the treaty for consideration forced the United States and Turkey to find another way to regularize their diplomatic relations.[1]

The Fight on the Treaty

Opposition to the Lausanne Treaty began almost as soon as it was signed. Enemies of the treaty were more vocal than its supporters, and they were able to mold themselves into highly effective pressure groups. With programs based on idealistic pronouncements designed to work on the consciences of the American people, these groups were able to assemble considerable support in the Senate. Traditional hatred of the "Terrible Turk" was an important basis for this strength. The Armenian problem was another, although not all Armenians in the United States opposed the

[1] *Christian Science Monitor* (Boston), January 19, 1927; Frank B. Kellogg to Mark L. Bristol, January 18, 1927, *Papers Relating to the Foreign Relations of the United States, 1927* (3 vols., Washington, 1942), III, 766 (hereafter cited as *FR 1927*). See *Congressional Record*, 69 Cong., 1 Sess., LXVII, pt. 6, 6250, for President Calvin Coolidge's message submitting the Lausanne Treaty to the Senate on May 3, 1924.

treaty. A moderate group, the Armenian-America Society, supported approval. The American Committee Opposed to the Lausanne Treaty (earlier called the American Committee for the Independence of Armenia) campaigned against ratification. Originally led by the prewar United States Ambassador to Germany, James W. Gerard, and dominated by Vahan Cardashian, a fiery Armenian-American, this group asked the Senate to reject the treaty.[2] Later, David Hunter Miller headed this committee, with Gerard and Albert Bushnell Hart serving as vice-chairmen. The organization's executive committee included such imposing names as Southern Methodist Bishop James Cannon, Jr., James M. Cox, Homer S. Cummings, Abram I. Elkus, Oscar S. Straus, and Ray Lyman Wilbur.[3]

The committee kept up a barrage of propaganda condemning the treaty. One publication, circulated during Senate consideration of the treaty, included such articles as David H. Miller's "For a Treaty Negotiated — Not Dictated," William T. Manning's "Duty and Honor," Henry Morgenthau's "A Treaty with a Red-Handed Despotism," and William S. Davis' "Why the Lausanne Treaty Should Not Be Ratified." The same pamphlet included sections on "Protests and Resolutions" and press comments on the Lausanne Treaty.[4] The American Committee Opposed to the Lausanne Treaty was the most active group lobbying against the formal resumption of Turkish-American relations.

Also influential was a group of 110 bishops of the Episcopal Church, which petitioned the Senate against the Lausanne Treaty. The bishops based their protest on an uninformed picture of conditions in Turkey and a conviction of the immorality of a treaty with a country which so clearly had demonstrated its opposition to minorities living within its borders.[5]

[2] Joseph C. Grew to Frederic R. Dolbeare (American Embassy, London), February 29, 1924, Joseph C. Grew MSS (Houghton Library, Harvard University, Cambridge, Mass.), 1924, vol. 3; Robert L. Daniel, "The Armenian Question and American-Turkish Relations, 1914–1927," *Mississippi Valley Historical Review*, XLVI (September, 1959), 263–264. As Daniel explains, the Armenia-America Society represented the Cilician Armenians, who advocated the expansion of Armenia into Cilicia after World War I. The American Committee for the Independence of Armenia represented the Caucasus-oriented Armenians.

[3] James W. Gerard to Calvin Coolidge, May 18, 1927, Calvin Coolidge MSS (Manuscript Division, Library of Congress, Washington), Box 193-A.

[4] The American Committee Opposed to the Lausanne Treaty, *The Lausanne Treaty and Armenia (Supplement)* (New York, 1927), *passim*, in DS 711.762 Protests/3. See also the *Christian Science Monitor*, January 3, 1927.

[5] Grew to Charles Slattery (Bishop Co-Adjutor of Massachusetts), April 7, 1926, in Joseph C. Grew, *Turbulent Era: A Diplomatic Record of Forty Years, 1904–1945*, ed. Walter Johnson (2 vols., Boston, 1952), I, 675; The American Com-

The Episcopal Church's lack of direct missionary interest in Turkey contributed to the weakness of its position. Joseph C. Grew, the treaty's chief architect, who became Undersecretary of State in 1924, tried with some success to clarify the situation for the bishops, who he felt had been misled by Armenian propaganda and a lack of information about Turkey itself. The United States would be in a better position to aid the minorities, Grew explained, if the treaty became effective. "Are we going to permit our righteous indignation over past injuries to exclude us effectively from opportunities to extend further help?" Grew asked one of the clergymen.[6] Grew's letters and talks with some of the Episcopalians caused them to withdraw their signatures from the petition. Bishop Charles Slattery of Massachusetts admitted he had signed without investigating the petition when Bishop William T. Manning of New York, a leader in the fight against the treaty, presented the document to him.[7] The Episcopal bishops, by bringing up moral issues, invoked an effective if misguided argument against ratification.

Opponents of the Lausanne Treaty had a very effective voice in the Senate, Democratic Senator William H. King of Utah. King summed up the opposition arguments in a resolution introduced on December 22, 1926, when the final Senate fight on the treaty opened. The core of the matter, according to King, was Armenia. He charged that in 1922 both President Warren G. Harding and Secretary of State Charles Evans Hughes had pledged to support the cause of Armenia but that their promises had been ignored in the Lausanne Treaty. He also referred to the Chester concession of 1923, granted to an American group which promised to undertake certain railroad projects in Turkey in return for mineral rights along the railroad's right-of-way. King maintained that the Turkish government granted this concession "with the avowed purpose of securing the moral and diplomatic support of the American delegation [at the Lausanne conference] to certain Turkish contentions as against the Allies." King aimed his third accusation against the Standard Oil Company, which he described as the most important and powerful supporter of the treaty. Standard Oil, King charged, was seeking an oil concession from Turkey in

mittee Opposed to the Lausanne Treaty, *The Lausanne Treaty and Armenia (Supplement)*, pp. 75–79 (text of the bishops' petition).

[6] Bishop Charles L. Brent to Kellogg, December 30, 1926, DS 711.672/531; Grew to Slattery, April 7, 1926, *Turbulent Era*, I, 675–676.

[7] Grew to Thomas Sergeant Perry (Grew's father-in-law), April 10, 1926, *Turbulent Era*, I, 677–678; Washington *Post*, January 6, 1927.

the provinces of Erzurum, Van, and Bitlis. Finally, King noted that the Turkish government had never ceased its "contemptuous disregard of treaty obligations" and "its cruel and despotic course toward Christian minorities within its borders." [8]

The opposition submitted no documentary proof of King's charges, and the State Department totally repudiated them. For example, Secretary of State Frank B. Kellogg pointed out to Senator William E. Borah of the Foreign Relations Committee that the State Department took no action to secure the Chester concession and that no communications concerning it had passed between the Turkish and American delegations at Lausanne. According to Kellogg, the Chester concession, which had been cancelled by the Turkish government in December, 1923, played no part in State Department thinking on the Lausanne Treaty. [9]

Antipathy toward the treaty caused its supporters in the State Department and Senate to delay formal action repeatedly in the hope that the vote, when finally taken, would be favorable. The treaty's proponents employed this strategy even though Americans in Turkey strongly urged an immediate decision and Turkish officials questioned the delay. [10] State Department officials, including Grew, became alarmed as the opposition became more vocal. Grew labeled those fighting against the treaty "armchair theorists" who were misinformed about the true situation in Turkey. Grew felt that United States approval and implementation of the Lausanne settlement would give the leaders of the new Turkey an opportunity to prove themselves sincere and responsible. [11]

Champions of the treaty both in Turkey and in the United States unfortunately were not so active as the opposition in publicizing their cause. Nevertheless, these people, and particularly Americans working in Turkey, were best qualified to pass judgment on the treaty and to describe accurately conditions under the Atatürk government. Missionary and com-

---

[8] *Congressional Record*, 69 Cong., 2 Sess., LXVIII, pt. 1, 910–911. See below, p. 130, for details about the Chester concession. King had made similar charges for several years before 1926.

[9] December 29, 1926, *Papers Relating to the Foreign Relations of the United States, 1926* (2 vols., Washington, 1941), II, 986–990.

[10] James L. Barton to Henry Cabot Lodge, May 16, 1924, William E. Borah MSS (Manuscript Division, Library of Congress, Washington), Box 543; Lodge to Barton, May 22, 1924, *ibid.*; Borah to Kellogg, March 4, 1926, *ibid.*, Box 546.

[11] Grew to Elbert F. Baldwin, February 11, 1924, Grew MSS, 1924, vol. 3; Grew to G. Howland Shaw, April 30, 1924, *ibid.*, 1924, vol. 4; Grew to Archibald Cary Coolidge, January 31, 1924, *ibid.*, 1924, vol. 3.

mercial interests favored ratification for one basic reason – their status would be legalized by full diplomatic recognition. As the president of Robert College in Istanbul expressed it, "We believed that the future welfare of all these interests depended upon the good will of the new government, and that we should accept its pledges and cooperate with it. The fact that all the well informed Americans in Turkey so strongly urged ratification was in itself a weighty argument." [12]

It is notable that the missionaries had reversed themselves from earlier days, when they had been hostile to the Turks and their government, partly because of their treatment of the Armenians. Indeed, the missionaries had made significant contributions to the development of the "Terrible Turk" stereotype. By 1923, however, the missionaries recognized that their former constituency, the Armenians, no longer existed in Turkey. They decided to carry on their work among the Turks themselves rather than withdraw completely. Thus, approval of the Lausanne Treaty was desirable and necessary.[13]

Individually and in groups the missionaries informed their American backers and the State Department about the need for the Lausanne Treaty, as did Boston-based officials of the American Board. The mission workers were concerned not only with their own particular problems but also with the broad questions of American relations with Turkey. American Board members meeting in Istanbul late in 1924 decided that "the efficiency of the American Embassy . . . is seriously handicapped" and that Admiral Mark L. Bristol "feels himself almost helpless in effecting anything of a useful nature under existing circumstances." [14] Admiral Bristol considered it his duty to cooperate with missionary and commercial interests in supporting their views and communicating them to Washington. Bristol encouraged various meetings which discussed the problems created by a lack of proper treaty relations. One such gathering in Istanbul on January 8, 1927, prepared a telegram to Chairman Borah of the Senate Foreign Relations Committee making it clear once again that Americans in Turkey

[12] Caleb Frank Gates, *Not to Me Only* (Princeton, 1940), p. 295.

[13] See below, pp. 147ff., for a detailed discussion of missionary attitudes and work in the interwar period. See also Daniel, "The Armenian Question and American-Turkish Relations, 1914–1927," p. 268.

[14] James L. Barton (Foreign Secretary, American Board) to Charles Evans Hughes, November 24, 1923, Coolidge MSS, Box 193-A; W. W. Peet et al. to Ernest W. Riggs, January 19, 1925, American Board of Commissioners for Foreign Missions MSS (Houghton Library, Harvard University, Cambridge, Mass.), ABC 16.9.1, vol. 3, no. 47.

unanimously endorsed the treaty.[15] The *Congressional Record* printed a petition of April, 1926, from various business, missionary, and educational interests in Turkey. Calling themselves "the American citizens most vitally concerned in Turco-American relations," the signers set forth two reasons why ratification of the treaty was indispensable — first, to regularize the position of American citizens according to Turkish law and to guarantee security in the conduct of operations; and secondly, to secure full diplomatic and consular protection.[16] Americans in Turkey clearly were not seeking special privileges and rights, harking back to the days of the capitulations. Rather, they wanted diplomatic equality which would provide recourse to and support from their government. For these people the capitulations were dead and forgotten.

Numerous other groups in the United States supported the Lausanne Treaty. The Foreign Policy Association issued a pamphlet in 1924 emphasizing the organization's opinion that ratification of the treaty "would be in the best interests of the United States and of the peoples of the Near East." "To treat the Turks as pariahs," the Association stated, "is to invite them to conduct themselves as such. To reject the settlement . . . is to perpetuate the psychology of war. . . . The way to terminate war is to make peace." The United States Chamber of Commerce, the New York State Chamber of Commerce, and the Boston Chamber of Commerce all came out strongly in support of the treaty. They realized that nonratification might seriously hamper trade between Turkey and the United States.[17]

Undersecretary of State Grew capably summarized the thinking of treaty supporters in a clear and concise letter to Senator Charles Curtis. Grew outlined "The Outstanding Reasons Why the Treaty with Turkey Should Be Ratified": (1) old treaties with Turkey are out of date and could not be used to protect American interests; (2) all of the powers except the United States had recognized the abolition of the capitulations; (3) all Americans in Turkey favored ratification of the treaty; (4) defeat of the treaty would harm rather than aid the Greek and Armenian minor-

[15] Hughes to Borah, January 10, 1925, Borah MSS, Box 546; Bristol, Confidential Diary, January 8, 1927, DS 867.00/1950.

[16] 69 Cong., 1 Sess., LXVII, pt. 8, 8407.

[17] *The Turco-American Treaty of Amity and Commerce Signed at Lausanne, August 6, 1923*, Foreign Policy Association Pamphlet No. 27, Series of 1923–1924, in Borah MSS, Box 546; Resident Vice-President, Chamber of Commerce of the United States of America (signature not legible), to Lodge, May 13, 1924, Borah MSS, Box 543; printed document, Chamber of Commerce of the State of New York, January 6, 1927, DS 711.672/535; *Christian Science Monitor*, January 7, 1927.

ities because the United States would not be in a position to give them even moral support; (5) territory for an Armenian national home could be detached from Turkey only by war; (6) the treaty would give Americans treatment equal to that accorded to nationals of the twenty-seven other governments which had concluded treaties with Turkey; and (7) the Turkey of Kemal Atatürk was no worse than the Turkey of Abdul Hamid. "If there was no ethical impropriety in our having formal treaty and diplomatic relations with the Governments of Abdul Hamid and the Young Turks, why should this impropriety be considered to exist now?" Grew asked Curtis.[18] Grew reflected the State Department conclusion that a realistic attitude toward conditions in Turkey was necessary. The moralistic thinking of the opposition, based partly on inaccurate information, would result in little good and perhaps considerable harm to the very groups which it sought to protect.

These pro and con arguments were the basis for the debate on the Lausanne Treaty between 1923 and 1927. Effective propaganda in the United States for the Armenian cause contributed significantly to the final defeat of the treaty. The Episcopal bishops argued that the United States had a moral obligation to Armenia. Senator King listed the failure of the treaty to fulfill American promises to Armenia as a major reason for its defeat.[19]

Another more valid reason for the treaty's demise was its failure to include naturalization provisions. The Turkish government still claimed the allegiance of thousands of naturalized American citizens of Ottoman origin, a fact which had long complicated Turco-American relations. During the Senate debate on the treaty there was discussion and adoption of a reservation guaranteeing that such persons would have the same rights as native Americans in Turkey. Advocates of the treaty opposed this reservation, pointing out that the naturalization question had been discussed without agreement at Lausanne and that the Turks were not likely to accept such a change.[20]

Senator Lawrence D. Tyson of Tennessee listed other reasons, or excuses, for defeat of the treaty. Tyson claimed the Democrats opposed the

[18] May 20, 1926, *Turbulent Era*, I, 679–681.

[19] "Why the Democrats Defeated the Turkish Treaty," *Literary Digest*, XCII (January 29, 1927), 10. See also Philip Marshall Brown, "The Lausanne Treaty," *American Journal of International Law*, XXI (July, 1927), 503.

[20] *Christian Science Monitor*, January 10 and 12, 1927; Kellogg to Bristol, January 11, 1927, *FR 1927*, III, 765.

43

settlement because the treaty of 1830 guaranteed more substantial benefits to American interests. Secondly, since American commercial interests were of great importance to the Turkish economy, the Turkish government would not antagonize them even if the United States rejected the treaty. Tyson also emphasized the effect of the flood of communications from church groups advocating defeat of the treaty; he neglected to point out that they were not from the Congregational Church, the only one active in Turkey.[21]

None of those responsible mentioned the most important reason for rejection of the Lausanne Treaty — domestic politics. Grew, speaking many years later to the American Philosophical Society, stated the problem:

It was a good treaty, from both the American and the Turkish points of view. . . . In some respects, indeed, it was more favorable to American interests even than the treaty negotiated by the Allies was to their interests because I simply outsat General Ismet. I brought it home to Washington, well pleased and expecting the accolade "well done thou good and faithful servant." But alas, alas, domestic politics intervened. There were still in our country elements which were dissatisfied that I had not been able to pull impossible rabbits from impossible hats.[22]

Grew observed on another occasion that the Lausanne defeat "was purely a question of domestic Democratic politics" since the Armenian element had influenced "a small but aggressive group of American senators and bishops."[23] In 1931, while Grew was Ambassador to Turkey, Senator Burton K. Wheeler of Montana told him that "he had voted against the Lausanne treaty since Senator [Claude A.] Swanson had asked him to do so as a personal favor but he hadn't known anything whatever about the real situation and he seemed distinctly regretful that he had taken this action."[24] Political division between Democrats and Republicans, then, was the most important single factor behind the defeat of the Lausanne Treaty.

[21] Memo of conversation, official of the Division of Eastern European Affairs (unidentified) and Lawrence D. Tyson, February 8, 1927, DS 711.672/578.

[22] "The Peace Conference of Lausanne, 1922–1923," *Proceedings of the American Philosophical Society*, XCVIII (February, 1954), 2. On the day the treaty was signed Grew made clear his fears that it would not be popular with the American people. See Grew to Hughes, August 6, 1923, *Turbulent Era*, I, 601–603.

[23] Editor's note, quoting from a 1936 letter from Grew to his daughter, Mrs. J. Pierrepont Moffat, *Turbulent Era*, I, 678–679.

[24] Diary, October 14, 1931, Grew MSS, 1931, vol. 3. Senator Swanson, the ranking member of the Senate Foreign Relations Committee, was a leading opponent of the treaty.

The chance to embarrass the incumbent Coolidge Administration with the defeat of an important treaty could not be ignored. The attitude of the State Department and of Americans in Turkey made no difference to opponents of the treaty.

Reactions to the Senate Decision

There was varied reaction to the defeat of the Lausanne Treaty. Although disturbed that relations with Turkey could not be restored on the basis of the Lausanne settlement, the State Department could gain solace from the fact that the American press generally looked with disfavor on the Senate action. The Washington *Post*, for instance, bluntly stated that the Senate had made an "astonishing blunder" and that the "net result" of its action would be the end of American business opportunities in Turkey.[25] The New York *Times*, though restrained in its comments, called upon Turkey to demonstrate to the world "the seriousness and honesty of her purpose." [26] According to the Atlanta *Constitution*, the economic interests of the United States from the trade angle had been dealt a "serious blow" by the Senate, which acted entirely on prejudice and intolerance. The Pittsburgh *Sun* facetiously called for a constitutional amendment to give the President the right to negotiate treaties "with the advice and dissent" of the Senate.[27] "Seldom has a decision in foreign affairs been taken with more irrelevant emotion and greater disregard for realities," editorialized the New York *Herald Tribune*, and the Philadelphia *Public Ledger* called the Senate action "a rather absurd performance." [28] The general tenor of these editorials was that the Senate, acting with petty and insignificant political grievances in mind, had done a real injustice to Turkey, a country genuinely striving to become one of the enlightened nations of the world.

Newspapers which approved the rejection of the treaty felt that Turkey should not yet be forgiven for past misdeeds. According to the Wheeling *Intelligencer*, "The Senate did right in rejecting the Lausanne Treaty

[25] January 20, 1927.
[26] January 20, 1927.
[27] Quoted in General Committee of American Institutions and Associations in favor of Ratification of the Treaty with Turkey, *American Public Opinion Condemns the Failure to Ratify the American-Turkish Treaty* (New York, 1927), pp. 1, 7, in DS 711.672/568. This pamphlet quotes ninety-two newspaper editorials, seventy-five of which criticized Senate action on the treaty.
[28] Quoted in Kellogg to Bristol, January 21, 1927, *FR 1927*, III, 770.

which . . . condones the wholesale crimes of the Kemal regime. Our State Department ought to have brains enough and prestige enough to make a treaty with Turkey which will protect the universal concepts of honor as well as actual and potential dollars." The Tampa *Tribune* applauded the Lausanne rejection as "quite in accord with the opinion of most private citizens of America who are influenced not exclusively by business considerations but more by humanity. The Turks, in their own peculiar way, are as unworthy of national recognition as Soviet Russia." [29] The *Christian Science Monitor*, certainly not reflecting the views of the Boston-based American Board, heartily applauded the Senate decision on the treaty. The settlement, it said, was a "replica" of the treaty forced upon the European Allies by the Turks, who took advantage of the situation to get concessions. "The representatives of the United States should never have become involved in this precipitate surrender of Europe to the Turk," the *Monitor* observed.[30]

Treaty advocates, particularly State Department officials most intimately connected with Turkish affairs, were immediately worried about the possible effect in Turkey of the treaty rejection, especially since Bristol had reported shortly before the Senate acted that the Turkish press was inspired with the idea that ratification of the treaty was assured. Kellogg hastily instructed Bristol discreetly to dispel this idea.[31] To impress on the Turks that the Senate action did not reflect majority sentiment in the United States, Secretary of State Kellogg sent Bristol quotations from various newspapers condemning the rejection of the treaty. Bristol was to give publicity to these editorials if necessary to assuage the feelings of the Turks.[32] Actually, when Turkish newspapers learned of the failure of the treaty they reacted mildly and with considerable understanding. This helped to blunt the disappointment and fears of Americans in Turkey and of the State Department. Sheldon L. Crosby, Counselor of Embassy in Istanbul, reported to Kellogg that, although the Turkish press was disappointed, its comments were "devoid of criticism or suggestions of retaliation." [33] The Istanbul *Vakit*, for instance, commented as follows:

The failure of the American Senate to ratify the treaty of Lausanne has

[29] Quoted in *American Public Opinion Condemns the Failure to Ratify the American-Turkish Treaty*, pp. 29, 31.
[30] January 25, 1927.
[31] Bristol to Kellogg, January 13, 1927, *FR 1927*, III, 765; Kellogg to Bristol, January 13, 1927, *ibid.*, 766.
[32] January 21, 1927, *ibid.*, 769–770.   [33] January 21, 1927, *ibid.*, 770.

been received here with calm. In connection with this incident, we should bear in mind, first, that the Americans residing in Turkey, including those valued friends of our country, Admiral and Mrs. Bristol, deeply regret this action, and, second, that the treaty was rejected by a minority vote, simply because the two-thirds majority required by the Constitution was not obtained. These two points mitigate the otherwise bad impression produced by the nonratification.[34]

The Turkish press soon forgot about the Lausanne Treaty, which assumed a "most obscure position" within a few days after its rejection.[35]

The Turkish government exhibited no alarm over Senate action on the treaty. As the Turkish Minister for Foreign Affairs pointed out later to Grew, new negotiations would give Turkey an opportunity to obtain a treaty more favorable to its own interest.[36] Turkish officials did puzzle, however, over the fact that a minority in the United States could dictate to the majority. President Atatürk expressed this sentiment in an impromptu speech delivered in the presence of Admiral and Mrs. Bristol in an Ankara club. Kemal emphasized that esteem in Turkey for the Bristols was not impaired, nor was there any fundamental reason why the United States and Turkey should not exist in complete harmony. He could not understand, however, "how it was possible in a country where culture and civilization form the keynote of the social fabric of the nation, that a fanatical minority could impose its will on an enlightened majority." [37] For a time rejection of the treaty put Americans in Turkey in an embarrassing position, but there was no retaliation by the Turks.[38] Furthermore, the United States and Turkey soon reached an agreement which eliminated the possible adverse effects of the defeat of the treaty.

The Restoration of Diplomatic Relations

The Department of State made no further attempt to secure Senate approval of the Lausanne Treaty, although Secretary Kellogg for a while

[34] Quoted in "Turkey and America," *The Living Age*, CCCXXXII (March 15, 1927), 491. See also Mark Lambert Bristol MSS (Manuscript Division, Library of Congress, Washington), Box 12, for a large collection of clippings and translations of articles appearing in the Turkish press on the treaty rejection and related matters.

[35] Charles E. Allen (Consul, Istanbul), Review of the Turkish Press, January 30–February 12, 1927, DS 867.9111/173.

[36] Conversation, Grew and Tevfik Rüsdü Aras, November 3, 1927, *Turbulent Era*, II, 745.

[37] Bristol, Confidential Diary, January 31, 1927, DS 867.00/1954.

[38] Gates, *Not to Me Only*, pp. 295–296; Charles T. Riggs, "Turkey, the Treaties and the Missionaries," *Missionary Review of the World*, L (May, 1927), 343.

kept the possibility in mind.[39] Bristol suggested that the treaty be resubmitted immediately, even though it had no chance for approval, to forestall the Turkish Grand National Assembly from discarding it and to strengthen his hand in the negotiations then under way. The Department of State rejected this suggestion, feeling that the Senate would resent such action so soon after it had spoken on the treaty.[40] In 1928, opponents of the treaty, fearing that the State Department would resubmit it to the Senate, called for hearings. Armenian interests, inspired and led by Vahan Cardashian, the Armenian-American lawyer from New York, petitioned for the hearing. Cardashian drew up a long legal brief reiterating the old charges that the Armenian cause had been bartered for oil at the Lausanne conference. Although Senator King, Cardashian's spokesman in the Senate, submitted a resolution calling for hearings, neither the Senate nor the State Department took any action.[41]

With the Treaty of Lausanne defeated, the State Department faced a major predicament: How was it to accomplish the urgently needed restoration of formal diplomatic relations with Turkey? Admiral Bristol as well as the Department had already given considerable thought to this problem. Secretary Kellogg advised Bristol on the same day the Senate acted on the treaty to proceed to Ankara and explain to Prime Minister Ismet Inönü and Foreign Minister Tevfik Rüsdü Aras that rejection of the treaty by no means implied an American desire to renounce all relations with Turkey. The executive branch of the government, Bristol was to point out, had done all it could to secure approval of the treaty and was now ready to restore diplomatic relations by a simple exchange of notes rather than a formal treaty. Kellogg gave Bristol permission to imply, if asked by the Turks, that the United States no longer recognized the capitulations. He was to "state that as a practical matter this subject had not arisen during the past few years. In this connection you should also state that the present

[39] Kellogg to Bristol, February 1, 1927, *FR 1927*, III, 784.

[40] Bristol to Kellogg, February 6, 1927, *ibid.*, 786–787; Kellogg to Bristol, February 8, 1927, *ibid.*, 789.

[41] Cardashian to Coolidge, February 9, 1928, DS 711.672 Protests/40; Cardashian to Borah, March 24, 1928, DS 711.672 Protests/47; New York *Times*, May 15, 1928. On the advice of the State Department, President Franklin D. Roosevelt on January 12, 1934, asked the Senate to return the Lausanne Treaty to him, a request honored three days later. Thus the treaty was finally dead. See William Phillips to Roosevelt, January 11, 1934, DS 711.672/628 ½; *Journal of the Executive Proceedings of the Senate of the United States of America*, 73 Cong., 2 Sess., LXXV, 87 (hereafter cited as *Sen. Ex. Journal*).

noncapitulatory regime in Turkey has twice been formally, although by implication, recognized by the Government of the United States . . ." through the note exchanges of February 18 and July 20, 1926.[42] Bristol, who did not think the United States should agree to the abrogation of the capitulations in this manner, wrote: "I have always found it an excellent idea while I have been here in Turkey to let sleeping dogs lie, and I see no good reason for changing my policy now." [43]

In his first conversation with Aras after rejection of the treaty, Bristol emphasized the problem of party divisions in the United States. As one of Bristol's aides recorded it,

He [Bristol] explained that the Senate's refusal of the Treaty was primarily traceable to an internal political situation, where the Administration suffered from a lack of conclusive majority. He admitted it to be most regrettable that such a subject as a Treaty should be made the butt of party politics, and then stated strictly confidentially that this amounts simply to another instance of where the merits of a question before the Senate are sometimes lost sight of in the length to which a minority party goes towards derogating the prestige and influence of an Administration and of the President.[44]

At this same meeting, Aras inquired about the possibility of resubmitting the Lausanne Treaty to the next session of the Senate. Aras really did not favor resubmission because two days later, when he suggested the negotiation of a simple treaty of amity, he made it clear to the Admiral that he preferred a new treaty. Bristol thought the Turks wanted to get rid of the Lausanne Treaty because it contained more favorable provisions than they wished to accord to other nations.[45]

The Aras-Bristol negotiations resulted in an agreement in mid-February, 1927. Aras argued for some time in favor of a formal treaty of amity, until Bristol convinced him that such a treaty would probably meet the same fate in the Senate as the Lausanne Treaty.[46] Ultimately, the

[42] Bristol, Confidential Diary, January 6, 1927, Bristol MSS, Box 26; Kellogg to Bristol, January 18, 1927, *FR 1927*, III, 766–768.

[43] Bristol, Confidential Diary, February 8, 1927, DS 867.00/1958.

[44] As recorded by Robert Treat, in Bristol's Confidential Diary, January 22, 1927, Bristol MSS, Box 26.

[45] Bristol to Kellogg, January 22, 1927, *FR 1927*, III, 772; Bristol to Kellogg, January 24, 1927, *ibid.*, 775–777. See Bristol, Confidential Diary, January 22, 1927, Bristol MSS, Box 26, for a résumé of Bristol's initial talk with Aras.

[46] See Bristol to Kellogg, March 16, 1927, DS 867.00/1961, for a group of excerpts from Bristol's diary covering the entire period of negotiations. See also Bristol, Confidential Diary, January 29, 1927, Bristol MSS, Box 26.

49

two negotiators decided on a simple exchange of notes and established a tentative formula for the agreement by January 30. When Bristol and Aras signed the notes on the afternoon of February 17, 1927, they also agreed to extend the modus vivendi on commercial relations between the two countries.[47] The first note contained these main points: (1) The United States and Turkey will establish diplomatic and consular relations and appoint ambassadors as soon as possible. (2) The two countries will regulate by treaties or conventions the commercial and consular relations and conditions of establishment and residence in their respective territories; if the Treaty of Lausanne is ratified by both countries by June 1, 1928, this requirement will be met; if the treaty is ratified, Article 31 shall be modified to provide that provisions of a temporary nature shall expire on the same date as they do in the Allied-Turkish treaty of July 24, 1923. (3) The United States and Turkey agree that the extradition treaty signed at Lausanne shall at a convenient time be submitted to both governments for ratifications. (4) Negotiations for a naturalization convention will start within six months after the Lausanne Treaty or new consular and establishment and residence conventions go into effect. (5) The question of claims will be handled in accordance with the exchange of notes of December 24, 1923; these notes will be effective six months after mutual ratification of both the new commercial and establishment and residence conventions, if the Lausanne Treaty is not ratified. (6) Pending the effective date of the consular and establishment and residence conventions or the Lausanne Treaty, the principles established above and the "essential provisions" of the Lausanne Treaty will be the basis reciprocally accorded the nationals of either country when they are in the territory of the other.[48]

The second note extended the modus vivendi on commercial relations for an additional fifteen months if necessary.[49] Not only did the two notes provide for the immediate necessities in Turco-American relations but also they established procedures for the future negotiation of other conventions and treaties. This was in line with the purposes of the State Department as Kellogg outlined them in an instruction to Bristol

[47] Bristol to Kellogg, January 30, 1927, *FR 1927*, III, 780; Bristol to Kellogg, February 17, 1927, *ibid.*, 799.

[48] Bristol to Aras, February 17, 1927, *ibid.*, 794–795. The original documents are in Bristol to Kellogg, April 1, 1927, DS 711.672/587.

[49] Bristol to Aras, February 17, 1927, *FR 1927*, III, 797–798.

during the negotiations. Kellogg's statement on American policy toward Turkey was indicative of his sincerity in trying to regularize Turco-American relations:

The Government of the United States is now looking at its relations with the Government of Turkey not in terms of months but in terms of years. It is animated only by an earnest desire to have friendly official contact with the Government of Turkey as quickly as possible and eventually to develop through such friendly contact comprehensive treaty relations between the United States and Turkey. A great deal has been accomplished in the last few months towards a better understanding of Turkey in the United States in spite of the failure of the United States Senate to ratify the treaty of August 6. American public opinion is unquestionably being favorably impressed by the good sense apparently displayed by Turkey in the face of the Senate's action.[50]

The Turks were pleased with the new arrangements. The State Department authorized Bristol to sign the proposed notes on February 15, 1927. That evening Admiral and Mrs. Bristol attended a dance at the Czechoslovak Legation in Ankara where the other guests included Aras and Prime Minister Ismet Inönü. Bristol described the event in his diary: "Tewfik Rouschdy Bey [Aras] asked Mrs. Bristol to tell Ismet Pasha that we had received authority to sign the notes. Ismet Pasha immediately became very much pleased over this news and expressed his pleasure to me. . . . Ismet Pasha was evidently feeling very jolly and entered quite into the spirit of the dance. There is no doubt that Ismet Pasha and Tewfik Rouschdy Bey were very pleased with the news that I had received." [51]

The exchange of notes was extremely significant because it restored formal diplomatic relations after a lapse of almost ten years. During this period the sole instrument of the United States government in Turkey was the High Commission, which operated in its later years under the sufferance of the Turkish government. As time passed Admiral Bristol felt more and more the need for a stable arrangement. American institutions and commercial interests operating in Turkey clamored for aid from their government; the sending of an ambassador to Turkey was a prerequisite for furnishing this aid. By restoring formal diplomatic relations, the agreement provided the official machinery for working out the details essential to more normal relations.

[50] February 8, 1927, *ibid.*, 790.
[51] Confidential Diary, February 15, 1927, Bristol MSS, Box 26.

Reaction to the Agreement in the United States

Friends of Turkey in the United States welcomed the new arrangements. In general, editorial comment hailed it as a victory for American interests in Turkey and, as the *Literary Digest* expressed it, "a slap on the Senate's collective wrist." The New York *Times* depicted the agreement as a tribute to Bristol and a "reflection of credit upon the Turkish authorities that in spite of the defeat of the Lausanne Treaty the relations of amity are again extended." [52] Curiously enough, the exchange of notes "passed virtually unnoticed by the press" in Turkey. One paper humorously observed, however, that Turkey owed a debt of gratitude to the Senate: "We want to sincerely thank the minority of the American Senate for having been unfriendly to us. We ourselves shall never be able to carry on propaganda in America but here are these dear Senators who, by their negative attitude, have afforded our two countries an excellent opportunity to know each other better and draw more closely together." [53]

The opposition in the United States to the exchange of notes, composed of the same elements who had fought the Lausanne Treaty, was loud and almost violent in its protests. The dominant personality was Vahan Cardashian. The general contents of the notes became public knowledge after their signature, although the texts were kept secret for almost a month.[54] Cardashian, who wasted no time in registering a clear protest with Secretary Kellogg, termed the exchange of notes "an arbitrary misuse of power by [the] executive" and "a calculated defiance of [the] senate." [55] In a subsequent letter to President Coolidge, Cardashian described the agreement as "(1) faithless, (2) high-handed, (3) purposeless, and (4) offensive and provocative." Cardashian asserted in his seven-page letter that Coolidge had robbed the Senate of its concurrent voice in the making of treaties and that the State Department supported "so-called missionaries," who were maintaining secular Turkish schools, and concession hunters interested in oil. Cardashian concluded, "The present Department of State . . . has resorted, in its handling of the Turkish situation, to the tactics commonly used at Quai d'Orsay by subordinates; and, in my opin-

[52] "Muddling Through with Turkey," *Literary Digest*, XCIII (April 9, 1927), 14; New York *Times*, February 20, 1927.
[53] Allen, Review of the Turkish Press, February 13–26, 1927, DS 867.9111/174.
[54] New York *Times*, February 19 and March 15, 1927; Kellogg to Bristol, February 14, 1927, *FR 1927*, III, 792–793; Grew (Acting Secretary of State) to Bristol, March 9, 1927, *ibid.*, 801; Bristol to Kellogg, March 11, 1927, *ibid.*, 802.
[55] February 19, 1927, DS 711.672 Protests/-.

ion, based upon my experience with it, it has not hesitated to draw upon, at times, quite freely, the methods of the Bolshevist Foreign Office."[56]

During the spring of 1927, Cardashian hounded President Coolidge and Secretary Kellogg with additional unfounded assertions.[57] He complained repeatedly about the projected exchange of ambassadors, on one occasion asking whether the Greeks and Armenians in the United States "would swallow so bitter a pill as a Turkish Ambassador." [58] He further threatened to obtain a "Writ of Prohibition" to enjoin Coolidge from exchanging ambassadors with Turkey. "It is most distressing," he wrote, "that the President of the United States should be led into doing a thing which is clearly in violation of the fundamental law of the land." [59]

In various cities Cardashian organized mass meetings which adopted resolutions protesting against the February, 1927, agreement and particularly attacking the proposed exchange of ambassadors. These meetings held in April, May, and June, 1927, flooded the Department of State and the White House with resolutions and other communications. Cardashian personally presided and spoke at meetings in several cities.[60] Cardashian received support from some of the same persons who had fought against the Lausanne Treaty — James W. Gerard, D. Parkes Cadman, William T. Manning, and others. Gerard, speaking for the American Committee Opposed to the Lausanne Treaty, again argued that the 1830 treaty was the sole legal basis for Turkish-American relations and that the new arrangement was illegal.[61] The State Department, though disturbed by the protests, ignored them. It was, of course, the President's constitutional right to send and receive ambassadors. Furthermore, the Department did not interpret the agreement of February, 1927, as a direct attempt to put the Lausanne Treaty into operation.[62]

Reflecting continued division within their ranks, not all Armenians in

[56] March 21, 1927, DS 711.672 Protests/2.
[57] See Cardashian to Kellogg, April 8, 1927, DS 711.672 Protests/4; Cardashian to Coolidge, April 25, 1927, DS 711.672 Protests/7; Cardashian to Kellogg, May 7, 1927, DS 711.672 Protests/10; and Cardashian to Coolidge, May 20, 1927, DS 711.672 Protests/12.
[58] To Kellogg, April 8, 1927, DS 711.672 Protests/4.
[59] To Coolidge, May 20, 1927, DS 711.672 Protests/12.
[60] See DS 711.672 Protests/7, /8, /9, /15, /16, /17, /18, /20, /22, /23, and /26.
[61] New York *Times*, June 23, 1927; D. P. Cadman and W. T. Manning to Kellogg, April 11, 1927, DS 711.672 Protests/5; Gerard to Coolidge, May 18, 1927, Coolidge MSS, Box 193-A.
[62] G. Howland Shaw (Chief, Near Eastern Division) to Arthur F. Newell, June 8, 1927, DS 711.67/59; Kellogg to Borah, March 31, 1928, DS 711.672/610a.

the United States supported Cardashian. A leading Armenian publication labeled him a "vainglorious charlatan" who was exploiting the Armenian cause for "personal aggrandizement." The article continued:

In order to mystify unsophisticated Armenians concerning his importance, he fabricates self-laudatory interviews with anonymous Senators, insinuates that he writes the material signed by the distinguished members of the American Committee Opposed to the Lausanne Treaty, sends fatuous and insolent letters to the Department of State; and, being unaware that Bishop William T. Manning, Senator William H. King, James W. Gerard and other prominent Americans were friends of Armenia long before they had heard of his existence, quotes them mendaciously to the effect that but for him they would not have taken any interest in the cause of Armenian independence.[63]

Admiral Bristol, commenting on this article, wrote: "It looks as if they are trying to chuck Kordashian or at least pave the way to shirk responsibility for him if anyone attempts to show him up in his true colors." [64]

The Appointment of Joseph Grew

The initial step toward implementing the agreement was the exchange of ambassadors. Joseph C. Grew's already long diplomatic career and his close association with problems in Turkish-American relations made him the person best qualified to represent the United States in Turkey. Thus, there was little surprise when rumors that he would get the position proved valid.[65] Also, there was evidence that Grew and Secretary of State Kellogg were not on the best of terms. The Frederick, Maryland, *News* reported this on March 19, 1927:

One of the most interesting bits of gossip about the State Department tells of a feud between Secretary of State Kellogg and Under-Secretary Joseph C. Grew. When Kellogg is away, Grew takes charge, but when Kellogg returns to his job he totally ignores Grew, according to some members of the department personnel. Some of the service men refer to the situation as a "sitting match," between the two men, believing that Kellogg doesn't want to resign lest Grew obtain control and perhaps succeed him, and that Grew has been doggedly fighting appointment as ambassador to Turkey

---

[63] "Thus Far and No Farther," *The New Armenia*, XIX (April–June, 1927), 17.
[64] To Shaw, July 1, 1927, DS 860j.01/587 ½.
[65] Grew to Thomas S. Perry, February 25, 1927, Grew MSS, 1927, vol. 4; Grew to Arthur B. Lane, April 16, 1927, *ibid.*, 1927, vol. 3; New York *Times*, May 18, 1927.

or some other post because of his desire to remain in a position of authority over all embassies and legations.[66]

Grew confirmed the truth of the assertions in the first part of this article in a later letter to a State Department colleague. Grew felt that Kellogg, who neither informed him nor consulted him on State Department business, did not respect his opinion.[67]

Also in the background of Grew's appointment was a possible investigation of appointment procedures in the Foreign Service growing out of alleged favoritism for social diplomats over consular officers. During the investigation by a Senate committee in 1928, Secretary Kellogg made it clear that Grew, as chairman of the Foreign Service Personnel Board, had not promoted himself, as charged, and that President Coolidge thought Grew was the only person in the State Department who could negotiate a new treaty with Turkey.[68] Grew felt that "a change was clearly indicated" in the undersecretaryship and that "new blood was clearly needed on the [Personnel] Board." [69] As he wrote to his uncle, "I am very keen about the job as there is some important constructive work to be done in Angora [Ankara] and I am keenly interested in the development of the new Turkey. . . . I wanted a working rather than a social post and Turkey fills the bill in that respect." [70]

After Admiral Bristol had secured Turkish approval, the State Department announced Grew's selection, and he received his formal commission and letter of credence on May 27, 1927.[71] Both Turks and Americans in Turkey heartily approved of Grew's selection. The Turkish press, commenting extensively, emphasized his role at the Lausanne conference as qualifying him for the post. One Istanbul paper, *Le Milliyet*, mentioned that he was a friend of Inönü's and that, in contrast to standard practice in regard to American ambassadors to Turkey, he was not Jewish.[72] The *Le-*

---

[66] Clipping, Grew MSS, 1927, vol. 2. Evidence does not support the allegations in the latter part of the statement. See also Waldo H. Heinrichs, Jr., *American Ambassador: Joseph C. Grew and the Development of the United States Diplomatic Tradition* (Boston, 1966), pp. 115–125.

[67] To William R. Castle, Jr., September 11, 1928, *Turbulent Era*, I, 652–653.

[68] Editor's note, *ibid.*, 698–699, 702–704.

[69] Grew to Alexander C. Kirk, July 15, 1927, *ibid.*, 705.

[70] To Henry S. Grew, May 25, 1927, Grew MSS, 1927, vol. 3.

[71] Kellogg to Bristol, May 9, 1927, *FR 1927*, III, 803; Bristol, Confidential Diary, May 16, 1927, DS 867.00/1971; Kellogg to Grew, May 27, 1927, DS 123 G 861/300A.

[72] New York *Times*, May 20, 1927.

vant Trade Review, published by the American Chamber of Commerce in Istanbul, voiced the sentiments of Americans in Turkey as entirely favorable to Grew's selection.[73]

In the United States there was a mixed reaction to Grew's appointment. Friends of Turkey and most of the press applauded the choice as logical and designed to strengthen Turkish-American relations. Many newspapers, such as the Washington *Evening Star,* saw particular merit in Grew's designation because he was a career diplomat rather than a social diplomat, and they also noted that the tradition of appointing Jews to the post had been broken. The practice of placing Jews in this position, the paper explained, was founded on the belief that Turkey, as a Muslim country, preferred non-Christian representatives from other nations.[74]

Grew's designation as ambassador gave Turkey's enemies in the United States another opportunity to proclaim loudly against the resumption of diplomatic relations. A few newspapers questioned the appointment of an ambassador after the Senate had rejected a treaty designed to restore diplomatic relations.[75] The most outspoken and radical opposition to Grew, as might be expected, came from Vahan Cardashian, who complained in a letter to Secretary Kellogg that "the appointment of Mr. Grew is an utterly insane thing to do. . . . Permit me to say that I detest lawlessness and crookedness particularly in high places. That is how Bolshevism came about." [76] James W. Gerard, again representing the American Committee Opposed to the Lausanne Treaty, contended in a letter to Kellogg that the February, 1927, agreement ignored the authority of the Senate. "Likewise," Gerard wrote, "it is difficult to understand why we should send an 'Ambassador' to Turkey — a primitive Asiatic country, with a population of 5,000,000, when we have reduced to a Legation our Embassy to Austria." [77]

Almost a year passed before the Senate confirmed Grew's appointment. President Coolidge gave him an interim appointment in May, 1927,

[73] "Arrival of Ambassador Grew," XV (September, 1927), 371–373.
[74] May 20, 1927, clipping in Grew MSS, 1927, vol. 2. See this volume for a large collection of newspaper clippings on the Grew appointment.
[75] "Now on Speaking Terms with Turkey," *Literary Digest,* XCIII (June 11, 1927), 13.
[76] May 21, 1927, DS 711.672 Protests/13.
[77] Made public on June 22, 1927, quoted in *Turbulent Era,* II, 710, n. 3. Gerard's population figure was inaccurate. The Turkish population was estimated at 14,500,000 in 1930. See Royal Institute of International Affairs, *The Middle East: A Political and Economic Survey* (2nd ed., London & New York, 1954), p. 559.

and sent his formal nomination as Ambassador Extraordinary and Pleni-potentiary to Turkey to the Senate on December 6, 1927. Although the speculation was that Grew's nomination would be confirmed with com-parative ease, four months elapsed before the Senate acted.[78] The Senate Foreign Relations Committee delayed action partly because of the immi-nent investigation of the Foreign Service Personnel Board, scheduled to begin after the 1927 holidays. Kellogg telegraphed reassurances to Grew, who was disturbed about the delay on his confirmation, especially as to how the Turkish government and press would react "when Senator King gets busy on the floor of the Senate." Writing to Hugh R. Wilson, Ameri-can minister to Switzerland, he said: "The Turks behaved very well when the Lausanne Treaty was rejected, and pretty well, when the Mouhtar Bey–Gerard incident occurred, but they are a little sore about it all and if more nasty things are said about them in the United States, the press is more than likely to blow up." [79] In a later letter to Wilson, Grew described the Personnel Board investigation as a means "to permit various disgrun-tled consular officers to be heard. . . . After they have finished with my reputation on the Personnel issue I then have to pass through still another Purgatory before eventually emerging into an alleged Heaven of national confidence and confirmed ambassadorship. In this second Purgatory we encounter a solid phalanx of democrats led by Senators Swanson and King and if we get through that I shall feel like the ship that makes port after many storms." [80]

Finally, on April 4, 1928, Chairman Borah of the Foreign Relations Committee favorably reported Grew's nomination, which the Senate ap-proved the next day. The State Department informed Grew of the Senate action, and the newspapers reported that the American colony in Turkey and Turkish officials had received the news with satisfaction.[81] But actual-ly, the struggle was not over. On April 6, Senator David A. Reed of Penn-sylvania, on behalf of Senator King, moved that Grew's confirmation be

[78] *Sen. Ex. Journal*, 70 Cong., 1 Sess., LXVI, pt. 1, 47; *Christian Science Moni-tor*, November 30, 1927; clipping, Washington *Evening Star*, November 27, 1927, Grew MSS, 1927, vol. 2.
[79] Kellogg to Grew, December 21, 1927, DS 123 G 861/322a; Grew to Hugh R. Wilson, December 29, 1927, Grew MSS, 1927, vol. 4. See below, pp. 60–62 for in-formation about the Mouhtar-Gerard incident.
[80] February 25, 1928, Grew MSS, 1928, vol. 2.
[81] *Sen. Ex. Journal*, 70 Cong., 1 Sess. LXVI, pt. 1, 643; diary, April 6, 1928, *Turbulent Era*, II, 772; clipping, Washington *Evening Star*, April 7, 1928, Grew MSS, 1928, vol. 4.

reconsidered. Apparently Senator Borah had promised King that the nomination would not be confirmed until King had a chance to speak on it. But both Borah and King were absent from the executive session which approved Grew's nomination. The result was Reed's motion, which the Senate approved on April 9. When the Senate reconsidered the nomination on April 13, after hearing remarks from King, Swanson, and Borah, it once again gave its consent.[82]

Grew felt that the mix-up resulted from another attempt by King to express his opposition to the restoration of official Turkish-American relations. Grew raised a good point in a letter to a fellow diplomat: "I at least, have the honor of being probably the only Federal official whose nomination has ever been confirmed twice. An interesting point of law would have arisen if King had been able to have the nomination voted down upon reconsideration. I hardly think that it would have been legal." [83] The Turkish Foreign Minister remarked to Grew at the time that his double confirmation was a significant sign of the consolidation of Turkish-American relations. What it actually represented, however, was a grandstand attempt to embarrass the Department of State in its implementation of Turkish policy. A further illustration of this tactic was the resolution which Senator King submitted to the Senate on April 10, 1928. Once again he complained that the February, 1927, agreement and the exchange of ambassadors was "a serious and unwarranted infringement by the Executive on the constitutional powers of the Senate and a violation of both the spirit and letter of the Constitution." The Senate took no action on this resolution.[84]

By the time of his confirmation, Grew had been in Turkey for seven months. He arrived with his family on September 18, 1927, after talks with American ambassadors in London, Paris, and Berne.[85] Bertha Carp, a veteran secretary at the Istanbul embassy, made some amusing remarks about the pending arrival of the Grew family: "Well the Grews are arriving Sunday with femme de chambre, valet de chambre, chambermaid, maitre d'hotel, and ninety nine more on his string. The van has arrived

[82] *Sen. Ex. Journal*, 70 Cong., 1 Sess., LXVI, pt. 1, 655–656, 671; Grew to Robert W. Bliss, June 9, 1928, Grew MSS, 1928, vol. 1; New York *Times*, April 8, 1928.

[83] To Bliss, June 9, 1928, Grew MSS, 1928, vol. 1.

[84] Conversation, Grew and Aras, April 19, 1928, *ibid.*, 1928, vol. 3; *Congressional Record*, 70 Cong., 1 Sess., LXIX, pt. 6, 6142–6143.

[85] Robert E. Olds (Undersecretary of State) to Grew, July 1, 1927, DS 123 G 861/301a; diary, September 9–18, 1927, *Turbulent Era*, II, 715.

and it took weeks to assure the Turks that the States is not contemplating war on them when they saw such a thing that weighed tons and tons with loaded stuff which had to pass 'unopened.' Finally we convinced them and then people came from all quarters to see this huge van and gaze at it." [86] After moving into the embassy, which Mrs. Grew immediately started to redecorate, Grew saw the Foreign Minister on September 22, 1927, and President Atatürk formally received him on October 12.[87]

The Grew appointment brought to a close a unique diplomatic career — that of Rear Admiral Mark L. Bristol. The wearer of many hats during his eight-year stay in Turkey, Admiral Bristol earned the deep confidence and respect of the Turkish government and people. Although a career naval officer, his success as a diplomat in Turkey overshadows his considerable accomplishments in the Navy. With the signing of the 1927 agreement and Grew's designation as ambassador, Bristol returned to naval service. The Navy Department, in fact, had asked the State Department in 1924 when it could expect the Admiral's return to full-time naval service. Bristol indicated then that he would be glad to remain in Turkey as long as necessary, but that he "would welcome an opportunity to complete his career in the Navy in an appropriate manner." Because President Coolidge preferred no change in the High Commissioner's office at the time, Bristol remained under State Department control. On March 19, 1927, Bristol received instructions to conclude his work in Turkey by June 1. He actually departed on May 24, leaving Sheldon L. Crosby as chargé d'affaires pending Grew's arrival.[88]

Congratulating Bristol on his work, Coolidge wrote that his success and the position he had established for the United States in Turkey were "notable in the annals of American diplomacy." Coolidge also congratulated him on his new position as commander-in-chief of the United States Asiatic Fleet.[89] Ahmed Emin Yalman, the prominent Turkish journalist, has paid high tribute to Bristol's work:

The choice of . . . Bristol as American high commissioner must be men-

[86] To Admiral and Mrs. Bristol, September 13, 1927, Bristol MSS, Box 12.
[87] Diary, September 27 and October 12, 1927, Grew MSS, 1927, vol. 1; diary, September 22, 1927, *Turbulent Era*, II, 719–722.
[88] Curtis D. Wilbur to Hughes, October 8, 1924, Coolidge MSS, Box 193; Hughes to Wilbur, December 22, 1924, *ibid.*; Hughes to Coolidge, December 22, 1924, *ibid.*; Coolidge to Hughes, December 22, 1924, *ibid.*; Kellogg to Bristol, March 19, 1927, *FR 1927*, III, 802; Sheldon L. Crosby to Kellogg, May 24, 1927, *ibid.*, 804.
[89] June 20, 1927, Bristol MSS, Box 12.

tioned as one of the few favorable outside factors against thousands of adverse ones in the first phase of the Turkish "National Struggle" . . . His activities from the beginning to the end of our struggle for independent national existence amounted, in effect, to almost an informal alliance between Turkey and the United States. . . . This American's concern for Turkey's fate in the critical years, 1919–23, can be considered the introductory phase of Turkish-American cooperation during and after World War II. . . . Admiral Bristol's persuasive words and constructive actions contributed greatly to the negotiation of peace in the Balkans and Middle East, where he saw, instead of a "powder barrel," a potential stronghold for international peace.[90]

Certainly, Bristol's work in Turkey laid the foundations for the successes experienced in Turkish-American relations in the years following his stay there.

Controversy over Ambassador Ahmed Mouhtar

To implement the new agreement with the United States, the Turkish government designated Ahmed Mouhtar as its ambassador on May 25, 1927, a choice which the United States government immediately approved.[91] Born about 1870, Mouhtar studied law in Istanbul and then entered the Ottoman foreign service. Joining the Nationalists after World War I, he served in 1921–1922 as Minister for Foreign Affairs and later became Turkish ambassador to the Soviet Union. At the time of his appointment to the United States he was a deputy for Istanbul in the Grand National Assembly. Welcoming the appointment, Grew described Mouhtar as an "old-school diplomat" and the "doyen of the Turkish diplomatic service," one well qualified to serve as Turkey's chief representative in the United States.[92]

One of Grew's first tasks after his arrival in Turkey was to persuade Mouhtar to depart for the United States. After Grew made many representations to Turkish officials, Mouhtar finally left for America in mid-November, 1927. Grew was never able to ascertain definitely the cause of the delay, though he speculated on numerous occasions that Mouhtar dreaded ocean travel. The Turkish government suggested that Mouhtar

[90] *Turkey in My Time* (Norman, Okla., 1956), pp. 78–79.
[91] Crosby to Kellogg, May 25, 1927, *FR 1927*, III, 804; Everett Sanders (Coolidge's secretary) to Kellogg, May 27, 1927, Coolidge MSS, Box 193.
[92] Crosby to Kellogg, June 4, 1927, DS 701.6711/191; Crosby to Kellogg, July 1, 1927, DS 701.6711/195; Grew to Shaw, October 19, 1927, Grew MSS, 1927, vol. 4.

could not go to Washington until arrangements were completed for hous-
ing and an embassy staff.[93]

When Mouhtar arrived in the United States on November 28, 1927,
the Cardashian-Gerard group greeted him with a storm of protest. Actually, these complaints began as soon as the Turkish government announced
Mouhtar's appointment.[94] For several days, beginning on November 27,
1927, Gerard released statements charging Mouhtar with responsibility
for the massacre of 30,000 Christians in the Alexandropol region of Armenia in August, 1920. He had been involved, Gerard maintained, in a
Turco-Soviet agreement in 1919 providing for the division of Armenia between the two nations, and this had led to the Alexandropol events. Gerard also reiterated two old points, that the exchange of ambassadors was
unconstitutional and that the State Department was still trying to facilitate
the granting of oil concessions in the Middle East to American interests.
Discounting the charges, the State Department stated that Turkey was
sending one of its most distinguished diplomats to the United States and
that the President had every right to receive him.[95]

The State Department was apprehensive about Mouhtar's safety after
Gerard's outburst. United States officials took him in a Coast Guard cutter
from his ship to the United States Barge Office on the Battery and then
twelve armored motorcycles escorted him to his train in New York. Upon
his arrival, Mouhtar denied the alleged massacre charges, stating that he
was not in Turkish government service at the time. When he arrived in
Washington, under constant secret service guard since leaving New York,
Mouhtar went to the Wardman Park Hotel, his temporary residence. The
State Department countered criticism of the elaborate precautions taken
to ensure Mouhtar's safety with the statement that it had arranged the ambassador's trip to Washington because he had no staff already assembled
to take care of the details.[96] Grew in Turkey fretted about the Armenian-
inspired threats against Mouhtar. He wrote in his diary, "If the Armenians
in the United States get old Mouhtar, the Government might just as well
send a battleship for my remains without waiting for the event, for it won't

[93] Diary, October 31 and November 13, 1927, Grew MSS, 1927, vol. 1; conversation, Grew and Aras, November 3, 1927, *Turbulent Era*, II, 744–745; New York
Times, November 15, 1927.
[94] Kellogg to High Commission, May 28, 1927, DS 701.6711/190.
[95] New York *Times*, November 28 and 29, December 1, 1927.
[96] *Ibid.*, November 29, 1927; Washington *Post*, November 29, 1927; Kellogg to
Grew, November 29, 1927, DS 701.6711/213A.

take long." Later, after being informed of Mouhtar's safe arrival in Washington, Grew wrote: "It is at least a relief to know that Mouhtar has arrived in Washington, although if some fanatic Armenian is out to get him, he can probably do it there as easily as in New York. If anything happens to Mouhtar, Gerard will have a lot to answer for, at least to his own conscience — if he has any, which I doubt." [97]

Although Gerard quieted down after Mouhtar's arrival, Cardashian continued the campaign against him. In a letter to the President, he labeled the Turkish ambassador an "undesirable alien," arguing that as a "war criminal and common felon" Mouhtar was barred from entrance into the United States by immigration laws. Cardashian ignored advice by the State Department not to publish these charges. The press paid little attention to him, and it was understood at the time that even Gerard refused Cardashian permission to use his name in connection with the charges.[98]

Although the Gerard-Mouhtar incident caused considerable anxiety for Grew in Turkey, the Turkish press showed restraint. It fully reported the events, but editorial comment, though critical, emphasized that the disturbance in the United States was the work of a minority and that partisan domestic politics played an important role.[99] Grew, however, made a hasty trip to Ankara, where he explained to Foreign Minister Aras that Gerard in no way represented the views of the United States government and that Mouhtar had been cordially received by government officials. "Tewfik Rushdi said that he cared only for the point of view of the American Government and that this outburst of a minority did not bother him at all," Grew recorded after this interview.[100] Later on, Aras observed that he was satisfied with Mouhtar's reception in Washington (the Gerard attack had resulted in a more cordial welcome from the United States government), and that Mouhtar was happy there. When President Coolidge received Mouhtar on December 5, 1927, he completed the formal re-establishment of Turkish-American relations.[101]

[97] Diary, November 29 and 30, 1927, Grew MSS, 1927, vol. 1.
[98] Cardashian to Coolidge, March 1, 1928, DS 711.672 Protests/43; Cardashian to Kellogg, March 5, 1928, DS 711.672 Protests/44; Kellogg to Grew, March 17, 1928, DS 711.672 Protests/46a.
[99] Grew to Kellogg, December 6, 1927, DS 701.6711/223; Allen, Review of the Turkish Press, December 1–4, 1927, DS 867.9111/206.
[100] Diary, December 10, 1927, *Turbulent Era*, II, 749. See also Grew to Bristol, December 23, 1927, Grew MSS, 1927, vol. 3.
[101] Diary, January 10, 1928, Grew MSS, 1928, vol. 3; New York *Times*, December 6, 1927.

1927 and the Future

The year 1927 marked the end of a decade's break in diplomatic relations and initiated a process which eventually made Turkey and the
United States staunch friends. The rejection of the Lausanne Treaty early
in 1927 constituted only a temporary setback. Opponents of the treaty, influenced by farfetched and fanatical charges by Armenians and their supporters and by partisan politics, were ill advised. At the price of harm for
the Armenian cause, the opposition elements worked against the well-con-
ceived plans of the Department of State and the wishes of those persons
most concerned — the American missionary and commercial interests in
Turkey. The Turks' magnanimity did much to soften the effects of the
treaty's rejection.

The United States obviously could not continue indefinitely without
formal relations with Turkey. Although Turkish-American trade was not
large, it was quite important to Turkey and to various American interests
operating there. Perhaps the United States could have succeeded in isolat-
ing itself from Turkey in 1927, but doing so would not have been practical
and, from Turkey's point of view, it would have been economically disastrous.

The alternative to the Lausanne Treaty was the exchange of notes of
February 17, 1927, an agreement which provided procedures for subsequent adjustment of Turkish-American relations. In this unique way, the
two governments were able to circumvent opposition in the United States.
The exchange of notes continued the long process of rapprochement, initiated by Admiral Bristol, between Turkey and the United States.

The appointments of Joseph Clark Grew and Ahmed Mouhtar were
the first major steps in implementing the 1927 agreement. Both countries
chose important and highly qualified diplomats, testifying to the emphasis
they placed on the resumption of relations. The diehard opposition in the
United States protested loudly, without lasting effect. Turkey, acting with
dignity and restraint, chose to recognize the honorable intentions of the
United States government rather than be misled by a small minority. Although Grew's work in Turkey over a period of almost five years somewhat overshadowed that of Mouhtar Bey in the United States, both diplomats proved their value and more than justified their selections.

Thus, 1927 was an important turning point in interwar Turkish-
American relations. During this year the United States began to orient its
Turkish policy in terms of years rather than days. American interests in

Turkey received guarantees of official government representation and protection which, as events proved, were very much needed. The same year saw the genesis of an altered public opinion of Turkey in the United States and almost the last stand of the embattled Armenian-Americans. The developments of the next twelve years were to prove decisive for American policy in Turkey and the Middle East.

❀ America Faces Turkey: The Framework of Turkish-American Relations in the Interwar Period

WHEN the United States re-established formal relations with Turkey in 1927, that nation was much different than it had been when Ambassador Elkus left in 1917. The decadent and sprawling Ottoman Empire had been transformed into a dynamic republic under the leadership of a national hero, Kemal Atatürk. Turkey's outlook on both domestic and foreign affairs was vastly different than it had been in the days of the Sultans. Relieved of many of the problems of the old Ottoman Empire, the new republic was able to chart a progressive and modernizing course. On the domestic scene, Atatürk instituted a series of sweeping political, social, religious, and economic reforms. Internationally, the Turks pursued a policy of peaceful coexistence after 1923. Turkey's domestic and international policies had as a basic purpose the restoration of the country to a position of influence and respect in the family of nations.

The Turkish reforms forced the American government and people to alter their thinking about Turkey. Some Americans had certain opinions which had to be dispelled before Turkish-American relations could become cordial. The governments of the two nations as well as private individuals and organizations dedicated themselves to the task of eliminating the invalid stereotype of the Turk. In this endeavor they were generally successful. The Turkish transformation also determined in part the character of the tasks of American diplomats in Turkey. A survey of the reform program as well as acquaintance with the careers and attitudes of these

65

diplomats is essential to an understanding of Turkish-American relations during the interwar period.

The Turkish Reform Movement

The nationalistic revolution which Atatürk led beginning in 1919 gained new momentum with the expulsion of the Greeks from Izmir in September, 1922. The event marked the climax of the struggle against foreign domination and confirmed the Nationalist rejection of the Treaty of Sèvres. Within a few months a settlement much more favorable to Turkey emerged from the Lausanne conference. Even before the Lausanne meetings, the Atatürk regime had begun its program to resurrect the Turkish people and nation. Kemal inaugurated a reform and modernization program which, over the next two decades, was to erase most of the vestiges of the Ottoman system. No other nation, with the possible exception of Japan, has been able to match the speed and success of Turkey in its westernization program, based most obviously on the principles of secularization and nationalism. Turkish reaction against a centuries-old Muslim heritage, coupled with extreme nationalism and admiration for Western methods, provided the impetus for Atatürk's reforms.[1]

The main instrument for the adoption of these far-reaching changes was the Halk Firkasi, the People's Party. Later renamed Cümhuriyet Halk Partisi, the Republican People's Party, this was the only durable political organization in Turkey until after World War II. Its origins went back to the "League for the Defense of the Rights of Anatolia and Rumelia," organized by Atatürk in May, 1919, although the party was not officially founded until September 9, 1923.[2] Through this organization and the Grand National Assembly, the Atatürk government instituted its reforms.

The changes began with a startling but inevitable step — the abolition

[1] Parts of this chapter, in slightly different form, appeared as "The 'Terrible Turk' and Turkish-American Relations in the Interwar Period," *Historian,* XXXIII (November, 1970), 40–53. Useful sources of information on the Turkish reform movement are Kemal H. Karpat, *Turkey's Politics: The Transition to a Multi-Party System* (Princeton, 1959); Bernard Lewis, *The Emergence of Modern Turkey* (London, 1961); Richard D. Robinson, *The First Turkish Republic: A Case Study in National Development* (Cambridge, Mass., 1963); Eleanor Bisbee, *The New Turks: Pioneers of the Republic, 1920–1950* (Philadelphia, 1951); Donald E. Webster, *The Turkey of Atatürk: Social Process in the Turkish Transformation* (Philadelphia, 1939).

[2] George Lenczowski, *The Middle East in World Affairs* (3rd ed., Ithaca, N.Y., 1962), p. 119. See also the London *Times,* Turkish Number, August 9, 1938.

of the Sultanate on November 1, 1922. Disturbed because the Allies had invited both the Ottoman and the Nationalist governments to the Lausanne conference, the Nationalists simply legislated their opposition out of existence. When the Sultan fled to Malta aboard a British battleship, the Grand National Assembly elected as Caliph his cousin, Abdul Mejid Effendi, who was stripped of all temporal powers and restricted to the spiritual leadership of Islam.[3] The Caliphate, representing a system incompatible with the new order, now became the rallying point for Kemal's opposition. This situation and the fact that the Caliphate was in theory a political as well as a religious institution made its continued existence dubious once Turkey became a republic on October 29, 1923. On March 3, 1924, the Grand National Assembly abolished the Caliphate, banished all members of the Ottoman ruling family, disbanded the commissariats for the Sheriat (Islamic law courts) and the Evkaf (Pious Foundations), and unified all government and Muslim schools under the Ministry for Public Instruction.[4] With these changes the Grand National Assembly erased the last serious internal threat to the Atatürk government and demonstrated its determination to separate church and state.

During the next eleven years many other steps were taken to curtail further the political influence of religion in Turkey. Administrative decrees on September 2, 1925, abolished religious orders, closed their houses, and regulated the wearing of religious garments. One of these decrees, by prohibiting the wearing of fezzes by government officials, laid the groundwork for the adoption of the Western hat, made compulsory for all male citizens on November 25, 1925. The fez was intimately connected with Islam since followers of Mohammed touched their covered heads to the ground when praying. In December, 1927, regulations requiring the use of the Turkish language in religious services became effective. On April 9, 1928, the Grand National Assembly eliminated from Article II of the Constitution of 1924 the sentence which read, "the state religion of Turkey is the religion of Islam." The secularization program continued on December 3, 1934, with a law prohibiting the wearing of religious garb outside mosques and churches, and on May 27, 1935, when

---

[3] Arnold J. Toynbee, *Survey of International Affairs, 1925* (3 vols., London, 1927–1928), I, 50–51; Lenczowski, *The Middle East in World Affairs*, p. 117.

[4] Toynbee, *Survey of International Affairs, 1925*, I, 56, 60, 572–575 (texts of the appropriate laws). See also *A Speech Delivered by Ghazi Mustapha Kemal, President of the Turkish Republic, October 1927* (Leipzig, 1929), pp. 681–686, for Atatürk's observations on these moves.

Sunday instead of the traditional Muslim Friday became the official weekly day of rest.[5]

The secularization effort, with emphasis on the downgrading of religion as a factor in national life, proceeded on the assumption that the Islamic tradition and practices had contributed many of the ills of the Ottoman Empire. Atatürk's government designed changes in the status of Islam to weaken the authoritarian hold of religion on the Turks and to make easier the nation's acceptance of a nationalistic westernization program. Professor Kemal Karpat has described the program as "rationalist, scientific-minded, anti-traditionalist, and anti-clericalist secularism." [6]

Many other far-reaching reforms accompanied the separation of church and state in Turkey. The adoption in 1926 of the Swiss civil code, the Italian penal code, and the German commercial code modernized the judicial system.[7] Also significant was replacement of the old Arabic script by a new Latin alphabet developed by a Turkish commission in 1928. Preceded by a vigorous educational campaign led personally by Atatürk, the alphabet and language reform was legalized on November 1, 1928. The Assembly had earlier approved legislation substituting the Western for the Islamic version of Arabic numerals.[8] A significant social change deemed of major importance by Atatürk was the emancipation of women. Women were instructed to discard the veil and adopt Western clothing. They were also admitted to institutions of higher learning and to many professions formerly restricted to men. Thus, the Turkish woman emerged from seclusion to take her place on an equal legal basis with men for the first time in Turkish history.[9]

[5] Toynbee, *Survey of International Affairs, 1925*, I, 72–75; Toynbee, *Survey of International Affairs, 1928* (London, 1929), pp. 206–207; Webster, *The Turkey of Atatürk*, pp. 127–129. The main objective of the Friday-to-Sunday change was to facilitate Turkey's relations with other nations in commerce, banking, and international political affairs.

[6] Karpat, *Turkey's Politics*, p. 271. For other views and information on the secularization program, see Charles C. Morrison, "Religion in Turkey," *Christian Century*, LII (July 3, 1935), 881; Wilfred Cantwell Smith, "Turkey: Islamic Reformation?" in *Islam in Modern Turkey* (New York, 1959); Niyazi Berkes, "Historical Background of Turkish Secularism," in Richard N. Frye, ed., *Islam and the West* (The Hague, 1957), pp. 41–68; Dankwart A. Rustow, "Politics and Islam in Turkey, 1920–1955," *ibid.*, pp. 69–107; and Niyazi Berkes, *The Development of Secularism in Turkey* (Montreal, 1964).

[7] Toynbee, *Survey of International Affairs, 1925*, I, 71; Lenczowski, *The Middle East in World Affairs*, p. 122; Webster, *The Turkey of Atatürk*, pp. 107–108.

[8] Toynbee, *Survey of International Affairs, 1928*, pp. 225–230.

[9] Toynbee, *Survey of International Affairs, 1925*, I, 76; Toynbee, *Survey of In-*

To eliminate confusion, a new law required all Turks to take surnames in 1934. At this time the Grand National Assembly bestowed on the President the name "Atatürk," meaning "Father of the Turk" or "first and foremost Turk." [10] Two other aspects of the reform movement concerned the educational and economic policies of the government.[11] They were designed, as were the other changes, to erase the traces of the Ottoman system and enable Turkey to establish itself as a self-sufficient, modern nation.

Most Americans reacted to these revolutionary changes with some skepticism about their durability, but in good faith and with considerable admiration. Armenian-Americans and others having special grievances continued their campaign of misrepresentation, contributing to the shortage of accurate information about Turkey in the United States. Although Kemal Atatürk was a dictator, he was benevolent, and his attitudes and programs contrasted significantly with other authoritarian leaders of the interwar era. As an American writer and religious leader pointed out during a visit to Turkey, Kemal countered criticism of his regime with the contention that he was "moving practically toward the goal of true democracy." The author explained further: "His dictatorship operates within the forms of democracy, and his declared policy is to allow democracy to increase and dictatorship to decrease." [12] Criticism of the Turkish President's private life, which at times received sensational publicity in the United States, was based on substantive evidence.[13] United States diplomatic representatives in Turkey reported privately to the State Department on Atatürk's affairs, confirming the reports, for instance, of his excessive drinking.[14] Such information caused some Americans to conclude that the reforms in Turkey were of little value. As one author put it: "Be not led

ternational Affairs, 1928, pp. 200–203; Webster, *The Turkey of Atatürk*, pp. 129–130, 275–277.

[10] Robert P. Skinner to Cordell Hull, November 28, 1934, DS 867.001 Atatürk, Kemal/1. See also Webster, *The Turkey of Atatürk*, p. 132.

[11] For a full discussion of these policies, see below, pp. 94–169.

[12] Charles C. Morrison, "Turkey's Dictator," *Christian Century*, LII (June 26, 1935), 849.

[13] See memo of conversation, Sumner Welles (Assistant Secretary of State) and Münir Ertegün (Turkish ambassador), November 5, 1938, DS 867.001 Atatürk, Kemal/61, and memo, Wallace Murray (Chief, Near Eastern Division), April 20, 1938, DS 867.001 Atatürk, Kemal/33, for examples of sensational publicity on Atatürk in the United States.

[14] Sheldon L. Crosby to Kellogg, August 10, 1925, DS 867.001 K31/2; Joseph C. Grew to Kellogg, July 16, 1928, DS 867.00/1999; G. Howland Shaw to Hull, September 21, 1935, DS 867.001 Atatürk, Kemal/17.

astray by the surface of things in the 'new' Turkey. The present regime is eager to be considered progressive; it does not wish to be blamed for the crimes of the former regime. But the leopard does not change his spots as easily as a Turk does his headgear. . . . The Turk is still much what he was, and there is little evidence that Turkey has essentially changed under that ardent disciple of Venus and Bacchus, Mustapha Kemal Pasha." [15]

One influential American whose estimate of Atatürk's program was not clouded by this puritanical approach was Ambassador Joseph C. Grew. In his diary he often expressed great admiration for Turkey's accomplishments. To achieve equality with European nations, Turkey discarded "the retarding trammels of orientalism" in an amazingly short time. Giving most of the credit to Atatürk, Grew observed that the Turkish revolution was due to "a keen and forceful nationalistic spirit," much like that prevailing in America in 1776.[16]

Americans in Turkey recognized the value and in general accepted the ideals of the Turkish reform movement, although there was considerable grumbling from some educators and commercial interests. This opposition was not directed toward the basic philosophy of the reforms, but rather toward the methods employed occasionally to accomplish them. Lynn A. Scipio, for many years Professor of Engineering and Dean of Robert College in Istanbul, wrote that Americans in Turkey "were decidedly in sympathy with the Nationalists." [17] President Caleb F. Gates of Robert College, noting Turkey's remarkable progress, told the College Board of Directors in 1927 that the Atatürk government was the best that he had seen during his forty-six years in Turkey.[18] Some American missionaries confessed difficulty in assessing the significance of the rapid Turkish reforms. "We are becoming almost accustomed to the somersaults of progress which keep Turkey in the limelight," the Turkey Mission of the American Board of Commissioners for Foreign Missions reported in 1925, but yet it is "difficult to so understand the significance of the changes." [19] A

[15] Harry A. Franck, "Steer Clear of Turkey," *The Outlook*, CXLVII (November 2, 1927), 274.
[16] Quoted in editor's note, Joseph C. Grew, *Turbulent Era: A Diplomatic Record of Forty Years, 1904–1945*, ed. Walter Johnson (2 vols., Boston, 1952), II, 708. See also Roger R. Trask, "Joseph C. Grew and Turco-American Rapprochement, 1927–1932," in Sydney D. Brown, ed., *Studies on Asia, 1967* (Lincoln, Neb., 1967), pp. 139–170.
[17] *My Thirty Years in Turkey* (Rindge, N.H., 1955), p. 177.
[18] New York *Times*, November 19, 1927.
[19] *The One Hundred and Fifteenth Annual Report of the American Board of Commissioners for Foreign Missions* [1925] (Boston, n.d.), p. 54.

year later the Board's Annual Report commented optimistically about the developments in Turkey:

Turkey is a continual surprise. The time-worn epithets of "sick man," "effete," "unchanging," which used to apply, no longer fit. Seldom, if ever, has a nation so rapidly introduced such a surprising series of drastic reforms as have actually been put in operation in Turkey within the past two years. What a psychological revolution, for example, is involved in the adoption by a Moslem country, accustomed to reckon time from the Hejira of Mohammed, of the date 1926 in all its civil documents instead of 1341! And how far reaching must inevitably be the results of the abolition of all Mohammedan religious courts, and all dervish orders, and of the printing of the Koran in Turkish, when it was never before allowed except in Arabic, and its circulation by the President of the Republic! Surely there is new hope for a people that can carry out these and many other reforms in so short a time, and it is a grave responsibility for the American Board that it has practically sole charge of the mission work in so progressive a country.[20]

The reform movement influenced the nature of the problems and work of American diplomatic representatives in Turkey. Confronted with this early example of Middle Eastern nationalism, the policy of the United States government was to allow the Turks to pursue their aims with as little interference as possible and with considerable encouragement. Although American diplomats in their efforts to protect American interests sometimes found Turkish officials exasperating, they did not find grounds for interfering with the legitimate moves and aims of the Turkish government. But the settlement of routine problems sometimes took months because of the nationalistic stubbornness of Turkish leaders, who were vigilant in protecting their country's honor and independence. Tevfik Rüsdü Aras, the Foreign Minister for much of the interwar period, sometimes puzzled American representatives. Grew, after trying for some time to get action on a particular problem, wrote:

My net impression is the Tewfik Rushdi Bey is a great theorist and a great talker, indiscreet, not very well informed of details. . . . Promises and assurances must always be taken with a grain, several grains, of salt. . . . In most countries the Minister for Foreign Affairs speaks authoritatively and finally for the Government, unless he makes some reservation before committing himself; this is distinctly not the case with Tewfik Rushdi Bey: he commits himself and the Government and then reverses himself and

[20] *The One Hundred and Sixteenth Annual Report of the American Board of Commissioners for Foreign Missions* [1926] (Boston, n.d.), p. 78

the Government later or doesn't even bother to rectify his statements. A new kind of diplomacy for me. It is at least an interesting study.[21]

Shortly after Grew wrote this, another embassy official acquainted with the Foreign Minister for three years wrote that Aras had "broadened considerably . . . in place of the rather vague and radical views which he held in the past." [22]

Grew noted other factors which made diplomatic work particularly trying in Turkey. One was the extreme difficulty of securing accurate information from Turkish officialdom. He confided to his diary that he often deplored "the lack of thoroughness of some of our despatches" but that it was impossible to improve them because of the lack of facts.[23] The other obstacle, and one typical of most Middle Eastern countries, was "baksheesh." "The longer I live in Turkey," Grew wrote, "the more I realize what an immense and nefarious part 'baksheesh' and personal pique play in the life of the country. . . . Contracts are given or withheld, Government favors are granted or refused, favorable or unfavorable reports are turned in according to the rake-off accorded by the interested parties to the subordinate officials responsible." Grew himself refused an opportunity to bribe a Turkish Finance Ministry official to submit a favorable report on a question of taxes on American schools in Turkey.[24] Since few Americans were willing to tender baksheesh, they were at a disadvantage compared with foreign interests, particularly in commercial matters. This problem was of little concern to Grew's successors in Turkey, however, if one can judge from their failure to mention it in their despatches to the State Department.

United States Diplomats in Turkey in the Interwar Period

Grew was the first American ambassador to Turkey after the re-establishment of diplomatic relations and the departure of Admiral Bristol in 1927. By the time he went to Turkey, Grew had already enjoyed a long and fruitful career in the Foreign Service. After graduation from Groton and Harvard, Grew began as a clerk in the Consulate General in Cairo in 1904. He served later in secondary posts in Mexico City, St. Petersburg, Berlin, and Vienna. After working with the Division of Western European

[21] Diary, February 29, 1928, *Turbulent Era*, II, 770.
[22] Crosby to Kellogg, October 13, 1928, DS 711.6712 Anti-War/28.
[23] March 12, 1930, *Turbulent Era*, II, 850–851.
[24] Diary, February 23, 1931, *ibid.*, 843.

Affairs and as Secretary of the American delegation at the Versailles conference, he became Minister to Denmark in 1920 and Minister to Switzerland in 1921. While in Switzerland he served as an American observer at the Lausanne conference and negotiated the Turco-American Treaty of Lausanne. During this period he diligently studied problems in Turkish-American relations and became acquainted with prominent Turkish officials, including Prime Minister Ismet Inönü. From March 7, 1924, until his appointment to the Turkey post in May, 1927, he was Undersecretary of State. One of his concerns in this position was to secure Senate approval of the Lausanne Treaty.[25] When he arrived in Turkey, Grew announced two general objectives: "to support American legitimate interests; and, to develop and strengthen to the uttermost the friendly relations between our two countries." [26] By the time he left Turkey, he had negotiated and signed two important treaties and ably supported American religious, educational, philanthropic, and commercial interests. Grew's efforts to make friendly and informal representations to the Turks rather than formal demands proved very successful. Noting in his diary that the State Department thought he should be more vigorous in support of American institutions, Grew defended his policy: "Our whole policy is to let the institutions and companies exhaust their legal or other remedies themselves before intercession by the Embassy; we thus reserve our ammunition and our representations carry much more weight than if we should continually intervene in small matters or before the lawyers have taken the first steps in major issues." [27] Since Aras appreciated his tactics, Grew added, "American institutions were more welcome in Turkey than the institutions of any other foreign Power." [28]

Ambassador Grew's interest in an efficiently functioning embassy led him to pay considerable attention to its everyday operations. His long diary observations on March 12, 1930, about the organization, quality, and quantity of despatches illustrate this concern.[29] A research program which Grew developed bore considerable fruit, even after he left Turkey. Embassy officials studied such topics as the administration of justice, the

[25] *Register of the Department of State, October 1, 1939* (Washington, 1939), p. 109.

[26] Diary, September 24, 1927, *Turbulent Era*, II, 724.

[27] August 11, 1931, Joseph C. Grew MSS (Houghton Library, Harvard University, Cambridge, Mass.), 1931, vol. 2.

[28] Memo of conversation, Grew and Aras, April 8, 1930, *Turbulent Era*, II, 852–853.

[29] *Ibid.*, 845–852.

press, political and social ideas, crime and mental disease, the influence of American educational institutions, and various economic subjects. The project results are scattered throughout the general records of the Department of State for the 1930s. Although one of Grew's successors complained that these "formidably voluminous reports . . . are of no earthly use to anyone and have been consigned to dusty oblivion," they were well received by the State Department.[30]

When Grew left Turkey on March 13, 1932, to accept President Herbert Hoover's appointment as Ambassador to Japan, he could speak of a vast improvement in relations between the United States and Turkey. Grew accounted for this change in an address to the American colony in Istanbul shortly before he left: the United States was one of Turkey's most "disinterested friends," with no "political row to hoe . . . no *arrière pensée* whatever in the practical friendship that we wish to show." American institutions in Turkey, Grew explained, were "a powerful and practical demonstration" of American friendship for Turkey.[31] Further tribute to the success of Grew's mission was paid by his Counselor of Embassy, G. Howland Shaw:

That these years have marked a great change in American-Turkish relations, that Mr. Grew's mission has been an outstanding success . . . is a matter of common knowledge. . . . The success of Mr. Grew's mission in the deeper and more lasting sense of the word is there to prove it. He has won the affection and admiration of the Turks and has represented the United States in Turkey in the truest sense of the word, not by practising a complicated art or science of diplomacy but by exemplifying day in and day out those qualities which win people the world over and draw them, not only to one's self as an individual, but to what one stands for, to what one respects. Perhaps, after all, diplomacy is at the same time a simpler and a more difficult thing than some of us imagine.[32]

[30] Grew to Henry L. Stimson, August 26, 1930, DS 124.676/96 (Grew's explanation of the research project). For examples of completed research see M. K. Moorhead, "Survey of Turkish-American Trade, 1931–1935," June 30, 1936, DS 611.6731/188; Robert D. Coe, "Ankara," October 1, 1934, enclosure in Skinner to Hull, November 14, 1934, DS 867.14/18; Skinner to Hull, November 14, 1935, DS 124.671/147.
[31] Diary, January 18, 1932, *Turbulent Era*, II, 909–910; address, March 11, 1932, *ibid.*, 916–917; diary, March 6–12, 1932, *ibid.*, 918–919.
[32] Shaw to Stimson, March 23, 1932, DS 123 G 861/475. For a detailed account of Grew's mission, see Trask, "Joseph C. Grew and Turco-American Rapprochement, 1927–1932," pp. 139–170. See also Waldo H. Heinrichs, Jr., *American Ambassador: Joseph C. Grew and the Development of the United States Diplomatic Tradition* (Boston, 1966), pp. 129–162.

Grew's successor in Turkey, appointed on March 17, 1932, was General Charles Hitchcock Sherrill, a lawyer and businessman whose only previous diplomatic experience was as Minister to Argentina from 1909 to 1911.[33] Sherrill's was a political appointment, made at the recommendation of prominent New York Republican leaders. Rumors suggested that he had contributed heavily to the Republican campaign fund for 1932.[34]

Sherrill apparently looked upon the Turkish assignment more as an opportunity to pursue his own projects than to represent American interests. Speaking before the American Club in Paris on his way to Turkey, Sherrill emphasized his interest in the mosaics in Istanbul's St. Sophia mosque but said little about basic problems in Turkish-American relations.[35] Among the results of his short stay in Turkey were a laudatory biography of Atatürk and a book on mosaics, including those at St. Sophia. His book on Kemal, incidentally, gave him an access to the Turkish President not enjoyed by other diplomats, a fact causing resentment among his foreign colleagues.[36]

American missionaries in Turkey, who worried that Sherrill would be more interested in commercial matters than in other problems, were pleasantly surprised to find him a regular churchgoer and genuinely concerned with the American Board's work. One missionary described Sherrill as a "complete surprise." "I think he's playing the game with great wisdom, & he may have a great influence for good in high places." [37] However, Sherrill's accomplishments in Turkey, other than his literary productions, were few. He did work toward suppression of the illicit drug traffic in Turkey

[33] *Register of the Department of State, July 1, 1933* (Washington, 1933), p. 253. Sherrill's military rank resulted from his service with the New York National Guard during World War I.

[34] New York *Times,* January 26, 1932; Grew to Shaw, February 13, 1932, Grew MSS, 1932, vol. 2.

[35] Sherrill to Stimson, May 20, 1932, DS 123 Sh 5/83 (copy of Sherrill's speech of April 21, 1932).

[36] Sherrill to Stimson, July 1, 1932, DS 867.001 K31/49; Skinner to Hull, May 29, 1935, DS 867.001 Atatürk, Kemal/12. See also Charles H. Sherrill, "My Interviews with the Gazi," *Asia,* XXXIV (March, 1934), 140–143. Sherrill's two books were *A Year's Embassy to Mustapha Kemal* (New York & London, 1934), and *Mosaics in Italy, Palestine, Syria, Turkey and Greece* (London, 1933).

[37] Ethel W. Putney to Mabel Emerson (American Board secretary), July 15, 1932, American Board of Commissioners for Foreign Missions MSS (Houghton Library, Harvard University, Cambridge, Mass.), ABC 16.5, vol. 15, no. 208 (hereafter cited as ABCFM MSS); Caleb F. Gates to Mark L. Bristol, April 25, 1932, Mark Lambert Bristol MSS (Manuscript Division, Library of Congress, Washington), Box 92; John K. Birge (American Board missionary) to Fred F. Goodsell (American Board secretary), August 28, 1932, ABCFM MSS, ABC 11.5.2, vol. 1.

and promoted the expansion of American commercial opportunities.[38] Since he spent two months in the fall of 1932 on leave in the United States, his actual residence in Turkey amounted to only eight months, giving him little time to work extensively on substantive problems in Turkish-American relations.[39] The least qualified of the four American ambassadors in Turkey between the wars, Sherrill accomplished little of lasting importance.

Sherrill submitted his resignation, according to custom, to President-elect Franklin D. Roosevelt on February 6, 1933. Much to his surprise, it was accepted on March 23, with the condition that he should transfer his office to his subordinates in the embassy immediately. Without elaboration, a State Department official later noted that Roosevelt "had some special reason for desiring an immediate transfer of the office." [40] It was not until several months after Sherrill left Turkey, and upon a request from his friend, Colonel Edward M. House, that President Roosevelt thanked Sherrill for his service in Turkey. The Turkish press, however, showed appreciation for Sherrill's work and praised him warmly when he left.[41]

The Roosevelt Administration returned to the practice, established at the time of Grew's appointment, of naming career diplomats to the Turkish post. Some representatives of American interests in Turkey suggested Admiral Bristol as Sherrill's successor, but the appointment went to Robert Peet Skinner of Ohio.[42] Born in 1866, Skinner entered the diplomatic service in 1897 as consul at Marseilles, France, and served as consul and consul-general in various posts until his appointment as Minister to Greece in 1926. At the time of his appointment to Turkey he was Minister to Es-

[38] "Turco-American Relations," *Current History*, XXXVIII (June, 1933), 379. See below, pp. 98–99, 176–177, for discussions of Sherrill's work on narcotics and commercial problems.

[39] New York *Times*, August 26 and October 2, 1932; Department of State, *Press Releases*, Weekly Issue No. 153 (September 3, 1932), p. 144.

[40] Sherrill to Stimson, February 6, 1933, DS 123 Sh 5/108 (enclosure is Sherrill's letter to Roosevelt); Hull to Sherrill, March 23, 1933, DS 123 Sh 5/115; memo, H. C. H. (unidentified) to Wilbur J. Carr, February 17, 1934, DS 123 Sh 5/148.

[41] Daniel C. Roper (Secretary of Commerce) to William Phillips (Undersecretary of State), October 27, 1933, DS 123 Sh 5/137 (about House's request); Marvin H. McIntyre (Roosevelt's secretary) to Phillips, November 3, 1933, DS 123 Sh 5/139 (enclosure is Roosevelt's letter to Sherrill, November 2, 1933); Charles E. Allen (Consul, Istanbul), Digest of the Turkish Press, March 19–April 1, 1933, DS 867.9111/395; New York *Times*, April 2 and 16, 1933.

[42] Asa K. Jennings to Bristol, December 3, 1932, Bristol MSS, Box 96; Stanley H. Howe to Bristol, April 1, 1933, *ibid.*

tonia, Latvia, and Lithuania. After receiving advance approval from the Turkish government, Roosevelt nominated Skinner on June 8, 1933, the Senate approved on June 10, and he arrived in Turkey on September 17.[43] Vahan Cardashian furnished proof, when Skinner was appointed, that some Armenians in the United States had not forgotten their hatred of Turkey. In a letter to Roosevelt, Cardashian wrote: "Permit me to say that exchange of ambassadors between America and Turkey is, on the authority of Jefferson, Madison and Hamilton, unconstitutional and, therefore, invalid, and it can be challenged by a court action." [44]

Skinner ably represented the United States in Turkey for almost three years. His major concern was the advancing of trade. He was especially interested in securing for American firms a share of the profits from the Turkish rearmament program of the mid-1930s. Skinner also contributed somewhat to the settlement in 1934 of the long-standing Turkish-American claims controversy.[45] He left Turkey in January, 1936, to retire from the Foreign Service.[46]

The last United States Ambassador to Turkey during the interwar period was John Van Antwerp MacMurray, who assumed the post on January 24, 1936. Considered one of the State Department's Far Eastern experts, MacMurray had served since 1907 in various Middle Eastern and Far Eastern nations and also in the Department as Chief of the Near Eastern Division, Chief of the Far Eastern Division, and Assistant Secretary of State. Like Skinner, he was Minister to Estonia, Latvia, and Lithuania at the time of his assignment to Turkey.[47] MacMurray's promotion to ambassadorial rank was well received. One Washington newspaper in an editorial described it as a "meritorious appointment" and commended Roosevelt's "devotion to the career principle in the United States' foreign service." [48] MacMurray welcomed the appointment; as he wrote to a State

[43] *Register of the Department of State, July 1, 1936* (Washington, 1936), p. 261; Shaw to Hull, June 5, 1933, DS 123 Sk 3/477; *Senate Executive Journal*, 73 Cong., 1 Sess., LXXIV, 144, 171; Shaw to Hull, September 17, 1933, DS 123 Sk 3/505.

[44] June 9, 1933, DS 711.672 Protests/52.

[45] See, for example, Skinner to Hull, June 13, 1934, *Foreign Relations of the United States, Diplomatic Papers, 1934* (5 vols., Washington, 1950–1952), II, 964–965 (hereafter cited as *FR 1934*). See below, pp. 99–102, for a discussion of the rearmament movement, and pp. 200ff. for information about the claims problem.

[46] Shaw to Hull, January 16, 1936, DS 123 Sk 3/567.

[47] *Register of the Department of State, October 1, 1939*, p. 142. Letters and other materials related to the appointment can be found in the John Van Antwerp MacMurray MSS (Princeton University Library, Princeton, N.J.), Box 148.

[48] Clipping, Washington *Evening Star*, January 12, 1936, in *ibid.*, Box 150.

Department friend, "There is . . . a thrill of satisfaction in reaching the ambassadorial grade; and Constantinople has always been, for me, one of those places just over the hill, which I felt I must get to." [49]

MacMurray did not expect his tasks in Turkey to be rigorous. In a letter summing up his initial impressions he wrote: "To tell the honest truth [if you won't give me away], this post promises to be less exacting than any I have had since the days of the Petersburg Embassy. There really seems to be less work than at Riga. So I look forward to spending very little time in the office, but playing around in the boat, swimming and picknicking & doing little trips along the Bosphorus & the Sea of Marmara." [50] In later years MacMurray recalled that his service in Turkey before the war was "singularly tranquil and uneventful. . . . I may be said to have held only a watching brief, in the afterglow of especial friendliness created by Admiral Bristol as High Commissioner and of Grew as our first Ambassador to the new Turkish regime." [51] Actually, MacMurray found plenty of important work to do. When offered appointment by President Roosevelt as Ambassador to China in 1937, MacMurray expressed a strong preference for the Turkish post. As he wrote to Secretary Hull, "under the present circumstances this mission offers more opportunity for constructive work." [52]

Furthermore, MacMurray was not pleased when the State Department detached him from the Turkey mission for several months in 1937 and 1938 to serve as Chairman of the Joint Preparatory Commission on Philippine Affairs. During this same period rumors that he might be appointed Ambassador to the Soviet Union disturbed him further. He expressed his feelings on both posts to a friend: ". . . there is some very distressing talk going on about my suitability for . . . [the Moscow] post. I begin to wonder whether being a willing horse does not, in this wicked world, result in one's being a goat. We are more than content with our post in Turkey; but I have had this wretched Philippine job, and I am likely to have it on my hands for at least a couple of months more." Actually, MacMur-

[49] MacMurray to Wilbur J. Carr, December 30, 1935, *ibid.*, Box 148.
[50] MacMurray to "Ef" [Mrs. J. Marvin Wright], March 27, 1936, MacMurray MSS, Box 151.
[51] MacMurray (Norfolk, Conn.) to Roger R. Trask, September 8, 1958.
[52] Hull to MacMurray, March 29, 1937, DS 123 M 221/543; MacMurray to Hull, March 30, 1937, DS 123 M 221/544. MacMurray's opinion of the China post was questionable in view of events taking place in the Far East at the time.

ray remained in Turkey until June 1, 1942, when he returned to Washington to serve as a Special Assistant to Secretary Hull.[53] The major accomplishment during MacMurray's term was the negotiation of a reciprocal trade agreement. Of course, MacMurray had to deal also with problems in Turkish-American relations caused by the coming of the war.[54]

A subordinate embassy official in Turkey deserving special mention is Gardiner Howland Shaw, who served from 1930 to 1937 as Counselor of Embassy. Shaw had earlier experience in Turkey, having served with Admiral Bristol's High Commission beginning in 1921 and later as First Secretary of Embassy from 1924 to 1926. He also attended the Lausanne conference. He returned to Turkey in 1930 after three years as Chief of the Division of Near Eastern Affairs.[55] Second in command in the United States embassy as counselor for seven years, Shaw dealt with everyday problems as well as larger issues in Turkish-American relations. Testimony to his value came from Ambassador MacMurray a few months after the latter assumed his post in Turkey:

. . . the public interest is actually better served by his maintaining the direct contacts with the officials of the Turkish regime. For, having been one of their comrades of Valley Forge days, so to speak, he has such relations with them as no American official except Joe Grew, and perhaps Admiral Bristol, has had or can hope to have; and that unique position, as a background to his understanding of conditions, his alert and discriminating sense of what is significant in the political and social development of this country, and his sound political judgment, enables him to accomplish things that are my envy and despair.[56]

When Shaw left Turkey in June, 1937, he became Chief of the Division of Foreign Service Personnel in the State Department.[57]

[53] *Register of the Department of State, October 1, 1939*, p. 142; Hull to MacMurray, July 14, 1937, MacMurray MSS, Box 161; MacMurray to Mahlon F. Perkins, January 11, 1938, *ibid.*, Box 165; *Register of the Department of State, October 1, 1942* (Washington, 1943), p. 195. MacMurray's successor was Laurence A. Steinhardt, Ambassador to the Soviet Union from 1939 through 1941. See the Laurence Adolph Steinhardt MSS (Manuscript Division, Library of Congress, Washington), Boxes 37–49 and Letterbooks 80–83 for pertinent materials.

[54] For information on the reciprocal trade agreement, see below, pp. 115–122; for complications in Turkish-American relations caused by World War II, see the last two chapters.

[55] *Register of the Department of State, October 1, 1939*, p. 180.

[56] MacMurray to Carr (Assistant Secretary of State), June 19, 1936, MacMurray MSS, Box 153.

[57] Hull to Shaw, June 8, 1937, DS 123 Sh 22/180.

Physical Problems of the Embassy

A major concern of American diplomats in Turkey was the problem of maintaining two embassies, one at Istanbul, in effect the summer capital, and the other at Ankara, where Atatürk established his headquarters after World War I. Turkish nationalism reflected itself in at least public insistence that Ankara function as the national capital. In fact, most Turkish government officials left Ankara to reside and work in Istanbul for several months each year. As Ambassador MacMurray put it, "The status of Ankara as the capital is a matter of dogma, which the Turks uphold with bigotry even while they take every opportunity to get away from the place." [58]

Although most foreign diplomats disliked residing in Ankara because of its harsh climate and interior location, all of the European nations established new embassies there when it became the capital.[59] Ambassador Skinner has explained the American situation as follows:

We ourselves had set up an insignificant embassy of a dozen rooms in the new capital and lamented the necessity of leaving our white marble mansion overlooking the Bosporus, in Istanbul, not to mention the fine embassy yacht and the possibility of a thousand excursions along the European shore, in a Sea of Marmara, among the islands and often to the Sweet Waters of Europe. It was not to be denied that there was plenty of social recreation which went along with the affairs of state in Constantinople for which the desert of Ankara was a poor substitute. The ambassadors had always lived in considerable state in Constantinople, the climate was agreeable, while existence in Ankara resembled life in one of our newly improvised cities in the Far West of an earlier generation.[60]

The Turkish government often pointed out to American officials its strong feeling that all embassies should be located in Ankara. Through the interwar period, however, the United States kept its main diplomatic establishment in Istanbul, in a building purchased in 1906 when the mission was raised to embassy rank.[61] The existence of a branch in Ankara caused many problems, including the necessity of having personnel there and in

[58] MacMurray to Keith Merrill, June 2, 1936, MacMurray MSS, Box 153.
[59] See Shaw to Hull, August 22, 1935, DS 867.01/205 for a description of the diplomatic exodus from Ankara during the summer.
[60] Robert P. Skinner (Belfast, Me.) to Roger R. Trask, August 24, 1958.
[61] Diary, November 3, 1927, Grew MSS, 1927, vol. 1; Skinner to Hull, November 14, 1935, DS 124.671/147; Lewis Heck, "Sidelights on Past Relations Between the United States and Turkey," *American Foreign Service Journal*, XVII (February, 1940), 110.

Istanbul at all times. On ceremonial occasions or when important problems developed, the American Ambassador had to make the trying and time-consuming rail trip from Istanbul to Ankara.[62]

Skinner, though preferring conditions in Istanbul, urged the State Department to establish a main embassy in a new building at Ankara. He was disturbed not only because of the inefficient use of personnel but also because the United States looked less responsive to Turkish nationalism than most other nations.[63] He was embarrassed that the United States embassy, in contrast to the "fine establishments" of European powers, could not accommodate more than ten persons at dinner: "in a new and growing capital like Ankara the social side of life plays a much more important role in government and politics than in the settled capitals of the western countries." [64] The fact that Skinner evicted lesser embassy officials from their living quarters in the small building in Ankara to make room for himself caused some grumbling but graphically illustrated the physical problem.[65]

After MacMurray arrived, he urged the State Department to improve the building in Istanbul and to build a new embassy in Ankara to facilitate the conduct of American business in the Turkish capital. MacMurray felt strongly enough on the embassy issue to point out in a personal letter to President Roosevelt that the inadequacy of the embassy building in Ankara was the only serious embarrassment in Turkish-American relations. MacMurray's reaction to the Istanbul building was interesting:

Our one grief is the monstrous residence — a Levantine version of an Italian palace, with big halls like station waiting rooms, with enormously high ceilings done in frescoes of mythological figures and sheep and flowers, but with precious little room or comfort for living purposes. It is, I am sure, the most blatantly un-American residence in which a representative of the U.S.A. ever had to live. It is rather the worse for being a bit shabby; but at its best it would still be, as one of my friends described it, like a chambermaid's dream of paradise.[66]

Although plagued by financial stringency forced by the Depression,

[62] Diary, September 21 and 22, 1927, *Turbulent Era*, II, 717–718; diary, March 12, 1930, *ibid.*, 845–846.

[63] Skinner to Hull, November 14, 1934, DS 867.41/18; Skinner to Hull, November 14, 1935, DS 124.671/147.

[64] Skinner to Hull, April 6, 1935, DS 123 Sk 3/543.

[65] Merrill to MacMurray, January 24, 1936, MacMurray MSS, Box 149.

[66] MacMurray to Carr, June 19, 1936, *ibid.*, Box 153; MacMurray to Roosevelt, December 1, 1936, *ibid.*, Box 156; MacMurray to Frederick L. Mayer, April 20, 1936, *ibid.*, Box 152 (source of the quotation).

the State Department responded to the Skinner and MacMurray recommendations by authorizing a survey, completed in August, 1936, of possible embassy sites in Ankara. After tedious negotiations with Turkish owners lasting more than two years, the United States purchased a new embassy site in January, 1939. Pending construction of the new building, MacMurray's staff moved the embassy in Ankara to new rented quarters in February, 1939. During the same period the Istanbul building was renovated and altered to house a consulate general which had had separate quarters until June, 1937. MacMurray had acceded to Turkish wishes by shifting the headquarters of the American diplomatic mission to Ankara. He felt that this transfer was one of his most important accomplishments in Turkey.[67]

The changes under MacMurray did not solve the basic problem of embassy accommodations. After MacMurray's successor, Ambassador Laurence A. Steinhardt, arrived in Turkey in 1942, he complained bitterly. In a letter to the Chief of the Division of Foreign Service Administration in the State Department, Steinhardt wrote:

When I was sent here, I was charged with keeping Turkey neutral if possible and seeing to it that they came into the war on our side if they were eventually forced to take a position. I expected to find an Embassy. Instead I found a second-class Consulate. . . . It was impossible for me to enter into this arena with the equipment and staff that I found here. . . . I do not know whether you have been shown any of my telegrams about the glassware. . . . For a mission in so vital a spot as Turkey is at the moment which possessed between the two buildings in Ankara and Istanbul only four finger bowls, three liqueur glasses, 7 wine glasses, 11 water glasses and 3 highball glasses, is not a mission at all.[68]

The "Terrible Turk" Stereotype

Although the Atatürk revolution created in large measure the environment in which American diplomats operated, Turkish-American relations also had to adjust to constraints imposed by attitudes within the United

[67] Hull to MacMurray, June 2, 1936, DS 124.671/150A; Captain H. M. Underwood to Hull, August 25, 1936, with enclosure, "Report on Embassy Sites, Ankara, Turkey, August, 1936," DS 124.671/166; MacMurray to Hull, February 4, 1937, DS 124.671/172; Robert F. Kelley to Hull, May 18, 1938, DS 124.671/273; MacMurray to Hull, December 2, 1938, DS 124.671/287; Kelley to MacMurray, January 18, 1939, DS 124.671/301; MacMurray to Hull, February 11, 1939, DS 124.671/302; MacMurray to Roger R. Trask, September 8, 1958.

[68] Steinhardt to Monnett B. Davis, May 8, 1942, in Steinhardt MSS, Letterbook 80.

States. A young Turkish woman, Selma Ekrem, described what she encountered on a trip to the United States after World War I: "Here in America lived a legend made of blood and thunder. The Terrible Turk ruled the minds of the Americans. A huge person with fierce black eyes and bushy eyebrows, carrying daggers covered with blood. I did not fit into the legend of the Terrible Turk and so I was not one. In fact many people were disappointed: to meet a real true Turk who turns out to be fair, meek and not very unlike an American." [69] Selma Ekrem had come face to face with the image of the "Terrible Turk." Turkish treatment of Armenians between the mid-1890s and the end of World War I earned the Turks this description, but it had little validity after the early 1920s. Nevertheless, Turkey's enemies worked hard to propagate the symbol of the Terrible Turk in order to prevent Turkish-American rapprochement.

Opponents of the Lausanne Treaty were particularly responsible for perpetuating the Ottoman stereotype. The Harvard historian Albert Bushnell Hart wrote that the Turks were "absolutely unfitted to be ranked and associated with civilized nations as an equal," and another writer described the Turk as an "evil genie" and a "scarecrow." [70] Armenians and their supporters in the United States helped to vilify the Turkish people and nation. In periodicals such as *The New Armenia* they counseled the world to beware of the Turks: "History has not maligned the Turk; the Turk has proved himself to be malignant. He has never confessed contrition nor made atonement for his crimes. To-day the Turk is the most sinister figure in Europe." [71] Written by a regional director of Near East Relief, this statement exemplifies the role of that organization in developing the Terrible Turk impression.

Friends of Turkey tried to counter these attacks with the truth, but they made little progress until 1927 and after in transforming the popular model of the Turk in the United States.[72] The State Department itself did much to paint a true picture of the new Turkey. Other persons, through

[69] *Unveiled: The Autobiography of a Turkish Girl* (New York, 1942, originally published 1930), p. 302.
[70] Albert B. Hart, "Reservations as to the Near Eastern Question," *Annals*, American Academy of Political and Social Science, CVIII (July, 1923), 120; Alex Aaronsohn, "The Powder Magazine of Europe — the Near East," *ibid.*, 127.
[71] E. Guy Talbot, "The Turk Malignant," *The New Armenia*, XIX (July–September, 1927), 41.
[72] See E. Alexander Powell, *The Struggle for Power in Moslem Asia* (New York & London, 1923), p. 18; Colby M. Chester, "Turkey Reinterpreted," *Current History*, XVI (September, 1922), 939–947; Arthur T. Chester, "History's Verdict on New Turkey's Rise to Power," *ibid.*, XIX (October, 1923), 79–86.

books, magazines, newspapers, and public addresses, worked toward the same goal,[73] believing that elimination of the Terrible Turk stereotype would be honest and just. Also changing the stereotype would remove some measure of the prejudice which had contributed to the defeat of the Lausanne Treaty and would establish strong foundations for Turkish-American friendship.

American diplomats in Turkey, especially Bristol, Grew, and Sherrill, worked actively to change the Turkish image in the American mind. Bristol's diary contains many entries showing his concern about inaccurate and false ideas of the Turks and their government. He encouraged Turkish officials to work to change American public opinion, and he tried himself to enlighten Americans who visited Turkey. In September, 1922, when Methodist Bishop James Cannon called in Istanbul, he showed Bristol a resolution he had written calling on the President, Secretary of State, and Congress to protect Christians in the Middle East from further persecution by the Turks. Bristol described his reaction:

He asked what I thought of it and I told him it was all right but it was undoubtedly based upon a misconception of the real conditions here in the Near East. . . . I laid great emphasis upon the fact that in my opinion there has been spread in America an entirely wrong impression of the situation in the Near East and that our relief committees and missionaries, as well as propaganda press of the Greeks and Armenians, have lent themselves to imparting this wrong information. . . . This seemed to make an impression on Bishop Cannon and he quite frankly admitted that I had given him an entirely new point of view, while at the same time he stated that he did not agree with me.[74]

Grew, always disturbed when anti-Turkish statements appeared in the American press, urged the Turkish government to undertake a public relations program in the United States. He tried to get articles by Turkish officials published in the United States and promoted the filming of a movie of Atatürk at his model farm outside Ankara.[75] Ambassador Sher-

[73] See Department of State, *Press Releases*, Weekly Issue No. 188 (May 6, 1933), pp. 320–325; *Christian Science Monitor*, January 24, 1928; and New York *Times*, May 29, 1928, for reports of various speeches on Turkey. An example of a book designed to dispel the "Terrible Turk" idea is Chester M. Tobin, *Turkey, Key to the East* (New York, 1944). Tobin first went to Turkey in 1924 to coach Turkey's Olympic track and field team. He remained in other capacities for several years.

[74] War Diary, September 23, 1922, Bristol MSS, Box 21. See this box for other materials relating to the problem of American public opinion on Turkey.

[75] Diary, February 15, 1928, *Turbulent Era*, II, 763–764; Grew to Shaw, August 1, 1928, DS 867.00/1998; Shaw to Grew, August 6, 1928, *ibid.*; diary, November 11,

rill devoted much time to informing Americans about Turkey. He spoke widely about Atatürk and Turkish progress during a leave in the United States in the fall of 1932. His literary effort, *A Year's Embassy to Mustapha Kemal*, though portraying Atatürk as a knight in shining armor who alone saved Turkey, helped to dispel the Terrible Turk idea. After an interview with Atatürk in which he outlined his project, Sherrill wrote: "I hope that this biographical and historical contact will prove useful to American interests during my service at this post. He [Kemal] seems to have me classified as a historian and especially as his biographer . . . rather than as a foreign Ambassador." [76] The State Department, unenthusiastic about Sherrill's writing, informed him that the Department "does not perceive how political implications can be readily avoided in the biography you contemplate writing." Consequently, Sherrill waited until his retirement to publish his book.[77]

American visitors to Turkey provided an important outlet for publicizing Turkey in the United States and a means of promoting closer ties between the two countries. Russell Boardman and John Polando, who in July, 1931, flew nonstop from New York to Istanbul in forty-nine hours to set a new world's record, were sensational and effective visitors. Received as heroes by the Turks, they were the subjects of adoration during their nine-day stay in Istanbul. Prime Minister İnönü gave them medals, and Atatürk himself entertained them. In a speech to Boardman and Polando, Atatürk said: "Heroes such as you are transforming nations into families whose members are interested in each other's mutual joys and sorrows. You have forged links of friendship between the great country of the New World, whose civilization we follow with admiration, and Turkey, the meeting ground of the East and West." [78] Grew, perhaps overly enthusiastic, recorded his impressions: "A tremendous fortnight, vivid, constructive, never to be forgotten. An event has occurred which has done more to consolidate the affections of Turkey for the United States than could have been accomplished by years of careful diplomacy." [79]

1930, Grew MSS, 1930, vol. 3; Grew to Jefferson Patterson (State Department), January 26, 1931, *ibid.*, 1931, vol. 1.
[76] New York *Times*, October 2, 1932; Sherrill to Stimson, July 1, 1932, DS 867.001 K31/49.
[77] William R. Castle, Jr., to Sherrill, August 1, 1932, DS 123 Sh 5/93.
[78] Diary, July 27–August 10, 1931, *Turbulent Era*, II, 890–899; Washington *Post*, July 31, 1931; New York *Times*, July 31, August 1 and 2, 1931 (source of the quotation).
[79] Diary, July 27–August 10, 1931, *Turbulent Era*, II, 889.

Grew saw in this event an opportunity to get favorable publicity for Turkey in the United States. In a letter to Boardman he wrote:

You certainly did help, in the highest measure, to strengthen the good will of Turkey for our country and thereby immensely aided our own work. If you can now, from time to time, give our own people a few plain facts about what modern Turkey is trying to accomplish and that the Turk himself is not such a bad sort of person and deserves the friendship and support of public opinion at home, you will be adding to the great work which you have already done. The real Turk, with all his good qualities, has never really been known or understood in our country. . . . He is . . . trying to do just about the same sort of thing that we were undertaking after 1776, and therefore he deserves our moral sympathy and support. You have so completely won the ear of the American people that whatever you say will be listened to with respect, and since the American people are the first in wanting to give a square deal when a square deal is needed and deserved, you can accomplish a lot if you will.[80]

The Boardman-Polando visit to Turkey was well publicized in the United States. When the fliers returned, a committee including the Turkish Ambassador, Ahmed Mouhtar, welcomed them, and President Hoover received them in the White House.[81]

An earlier visit to Turkey by Mrs. Evangeline Lindbergh, the mother of Charles A. Lindbergh, produced less spectacular, but still useful, results. Mrs. Lindbergh arrived in September, 1928, to teach for a semester at Istanbul Woman's College. During her stay the Turkish Aviation League presented to her a medal for her son. Grew, again showing great enthusiasm, wrote Mrs. Lindbergh when she returned to the United States that "your visit has done more to develop the friendly attitude of the Turks toward the United States than any other event since I came here." After she returned to Detroit, Mrs. Lindbergh made a long statement explaining Turkish westernization and lauding its achievements.[82]

In February, 1927, a group of six hundred American students aboard the "floating university" steamship *Ryndam* visited Istanbul. The *Christian Science Monitor*, reporting their enthusiastic reception, noted that the students were "eager to remedy what they describe as erroneous opinions

[80] October 12, 1931, Grew MSS, 1931, vol. 1.

[81] Washington *Post*, July 31, August 1, 27, and 29, 1931; New York *Times,* July 31, August 1 and 2, 1931.

[82] Diary, September 14 and December 29, 1928, Grew MSS, 1928, vol. 3; diary, January 9, 1929, *ibid.*, 1929, vol. 3; Grew to Evangeline Lindbergh, January 25, 1929, *ibid.*, 1929, vol. 2; clipping, Detroit *News*, February 23, 1929, *ibid.*, 1929, vol. 4.

on the present day Turkey, entertained by anti-Turkish circles in the United States." [83] The impression gained by American visitors in Turkey contrasted greatly with the anti-Turkish propaganda circulated in the United States. Publication by these visitors of more up-to-date views helped to break down old notions.

The Work of the American Friends of Turkey

The most effective effort to dispel Turcophobia and promote Turkish-American friendship was made by the "American Friends of Turkey." Asa K. Jennings, formerly Secretary of the International Committee of the Young Men's Christian Association in Turkey and later the planner of various American relief projects there, was the moving force behind this group. Between 1922 and 1930 in Turkey, Jennings organized local "Turkish-American Clubs" which worked on such projects as orphanages, playgrounds, and night schools.[84] Inspired by Jennings' work, William H. Hoover, head of the Hoover Vacuum Cleaner Company, convened a meeting in New York on June 11, 1930. Among those present were John H. Finley, associate editor of the New York *Times*; Albert W. Staub of the Near East Colleges Association; Dr. Stephen P. Duggan of the Institute for International Education; James E. West of the Boy Scouts of America; Mary Mills Patrick, former president of Istanbul Woman's College; and Jennings. The group decided to incorporate a new organization, the American Friends of Turkey. Designated executive vice-president, Jennings returned to Turkey and, with the cooperation of the Turkish government, organized a "Mixed Commission" of six Turkish and three American members to coordinate the corporation's work. Included on this commission was G. Howland Shaw, counselor of the American embassy.[85] Commenting on the new organization, the New York *Herald Tribune* observed:

The purpose of the association . . . seems a sharp departure from the spirit of the earlier American missionary effort, which scarcely thought of inviting the Turk to participate as it rescued its brands from the fires of Near Eastern want and ignorance. The new association has taken "turkophile" as its cable address. Would it have been possible a generation ago,

[83] February 2, 1927.
[84] American Friends of Turkey, Inc., *American Friends of Turkey* (New York, 1931), pp. 1–14, in Bristol MSS, Box 96. This twenty-three–page pamphlet explains the origin and work of the group.
[85] *Ibid.*, pp. 14–16.

when every newspaper cartoonist in the country represented "Turkey" as a sinister figure with an enormous paunch, a sharp scimitar and the vulture-like countenance of Abdul Hamid?[86]

Originally, the American Friends of Turkey emphasized projects in Turkey. The Turkish government established the "Hayir Islerine Yardim Cemiyeti," or "Society for the Promotion and Support of Good Works," to operate in conjunction with the American group.[87] By 1935, the American Friends had undertaken many worthwhile projects, including model playgrounds, prenatal, baby, and dental clinics, sports fields, and libraries. The group promoted popular education by cooperating with the Turkish Educational Association in translating and publishing literature in the new alphabet, sending graduate students to the United States, and developing an experimental kindergarten and primary school, based on the methods of progressive education, in Ankara. Beryl Parker of New York University directed the latter project.[88] Other activities included the presentation of six purebred cattle to President Atatürk, a tour in the United States by a Turkish debating team, and the organization in Turkey of a school for juvenile delinquents.[89]

Because financial difficulties in the mid-1930s prevented an expansion of its program in Turkey, the American Friends of Turkey concentrated on activities in the United States. Admiral Bristol's election as president in 1932 to replace William Hoover enhanced the organization's prestige. Support of students from Turkey in the United States was an important project during these years.[90] More significant was a publicity campaign to promote Turkish-American friendship and understanding. Much attention went to yearly celebrations of the Turkish national holiday on October 29. On the ninth anniversary of the Turkish Republic in October, 1932, the American Friends of Turkey sponsored a luncheon meeting at the Town Hall Club in New York, where the speakers included Turkish

[86] Clipping, July 27, 1930, enclosure in Jennings to Bristol, July 29, 1930, Bristol MSS, Box 96.

[87] *American Friends of Turkey*, p. 15.

[88] Asa W. Jennings, *American Friends of Turkey, Inc., Report of the Executive Vice-President, May 27th, 1935*, pp. 2–3, in Bristol MSS, Box 96. Asa W. Jennings succeeded his father, Asa K. Jennings, when he died. See also Asa W. Jennings to Murray, July 20, 1933, DS 867.42711/4 and Shaw to Hull, April 26, 1933, DS 867.42711/1 for information on Parker's work.

[89] Jennings, *American Friends of Turkey, Inc., Report of the Executive Vice-President, May 27th, 1935*, pp. 2–3.

[90] *Ibid.*, p. 4; Asa K. Jennings to Bristol, May 9, 1932, Bristol MSS, Box 96; Asa K. Jennings to Bristol, August 3, 1932, *ibid.*

Ambassador Ahmed Mouhtar and Wallace Murray, Chief of the Near Eastern Division of the State Department.[91] A much more elaborate celebration occurred on the tenth anniversary in 1933. A large committee headed by former Ambassador to Turkey Abram I. Elkus (1916–1917) arranged an imposing dinner at the Waldorf Astoria Hotel in New York. Well publicized in advance by the New York press and by Lowell Thomas, the radio commentator, the three hundred guests heard talks by Ahmed Mouhtar, Wallace Murray, and Charalambos Simopoulos, Greek Ambassador to the United States. The gathering also received messages from Presidents Roosevelt and Atatürk.[92]

The educational, philanthropic, and public relations work of the American Friends of Turkey was an outstanding aid to the cultivation of understanding in the United States and to the development of Turkish-American friendship. The governments of both countries recognized the organization's value. In reviewing its work in 1937, Asa W. Jennings wrote:

There was a time when Turkey was greatly misunderstood in the United States. Americans, however, have now come to a fuller realization of the vast changes which have taken place in Turkey since the declaration of the Republic, in spite of the fact that the Turkish Government has never engaged in any propaganda activities whatsoever in this country. Turkish leaders are most sincere in their efforts to modernize and develop their country. Their accomplishments testify to the success with which they have met. We have been exerting every effort to bring about a better understanding in the United States of the accomplishments of the Turkish Republic.[93]

Turkish Efforts to Eliminate the Terrible Turk Stereotype

The Turkish government's cooperation with the American Friends of Turkey indicated a desire to improve its reputation in the United States,

---

[91] Stanley Howe (official, American Friends of Turkey) to Stimson, October 17, 1932, DS 811.43 American Friends of Turkey/5; Asa W. Jennings to Murray, October 31, 1932, DS 811.43 American Friends of Turkey/12.

[92] New York *Times*, January 22, February 16, October 28 and 30, 1933; Rayford W. Alley (official, American Friends of Turkey) to Phillips, September 18, 1933, DS 811.43 American Friends of Turkey/14; Phillips to Alley, October 3, 1933, DS 811.43 American Friends of Turkey/17; Asa W. Jennings to Bristol, October 6, 1932, Bristol MSS, Box 96; Jennings to Bristol, October 31, 1933, *ibid.*; Department of State, *Press Releases*, Weekly Issue No. 214, November 4, 1933, pp. 249–250 (text of Murray's speech at the dinner).

[93] *American Friends of Turkey, Inc., Report of the Executive Vice-President, May 26th, 1937*, p. 4, Bristol MSS, Box 96.

but there were limits to what could be done. A shortage of funds restricted Turkey's efforts throughout this period, as did the absence of diplomatic representation, at least until 1927. Only two ambassadors represented Turkey during the period from 1927 through 1944. The first, Ahmed Mouhtar, served until April, 1934, when he retired from the Turkish Foreign Service. His successor, Mehmet Münir Ertegün, was Turkish Ambassador in London at the time of his new assignment.[94] Mouhtar and Ertegün confined their activities in the United States to the normal requirements of diplomatic representation, since practically all negotiations for treaties and other agreements took place in Turkey. Both ambassadors, by capably conducting the affairs of their country in the United States, contributed to the improvement of Turkey's public relations.

Occasional Turkish participation in American exhibitions helped in a small way.[95] The flow of unofficial Turkish visitors to the United States was not extensive, but the few who came were well received. Perhaps the most distinguished was Halidé Edib Adivar, an outstanding feminine leader of the Turkish revolution who wrote extensively about it. She made a good impression and did much to publicize the vast improvements in Turkey when she appeared at the Williamstown, Massachusetts, Institute of Politics in August, 1928.[96]

The Turkish government worked actively to prevent the dissemination of distorted information about Turkey in the United States. Most interesting were efforts to stop the filming of Franz Werfel's novel, *The Forty Days of Musa Dagh*. The Turkish government became alarmed in November, 1934, when it learned that an American company planned to produce this story about Turkish mistreatment of Armenians. The State Depart-

[94] Memo of conversation, Phillips and Ahmed Mouhtar, March 12, 1934, DS 701.6711/334; Department of State, *Press Releases*, Weekly Issue No. 236, April 7, 1934, p. 188. Ahmed Mouhtar died of pneumonia soon after his return to Turkey. See Allen and Howard Elting, Jr. (Vice-Consul, Istanbul), Digest of the Turkish Press, June 17–July 14, 1934, DS 867.9111/419. Ertegün died in Washington on November 11, 1944. His remains were returned to Turkey with full honors on the U.S.S. *Missouri* in 1946. See *Foreign Relations of the United States: Diplomatic Papers, 1944* (7 vols., Washington, 1965–1967), V, 915–917.

[95] See the New York *Times*, December 24, 1927, about Turkish participation in the Oriental Exposition at Madison Square Garden, New York, and *ibid.*, May 7 and July 23, 1939, for Turkey's activities at the New York World's Fair.

[96] See Halidé Edib [Adivar], *Turkey Faces West: A Turkish View of Recent Changes and Their Origin* (New Haven, 1930); diary, September 21, 1928, *Turbulent Era*, II, 793; Grew to Kellogg, July 25, 1928, DS 867.00/2000; diary, July 27, 1928, Grew MSS, 1928, vol. 3; Grew to Kellogg, August 10, 1928, DS 867.00/2001; New York *Times*, August 3, 4, and 10, 1928.

ment, after representations by the Turkish Ambassador and Foreign Minister, suggested to film industry officials that the filming of Werfel's novel would be "detrimental to the cordial feelings between the two peoples." Because of Turkish and State Department pressure, the Metro-Goldwyn-Mayer Company agreed not to make the picture.[97] In the meantime, the excited Turkish press threatened a boycott of all American films in Turkey.[98] The Armenian population in Istanbul, fearing retaliation by the Turks, publicly burned a picture of Werfel and a copy of his book. After President Atatürk died in November, 1938, new rumors that the film would be made again disturbed the Turkish Ambassador and caused the State Department to renew its pressure on motion picture interests.[99]

Its response to the Musa Dagh matter demonstrated the Turkish government's interest in preventing adverse publicity in the United States. The Turks were also touchy about articles appearing in American publications maligning Atatürk. In April, 1938, when the magazine *Ken* published an article, "Atatürk, Hoodlum as Hero," a State Department official noted that "unbridled license of this kind in attacking a foreign chief of state . . . will seriously affect our present most friendly relations with the Republic of Turkey and gravely compromise American interests as a whole in that country." After the Turkish Ambassador protested against the article, President Roosevelt instructed the Attorney-General to consider prosecution of the magazine. Later, the Ambassador, expressing Atatürk's appreciation for Roosevelt's personal interest, asked that no legal action be taken.[100] Critical articles about Atatürk in a Washington newspaper

[97] Memo, Murray, November 16, 1934, on conversation with Ambassador Münir Ertegün, DS 811.4061 Musa Dagh/1; Shaw to Murray, November 27, 1934, DS 811.4061 Musa Dagh/6; Ertegün to Murray, April 22, 1935, DS 811.4061 Musa Dagh/10; Ertegün to Hull, September 5, 1935, *Foreign Relations of the United States: Diplomatic Papers, 1935* (4 vols., Washington, 1953), I, 1053–1054; Murray to Will H. Hays (President of Motion Picture Producers and Distributors of America), September 7, 1935, *ibid.*, 1054–1055; Ertegün to Murray, October 4, 1935, *ibid.*, 1055–1056.

[98] Thomas Burke (Chief, Specialties–Motion Picture Division) to Frederick L. Herron (Motion Picture Producers and Distributors of America), June 4, 1935, file 281 Turkey (Record Group 151, Records of the Bureau of Foreign and Domestic Commerce, National Archives, Washington); Skinner to Hull, June 4, 1935, DS 811.4061 Musa Dagh/17; Shaw to Hull, September 10, 1935, DS 811.4061 Musa Dagh/35.

[99] Skinner to Hull, December 24, 1935, DS 811.4061 Musa Dagh/49; Ertegün to Murray, December 12, 1938, DS 811.4061 Musa Dagh/54; memo of conversation, Paul H. Alling (Near East Division) and Herron, January 11, 1939, DS 811.-4061 Musa Dagh/63.

[100] Memo, Murray, April 20, 1938, DS 867.001 Atatürk, Kemal/33; memo of

and *Life* magazine brought similar protests from the Turkish Ambassador. The appearance of the latter article, shortly before the Turkish President's death, was especially inappropriate.[101]

Rapprochement

An assessment of this combined Turkish-American campaign during the interwar years to eliminate the Terrible Turk stereotype and improve the reputation of Turkey in the United States reveals a profound change in American public opinion. Although traces of the old prejudice remained, most Americans with opinions about Turkey respected and admired its efforts to become a modern and progressive nation. When Kemal Atatürk died on November 10, 1938, there was general recognition in the United States that a great leader had passed from the world scene. The New York *Times* editorialized that Atatürk "was without doubt one of the ablest national leaders of the post-war period. . . . As a result of his rule the diminished Turkey of today is not only a healthier but a stronger and more stable nation than the vast suzerainty of the Sultans." Another writer remarked, "It is hard to find this man's counterpart in history. . . . He has been a Washington at Valley Forge and a Peter the Great bludgeoning his people into modernity." [102] By 1939, the kind of propaganda earlier circulated by Armenians and other enemies of Turkey was rare in American publications.

The restoration of harmony and friendly relations between the United States and Turkey by the end of the interwar period would not have been possible if both countries and their governments had not worked hard toward that end. There were obstacles, both in Turkey and the United States, to rapprochement. The Turkish program, emphasizing domestic

conversation, Sumner Welles (Undersecretary of State) and Ertegün, April 22, 1938, DS 867.001 Atatürk, Kemal/32 ½; memo, Murray to Welles, Adolf A. Berle (Assistant Secretary of State), and Hull, May 11, 1938, DS 867.001 Atatürk, Kemal/46.

[101] Memo, Murray to Welles, Berle, and Hull, May 13, 1938, DS 867.001 Atatürk, Kemal/39 ½; memo, Alling to Welles, October 31, 1938, DS 867.001 Atatürk, Kemal/58; memo of conversation, Welles and Ertegün, November 5, 1938, DS 867.001 Atatürk, Kemal/61. The articles referred to were in the Washington *Times*, May 12, 1938, and *Life*, October 31, 1938.

[102] Heck, "Sidelights on Past Relations Between the United States and Turkey," p. 114; Roosevelt to Abdul Halik Renda (Provisional President of Turkey), November 10, 1938, DS 867.001 Atatürk, Kemal/64; Marguerite Arnold, "Elegy for Atatürk," *New Republic*, XCVIII (May 3, 1939), 375; New York *Times*, November 11, 1938; William Gilman, "Turkey with Western Dressing," *Current History*, XLIX (November, 1938), 37.

reform and moderation and responsibility in international politics, aided in the improvement of relations with the United States as well as with other nations.

The basic objective of the United States was to protect its traditional missionary, philanthropic, cultural, and economic interests in Turkey. The political disinterest of the United States in the Middle East region facilitated the improvement of relations with Turkey. Important also was the high quality and effectiveness of United States diplomatic representatives in Turkey.

✣ The Economic Dimension: Commercial Relations Between the Wars

HISTORICALLY, the earliest links between Turkey and the United States had been made by traders, and commercial exchange traditionally had been one of the main areas of interest in Turkish-American relations. There was no substantial increase in volume between the wars, but bilateral trade remained a significant concern of the two nations. There were important markets in the United States for certain Turkish products. The Turks not only wanted some particular American commodities but also worked to expand trade as one phase of their extensive program of economic modernization and development.

World War I and the breaking of diplomatic relations in 1917 temporarily disrupted Turkish-American commercial relations. Although trade was resumed in 1919, it operated without formal guarantees for ten years, until the two nations negotiated a commercial treaty in 1929. This treaty prevailed until 1939 when a reciprocal trade agreement became effective. Turkish-American trade in the interwar years was affected both by Turkish economic nationalism and the impact of the post-1929 depression on both nations. Another significant influence was Turkey's political position in the Middle East and Europe, particularly in the late 1930s as World War II loomed on the international horizon. This chapter pays some attention to the products involved, but the emphasis is on factors affecting trade and the diplomacy of commercial relations.[1]

---

[1] See Leland James Gordon, *American Relations with Turkey, 1830–1930: An Economic Interpretation* (Philadelphia, 1932), pp. 72–113, and Mustafa Nebil Kazdal, "Trade Relations Between the United States and Turkey, 1919–1944," (Ph.D.

Turkish Commercial Policy

Various Turkish administrative procedures, including sanitary standards and port regulations, complicated trade relations with the United States. For example, the Turkish consulate general in New York often aroused the ire of American exporters because of its regulations on certificates of origin indicating the country of origin of goods being shipped to Turkey. If these certificates were not visaed by the consul general, regardless of the location in the United States from which the shipment was actually made, they would not be accepted by Turkish customs authorities.[2]

Another source of discouragement for United States companies was Turkish imitation of American products and trademarks. One example was the infringement of the Kolynos Toothpaste Company's trademark. Turkish courts in 1927 and 1928 dismissed the Kolynos suit against Turkish imitators despite the obvious use of its trademark.[3] Such practices hardly encouraged Americans to expand their commercial efforts in Turkey.

United States sanitary standards affected the packing of figs in the Izmir area and caused much diplomatic controversy. In 1927, the Bureau of Chemistry of the Department of Agriculture ruled that no more than ten per cent of any shipment of dried fruits to the United States could be affected by worms and insects. The Turkish Foreign Office protested to High Commissioner Bristol that the regulation, if enforced, would have a detrimental effect on the fig trade. Even earlier, a Turkish-American advisory board had been established to aid the United States consulate at Izmir in ensuring sanitary measures in *hans*, the fig-packing establishments.[4] Turkish packers greatly resented inspection of their *hans*. Consid-

thesis, Indiana University, 1946), pp. 61–70, 78–90, for detailed analyses of the products involved in Turkish-American trade.

[2] United States Department of Commerce, Bureau of Domestic and Foreign Commerce, *Commerce Reports*, XXX (September 26, 1927), 830 (hereafter cited as *Commerce Reports*); "Certificates of Origin for Turkey," *Levant Trade Review*, XVI (September, 1928), 342.

[3] Edward S. Rogers (counsel, Kolynos Company) to Wallace Murray (Chief, Near Eastern Division), October 6, 1928, DS 867.543 Kolynos/1. An enclosure in this document reviews several trademark infringement cases in Turkey. See Joseph C. Grew to Frank B. Kellogg, January 30, 1929, DS 867.543 Kolynos/7.

[4] Mark L. Bristol to Kellogg, April 12, 1927, DS 611.674 Figs/9; Samuel W. Honaker (Consul, Izmir) to Kellogg, September 25, 1926, DS 611.674/62. See also Honaker to Kellogg, February 20, 1926, DS 611.674/56 for a comprehensive description of the fig and raisin industries in Turkey.

ering the regulations a remnant of the capitulations, the Izmir press complained about the "dictatorial" methods used to enforce them. Ambassador Grew and Consul Herbert S. Bursley at Izmir eventually advised discontinuance of the inspections because of this friction. But the United States government followed the advice of Louis G. Michael, a Department of Agriculture attaché, who urged, after an inspection, that they be continued.[5]

The lack of a formal parcel post arrangement was another commercial handicap. Eventually, Turkish and American post office officials, with aid from the United States embassy in Turkey, negotiated a parcel post convention, effective in August, 1935. The convention, by regulating the contents of parcels and establishing insurance and postal rates, eliminated another impediment to the interchange of goods between Turkey and the United States.[6]

These petty administrative restrictions and problems often slowed trade between the two countries. But even if they had not existed, the volume probably would not have been appreciably higher. Turkey's economic policies, which diverged considerably from United States practice, unintentionally discouraged trade. Until August, 1929, Turkey's foreign trade was subject to the commercial provisions of the Allied Treaty of Lausanne, which prohibited tariff increases. Once free of these restrictions, the Turkish government applied higher tariff coefficients and revised its rates upward effective October 1, 1929. The higher duties brought protests from American exporters who complained that they had been given no warning and that shipments made before the changes went into effect were being admitted to Turkey only after payment of the higher rates. Secondhand clothing dealers in the United States, for example, pleaded with the State Department to arrange for suspension of the new duties until clearance of prior shipments. The State Department decided not to make for-

[5] George W. Renchard (Vice-Consul, Izmir) to Henry L. Stimson, September 9, 1931, DS 611.674/107; Bursley to Stimson, September 28, 1931, DS 611.674/109; Grew to Stimson, January 25, 1932, DS 611.674/113; Louis G. Michael to L. A. Wheeler (Department of Agriculture), November 11, 1932, DS 611.674/135.

[6] Robert W. Bliss (State Department) to Bristol, September 5, 1922, DS 811.71567/27; Grew to Kellogg, February 13, 1928, DS 811.71567/37; Charles H. Sherrill to Stimson, June 14, 1932, DS 811.71567/40; Walter F. Brown (Postmaster General) to Stimson, July 29, 1932, DS 811.71567/42; R. Walton Moore (State Department) to Robert P. Skinner, February 2, 1934, DS 811.71567/60; James A. Farley (Postmaster General) to Hull, undated but received December 5, 1935, DS 811.71567/66 (copy of the parcel post convention included).

mal representations because the increases were legal and applied equally to all countries.[7]

The Turkish government relied on the 1929 tariff schedule until November, 1931, when the Council of Ministers established monthly quotas for almost all imports. The Turkish government devised the quota system to ensure a favorable trade balance, which presumably would help to stabilize the value of the Turkish pound. In the eight years before 1931, Turkey's foreign trade showed an excess of exports over imports only in 1930.[8] Under the new system, periodic quota lists were to be published twenty days before they went into effect. American firms, which could not ship their goods to Turkey in such a short time, protested. Grew, in informal talks with Tevfik Rüsdü Aras, the Turkish Foreign Minister, arranged for publication of the lists ninety days in advance. Grew reported that the Turkish government intended only "minimum hardship" for American trade, since the trade balance with the United States normally was favorable to Turkey. Grew believed that the Turkish government would not apply the quotas "impartially" to all countries. "I am beginning to suspect that Japanese dumping was in a large measure responsible for the sudden restricting of importation," Grew observed.[9]

Turkey's trade policy also included exchange control and a compensation system. On February 20, 1930, the Grand National Assembly passed

[7] M. S. Anderson, *The Eastern Question 1774–1923: A Study in International Relations* (London, Melbourne, Toronto, & New York, 1966), p. 374; F. B. Keljikian (clothing dealer) to Department of State, September 7, 1929, DS 667.113 Second Hand Clothing/1; Sheldon L. Crosby (Secretary of Embassy, Istanbul) to Stimson, October 8, 1929, DS 667.113 Second Hand Clothing/16; Keljikian, N. Abarian, and Isaac Sackstein to Stimson, September 19, 1929, DS 667.113 Second Hand Clothing/6; W. R. Castle, Jr. (Assistant Secretary of State) to Keljikian, November 15, 1929, DS 667.113 Second Hand Clothing/25; *Commerce Reports*, XXXII (October 28, 1929), 250; *Christian Science Monitor* (Boston), October 2, 1929; Kazdal, "Trade Relations Between the United States and Turkey," pp. 33–35.

[8] Conversation, Grew and Tevfik Rüsdü Aras, December 2, 1931, Joseph C. Grew MSS (Houghton Library, Harvard University, Cambridge, Mass.), 1931, vol. 2; Grew to Stimson, November 16, 1931, DS 667.006/11; United States Tariff Commission, *Trade Agreement Between the United States and the Republic of Turkey: Digests of Trade Data with Respect to Products on Which Concessions Were Granted by the United States* (Washington, 1939), p. 12 (hereafter cited as U.S. Tariff Commission, *Trade Agreement Digest*).

[9] Grew to Stimson, November 27, 1931, DS 667.006/12; Henry Chalmers (Chief, Division of Foreign Tariffs, Bureau of Foreign and Domestic Commerce) to F. M. Moffat (President, Tanners Council of America), December 12, 1931, file 252 Turkey (Record Group 151, Records of the Bureau of Foreign and Domestic Commerce, National Archives, Washington) (hereafter cited as FDC Records); Grew to Stimson, December 15, 1931, DS 667.006/18.

a bill prohibiting the export of gold and giving the government exclusive control over exchange payments. Although foreign companies needed government permission to convert Turkish currency into their own exchange, most American firms in Turkey were not immediately inconvenienced by the exchange control. The Standard Oil Company of New York, however, because of the large amounts involved, experienced difficulty. An American embassy official suggested that "it is not impossible that the law was drafted expressly to prevent that Company from making excessively large purchases of foreign exchange." The Turkish government in 1932 and again in 1935 relaxed the exchange rules for countries like the United States with which Turkey had a favorable balance of trade. The exchange policy caused no serious problems for American interests until 1937.[10]

A compensation system begun by Turkey in 1932 resulted in a series of bilateral agreements with many foreign countries, not including the United States. The arrangements permitted the importation of products, quota or nonquota, if they were compensated for by the export of specified goods, including rugs, mohair, and tobacco. Coupled with the compensation system were clearing agreements involving government supervision of trade accounts to control the flow of exchange between Turkey and its trade partners. These regulations did not apply to the United States because until 1937 there was no threat that the balance of trade between the two countries would be adverse to Turkey.[11]

Efforts to Expand Trade

United States ambassadors Charles H. Sherrill (1932–1933) and Robert P. Skinner (1933–1936), both vitally concerned about commercial matters, worked hard to expand Turco-American trade. Sherrill felt that the quota system would defeat his avowed purpose of doubling trade.

[10] Grew to Stimson, February 26, 1930, DS 867.5151/17; David Williamson (Third Secretary of Embassy) to Stimson, May 5, 1930, DS 867.5151/22 (source of the quotation); Kazdal, "Trade Relations Between the United States and Turkey," pp. 36–38; Sherrill to Stimson, May 20, 1932, DS 667.0031/15; G. Howland Shaw (Counselor of Embassy) to Stimson, October 25, 1932, DS 867.5151/39; United States Tariff Commission, *Extent of Equal Tariff Treatment in Foreign Countries*, Report No. 119, 2nd Series (Washington, 1937), p. 74.

[11] Sherrill to Stimson, July 16, 1932, DS 667.006/24; Frederick T. Merrill, "Twelve Years of the Turkish Republic," *Foreign Policy Reports*, XI (October 9, 1935), 196; U.S. Tariff Commission, *Extent of Equal Tariff Treatment in Foreign Countries*, pp. 71–74.

In talks with Turkish officials he urged a relaxation of quotas on shipments from the United States. The quotas, he told Foreign Minister Aras, rendered him "helpless to plead . . . [Turkey's] cause at home because of injury done to American trade." [12] Sherrill placed importance on trade volume because he felt "the American people deserve more than they are getting for what is expended upon this Embassy," which he estimated at $191,445 for 1931. "When I saw those figures . . . ," he confessed to Secretary Stimson, "I was conscience-stricken and became even more determined than before that our people shall get more for their money than at present." [13] Sherrill's talks with Turkish officials proved effective; in January, 1933, Turkey abolished quota restrictions on American goods equal to the value of American purchases of Turkish products. This decree, however, had no appreciable effect on the volume of Turkish-American trade.[14]

Skinner's determination to expand sale of American commodities to Turkey received little encouragement from the Department of State. The ambassador fretted over the adverse balance of trade and the fact that, in contrast with United States firms, European companies worked actively to build up trade with Turkey. Skinner lamented the fact that German commercial representatives were "as active as flies about a honey pot and very properly engaged in making any commercial arrangements which may be feasible." The State Department refused Skinner permission to discuss the trade problem formally with Turkish authorities and told him to "avoid making any definite assertion or intimation that unless the Turkish Government sees to it that our trade with Turkey approaches more nearly to a balance, we will take restrictive action to that end." [15] One State Department official complained about Skinner's (and Sherrill's) "narrow one-sided commercial travelers' view of commercial relations." Another observed that "the function of the Department of State and of American diplomatic representatives is something more than merely act-

[12] Sherrill to Stimson, August 23, 1932, DS 667.116/17; Sherrill to Stimson, August 29, 1932, DS 667.116/20. This was just before Sherrill's leave in the United States.
[13] August 29, 1932, DS 667.116/20.
[14] Sherrill to Stimson, January 19, 1933, DS 667.116/32; New York *Times*, January 26, 1933; memo, Henry S. Villard, "American Trade with Turkey under the Decree of January 25, 1933," January 6, 1934, DS 667.116/62.
[15] Skinner to Hull, March 19, 1934, *Foreign Relations of the United States: Diplomatic Papers, 1934* (5 vols., Washington, 1950–1952), II, 940–942 (hereafter cited as *FR 1934*); Murray to Skinner, June 7, 1934, *ibid.*, 948.

ing as salesmen for American goods. It is clearly incumbent upon the Department and upon our foreign representatives to seek to proceed in this matter on statesmanlike rather than purely commercial conceptions and principles." The State Department, acknowledging the "troublesome question of credit and finance" in Turkey, felt that the initiative in expanding trade should be left to private commercial interests. The Department's cautious policy would absolve it from responsibility if such arrangements did not succeed.[16]

Ambassador Skinner looked on the Turkish rearmament program of the mid-1930s as a lucrative opportunity for American firms. Although reporting his "regret that Turkey is arming actively and heavily" because it feared Benito Mussolini's Italy, he outlined Turkish armament needs and suggested that the Department of State "bring these facts discreetly to the attention of our manufacturers."[17] The visit of Ahmed Emin Yalman to the United States in July, 1934, emphasized Turkish interest in the purchase of arms.[18] The State Department looked with clear disfavor on Skinner's proposals and the desire of American firms to sell military goods to Turkey. When in 1934 Ralph E. Flanders, president of the Jones and Lamson Machine Company of Springfield, Vermont, expressed his hopes of selling machinery to Turkey for the maintenance and repair of small arms, the Department refused to sanction the project. Flanders asked the Department to recommend that the Export-Import Bank grant his company a loan to finance the order. George Peek, Special Adviser to the President on Foreign Trade, agreed with Secretary of State Cordell Hull that the loan could not be sanctioned because the products Flanders intended to sell to Turkey were within the category of "arms and munitions" of war.[19]

Ambassador Skinner felt that the Flanders project should be approved. He believed that war goods should not be sold, but the products Flanders wished to sell could be used for peaceful purposes. Skinner

[16] Memo, Henry L. Deimel to Murray, Paul H. Alling, and Villard (all of the Near East Division), April 27, 1934, DS 611.6731/160; memo, Alling, May 22, 1934, DS 611.6731/161; Hull to Skinner, August 2, 1934, *FR 1934*, II, 954–956.

[17] Skinner to Hull, May 22, 1934, *ibid.*, 960–961; Skinner to Hull, June 13, 1934, *ibid.*, 964–965.

[18] Memo, Murray, July 27, 1934, *ibid.*, 953–954. Yalman, primarily a journalist, represented a number of United States firms in Turkey at this time.

[19] Ralph E. Flanders to Hull, September 26, 1934, *ibid.*, 965–967; Hull to George Peek, October 1, 1934, *ibid.*, 967; Peek to Hull, October 9, 1934, *ibid.*, 968. Flanders served as a United States Senator from Vermont from 1946 to 1959.

feared that orders not accepted in the United States would go to European countries "whose representatives are in Ankara doing their utmost to prevent purchases in the United States." [20] Skinner's definition of arms and munitions excluded "any articles of manufacture . . . which had been produced and perfected for normal peace time purposes, which are commonly offered for sale in the principal industrial countries of the world, even when such articles are being contracted for by the military branch of the Government of the importing country." The State Department concurred in this definition but felt that the export financing of such products should be avoided "when there is danger that, in case of war, this Government could be justly criticized for assisting in the military preparation of one of the parties thereto." The State Department repeatedly reminded Skinner that it could not encourage the export of arms and munitions.[21] The Department discouraged several firms, including General Motors Export Corporation, Curtiss-Wright, and the Glenn L. Martin Company, from selling such products to Turkey during this period.[22]

Skinner's campaign to obtain a share of the profits from Turkish rearmament began about the same time that a committee headed by Senator Gerald P. Nye of North Dakota launched an investigation of the munitions industry. The State Department could hardly have encouraged Skinner under the circumstances, when public opinion was being stirred up by these investigations designed to disclose the role of the munitions industry in promoting the United States entrance into World War I. During the probe there were many references to American firms which had interests in Turkey during and after the war. Testimony before the Nye committee disclosed, for example, that a 1928 conference in Washington involving Turkish diplomats, United States naval officers, and manufacturing interests considered the sale of arms to the Turkish government. Witnesses before the committee charged that the United States Navy cruiser *Raleigh* went to Istanbul in 1929 to demonstrate guns made by an American

[20] Skinner to Hull, November 5, 1934, *ibid.*, 969–970.

[21] Skinner to Hull, January 9, 1935, *Foreign Relations of the United States: Diplomatic Papers, 1935* (4 vols., Washington, 1953), I, 1046–1047; William Phillips to Skinner, March 18, 1935, *ibid.*, 1050; Hull to Skinner, January 15, 1935, *ibid.*, 1049; Phillips to Skinner, February 23, 1935, *ibid.*, 1050.

[22] Memo, Murray, January 11, 1935, *ibid.*, 1048–1049 (General Motors); Skinner to Hull, April 6, 1934, DS 867.796 Curtiss/22; Glenn L. Martin to Hull, July 20, 1934, DS 867.248 Martin Company, Glenn L./1; George H. Dern (Secretary of War) to Hull, August 16, 1934, DS 867.248 Martin Company, Glenn L./4.

firm.[23] Furthermore, the committee was told, General Douglas Mac-Arthur, Army Chief of Staff, visited Turkey in 1932 to promote the sale of American military equipment. MacArthur informed the committee that there was "absolutely no foundation" to these charges.[24]

Because of the climate of opinion in the United States, at that time generally isolationist, Skinner was unsuccessful in promoting opportunities for American armament companies, but he was able to facilitate the entrance of other products into Turkey. In July, 1934, the Turkish government extended to the United States all commercial advantages which it had accorded by agreement to other countries. Skinner reported that the concession, applying mainly to products not subject to quota restrictions, put the United States "in a more favorable position as respects the importation of American goods into this country than we have been at any time since the inauguration of the policy of restrictions." [25]

Exchange Difficulties

On November 20, 1936, the Turkish government abolished the quota system begun in 1931. A new decree established five categories of Turkish imports: (1) a free list; (2) goods, amounting to about 65 per cent of Turkey's imports, which could enter without quota restrictions if they came from a country having a clearing agreement with Turkey or whose balance of trade was consistently favorable to Turkey; (3) goods importable only with specific permission from an appropriate Turkish ministry; (4) merchandise authorized for import in bilateral agreements with the Turkish government; and (5) a list of commodities not open to import. Included in the third category were household insecticides, tractors, agri-

[23] United States Senate, *Hearings Before the Special Committee Investigating the Munitions Industry*, 73 and 74 Cong. (12 vols., 40 parts, Washington, 1934–1943), I, pt. 1, 249–252, pt. 2, 497–510. See also the *Christian Science Monitor*, September 7 and 8, 1934. Turkish Ambassador Münir Ertegün wrote to Secretary Hull for information about the 1928 charges. See Ertegün to Hull, September 11, 1934, *FR 1934*, I, 430.

[24] *Hearings Before the Special Committee Investigating the Munitions Industry*, I, pt. 4, 829–830, pt. 5, 1080–1081; *Christian Science Monitor*, September 13 and 14, 1934. See Shaw to Stimson, September 29, 1932, DS 867.20111/8 for a report on MacArthur's visit to Turkey. While there he attended a military review and talked with Kemal Atatürk. Shaw observed in this despatch: "It is probable that as a result of General MacArthur's visit the Turks will send some of their officers to the United States for courses of study with the General Staff, with the Navy and with the Army and Navy Air Services."

[25] To Hull, July 21, 1934, DS 667.116/83.

cultural implements, and cotton yarn, all imported from the United States; goods such as leather, canned food, cotton textiles, chewing gum, and toothpaste were in the last group. Despite restrictions on these products, the abolition of quotas meant that most American goods could enter Turkey without hindrance. This situation would exist, however, only as long as the trade balance remained in Turkey's favor.[26]

Because the balance was in Turkey's favor, American exporters experienced few difficulties until late 1937 in converting Turkish currency into dollars. Turkey's clearing arrangements with other nations did not work well, however, and Turkish importers began in 1937 to buy larger quantities from United States sources. The assistant commercial attaché in Istanbul predicted early in 1938 that, unless exports to the United States were expanded as well, the favorable balance of trade Turkey enjoyed would be sacrificed. If this happened, "the exchange facilities at present accorded local importers of American merchandise will become increasingly difficult to maintain." The attaché's prediction came true on May 11, 1938, when the Turkish government suspended all foreign exchange payments, apparently because of expansion in imports from the United States. American firms doing business in Turkey either had to stop sales or wait indefinitely for dollar exchange.[27]

Even before the exchange decree American firms had begun to complain to the State Department about a lag in exchange payments. The Socony-Vacuum Oil Company, for instance, pointed out that it was owed arrears of $891,000 as of December 31, 1937.[28] With the exception of daily exchange payments to three American oil companies, evidently to ensure a continued flow of their products to Turkey, all foreign exchange transfers were prohibited between May and July, 1938, when the government resumed the issue of exchange permits. It granted the permits only sporadically for the rest of the year, causing a temporary halt in the import of most American products. Arrears owed to American firms were more than $4,000,000 on December 21, 1938. American purchases of Turkish tobacco, beginning in mid-November, 1938, provided over $7,500,000 in

[26] John V. A. MacMurray to Hull, January 14, 1937, DS 667.006/43; S. Walter Washington (Chargé d'Affaires) to Hull, August 12, 1937, DS 667.006/46.

[27] John A. Embry, "Economic Conditions in Turkey During 1937," Special Report No. 137, February 2, 1938, FDC Records, file 128X Istanbul (source of the quotation); Robert F. Kelley (First Secretary of Embassy) to Hull, May 11, 1938, DS 867.5151/83; *Commerce Reports*, XLI (August 6, 1938), 690.

[28] H. D. Green (Socony-Vacuum Company) to Hull, February 11, 1938, DS 611.6731/313.

dollar exchange to Turkey within a few weeks, but arrears of more than $1,300,000 still existed in February, 1939.[29] Not until late in 1939 was Ambassador MacMurray able to report that all 1938 exchange arrears had been liquidated. By this time exchange payments had been made for applications filed up to February 20, 1939.[30] The exchange situation was a major issue in discussions for a reciprocal trade agreement in 1938 and 1939.[31]

Trade Volume and Products

There was little overall change in either volume or the products involved in Turkish-American trade during the interwar period. As the table on page 105 indicates, after the comparative boom in the immediate postwar years, the volume in the 1920s approximated what it had been in the five years before World War I. A significant drop in exports from the United States to Turkey for a few years after 1930 reflected the world economic crisis and Turkey's quota system.

The table on page 106 lists the principal Turkish products imported into the United States. Cigarette leaf tobacco, used for blending with American tobacco, was consistently the most important individual commodity. In 1938, cigarette leaf tobacco accounted for 73 per cent of the total value of United States imports from Turkey.[32] Two factors explain the significant decrease in the import of handmade oriental rugs and figs: high United States tariff rates and increasing domestic production.[33] Chrome ore was the most important new import from Turkey. In 1930, several American companies indicated their interest in Turkey's chrome supply. One corporation, the American Smelting and Refining Company, spent several years studying chrome prospects in Turkey. In 1937, the Eti Bank, in charge of Turkish mineral development, intensified its efforts to

[29] Kelley to Hull, May 18, 1938, DS 867.5151/84; MacMurray to Hull, July 5, 1938, DS 611.6731/596; MacMurray to Hull, February 20, 1939, DS 611.6731/528.

[30] MacMurray to Hull, November 11, 1939, *Foreign Relations of the United States: Diplomatic Papers, 1939* (5 vols., Washington, 1955–1957), IV, 880.

[31] United States Department of Commerce, Bureau of Foreign and Domestic Commerce, *Trade of the United States with Turkey in 1938* (Washington, 1939), p. 1. Because of the bearing of the exchange problem on the trade agreement and its operation, further discussion is deferred until the agreement is analyzed. See below, pp. 115–125.

[32] U.S. Tariff Commission, *Trade Agreement Digest*, p. 1. See Kazdal, "Trade Relations Between the United States and Turkey," p. 112, for a table showing percentages of United States exports from Turkey represented by tobacco, 1919–1938.

[33] Kazdal, "Trade Relations Between the United States and Turkey," p. 74.

Turkish-American Trade, 1914–1941[a]

Year	Imports from Turkey	Exports to Turkey	Balance
1910–1914 (ave.)	$19,251,000	$ 3,348,000	$15,903,000
1914	20,843,077	3,328,519	17,514,558
1915	12,228,707	994,120	11,234,587
1916	864,485	42,169	822,316
1917	335,590	167,515	168,075
1918	222,039	305,557	83,518[b]
1919	37,003,002	25,231,722	11,771,280
1920	39,766,936	42,247,798	2,480,862[b]
1921	13,246,638	23,947,110	10,700,472[b]
1922	21,693,000	16,466,000	5,227,000
1923	13,009,000	3,470,000	9,539,000
1924	14,621,000	3,665,000	10,956,000
1925	14,648,000	3,380,000	11,268,000
1926	16,832,000	2,927,000	13,905,000
1927	20,070,000	4,027,000	16,043,000
1928	18,388,000	4,242,000	14,146,000
1929	12,166,000	5,810,000	6,356,000
1930	11,638,000	4,385,000	7,253,000
1931	8,085,000	1,713,000	6,372,000
1932	5,388,000	1,539,000	3,849,000
1933	8,189,000	1,343,000	6,846,000
1934	7,161,000	2,722,000	4,439,000
1935	7,780,000	4,456,000	3,324,000
1936	9,811,000	6,222,000	3,589,000
1937	17,855,000	14,916,000	2,293,000
1938	18,958,000	13,218,000	5,740,000
1939	19,836,000	8,313,000	11,523,000
1940	13,888,000	8,274,000	5,614,000
1941	10,718,000	6,810,000	3,908,000

SOURCE: United States Department of Commerce, Bureau of Foreign and Domestic Commerce, *Foreign Commerce and Navigation of the United States . . . [1914–1941]* (Washington, 1915–1944).

[a] Figures beginning in 1922 are to the nearest thousand. Statistics for 1914–1917 are for the fiscal year, ending June 30 of each year; statistics for years beginning in 1918 are for the calendar year.

[b] Favorable to the United States.

---

sell chrome ore in the United States.[34] Expanding needs and the Turkish desire to sell explain the increase in American purchase of chrome ore.[35]

[34] Joseph S. McGrath (Minerals Division, Bureau of Foreign and Domestic Commerce) to Julian E. Gillespie, May 12, 1930, FDC Records, file 272 Turkey; Jefferson Patterson (Chargé d'Affaires) to Stimson, June 29, 1930, DS 867.63/37; Gillespie to Ilhami N. Pamir (Director-General, Eti Bank), June 1, 1937, FDC Records, file 272 Turkey.

[35] See *Foreign Relations of the United States: Diplomatic Papers, 1940* (5 vols.,

Principal United States Imports from Turkey, 1914–1941 (in Dollars) [a]

Product	1914	1920	1927	1929	1931	1933	1935	1937	1939	1941
Canary seed	....	....	9,504	49,105	159,249	71,655	106,545	222,154	61,804	....
Chrome ore	....	19,422,318	....	17,819	44,609	495,150	267,294	750,509	323,704	1,099,723
Cigarette leaf tobacco	9,837,473	....	9,953,000	10,366,000	5,963,000	4,367,000	3,666,000	8,807,000	11,212,205	11,252,794
Emery ore	256,084	111,403	35,142	53,997	12,515	6,398	28,618	47,932	17,190	....
Figs	719,022	1,949,463	1,383,000	1,168,000	447,000	397,000	256,000	221,000	159,476	18,205
Filberts	....	917,991	809,200	234,089	357,945	201,058	153,062	96,517	285,886	38,327
Hareskins	....	....	203,368	308,021	53,615	48,079	59,921	137,052	60,864	61,329
Licorice extract	....	....	....	....	....	6,156	1,636	9,398	11,406	....
Licorice root	839,521	955,417	739,994	663,188	483,007	168,142	346,795	421,068	701,480	164,040
Marten skins	....	....	49,956	155,519	50,206	29,281	20,927	132,537	168,971	230,639
Meerschaum, crude	....	51,473	....	3,239	724	155	....	5,136	12,191	14,431
Mohair	....	....	486,556	436,736	....	208,259	....	354	25,715	....
Opium	1,500,355	1,191,129	410,628	244,617	231,161	137,660	63,292	163,421	289,059	386,670
Pistachios	....	....	14,809	....	73	12,907	6,022	6,727	19,405	57,370
Poppy seeds	....	....	2,875	32,025	18,643	13,380	2,226	....	12,896	244,283
Raisins	119,156	1,215,686	71,079	43,427	37,875	19,808	16,337	26,491	16,916	2,282
Rugs, handmade	1,404,987	2,055,327	2,788,400	1,908,000	327,000	137,000	38,000	44,000	16,620	....
Sheep, lamb, and goat casings	....	....	419,000	553,000	397,000	616,000	160,000	560,000	265,211	....
Valonia, crude	....	....	174,694[b]	267,089	251,855	236,276	313,512	364,941	236,494	....
Valonia, extract	....	....	....	47,830	107,768	125,868	69,400	25,908	18,477	....

SOURCE: U.S. Tariff Commission, *Trade Agreement Digest*, pp. 23–109; United States Department of Commerce, Bureau of Foreign and Domestic Commerce, *Foreign Commerce and Navigation*, 1915, 1920, 1927, 1939, 1942.

[a] Omissions indicate either no data available or no imports. Statistics for 1914 are for the fiscal year ending June 30, 1914; all other statistics are for the calendar year.

[b] Figures for crude and extract valonia are combined.

United States Exports to Turkey, by Commodity Groups, 1923–1941 (in Dollars)

Commodity Group	1923	1925	1927	1929	1931	1933	1935	1937	1939	1941
Animals and animal products, edible...	...	...	31,978	9,498	2,180	...	378	5,463	45,380	...
Animals and animal products, inedible..	...	...	601,925	269,017	211,966	2,703	227,613	1,025,410	451,448	20,850
Vegetable food products and beverages..	1,106,325	507,956	518,580	552,769	81,847	9,931	20,885	50,708	26,301	28,504
Vegetable food products, inedible, except fiber and wood	75,010	70,210	226,549	259,298	90,890	101,105	344,985	549,381	350,872	360,702
Textiles	647,448	395,117	164,524	139,698	39,501	54,038	117,151	1,361,603	263,487	169,214
Wood and paper	26,838	19,920	27,360	29,682	11,096	11,611	36,081	83,456	65,965	5,834
Nonmetallic minerals	514,570	366,393	99,927	207,341	84,887	204,123	713,945	1,416,520	1,710,268	250,958
Metals and manufactures, except machinery and vehicles	138,786	284,662	529,405	621,683	45,653	237,240	422,864	3,758,973	852,306	1,241,876
Machinery and vehicles	252,682	653,281	1,209,450	2,900,286	956,072	584,180	1,830,945	5,999,552	3,979,865	2,716,880
Chemicals and related products	33,612	21,504	45,794	109,524	84,045	39,563	126,198	393,236	236,038	267,459
Miscellaneous	135,529	465,115	485,592	642,861	76,321	53,252	505,878	211,289	270,285	1,673,147

SOURCE: United States Department of Commerce, Bureau of Foreign and Domestic Commerce, *Foreign Commerce and Navigation*, 1923, 1925, 1927, 1929, 1931, 1933, 1935, 1937, 1939, 1941.

The table on page 107 indicates the volume of American exports to Turkey by the commodity groups established by the United States Department of Commerce. The large expansion in exports to Turkey after 1935 is explained by several factors: (1) increased Turkish demand for automotive products, sewing machines, and electric refrigerators; (2) diversion to the United States of orders usually given to European countries, in some cases because of the unsatisfactory operation of Turkey's bilateral clearing agreements; and (3) the shift in production in European countries to armaments, a development which increased Turkish dependence on American cotton yarns, other textiles, iron and steel goods, and petroleum products.[36] The table shows that exports of animal and vegetable products to Turkey remained relatively stable in value, whereas minerals, metals, machinery, vehicles, and chemicals products increased significantly. This accounts for the doubling in value of exports in 1939 as compared with 1927.

Turkish-American trade was more important to Turkey than it was to the United States. In 1927, for example, 3.9 per cent of Turkey's imports came from the United States; in 1938, 10.5 per cent. Exports, on the other hand, showed a percentage decrease. In 1927 Turkey sent 15.5 per cent of her exports to the United States; in 1938 the figure had fallen to 12.3 per cent. United States trade with Turkey, however, was a small part of the nation's total foreign trade. Trade with Turkey required substantial attention from the Department of State, but its monetary value never reached large figures and was relatively small in comparison with trade with many other nations.[37]

The Diplomacy of Commerce: The Treaty of 1929

A major concern of the Department of State in the interwar period was the negotiation of formal agreements to regulate Turkish-American commercial relations. Pending action on the Lausanne Treaty, a modus vivendi first arranged in February, 1926, governed Turkish-American trade relations. After Senate rejection of the Lausanne Treaty, Admiral Bristol on February 17, 1927, secured the renewal of the 1926 modus vivendi.

Washington, 1955–1958), III, 944–957, for documents on Turco-American negotiations for chrome ore purchases after the start of World War II. Later volumes in the *Foreign Relations* series contain additional documents.

[36] Department of State, *Press Releases*, XX (April 8, 1939), 269.

[37] U.S. Tariff Commission, *Trade Agreement Digest*, pp. 14–15; Kazdal, "Trade Relations Between the United States and Turkey," p. 110.

Ambassador Grew arranged for another extension of this measure on May 19, 1928.[38]

The State Department considered the feasibility of negotiating a formal trade treaty with Turkey in 1928. Secretary Kellogg felt, however, that such a treaty should be postponed to avoid "any action that might encourage further anti-Turkish agitation in the United States and . . . compromise the growing sentiments of friendliness toward Turkey." Kellogg recommended instead an exchange of notes "according mutual unconditional most-favored-nation treatment in customs matters without a definite time limit as to its duration," an arrangement which would give Turkey and the United States ample time for the negotiation of a treaty.[39] Grew, who emphatically opposed this procedure, felt that the United States should not "risk jeopardizing the whole structure of friendly relations and confidence" that it was cultivating in Turkey. "If I have to tell the Ruschdi [the Turkish Foreign Minister]," Grew wrote to a State Department friend, "that we are frankly unwilling to negotiate a treaty with Turkey for fear of stirring up further anti-Turkish agitation among the public and the Senate, are they going to bear with us sympathetically or are they going to climb up on their high horse? You can guess as well as I can." [40] Fortunately Kellogg's proposal never reached the Turkish government. Early in 1929 Foreign Minister Aras committed himself to the most-favored-nation formula in any future commercial treaty with the United States.[41]

The decision to delay negotiation of a commercial treaty necessitated another extension of the modus vivendi. Although a 1927 Turkish law specified that such arrangements would not be legal after April 10, 1929, Aras secured permission from the Grand National Assembly to extend the arrangement with the United States until April 10, 1930.[42] The modus vivendi subsequently adopted on April 8, 1929, was substantially the same as the previous arrangements. The original modus vivendi, according to its terms, applied pending the conclusion of a "Commercial Convention." In

[38] Grew to Kellogg, May 22, 1928, *Papers Relating to the Foreign Relations of the United States, 1928* (3 vols., Washington, 1942–1943), III, 953 (hereafter cited as *FR 1928*).

[39] Kellogg to Grew, December 26, 1928, *ibid.*, 962–963.

[40] To G. Howland Shaw, February 27, 1929, Grew MSS, 1929, vol. 2.

[41] Conversation, Grew and Aras, February 17, 1929, in Joseph C. Grew, *Turbulent Era: A Diplomatic Record of Forty Years, 1904–1945*, ed. Walter Johnson (2 vols., Boston, 1952), II, 801.

[42] *Ibid.*, 800–802; Grew to Kellogg, March 24, 1929, *Papers Relating to the Foreign Relations of the United States, 1929* (3 vols., Washington, 1943–1944), III, 810 (hereafter cited as *FR 1929*).

the new instrument the Turks insisted upon altering this phrase to read "Convention of Commerce and Navigation." Grew thought at first that this was an attempt to "kill the Treaty of 1830 for good and all. . . . A new treaty of commerce and navigation would undoubtedly cancel certain old capitulatory rights, the fiction of which the Senate seems desirous of preserving (in alcohol)." Later Aras assured Grew that the change was made to conform with similar notes exchanged by Turkey with other powers. The State Department lodged no objection, although it retained the idea that a simple commercial treaty would eventually be negotiated.[43]

Soon after he arrived in Turkey in 1927, Grew expressed his opinion that the Turks should not be approached on treaty matters with a "hat-in-hand" attitude and that the United States "should keep free from any 'knocking at the door' tendency. Let Turkey do the knocking for a change." Grew felt there would be profit for the United States in giving Turkey time to familiarize itself with standard treaty forms through negotiations with other countries.[44] When the Turkish Foreign Minister suggested talks for a commercial treaty less than a year later, Grew welcomed the suggestion, not only because it would formalize Turkish-American commercial relations but also because Senate approval of the treaty "would . . . pave the way for the eventual submission to that body of other instruments effectually regularizing the general relations between the United States and the Turkish Republic." [45]

In March, 1929, the State Department, after assurances that the Senate would accept a simple commercial treaty, authorized Grew to continue his talks with the Turks, but cautioned him to avoid "premature publicity." [46] During these preliminary sessions the Turks suggested the application of most-favored-nation treatment not only to customs matters but also to navigation. Henry L. Stimson, Kellogg's successor as Secretary of State in 1929, had reservations about the profitability of extending most-favored-nation treatment to Turkey in spite of the fact that Grew had already so committed the United States. Grew believed that withdrawal of

[43] Grew to Stimson, April 9, 1929, *FR 1929*, III, 814–818; diary, April 2, 1929, Grew, *Turbulent Era*, II, 805–807; Grew to Stimson, April 4, 1929, *FR 1929*, III, 813–814; Stimson to Grew, April 3, 1929, *ibid.*, 813.

[44] Grew to Shaw, November 21, 1927, Grew MSS, 1927, vol. 4.

[45] Grew to Kellogg, October 2, 1928, *FR 1928*, III, 961; Grew to Kellogg, February 25, 1929, *FR 1929*, III, 807–808.

[46] Memo of conversation, Shaw with Senators William E. Borah and Hiram Johnson, March 16, 1929, DS 611.6731/123; Kellogg to Grew, March 18, 1929, *FR 1929*, III, 809.

his offer would be "an open breach of faith," leaving him no choice "but to resign definitely and get out. This would not be in the nature of an heroic gesture but simply because my position vis-à-vis the Turkish Government might be so weakened as to make it undesirable for me to remain." Stimson finally approved negotiations on the basis of the most-favored-nation formula after G. Howland Shaw, Chief of the Near Eastern Division, assured him that no disadvantage would result from according Turkish products such treatment. Stimson later agreed that navigation matters could be covered in the treaty.[47]

Formal talks took place between September 8 and October 1, 1929, on the basis of a draft treaty submitted by the Department of State. Although the Turkish delegation requested many minor changes and clarifications, the treaty was negotiated with comparative ease.[48] Grew described the sessions with the Turks as follows:

Practically all of our conferences were informal and there was no initialing of paragraphs or anything of that kind, and no stenographers were present except at the opening plenary session. Once a point had been orally accepted, no matter how informally, we simply put it aside and it appeared in the final text. In fact, after the first plenary session the negotiations developed into a series of informal conversations which made them much simpler and more agreeable and both sides were able to talk much more openly and freely than if the discussions had been formal.[49]

Grew believed that Turkey was willing to accept the treaty for several reasons: its balance of trade with the United States was favorable; it wanted to interest sound American companies and capital in its public works program; it realized the "moral prestige" which would accompany the pact; and it "understands the danger of another rebuff in the United States Senate and does not want to jeopardize the treaty's ratification by insisting upon unreasonable provisions with us."[50]

[47] Grew to Stimson, June 6, 1929, *FR 1929*, III, 820; Grew to Shaw, June 19, 1929, Grew MSS, 1929, vol. 2 (source of the quotation); Shaw to Stimson, July 8, 1929, DS 711.672 (1929)/3 ½ (Stimson's approval is handwritten on this document); Stimson to Grew, August 6, 1929, *FR 1929*, III, 821.

[48] Grew to Stimson, September 8, 1929, *FR 1929*, III, 825; Grew to Stimson, September 11, 1929, *ibid.*, 825–829; Grew to Stimson, September 24, 1929, *ibid.*, 832–833; Grew to Stimson, September 25, 1929, *ibid.*, 833–835. See also diary, September 8, September 10, and September 14–October 1, 1929, Grew, *Turbulent Era*, II, 832–837, for a summary of the treaty negotiations.

[49] Diary, September 14–October 1, 1929, Grew, *Turbulent Era*, II, 836–837.

[50] *Ibid.*, 835. Grew expressed the same sentiments in a letter to Shaw, October 12, 1929, Grew MSS, 1929, vol. 2.

Article I of the short treaty pledged both countries to accord most-favored-nation treatment in regard to import duties, export duties, and "other duties and charges affecting commerce." Excluded were advantages the United States might extend to its territories and possessions and the Panama Canal Zone and Cuba, or which Turkey might accord to countries detached in 1923 from the former Ottoman Empire. In Article II the United States and Turkey guaranteed each other treatment equal with other countries in matters of prohibitions or restrictions on imports and exports. Article III guaranteed United States vessels in Turkish waters and Turkish vessels in American waters the same treatment as national vessels. Coastwise traffic, bounties to national merchant marines, and fishing in territorial waters were excluded from national treatment. Article IV confirmed each country's right "to impose prohibitions or restrictions of a sanitary character designed to protect human, animal or plant life, or regulations for the enforcement of police or revenue laws." The final article established procedures for ratification, and set the duration of the treaty at three years and then indefinitely until one year after either country signified its intention to terminate it.[51]

The formal minutes of the October 1, 1929, meeting when the treaty was signed clarified certain articles particularly disputed during the negotiations. The Turkish delegation interpreted the phrase "other duties and charges affecting commerce" in Article I to mean duties pertaining to import, export, and consumption taxes, but not to internal taxes levied on incomes and profits. The Turks also agreed to omit from Article II the sentence, "It is understood that the High Contracting Parties shall have the right to apply these prohibitions or restrictions to products favored by premiums or subsidies, either openly or secretly." Grew insisted on this omission because the United States never granted premiums or subsidies of this sort. The minutes also explained that ships of either country could pass from port to port in the other's territory for the loading or unloading of passengers and cargoes.[52]

The signing of this new commercial treaty elated Secretary Stimson and other State Department officials.[53] In view of the fate of the Lausanne

[51] Text of the treaty, *FR 1929*, III, 838–840. The original English and Turkish texts are enclosed in Grew to Stimson, October 2, 1929, DS 711.672 (1929)/27. Note the relevance of Article IV to the United States practice of inspecting Turkish fig packing *hans*.

[52] Text of the minutes, *FR 1929*, III, 841–842.

[53] See Stimson to Grew, October 2, 1929, DS 711.672 (1929)/26 ½; Shaw to Grew, October 2, 1929, DS 711.672 (1929)/26.

Treaty, there was some apprehension about securing Senate approval. Grew, worried about his own position in Turkey, wrote to Shaw: "Let us pray. If the Senate refuses this treaty, I don't see how I can continue to face the Turkish Government — and I don't believe I could or would." [54] The Department of State enlisted support for the treaty from the Department of Commerce. Julius Klein, Assistant Secretary of Commerce, pledged his aid if necessary, but agreed that "it would be unwise . . . to evince any unusual interest in the treaty until . . . opposition shall have arisen." Julian E. Gillespie, the commercial attaché in Turkey who helped negotiate the treaty, returned to the United States on leave in December, 1929. Grew informed Wallace Murray of the Near East Division that Gillespie could be "of material assistance" if a fight developed over the treaty. [55]

The State Department made extensive efforts to explain the treaty to Senate leaders. Wallace Murray and Joseph P. Cotton, Undersecretary of State, discussed the proposed pact with Chairman William E. Borah of the Senate Foreign Relations Committee on December 23, 1929. Borah expected no resistance except possibly from Senator Claude A. Swanson of Virginia. [56] As Borah predicted, Swanson and his Armenian friend, Vahan Cardashian, provided the only serious opposition to the treaty. Swanson sent Cotton a long memorandum, prepared by Cardashian, reiterating the old arguments about the sacrifice of Armenia after World War I. Cardashian suggested a reservation to the treaty as follows: "The Senate advises and consents to the ratification of the Treaty with the understanding that nothing therein is to be construed as a recognition or acceptance of the territorial status of Turkey, or of any matter which is not expressly embodied in the Treaty." Cardashian still maintained the fiction of an independent Armenia. Cotton wrote Swanson that Cardashian was "trying to becloud the issue by leading off into a theoretical discussion of matters which have nothing to do with the present treaty and rehashing old stuff which has all been gone over. If we begin discussing it he will never get through." In a letter to Borah, Cardashian claimed that the 1830 treaty had to be terminated by Senate action or a special proclamation of the

[54] October 12, 1929, Grew MSS, 1929, vol. 2.
[55] Memo of conversation, Murray and Julius Klein, November 13, 1929, DS 711.672 (1929)/31; Grew to Stimson (for Murray), December 6, 1929, DS 711.672 (1929)/41.
[56] DS 711.672 (1929)/42. See also memo, Murray, "The American-Turkish Treaty of Commerce and Navigation of October 1, 1929," January 7, 1930, William E. Borah MSS (Manuscript Division, Library of Congress, Washington), Box 546.

President before the new treaty could become effective. The treaty, he maintained, "will invade upon lands, now under Turkish control, which belong to Armenia." [57]

Although the opposition was limited, the Senate did not act on the treaty for more than two months after President Hoover submitted it for advice and consent. On February 17, 1930, Cotton reminded Borah that since the modus vivendi with Turkey would expire on April 10, 1930, approval of the treaty was of immediate importance. The same day the Senate, without debate, consented to ratification of the treaty.[58] Speaking many years later, Grew described his feelings: "By that time the Armenians . . . had shot their bolt, and, while this second treaty was not one-half as favorable to American interests as the first one [1923], it passed the Senate *viva voce* without even a tallied vote. Such are politics! But I was satisfied." [59] The Turkish Minister for Foreign Affairs was delighted with Senate approval of the treaty. The Turkish press recorded its satisfaction and suggested that passage of the treaty implied endorsement of the rejected Lausanne Treaty and the subsequent executive action renewing diplomatic relations.[60]

The 1929 treaty of commerce and navigation was a significant milestone in the program of regularizing Turkish-American relations. It also was a major diplomatic accomplishment for Ambassador Joseph Grew. For the first time since 1917, a formal treaty governed commercial relations with Turkey. Although the modus vivendi beginning in 1926 had served its purpose well, commercial interests could now feel more secure when backed by formal treaty guarantees. The new commercial treaty was the first in a series of settlements designed to accomplish piecemeal what the Lausanne Treaty would have done at one stroke.

[57] Swanson to Cotton, February 3, 1930, DS 711.672 (1929)/48; Cotton to Swanson, February 6, 1930, *ibid.*; Cardashian to Borah, February 5, 1930, Borah MSS, Box 547.

[58] Cotton to Borah, February 17, 1930, *ibid.*; *Congressional Record*, 71 Cong., 2 Sess., LXXII, pt. 4, 3779–3780. The Grand National Assembly ratified the treaty on April 12, 1930, and ratifications were exchanged on April 22. The modus vivendi, due to expire on April 10, was renewed on April 8 to cover the period before the exchange of ratifications. See Grew to Stimson, April 12, 1930, DS 711.672 (1929)/61, and *FR 1929*, III, 842n.

[59] "The Peace Conference of Lausanne, 1922–1923," *Proceedings of the American Philosophical Society*, XCVIII (February, 1954), 2.

[60] Grew to Stimson, February 20, 1930, DS 711.672 (1929)/52; Charles E. Allen (Consul, Istanbul), Review of the Turkish Press, February 20–March 19, 1930, DS 867.9111/270.

The Diplomacy of Commerce: The Reciprocal
Trade Agreement of 1939

The treaty of October 1, 1929, served as the basis of Turkish-American commercial relations until 1939, when it was replaced by a new pact based on the Reciprocal Trade Agreements Act of June 12, 1934. The possibility of supplanting the 1929 treaty was first suggested by a Turkish official in November, 1936. The State Department at that time was studying the status of Turkish-American trade and Turkish commercial policy, but was not yet ready for a new agreement, "particularly as there do not appear to be any vital problems pressing for settlement at this time in our commercial relations with Turkey." [61] In May, 1937, the Department informed Ambassador John V. A. MacMurray that a "country committee," including representatives from various government departments and agencies, had been established to examine the feasibility of a trade agreement with Turkey. About the same time the Turkish Minister for Foreign Affairs proposed negotiation of reciprocal tariff reductions.[62] MacMurray reported that the Turks were anxious to open negotiations: "I learn that this desire for haste has even raised the question of denouncing our existing commercial treaty in order to expedite new negotiations." The Turks, MacMurray said, would be willing to grant concessions on certain imports in order to increase exports to the United States of such products as carpets, wool, mohair, filbert nuts, figs, and raisins.[63] The Turkish government obviously wanted to increase exports immediately as a means of supplementing the dollar exchange at its disposal.

Furthermore, the Turkish government was sympathetic with the purposes of the reciprocal trade program. The United States commercial attaché in Turkey reported that Turkey admired the program and was "anxious and willing to turn toward that group of countries headed by the United States who favor a more progressive trade policy." Expressing similar views in the Istanbul *Tan* on November 22, 1937, the Turkish journalist Ahmed Emin Yalman noted that the United States and Turkey were "faithful and earnest companions on the road to peace. . . . Our Gov-

---

[61] MacMurray to Hull, November 6, 1936, *Foreign Relations of the United States: Diplomatic Papers, 1937* (5 vols., Washington, 1954), II, 941 (hereafter cited as *FR 1937*); R. Walton Moore (Acting Secretary of State) to MacMurray, November 19, 1936, *ibid.*, 941–942.

[62] Francis B. Sayre (for Hull) to MacMurray, May 3, 1937, *ibid.*, 942–943; MacMurray to Hull, May 4, 1937, *ibid.*, 943.

[63] MacMurray to Hull, May 8, 1937, *ibid.*, 944.

ernment has considered Mr. Roosevelt's endeavors regarding the new commercial treaties as . . . an invitation for collaboration in the cause of peace." [64]

By August, 1937, the State Department decided that a basis existed for trade negotiations with Turkey.[65] A major factor delaying this decision was Turkey's extensive use of bilateral clearing and compensation agreements. Herbert Feis, the State Department economic adviser, believed that the United States should protect itself against these agreements which were "of a characer that could be indefinitely extended so as to curtail substantially the possible market for American goods in Turkey even though we had most-favored-nation promise in its ordinary form." Feis was especially concerned about the steady increase in Germany's trade with Turkey. The State Department decided, however, not to raise questions about Turkey's trade systems until negotiations for a trade agreement actually started.[66]

Another important prerequisite was Turkish acceptance of the most-favored-nation principle as a basis for the agreement. On October 23, 1937, the Turks agreed to the principle in regard to customs duties on United States goods, and three days later, after a request from the embassy, accepted an expanded formula reading "most favored nation treatment extending not only to customs duties but to all forms of commercial restriction and control." [67]

After disposition of these questions, the State Department followed its standard procedure in initiating trade agreement talks. The Department issued a preliminary announcement of the contemplated accord on November 3, 1937, inviting interested parties to submit suggestions on products to be considered in the deliberations. A formal announcement on January 12, 1938, set deadlines for the presentation of these views and scheduled a public hearing by the Committee on Reciprocity Information.[68] The

[64] Gillespie to Shaw, May 12, 1937, FDC Records, file 449.0; Kelley to Hull, November 27, 1937, DS 611.6731/238 (contains a translation of Yalman's article).
[65] Hull to S. Walter Washington (Chargé d'Affaires), August 13, 1937, *FR 1937*, II, 947; memo, Harry C. Hawkins (Chief, State Department Division of Trade Agreements) to Herbert Feis, August 3, 1937, DS 611.6731/211.
[66] Memo, Feis to Hawkins, August 4, 1937, DS 611.6731/210; memo, Feis to Hawkins, June 1, 1937, *FR 1937*, II, 944–945; memo, Hawkins, August 6, 1937, DS 611.6731/209. See also Feis to MacMurray, May 3, 1937, in the John Van Antwerp MacMurray MSS (Princeton University Library, Princeton, N.J.), Box 159.
[67] Hull to Washington, August 13, 1937, *FR 1937*, II, 947; Kelley to Hull, October 26, 1937, *ibid.*, 950–951.
[68] *Commerce Reports*, XL (November 6, 1937), 887, and XLI (January 22,

announcements brought little reaction from American interests. One exception was California fig and raisin growers, who flooded the State Department and the President with protests against a decrease in duty on Turkish figs and raisins. A. P. Giannini, Chairman of the Board of the Bank of America, San Francisco, explained to Hull the difficulties which would confront California raisin growers. He also sent him the text of an editorial of January 24, 1938, in the San Francisco *Chronicle* calling on California raisin and fig interests "to leap to the defense" of their industry. "It would be asking a good deal of California fig growers," the paper said, "to expect them to compete on equal terms with the Turkish peasant, even for the high-minded purpose of enabling him to buy an American brass bed." [69]

The Armenian-American League of California protested to President Roosevelt that the trade agreement would "bankrupt" the California raisin industry, an opinion which Senators Hiram W. Johnson and William G. McAdoo of California reiterated in letters to Hull. On the other hand, some United States importers of Turkish goods asked for reductions in tariff duties. The National Confectioners Association, noting its members' large use of shelled filberts, suggested a decrease in the duty on them. [70]

Although the original intention was to conduct the bargaining for the trade agreement in Washington, the State Department acquiesced in a Turkish request that the negotiations take place in Ankara. Henry J. Wadleigh of the State Department Division of Trade Agreements and Norman R. Burns of the United States Tariff Commission joined Julian E. Gillespie and Robert F. Kelley on the United States delegation. [71] The meetings of the delegations began on March 29, 1938, and continued intermittently until April 1, 1939, when the trade agreement was signed. [72] Several im-

1938), 88; Department of State, *Press Releases*, XVII (November 6, 1937), 356–361, and XVIII (January 15, 1938), 108–112.

[69] A. P. Giannini to Hull, January 24, 1938, DS 611.6731/270.

[70] James B. Boone (Armenian-American League) to F. D. Roosevelt, January 31, 1938, DS 611.6731/278; Hiram W. Johnson to Hull, February 3, 1938, DS 611.6731/286; William G. McAdoo to Hull, February 4, 1938, DS 611.6731/293. Practically all California congressmen registered similar protests. See also W. Parker Jones (General Counsel, National Confectioners Association) to Hull, November 12, 1937, DS 611.6731/229.

[71] Kelley to Hull, January 17, 1938, *Foreign Relations of the United States: Diplomatic Papers, 1938* (5 vols., Washington, 1954–1956), II, 1052–1053 (hereafter cited as *FR 1938*); Hull to Kelley, January 28, 1938, *ibid.*, 1054; Hull to Kelley, March 7, 1938, *ibid.*, 1055.

[72] Kelley to Hull, May 3, 1938, DS 611. 6731/379; MacMurray to Hull, April 1, 1939, *FR 1939*, IV, 865.

portant issues delayed conclusion of the talks and on occasion even threatened to cause their failure.[73] The question of the specific products to be dealt with in the agreement was decided with comparative ease. Of the products considered, tobacco and rugs provoked the most discussion. The Turks at first asked for a reduction in the tobacco duty and then withdrew the request. The State Department had unsubstantiated information that American tobacco companies in Turkey opposed a reduction in duty in order to prevent smaller companies from competing in the trade, and that these firms influenced the Turkish delegation. The United States delegation informed the State Department that it had no indication that this was true but that the Turks opposed any reduction which would be generalized to other countries. The existing rate had been in effect for sixty years, the Turks pointed out, and a reduction would be of no value to Turkey if it were extended, for instance, to Greece, Russia, and Bulgaria, countries which would then probably compete successfully with Turkey in the tobacco trade. Later the Turks for unexplained reasons reversed themselves again and accepted a 5 per cent reduction in the tobacco duty.[74] Perhaps the Turkish government realized that a reduction would not affect its relative position among tobacco-producing countries in its area.

The Turks wanted a more substantial reduction on rugs than the United States originally offered. Ambassador MacMurray reported that both Prime Minister Celal Bayar and Numan Menemencioglu, Secretary General of the Turkish Foreign Office, considered further cuts on rugs essential to the successful conclusion of the agreement. The State Department, after studying the frequent Turkish requests, agreed on December 13, 1938, to reduce the rug duty. The United States based its reluctance to grant this concession on the fact that Turkey was not its principal sup-

[73] In June, 1938, the Turks suggested that the negotiations be suspended since Turkey would receive "neither material nor moral advantages" from the agreement as proposed by the United States. Hull instructed the American delegation to continue talks with the Turks. Later he considered making a personal appeal to high Turkish officials to expedite success of the negotiations, but this action was not actually taken. See MacMurray to Hull, June 8, 1938, *FR 1938*, II, 1057–1061; Hull to MacMurray, June 15, 1938, *ibid.*, 1061–1063; MacMurray to Hull, June 17, 1938, *ibid.*, 1063–1064; Hull to MacMurray, September 23, 1938, *ibid.*, 1083; MacMurray to Hull, October 12, 1938, *ibid.*, 1087–1089.

[74] MacMurray to Hull, September 16, 1938, DS 611.6731/433 (enclosure no. 1, conversation among Kelley, Gillespie, and Turkish delegation members, August 16, 1938); Hull to Embassy, September 8, 1938, DS 611.6731/422; MacMurray to Hull, September 14, 1938, DS 611.6731/426; MacMurray to Hull, December 21, 1938, DS 611.6731/492 (enclosure no. 2, conversation between Turkish and American delegations, December 12–17, 1938).

plier of oriental rugs. A reduction would necessitate the generalization of the concession and a subsequent loss in revenue for the United States.[75]

The most important disputes during the negotiations related to conflicting Turkish and American commercial procedures. The Turks, though sympathetic with the purposes of the reciprocal trade program, were reluctant to bind themselves to procedures restricting their freedom of action in commercial matters. Contrary to American practice, the Turkish government wanted the right to place quota restrictions, impose higher duties at will, and levy internal taxes on products imported into Turkey. The final arrangement, however, contained assurances against import restrictions on schedule items, except under limited conditions. Turkey promised to apply equally to all countries any restrictions against nonscheduled items. National treatment was guaranteed with regard to internal taxes.[76] The negotiators also had to decide whether the concessions made by both countries would be percentage reductions, as Turkish law required, or specified monetary rates. The United States conceded on this point.[77] Turkey also wanted to insert in the trade agreement a so-called "Balkan Clause" to exclude certain trade concessions made to Balkan countries from generalization to the United States. After the United States refused to accept such a provision, the Turks consented to its omission.[78]

The most complicated problem facing the negotiators was the exchange provision, which was especially important because of the exchange arrears situation of 1937 and 1938. In an effort to acquire foreign ex-

[75] MacMurray to Hull, December 3, 1938, DS 611.6731/464; Kelley to Hull, December 11, 1938, DS 611.6731/467; Sumner Welles (Acting Secretary of State) to Embassy, December 12, 1938, DS 611.6731/467; MacMurray to Hull, December 13, 1938, DS 611.6731/484 (enclosure no. 4, telephone conversation, Kelley and Numan Menemencioglu, December 5, 1938); Welles to Embassy, December 13, 1938, DS 611.6731/467.

[76] MacMurray to Hull, June 27, 1938, DS 611.6731/407; Hull to Embassy, April 6, 1938, DS 611.6731/356; MacMurray to Hull, June 10, 1938, DS 611.6731/401; MacMurray to Hull, March 11, 1939, *FR 1939*, IV, 862–863; Welles to MacMurray, March 18, 1939, *ibid.*, 863–864; Kelley to Hull, March 22, 1939, *ibid.*, 864; *Commerce Reports*, XLII (April 22, 1939), 383.

[77] Kelley to Hull, May 30, 1938, DS 611.6731/394; MacMurray to Hull, June 10, 1938, DS 611.6731/401; memo of conversation, Vernon L. Phelps, Charles F. Darlington (Division of Trade Agreements) and Münir Ertegün, June 1, 1938, DS 611.6731/388; Hull to MacMurray, June 25, 1938, *FR 1938*, II, 1064–1066; Department of State, *Press Releases*, XX (April 8, 1939), 270.

[78] Kelley to Hull, December 11, 1938, DS 611.6731/467; Welles to Embassy, December 13, 1938, DS 611.6731/467; MacMurray to Hull, December 21, 1938, DS 611.6731/492; Hull to MacMurray, January 19, 1939, *FR 1939*, IV, 861–862; MacMurray to Hull, March 28, 1939, *ibid.*, 865.

change, Turkey usually limited exchange for import payments to a coun-try to a maximum of 80 per cent of the value of Turkish exports to the same country. The United States indicated it would not accept such re-strictions which might prohibit or at least delay payments for American sales.[79] The Turkish Foreign Minister explained that his country's ex-change problem was complicated by the seasonal character of its exports to the United States, particularly in regard to tobacco. He suggested a clause whereby Turkey would promise to pay for American imports within a specific period after their purchase, for example two years.[80] Unwilling to accept this proposal, the United States advanced its own exchange for-mula on July 28, 1938:

Turkey would undertake to make available for payments for commercial imports of merchandise of American origin, as a minimum, an amount of exchange sufficient to pay for a proportion of Turkey's total imports from all countries equivalent to the proportion of the total imports supplied by the United States in the three-year period 1935–1937.

. . . .

The three-year period 1935–1937 has been selected as the base period since it is believed that this would result in approximately the same amount of exchange being made available for commercial imports of articles of American origin as would be made available under the 80 per cent clause which has been proposed by the Turkish Government.[81]

In other words, Turkey each year would make available exchange to pay for American imports in an amount equal to 10.91 per cent, the propor-tion of total Turkish imports from the United States in the proposed base years. Turkey ultimately accepted this formula, subject to the provision that the value of imports resulting from utilization of credits from Great Britain (May, 1938) and Germany (October, 1938) would be excluded from the figure representing total Turkish imports. Turkey insisted upon these exceptions since the credits would temporarily increase its imports, thus forcing it to make available a much larger amount of exchange for im-ports from the United States.[82] The United States believed that the new

[79] MacMurray to Hull, June 10, 1938, DS 611.6731/401; memo of conversa-tion, Phelps, Darlington, and Ertegün, June 1, 1938, DS 611.6731/388.

[80] MacMurray to Hull, August 1, 1938, DS 611.6731/419 (enclosure no. 1, con-versation among Kelley, Aras, and Nebil Bati [Acting Secretary General, Turkish Foreign Office], July 12, 1938).

[81] MacMurray to Hull, August 1, 1938, DS 611.6731/419 (enclosure no. 2, con-versation, Kelley and Nebil Bati, July 28, 1938).

[82] MacMurray to Hull, September 16, 1938, DS 611.6731/433 (enclosure no. 1,

arrangement, by providing for the granting of exchange permits in the chronological order of the applications, would alleviate the arrears situation. The Department of Commerce cautioned American exporters, however, "to follow as closely as possible the course of Turkey's total import trade and the proportion of such trade represented by American goods," since there was no guarantee that Turkey would provide exchange in excess of the amount specified in the agreement.[83]

Other than the provisions already outlined, an important aspect of the trade agreement was the tariff reductions granted on specified products.[84] The United States made concessions on a much larger volume of goods than Turkey, but the Turkish percentage reductions were greater than those granted by the United States. The American tariff concessions were on a total of twenty-one items, which represented 91.6 per cent of total imports from Turkey in 1938. Duty reductions were granted on cigarette leaf tobacco, seedless raisins, shelled filberts, handmade oriental rugs, shelled and unshelled pistachios, canary seed, valonia extract, licorice extract, cymbals, and crude meerschaum. The duty on poppy seed was frozen. Crude licorice root; valonia, sheep, lamb, and goat casings; hare and marten skins; chrome and emery ore; and crude borax were bound on the free list. The most important reduction, amounting to over 14 per cent, was on cigarette leaf tobacco.[85] The Turkish government granted reductions on forty-four items, twenty of them for more than 50 per cent. The goods involved represented 45 per cent of Turkey's total imports from the United States. The most significant reductions were on motor vehicles and parts, refrigerators, radios, typewriters and ribbons, calculating machines, sewing machines, cattle hides, goat and kid upper leather, iron and steel galvanized sheets, filing cabinets, asbestos brake

memo of conversation among Kelley, Gillespie, Menemencioglu, and Enver Yelkenci [American Section, Turkish trade office], August 16, 1938); MacMurray to Hull, October 24, 1938, DS 611. 6731/447 (enclosure no. 1, memo of conversation among Kelley, Gillespie, Henry J. Wadleigh, Norman R. Burns, Menemencioglu, and Birhan Zihni Sanur [Turkish delegation member], October 19, 1938); Sükrü Saracoglu to MacMurray, April 1, 1939, in U.S. Tariff Commission, *Trade Agreement Digest*, p. 124 (text of the note explaining the exchange provision).

[83] *Commerce Reports*, XLII (April 8, 1939), 321.

[84] See U.S. Tariff Commission, *Trade Agreement Digest*, pp. 113–123, for text of the trade agreement and accompanying schedules. See *Commerce Reports*, XLII (April 22, 1939), 383–384, and Department of State, *Press Releases*, XX (April 8, 1939), 266–287, for analyses of the agreement.

[85] U.S. Tariff Commission, *Trade Agreement Digest*, pp. 1, 8.

lining, rubber thread, plastic construction materials, liquid waterproofing preparations, insecticides, toothpaste, and lubricating oil.[86]

There was no apparent opposition in the United States to the signing of the trade agreement on April 1, 1939.[87] Since it was an executive agreement, it did not come before the Senate. But this fact alone does not explain the lack of opposition. By this time, Armenian elements in the United States had ceased to protest against American relations with Turkey. The State Department records and other sources yield no evidence of protests from nationality groups or commercial interests other than those which came from California raisin and fig growers when the agreement was first proposed. The real significance of the agreement, according to the press, was political rather than economic. The *Christian Science Monitor* observed that the pact "has thrown another link of the free economic system across the path of totalitarian economic expansion." The Hull idea of "free economy" and the German concept of "regulated economy" came into "direct conflict" in Turkey. The signature of the agreement meant that, although Germany had some influence in Turkey, "the Hull trade doctrines also have a position at the Dardanelles." [88] According to the *Washington Post*, the pact "is expected to put a dent in Nazi Germany's flourishing export business" with Turkey. By reducing tariffs and committing Turkey to unconditional most-favored-nation treatment, the trade agreement "places a barrier in the way of German efforts to monopolize the Turkish market." [89]

The Exchange Problem

The trade agreement did not operate so well as expected. The Turkish ambassador to the United States pointed out that after the pact became operative "Turkish exports to the United States had practically ceased." The ambassador suggested three reasons for this: (1) Germany, by offer-

---

[86] *Ibid.*, pp. 1, 3–4.

[87] On April 5, 1939, President Roosevelt proclaimed the agreement provisionally effective on May 5, 1939. The reductions were generalized to all countries having trade agreements with the United States based on most-favored-nation treatment except Germany, which discriminated against American commerce and thus disqualified itself. See MacMurray to Hull, April 1, 1939, *FR 1939*, IV, 865–866; U.S. Tariff Commission, *Trade Agreement Digest*, pp. 1, 125. The trade agreement was the first with a Middle Eastern nation and the twenty-first under the Trade Agreements Act of June 12, 1934.

[88] April 3, 1939.

[89] April 2 and 3, 1939.

ing higher prices for Turkish raw products, forced American buyers out of the market and cut down the amount of American exchange flowing to Turkey; (2) Turkey had generalized the reductions made in the trade agreement, enabling German exporters to sell more goods in Turkey; and (3) Turkish merchants, in order to buy American goods, had to offer a premium of up to 40 per cent above the official exchange rate on dollar exchange.[90] To alleviate this situation, the ambassador offered to allot for Turkish sales to American sources, exclusive of tobacco, an amount in Turkish currency higher than the official rate. This procedure would provide American purchasers with more Turkish exchange and enable them to buy more Turkish goods at lower prices.[91]

The complicated exchange problem contributed much to the slowness of Turkish-American trade. Not only did Turkish interests have to pay the premium, but the arrears situation, contrary to the result expected from the trade agreement, became worse. Ambassador MacMurray reported about a month after the agreement became effective that more than $350,-000 for 1938 imports from the United States was still in arrears and that the Turkish government was not making exchange available for current imports.[92] The United States rejected the Turkish offer of a more favorable exchange rate for dollars transferred to Turkey in payment for purchases other than tobacco. This, the Treasury Department advised, would be considered a bounty under Section 303 of the Tariff Act of 1930, and would require countervailing charges on dutiable imports from Turkey benefiting from such premiums. Only by applying the premium uniformly could the plan be made acceptable to the United States. This the Turks were not willing to do.[93]

The exchange problem continued unsolved during 1939. The Turkish government, as in 1938, granted daily exchange allotments to American oil companies but only periodically permitted others to buy dollar exchange. After receiving protests from American business interests, the State Department instructed embassy officials to discuss the situation with the Minister for Foreign Affairs. The Department was particularly disturbed because Turkey was not granting exchange, as the trade agreement

[90] Memo of conversation, Paul H. Alling (Near East Division) and Ertegün, July 29, 1939, *FR 1939*, IV, 872–873.
[91] *Ibid.*, 873.
[92] To Hull, June 12, 1939, *ibid.*, 868–869.
[93] Memo of conversation, George V. Allen, Murray, and Ertegün, August 9, 1939, *ibid.*, 873–874; Hull to MacMurray, August 26, 1939, *ibid.*, 879–880.

123

provided, in the chronological order of requests.[94] The exchange problem was further complicated by the outbreak of World War II in September, 1939, and the reluctance of American interests to deal with Turkey when they had no guarantee that dollar payment would be forthcoming.[95]

On December 2, 1939, Nazmi Topcioglu, the Turkish Minister of Commerce, delivered a radio address outlining plans to spur trade with the United States. The Turkish clearing and compensation systems with other countries, he explained, had increased Turkish domestic prices well above the world market price. To eliminate the difference between Turkish domestic prices and the world market price, and thus increase exports to the United States, the Minister proposed the application of a compensation premium to American trade. As he explained it, "The American compensation premium will be approximately 25 per cent, consequently every exported article will receive a premium in this proportion and every imported article will pay a premium in the same proportion. The application of this system will make possible the cash payment of the counter value of imported goods and thereby blocked funds will be avoided." [96] As outlined by the United States Department of Commerce, the new system increased the buying rate of the dollar by 25 per cent, the increase representing the premium paid on goods exported from Turkey to the United States. Similarly, the dollar would be worth 25 per cent less when used to pay for goods imported into Turkey from the United States. The idea was to increase the sale of Turkish goods in the United States and discourage the purchase of American goods in Turkey.[97]

When the Turks put the new system into effect on December 15, 1939, holders of exchange permits refused to pay the premium required in Turkey, which meant that all exchange payments stopped even though permits were issued. The Turks also proposed freeing exchange for all permits issued before December 15, 1939, at the new rate. They eventually agreed to grant exchange for prior applications at the old rate, but new imports in 1940 had to pay the premium in order to get dollar exchange.[98]

[94] W. H. Lukens (Export Manager, R. M. Hollingshead Corporation) to Murray, June 26, 1939, DS 611.6731/599; Hull to Embassy, July 10, 1939, DS 611. 6731/599.

[95] *Commerce Reports*, XLII (October 14, 1939), 920–922.

[96] Quoted in MacMurray to Hull, December 4, 1939, *FR 1939*, IV, 882–883.

[97] *Commerce Reports*, XIII (December 16, 1939), 1180. See Kazdal, "Trade Relations Between the United States and Turkey," pp. 179–180, for a discussion of this compensation system.

[98] MacMurray to Hull, December 19, 1939, *FR 1939*, IV, 890; MacMurray to

The arrears situation continued in 1940 when the Turkish government only periodically issued exchange permits. The Turks requested a loan of $6,500,000 from the Export-Import Bank in December, 1939, to provide money to pay the arrears and enable them to meet current demands through income from sales to the United States. Although Ambassador MacMurray recommended granting the loan, the Bank explained that no funds were available for such a purpose. Late in 1940 MacMurray reported that all exchange arrears for 1939 had been paid but that permits had been issued for only the first three months of 1940.[99] The arrears situation carried over and remained unsolved after United States entrance into World War II. Because the trade agreement failed to eliminate this serious problem, Turkish-American trade at the end of the period under consideration was in a very unstable state.

Conclusion

During the interwar period trade remained a significant area of Turkish-American relations. World War I, the Turkish nationalist revolution under Atatürk, the depression of the 1930s, and the international situation before United States involvement in World War II were notable conditioners of Turkish-American commercial relations. For Turkey, which relied on the United States for many commodities, trade was high on the list of diplomatic problems. For the United States, trade was probably no more important than several other aspects of its relations with Turkey.

The leaders of Republican Turkey were convinced that their nation had to have a favorable balance of trade to provide funds for programs of domestic development. This meant not only an overall favorable balance but favorable balances with each trade partner — thus the imposition of quotas, bilateral compensation treaties, clearing agreements, and rigid exchange controls. Because the balance in Turkish-American trade was usually in Turkey's favor, this nationalistic trade program created few serious problems between the two countries until the late 1930s, when the balance began to shift. The reaction of the United States to Turkey's economic nationalism as reflected in its trade policies was one of patience and under-

Hull, December 20, 1939, *ibid.*, 890–891; Hull to MacMurray, December 22, 1939, *ibid.*, 891; MacMurray to Hull, January 13, 1940, *FR 1940*, III, 964.

[99] MacMurray to Hull, December 12, 1939, *FR 1939*, IV, 886; memo of telephone conversation, George V. Allen and Warren L. Pierson (President, Export-Import Bank), December 19, 1939, DS 611.6731/659; MacMurray to Hull, December 10, 1940, *FR 1940*, III, 988–989.

standing, even when the complicated exchange arrears situation developed as World War II approached.

The successful negotiation of two major commercial agreements, in 1929 and 1939, illustrated mutual concern with trade and the hope that it would expand to the benefit of both nations. The 1929 treaty was significant not only because it regularized trade relations but also because it was the beginning of a series of agreements aimed at eliminating the various disarrangements resulting from World War I and the severing of diplomatic relations in 1917. The 1939 reciprocal trade pact was a significant part of Secretary of State Hull's program to reduce world tension and promote prosperity by the removal of economic barriers.

Reaction in the United States to the two trade arrangements illustrated the change in public attitudes toward Turkey. There was some dissent on the 1929 treaty, mainly from Armenian elements led by Vahan Cardashian, but the comparative ease in securing Senate approval indicated a more favorable response to the new Turkish Republic. The reciprocal trade agreement of 1939 aroused no significant controversy in the United States, and there were few traces of the old stereotyped responses to Turkish affairs prevailing in earlier decades.

Although some problems remained, one can conclude that the efforts of the two nations to improve relations in the area of commerce contributed to the restoration of friendly ties between Turkey and the United States. Another aspect of the economic dimension, United States technical aid and investment in Turkey, which also contributed significantly to Turkish-American rapprochement, is the subject of the next chapter. It must be considered along with trade in an analysis of Turkish-American economic relations between the two world wars.

❦ The Economic Dimension: Investments and Technical Aid

SINCE the end of World War II, the influence of the United States in determining the nature of economic development in the Republic of Turkey has been obvious.[1] The significant American economic impact in Turkey since 1945 has been partly the result of vastly expanded political influence there.[2] Although the demands of international politics after 1945 have been of prime significance to both the United States and Turkey, part of the historical basis for the American role in Turkish economic development in this period was established during the interwar era. Ironically, from the early 1920s to 1939, the political noninvolvement of the United States was a factor of great weight in determining the American role in Turkish economic development. The absence of political aspirations after World War I in the new Republic of Turkey made it possible for United States business and financial interests to operate there with some influence and success.

The Framework of Economic Relations

It was not until 1927 that these interests could be established on a sound basis. Although the resumption of formal diplomatic relations in that year facilitated the development of American business interests in Turkey, there was another prerequisite for this activity: the ability of the

[1] This chapter in slightly different form appeared as "The United States and Turkish Nationalism: Investments and Technical Aid During the Atatürk Era," in *Business History Review*, XXXVIII (Spring, 1964), 58–77.

[2] Kemal H. Karpat, *Turkey's Politics: The Transition to a Multi-Party System* (Princeton, 1959), p. 300.

United States and its citizens in Turkey to adapt to Turkish nationalism, perhaps summed up best by Kemal Atatürk's popular slogan, "Turkey for the Turks." Inspired by the ideas of Ziya Gökalp and other intellectuals and by historical events, nationalism became one of the basic guides for the Turkish Republic after World War I.[3]

The United States made cautious efforts not to interfere in the Turkish domestic and international situations. In its diplomatic dealings with Turkey the State Department insisted that its representatives do nothing to counteract the aims of Turkish nationalism. Official or private efforts to resist the strong nationalistic feelings and policies in Atatürk's country would have resulted in failure for American diplomatic and business efforts. The Turkish government was receptive to representatives from countries like the United States who made no attempt to resist developments influenced by Turkey's brand of nationalism.

Etatism, the ideology of Turkish economic policy, was closely associated with nationalism. Etatism in practice meant increased state control and ownership in the economic sphere without completely shutting the door to private enterprise. As Richard D. Robinson has observed, "étatism grew as a result of the compelling need for accelerated economic development, the failure of private enterprise to maintain the desired pace, the non-availability of foreign capital, and the ambition of empire-building bureaucrats."[4] In 1931, when the Republican People's Party explained its six basic principles, it justified étatism as follows: "Although considering private work and activity a basic idea, it is one of our main principles to interest the State actively in matters where the general and vital interests of the nation are in question, especially in the economic field, in order to lead the nation and the country to prosperity in as short a time as possible."[5] It was within the confines of étatism that United States economic interests had to operate, and they did so reasonably well.

[3] For information on Turkish nationalism, see *ibid.*, pp. 84–90, 251–254; Niyazi Berkes, ed., *Turkish Nationalism and Western Civilization: Selected Essays of Ziya Gökalp* (New York, 1959); Uriel Heyd, *Foundations of Turkish Nationalism: The Life and Teachings of Ziya Gökalp* (London, 1950); Richard D. Robinson, *The First Turkish Republic: A Case Study in National Development* (Cambridge, Mass., 1963), pp. 65–91; Bernard Lewis, *The Emergence of Modern Turkey* (London, 1961), pp. 234–287; Donald E. Webster, *The Turkey of Atatürk: Social Process in the Turkish Transformation* (Philadelphia, 1939), pp. 163–165; and Lord Kinross, *Atatürk: A Biography of Mustafa Kemal, Father of Modern Turkey* (New York, 1965).

[4] *The First Turkish Republic*, p. 111.

[5] Quoted in Lewis, *Emergence of Modern Turkey*, p. 280.

Similarly, the United States succeeded in its economic relations with Turkey because it was sympathetic with Turkey's westernization program. Turkey could logically turn to the politically disinterested United States for aid and advice in a program which placed priority on economic development. Turkey did not rely exclusively on the United States but accepted support from other countries, including England, France, Germany, and the Soviet Union. There were periods, however, when advice and aid were sought mainly from American sources, essentially because of the political detachment of the United States and its citizens.

American economic activity in Turkey during the interwar period was in three major areas: investment of capital in Turkish projects, operation of United States commercial and industrial firms in Turkey, and employment of technical experts and advisers. The resulting direct interaction of many Americans with the Turkish leaders and people contributed to Turkey's economic progress as well as to the strengthening of Turco-American friendship.

Not until the decade of the 1930s did American and other foreign investors become genuinely interested in Turkey. Various domestic and international obstacles stood in the way of any extensive economic penetration of the new republic in its early years. Extremely important was the Atatürk government's fear of external political domination, which delayed the direct operation of foreign enterprises in Turkey and the advancing of credit. Because of difficulties experienced by the Ottoman Empire, particularly the capitulations, the Turks tended to judge considerations of a national character from a political rather than from an economic standpoint. They were extremely cautious about permitting the entry of foreign capital under conditions which might prevent adequate Turkish control and supervision and bring about a recurrence of the chaotic situation before World War I.[6] After an unsuccessful venture at granting a foreign concession in 1923, the Turkish government resolved to develop its economy for the time being without resort to foreign capital. Not until late in the decade did Turkey seriously consider the possibility of foreign loans.[7]

[6] Samuel Goldberg, "General Developments in Turkey" (mimeographed letter, European section, Division of Regional Information, Bureau of Foreign and Domestic Commerce) to District Office Managers, December 28, 1927, FDC Records, file 449.0. See also D. C. Blaisdell, "American Investment in Turkey: A Forecast," *Levant Trade Review*, XV (December, 1927), 525.

[7] Hedley V. Cooke, *Challenge and Response in the Middle East: The Quest for Prosperity, 1919–1951* (New York, 1952), pp. 268–269.

The 1923 fiasco was the ill-fated "Chester concession" for the construction of an extensive railway network with mineral rights along the railroad's right-of-way. Rear Admiral Colby M. Chester, at the head of a group calling itself the Ottoman-American Development Company, opened negotiations with the Turkish government in 1908. The Turks finally granted the concession in April, 1923, but then canceled it seven months later when it became evident that the terms of the contract would not be met because of dissension among the officials of the Chester group and their inability to raise the capital needed for the project.[8] Although the Ottoman-American Development Company and its successors continued for years to insist on the legality of the concession, the Turks considered it completely invalidated in 1923.[9] According to Ambassador Grew, the Chester case "left a very unfortunate impression on the Turkish Government and materially injured Turkish faith in American business concerns." [10]

Memory of the poor credit rating of the old Ottoman government was another element slowing down American investment in Turkey. To improve its credit and facilitate payment of its extensive debts, the Ottoman government established the Council for Administration of the Ottoman Public Debt in December, 1881. This organization, including members from several European countries, helped to encourage the entrance of European capital into Turkey before World War I, but it was not able to liquidate the original debt.[11] In the Allied Lausanne Treaty, the Atatürk gov-

[8] K. E. Clayton-Kennedy (Ottoman-American Development Company) to Charles Evans Hughes, July 25, 1923, *Papers Relating to the Foreign Relations of the United States, 1923* (2 vols., Washington, 1938), II, 1215–1241 (includes documents on the concession); Bristol to Hughes, December 21, 1923, *ibid.*, 1251; John A. DeNovo, "A Railroad for Turkey: The Chester Project, 1908–1913," *Business History Review*, XXXIII (Autumn, 1959), 300–329; John A. DeNovo, *American Interests and Policies in the Middle East, 1900–1939* (Minneapolis, 1963), pp. 58–87, 210–228.

[9] During the 1930s, Henry Woodhouse, who took over the "rights" of the Ottoman-American Development Company, tried to sell his nonexistent concession to the Standard Oil Company of New Jersey and the Socony-Vacuum Oil Company. He claimed that lands in Iraq under the control of the Turkish Petroleum Company, in which the two American firms participated, really belonged to his company. See Woodhouse to Hull, September 21, 1935, DS 867.602 OT81/496.

[10] Diary, July 30, 1930, Joseph C. Grew MSS (Houghton Library, Harvard University, Cambridge, Mass.), 1930, vol. 3.

[11] Memo, K. Carlson (State Department), "The Ottoman Public Debt," June 28, 1929, DS 867.51/387 ½ (survey of the history of the Ottoman Public Debt); Sydney Nettleton Fisher, *The Middle East:A History* (New York, 1959), pp. 327–329; M. S. Anderson, *The Eastern Question 1774–1923: A Study in International Relations* (London, Melbourne, Toronto, & New York, 1966), p. 226.

ernment accepted responsibility for part of the Ottoman debt, estimated at about 40 per cent of the total, but Turkey's inability to meet interest and principal payments forced periodic revision of these obligations.[12] When President Hoover announced a moratorium on war debts in 1931, the Turkish government asked that the moratorium be applied to the Ottoman debt. As Ambassador Grew explained to the Turkish Minister for Foreign Affairs, this was not possible because the moratorium applied only to intergovernmental debts contracted during World War I.[13] The unsettled condition of the Ottoman debt undermined confidence in Turkey's ability to meet other financial obligations and discouraged potential American and European investors. In the mid-1930s, when Turkey embarked upon an extensive public works and armaments program, its financial resources and ability to meet new contracts were questioned. Ambassador Robert P. Skinner assured the State Department that Turkey's credit was good, but another State Department official thought "it might be well for American firms to think twice before undertaking extensive works in Turkey." [14]

Various banking and labor laws contributed their share to the difficulties of investment in Turkey. Numerous European banks existed in Turkey, but the American Express Company, which established a branch in Istanbul in 1921, was the only American banking institution. It experienced considerable difficulty in 1933, when a new banking law required a deposit of $500,000 with the government as a prerequisite for doing business in Turkey. The company complained that investment of this amount would be unprofitable overcapitalization.[15] This law and others help to ex-

[12] Arnold J. Toynbee and Kenneth P. Kirkwood, *Turkey* (London, 1926), p. 237; Grew to Henry L. Stimson, November 28, 1930, DS 867.51/433; G. Howland Shaw to Hull, May 29, 1933, DS 867.51/529. See also Mustafa Nebil Kazdal, "Trade Relations Between the United States and Turkey, 1919–1944" (Ph.D. thesis, Indiana University, 1946), pp. 42–44, for a discussion of the revisions of the Ottoman debt settlement.

[13] Grew to Stimson, July 15, 1931, DS 867.51/448; Daily Report, Wallace Murray (Chief, Near Eastern Division), July 24, 1934, DS 867.51/575.

[14] Robert P. Skinner to Hull, June 28, 1934, *Foreign Relations of the United States: Diplomatic Papers, 1934* (5 vols., Washington, 1950–1952), II, 950; memo, Henry S. Villard (Near East Division), July 11, 1934, DS 611.6731/164.

[15] Frederick P. Small (President, American Express Company) to Hull, May 9, 1933, DS 867.516/71; Shaw to Hull, July 17, 1933, DS 867.516/78; Shaw to Hull, August 4, 1933, DS 867.516/80; Kazdal, "Trade Relations Between the United States and Turkey," pp. 97–98. The State Department documents noted here imply that the Bank suspended operations, but there is no proof that it did so immediately. Kazdal says its operations continued. Professor Sydney Fisher (letter to Roger R. Trask, May 4, 1965) says the bank was not functioning by 1936.

plain the lack of adequate banking facilities in Turkey, a particular hardship for American business interests.

As far as was practical, Turkish labor policy restricted all jobs to Turkish workers. According to legislation passed in June, 1932, effective three years later, most occupations were not open to foreigners. Although the new law affected few Americans, thousands of non-Turkish workers, the majority of them Greek, were discharged from their jobs. American firms operating in Turkey also had to comply with a comprehensive labor law passed in June, 1936, regulating contracts, working conditions, and labor relations in all establishments employing ten or more persons.[16] American companies were not, therefore, entirely free to hire American or European personnel or to regulate labor conditions as they wished.

Turkish Interest in American Loans

Although the investment field was not attractive to American capital, the Turkish government, particularly after 1929, made attempts to lure private American capital to Turkey and considered the possibility of seeking loans from the United States government. Prime Minister Ismet Inönü and Foreign Minister Tevfik Rüsdü Aras expressed to Grew in April, 1930, their hopes of securing capital from American sources. Aras told Grew that "the United States was the only country to which Turkey could turn for financial help without some *arrière-pensée* and that the Turkish government would therefore welcome any cooperation that I [Grew] might be disposed to give." After Grew returned in July, 1930, from a trip to the United States, he advised the Foreign Minister that the Turks should take the initiative in efforts to attract American capital to Turkey. Grew suggested as a first step that a financial mission be sent to the United States to study the situation and make contacts.[17]

When Julius Klein, Assistant Secretary of Commerce, visited Turkey later in 1930, Turkish officials again indicated interest in a loan, and talked about sending such a financial mission. On October 7, 1931, a delegation headed by Sükrü Saracoglu, former Minister of Finance, left for the

[16] Charles H. Sherrill to Stimson, June 29, 1932, DS 867.504/4; Shaw to Hull, June 12, 1933, DS 867.504/9; Skinner to Hull, June 30, 1934, DS 867.504/11; John V. A. MacMurray to Hull, November 3, 1936, DS 867.504/24. See also Karpat, *Turkey's Politics*, pp. 74, 109.

[17] Conversation, Grew and Ismet Inönü, April 9, 1930, Grew MSS, 1930, vol. 3; conversation, Grew and Tevik Rüsdü Aras, April 22, 1930, *ibid.*; conversation, Grew and Aras, July 24, 1930, *ibid.*

United States, hoping to make contacts, obtain a private loan of from $50,000,000 to $100,000,000 for public works and bank credits, and interest Americans in the development of the cotton industry in Turkey.[18] Grew sent a letter to J. Pierpont Morgan introducing Sükrü Saracoglu, although he told Turkish officials before the mission left that it was unlikely that a loan could be obtained in the United States at the time. Grew observed that Saracoglu's trip "affords an excellent opportunity to develop favorably the relations of the two countries and that while he may return to Turkey a sadder and wiser man in so far as the American money market is concerned, his observations of American business conditions, systems and methods will prove useful to his own country." [19]

Sükrü Saracoglu's trip provoked protests from two sources. A representative of the Ottoman debt bondholders wrote Secretary of State Stimson that no consideration should be given to a loan to Turkey and suggested that the United States should "require Turkey to first bring order into her situation. It will justly consider that before fresh obligations are incurred it is morally necessary that the unfortunate and deceitful past be liquidated." The other outburst came from Vahan Cardashian. Believing that the mission intended to enlist American money and experts to develop railroads in Armenia, Cardashian wrote: "The American people, who have forgiven, and who may be called upon further to forgive, billions of dollars due them from the European nations, would be more than surprised to learn that a few of their fellow-citizens are disposed to rob the Poor-Box, — a few pennies from the Armenians, and, in the process, destroy the Armenians' last hope and supreme ideal." [20]

No loan from public or private sources resulted from Saracoglu's mission, although the Turkish government was pleased with his cordial reception and felt that a basis had been laid for future business.[21] The Turkish government made no direct requests for loans from the United States government until 1939. Because of a critical dollar exchange shortage in Turkey, the Turks admitted several times during reciprocal trade agreement

[18] Grew to Stimson, November 12, 1930, DS 867.51 Shukri Bey Mission/1; Grew to Stimson, September 23, 1931, DS 867.51 Shukri Bey Mission/3; editor's note in Grew, *Turbulent Era: A Diplomatic Record of Forty Years, 1904–1945*, ed. Walter Johnson (2 vols., Boston, 1952), II, 907n.
[19] Grew to J. Pierpont Morgan, October 5, 1931, Grew MSS, 1931, vol. 1; Grew to Stimson, October 5, 1931, DS 867.51 Shukri Bey Mission/23.
[20] A. Vignau-Lous to Stimson, October 11, 1931, DS 867.51/452; Vahan Cardashian to Stimson, November 10, 1931, DS 867.51 Shukri Bey Mission/43.
[21] Diary, January 5, 1932, Grew, *Turbulent Era*, II, 908.

negotiations in 1938 and 1939 that they would welcome a credit from the Export-Import Bank. Because the Bank had no funds available for the purpose, it turned down Turkey's formal request made in December, 1939.[22] European countries, because of their more extensive economic relations with Turkey and their political aspirations, were more willing than the United States to extend credits. A Soviet loan was granted in 1934, and large British and German advances were arranged in 1938.[23]

American Interest in Investment in Turkey

Although public loans were not forthcoming from the United States, by 1927 a substantial number of American firms had become interested in investment in Turkey. Officials of Ulen and Company of New York, for instance, negotiated with the Turkish government in 1927 concerning a loan for the construction of municipal improvements in Ankara and harbor installations at Samsun on the Black Sea and Mersin on the Mediterranean coast. The talks broke down in May, 1927, because Major James F. Case of Ulen and Company and the Turks could not agree on the extent of Turkish guarantees for the projected loan. Without proper security it would have been impossible to sell bonds in the United States to finance the loan.[24] Sheldon L. Crosby, chargé d'affaires at Istanbul, reported that Turkish officials thought the Ulen terms were "unduly onerous" and that it was "at this stage of the economic development of the country, unwise for the Government to enter into a long-term contract whereby a large proportion of the governmental revenues for public works would be assigned to a foreign firm hitherto untried in Turkey." Crosby also disclosed that the Ulen representative "experienced much dissatisfaction with Turkish methods of doing business." [25]

The plans of another American-backed company interested in the ex-

[22] Robert F. Kelley to Hull, October 26, 1937, *Foreign Relations of the United States: Diplomatic Papers, 1937* (5 vols., Washington, 1954), II, 952; memo of telephone conversation, George V. Allen (Near East Division) and Warren L. Pierson (President, Export-Import Bank), December 19, 1939, DS 611.6731/659.

[23] Skinner to Hull, March 17, 1934, DS 867.50 Three Year Plan/3; MacMurray to Hull, October 19, 1938, DS 867.51/666 (about the German credits); Herschel V. Johnson (Counselor of Embassy, London) to Hull, June 11, 1938, DS 867.51/647 (about the English credits).

[24] C. M. Bounell (Vice President, Ulen and Company) to Department of State, April 25, 1927, DS 867.51 UL2/-; Sheldon L. Crosby to Kellogg, May 26, 1927, DS 867.51 UL2/1; Charles E. Allen (Consul, Istanbul), Review of the Turkish Press, May 22–31, 1927, DS 867.9111/183; New York *Times*, May 24 and 29, 1927.

[25] To Kellogg, June 6, 1927, DS 867.51 UL2/2.

ploitation of Turkish oil and in railroad construction also failed. The State Department received information in January, 1928, that the American Oriental Bankers Corporation of Delaware, working through German interests, had concluded a contract for a loan of $30,000,000 to Turkey. Later, Marcus Reich, representing the company, told Ambassador Grew that this loan for the establishment of a state bank in Turkey had been signed on December 22, 1927, and that it had been approved by the Federal Reserve Board. Both assertions later proved to be false.[26] Although they showed interest in the American Oriental Bankers Corporation, the Turks terminated the negotiations in September, 1928, when they became convinced, as was the State Department, that the company was "of apparently unsavory reputation" and had no serious financial backing.[27]

Still another American firm investigated the possibilities of investment in Turkey in 1927. The Fox Brothers International Corporation of New York apparently signed a preliminary contract for the construction of railroad locomotive shops at Kayseri in central Turkey. According to the *Christian Science Monitor*, this would be "the first major movement of American capital to Turkey in recent years." There was considerable delay in signing the final contract, since the Turkish government was not satisfied with the company's financial demands. Grew reported to the State Department in April, 1928, that the final terms of the contract had been signed by the company and the Turkish government, but there is no evidence that the contemplated projects were ever undertaken.[28]

The Turkish government received its first substantial loan from a United States source in 1930. The origins of this arrangement go back to 1925, when the Turks granted a monopoly in the match industry to a Belgian group. The Belgians eventually sold their interests to Ivar Krueger, head of the Swedish International Match Company, which then trans-

[26] D. C. Poole (Chargé d'Affaires, Berlin) to Kellogg, January 4, 1928, DS 711.67/63; diary, conversation with Marcus Reich, January 31, 1928, Grew MSS, 1928, vol. 3; diary, February 2, 1928, *ibid.*; memo, Wallace Murray, "The American-Oriental Bankers' Corporation," March 7, 1928, DS 867.51 A.O.B. Corporation/14.

[27] Kellogg to Embassy, May 2, 1928, DS 867.51 A.O.B. Corporation/23; Grew to Kellogg, September 27, 1928, DS 867.51 A.O.B. Corporation/32; memo, Murray, "The American-Oriental Bankers' Corporation," March 7, 1928, DS 867.51 A.O.B. Corporation/14.

[28] Grew to Kellogg, October 26, 1927, DS 867.77 Fox Brothers/1; *Christian Science Monitor* (Boston), November 16, 1927; Grew to Kellogg, March 14, 1928, DS 867.77 Fox Brothers/14; Grew to Kellogg, April 25, 1928, DS 867.77 Fox Brothers/21.

ferred the match monopoly to a subsidiary, the American-European Match Company of New York. The Turkish government, believing that the sale was a trick by the Belgians to obtain delay in implementing their contract, canceled the concession.[29] Thereupon, the Turkish-American Investment Corporation, chartered in Delaware and affiliated with the Swedish match trust, negotiated a new agreement with the Turkish government. In a contract approved on June 15, 1930, the corporation agreed to lend $10,000,000 to Turkey in return for a twenty-five–year match monoply. The security for the loan was Turkish government promissory notes at 6.5 per cent interest. In addition, the Turkish-American Investment Corporation was to pay £T1,800,000 annually to the Turkish government for the match monopoly. The Turks planned to meet their semiannual promissory notes in dollar exchange with a portion of the money received in these payments.[30]

The Turkish-American Investment Corporation actually shipped $8,500,000 in gold bars to the Turkish government. In 1932 when its parent organization went bankrupt, the corporation still had not paid the remaining $1,500,000 of the loan, and had no plans to do so in the future. To compensate for this default, an agreement with the corporation released the Turkish government from its semiannual payments for six years, until July 1, 1938.[31] When the 1938 payment became due, the Turkish government was unable to meet its obligations because of the shortage of dollar exchange. As a matter of fact, the State Department even earlier had been asked by the Turkish-American Investment Corporation to aid in freeing exchange owed them. Instead of meeting the July 1, 1938, note in dollars, the Turkish government asked the company to reserve the amount due in Turkish currency before making its regular payment of £T1,800,000. At first the corporation refused, but later accepted this arrangement when it became evident that Turkey would not remit in

[29] Julian E. Gillespie (Commercial Attaché, Istanbul), Special Report No. 5, "Turkey Obtains $10,000,000 Loan in Return for Match Monopoly," July 10, 1930, DS 867.51 Turkish-American Investment Corporation/9.

[30] Jefferson Patterson (Chargé d'Affaires) to Stimson, June 16, 1930, DS 867.51 Turkish-American Investment Corporation/1; Patterson to Stimson, June 17, 1930, DS 867.51 Turkish-American Investment Corporation/5.

[31] Wilbur J. Carr (Acting Secretary of State) to Embassy, April 27, 1932, DS 867.51 Turkish-American Investment Corporation/13; memo of conversation, George V. Allen, Murray, and Paul H. Alling (all of the Near East Division) and Louis E. Stern (Treasurer, Turkish-American Investment Corporation), July 7, 1938, DS 867.51 Turkish-American Investment Corporation/100.

any other form.[32] The activities of the Turkish-American Investment Corporation during the 1930s, therefore, were not carried on with complete harmony and success. But the firm's large investment and its control of the match monopoly were a significant example of American participation in the development of the Turkish economy.

Operations of American Companies in Turkey

Several well-known American companies established large-scale operations in Turkey during the period. Some oil and tobacco companies actually had facilities there for years before 1927. The Standard Oil Company of New York, one of the largest American firms in Turkey, often found it necessary to ask the United States embassy for aid. Standard Oil's troubles arose from the imposition of taxes on installations in various locations in Turkey. In 1931 when unexplained taxes were levied against Standard Oil, Grew asked the Foreign Office for clarification. "In the note," Grew wrote in his diary, "I referred to the expressed desire of the Turks to cultivate close commercial relations with the United States and pointed out that this was not the way to accomplish that desire." [33] Another incident occurred in 1927, when the Turks required the company to abandon its Izmir warehouse because it was located in a military zone.[34]

The Ford Motor Company experienced less trouble when it established a potentially important new project in Turkey. Early in 1929, the Turkish Grand National Assembly approved a contract signed in November, 1928, by Sükrü Saracoglu, Minister of Finance, and William G. Collins of Ford Motor Company Exports, Inc., granting Ford a concession to construct and operate an assembly plant in a free zone within Istanbul. Materials brought into the zone were to be exempted from all customs duties and import taxes, but no completely assembled automobiles could be

[32] Kelley to Hull, January 24, 1938, DS 867.51 Turkish-American Investment Corporation/85; MacMurray to Hull, June 30, 1938, DS 867.51 Turkish-American Investment Corporation/94; memo, Francis X. Ward (Legal Adviser, State Department) to George V. Allen, August 16, 1938, DS 867.51 Turkish-American Investment Corporation/110. According to Kazdal, "Trade Relations Between the United States and Turkey," p. 199, the Turkish government paid off its indebtedness to the Turkish-American Investment Corporation by July, 1943.

[33] August 21, 1931, Grew MSS, 1931, vol. 2. For details of other Standard Oil tax troubles, see Grew to Stimson, January 15, 1930, DS 867.5123 Standard Oil/8; Grew to Stimson, April 16, 1930, DS 867.5123 Standard Oil/16.

[34] Diary, conversation, Grew and Clinton D. Campbell (General Manager, Standard Oil Company, Turkey), November 26, 1927, Grew MSS, 1927, vol. 1; diary, conversation, Grew and Campbell, December 14, 1927, *ibid.*

brought in by the company. The contract required Ford to hire at least 60 per cent Turkish employees within two years after operations began, and 75 per cent within six years. In return for the economic advantages gained, the Turkish government promised to pay to the company a premium of $30 for every vehicle imported into Turkey from the assembly plant in the free zone.[35] The factory began operations early in 1930, and became the central supply point for Ford products in Turkey and the Balkan area. The operation of the factory contributed to some expansion in the export of automotive products from the United States to Turkey. For example, Julian Gillespie, the commercial attaché in Istanbul, reported that the large expansion in shipment of tires to Turkey in 1930 was due to the Ford plant. Gillespie estimated that 7,500 vehicles would be assembled during 1930.[36]

The world depression, trade restrictions in countries around Turkey, and devaluation of the dollar contributed to an operating deficit at the plant, estimated by a Ford official at about $1,000,000 between 1929 and 1936. In the mid-1930s the plant suspended assembly operations except for the final preparation of almost complete autos shipped from the United States for sale in Turkey. In these years the plant sold between 450 and 600 cars per year.[37]

The Turkish government's interest in aircraft during the 1930s accounts for the attraction of the Curtiss-Wright Corporation to Turkey. In 1929, the Curtiss group began negotiations on a contract permitting them to assemble aircraft in Turkey and also to ship completed units from the United States. To demonstrate the efficiency of Curtiss products, four planes visited the country in May, 1930. In January, 1932, after three years of negotiations, the Turkish government ordered eighteen Curtiss-Wright planes, and a subsequent contract leased to the company an airplane factory at Kayseri, where a portion of the planes ordered would be assembled. The factory, incidentally, had been started earlier by a German aircraft manufacturer, the Junkers Company, whose contract had been

[35] "Constantinople Ford Assembly Plant," *Levant Trade Review*, XVII (February, 1929), 43–47.
[36] Gillespie to Director, Bureau of Foreign and Domestic Commerce, December 15, 1930, FDC Records, file 254.1 Turkey. Although evidence is not available, apparently the Ford plant assembled many fewer cars than the Gillespie estimate.
[37] MacMurray, memo of conversation with A. L. Molossi (Manager of the Ford plant), March 12, 1936, in the John Van Antwerp MacMurray MSS (Princeton University Library, Princeton, N.J.), Box 151.

canceled because the company had not complied with its terms.[38] This first order for Curtiss-Wright planes initiated a substantial investment by that company in Turkey. Curtiss-Wright personnel also helped the Turks to make aerial surveys, planned commercial air routes, and aided in the establishment of airmail service.[39]

Another potential outlet for American capital was the development of Turkish mineral resources. Several American oil groups, including the Texas Company, the Vacuum Oil Company, and the Benedum Trees Oil Company, showed interest in obtaining oil concessions in Turkey. None materialized, mainly because no significant oil deposits were found, although the government conducted extensive explorations.[40] Similarly, no important projects emerged from the interest of American companies in Turkish copper and chrome mines.[41]

American Technical Experts in Turkey

The investment of capital and the operation of manufacturing enterprises were not the only evidence of United States participation in Turkish economic development. The government of Turkey employed American technical advisers directly in many different fields of the Turkish economy. Since the Department of State and other departments aided in the recruit-

[38] Diary, February 8, 1932, Grew MSS, 1932, vol. 3; Grew to Stimson, March 11, 1932, DS 867.796 Curtiss/7. The efficiency of American aircraft was demonstrated by the record nonstop flight of Russell Boardman and Jon Polando from New York to Istanbul in July, 1931. Their plane was equipped with a Wright motor. See diary, July 27–August 10, 1931, Grew, *Turbulent Era*, II, 890–899; Washington *Post*, July 31, 1931; New York *Times*, August 1 and 2, 1931. Also see above, pp. 85–86.

[39] Sherrill to Stimson, June 17, 1932, DS 867.796 Curtiss/14; Skinner to Hull, November 9, 1933, DS 867.796 Curtiss/18; Skinner to Hull, December 6, 1933, DS 867.796 Curtiss/20.

[40] Memo of conversation, G. Howland Shaw and T. K. Schmuck (Texas Company), March 16, 1927, DS 867.6363/122; memo of conversation, Shaw and John C. Case (Vacuum Oil Company), December 6, 1928, DS 867.6363/130; H. C. McEldowney to Department of State, April 1, 1930, DS 867.6363/133 (about Benedum Trees Company); Kelley to Hull, November 18, 1937, DS 867.6363/158 (enclosure no. 1, article by Cevat Eyup Tashman, Director of the Turkish Institute of Mineral Research, Ministry of Economy, on petroleum explorations in Turkey).

[41] Memo of telephone conversation, Murray and Charles D. Hilles (American Smelting and Refining Company), November 15, 1929, DS 867.63/31; Fred Searles, Jr. (Newmont Mining Corporation) to Shaw, April 12, 1929, DS 867.6452/1. In 1936, the Turkish government expropriated (with compensation) a chrome mine at Fethiye operated by an American, Rufus W. Lane. The author could not determine when Lane acquired the mine. See MacMurray, memo of conversation with Sir Percy Loraine (British ambassador to Turkey), undated [1936], MacMurray MSS, Box 152; MacMurray to Lane, May 20, 1936, *ibid.*

ing of these specialists, their employment was unofficially sanctioned by the United States government. Not only did this technical assistance from the United States contribute a great deal to the development and administration of the Turkish economy, but also it played an important role in the expansion of Turkish-American friendship.

One indication of the great Turkish interest in industrial and agricultural modernization and expansion in the 1930s was the Five-Year Plan beginning in 1934.[42] To facilitate its economic development Turkey turned to foreign technical advisers to fill positions for which no native experts were available. There were precedents for employing Americans in special advisory capacities going back to 1831. In that year, Commodore David D. Porter, the first official American diplomatic representative in Turkey, arranged the hiring of an American shipbuilder, Henry Eckford, to advise and aid in the construction of Turkish naval vessels. In 1846, in response to a request from the Sultan, James B. Davis and J. Lawrence Smith went to Turkey. Davis established an experimental cotton farm and brought the first Angora and Cashmere goats into Turkey from Persia. Smith, interested in minerals, discovered deposits of emery ore, which later were exploited by the Turkish government.[43] In 1923 and 1924, Admiral Bristol reported on several occasions the interest of the Turkish government in hiring American experts in various advisory positions. The Turks especially desired the services of Edwin W. Kemmerer of Princeton University as a financial adviser, but because of other commitments he was unable to accept the offer. John Dewey, who went to Turkey in 1924 to study the Turkish educational system, was the forerunner of the technical assistants of the 1930s.[44]

The Turks were interested in engaging American technical advisers for two basic reasons. First, the Turkish government admired the efficiency of Americans and their methods. But more important was the absence of American political aspirations in Turkey and the entire Middle East.

[42] Cooke, *Challenge and Response in the Middle East*, pp. 268–271; Karpat, *Turkey's Politics*, p. 87. See also Kelley to Hull, March 10, 1938, DS 867.50 Five Year Plan/21, for a summary of progress made under the Five Year Plan.

[43] Merle E. Curti and Kendall Birr, *Prelude to Point Four: American Technical Missions Overseas, 1838–1938* (Madison, Wis., 1954), pp. 22–24, 154–155; David H. Finnie, *Pioneers East: The Early American Experience in the Middle East* (Cambridge, Mass., 1967), pp. 70–81, 111. See above, pp. 6–7.

[44] Bristol to Hughes, April 4, 1924, DS 867.01A/12; Bristol to Hughes, June 13, 1924, DS 867.51A/2; Grew (Acting Secretary of State) to Bristol, July 9, 1924, DS 867.51A/6; Bristol to Hughes, June 24, 1924, DS 867.01A/31.

Because they were politically disinterested, Americans were most likely to study Turkey's problems from the standpoint of the country's real needs. This factor above all accounted for the widespread use of American advisers in many fields during the 1930s. American diplomatic representatives in Turkey, especially Counselor of Embassy G. Howland Shaw and Commercial Attaché Julian E. Gillespie, were influential in the hiring of Americans.[45]

During 1932, the Turkish government, through Ambassador Charles H. Sherrill, invited several technical experts from the United States. In July, 1932, Sherrill forwarded requests for a counselor on customs administration and law and an adviser on the cost and technical operation of railroads. Upon the receipt of Sherrill's despatch, the State Department sent letters inviting nominations for the positions to several government agencies, including the Treasury Department, the Commerce Department, the United States Tariff Commission, and the Interstate Commerce Commission.[46] Subsequently, the Turks hired Robert H. Vorfeld of the Tariff Commission as customs adviser and Charles E. Bell as railway expert. The Turkish government was highly pleased with the work of Vorfeld, who spent a year in Turkey. The Turkish ambassador told a State Department official that if other American experts in Turkey proved as successful as Vorfeld, "it would assure in the future a really friendly attitude on the part of Turkey toward this country and should lead to far greater commercial relations." [47] Bell spent some time in Turkey studying the Railway Administration. When his original contract expired, the Turkish government offered to retain him as personal adviser to the Minister of Communications, but he was not rehired because of his high salary requests.[48]

[45] Robert L. Baker, "State Planning in Turkey," *Current History*, XXXVIII (July, 1933), 505; New York *Times*, May 28, 1933, and January 20, 1935; Curti and Birr, *Prelude to Point Four*, p. 183; "Turco-American Relations," *Current History*, XXXVIII (June, 1933), 379; Sherrill to Stimson, July 1, 1932, DS 867.01A/58.

[46] Sherrill to Stimson, July 1, 1932, DS 867.01A/57 (attached are carbon copies to the above offices, all dated July 7, 1932, signed by W. R. Castle, Jr.).

[47] Robert H. Vorfeld to Henry S. Villard (Near East Division), October 19, 1932, DS 867.01A/73 (attached is correspondence between Vorfeld and Ahmed Mouhtar, Turkish ambassador in Washington, who handled the hiring of Vorfeld); Sherrill to Stimson, January 19, 1933, DS 867.01A/97; memo of conversation, Castle and Ahmed Mouhtar, January 24, 1933, DS 867.01A/91. Bell was a former transportation director of the United States Food Administration. See the New York *Times*, May 5, 1933.

[48] Memo, Murray, May 19, 1934, DS 867.01A/132; Skinner to Hull, February 18, 1935, DS 867.01A/140.

Celal Bayar, Minister of National Economy, sought additional American advisers late in 1932. Of the six different posts open at this time, the most important was for a person to make a "general economic survey" of Turkey. The Turks also desired a permanent economic adviser and four specialists to work for the Departments of Mines, Industry, and Commerce in the Ministry of National Economy.[49] Wallace Clark, who took one of the openings, headed a team which made a survey of Turkish tobacco, alcohol, and salt monoplies during the spring of 1933. After learning of the opening from Julian Gillespie, Clark went to Turkey and negotiated his own contract. When his study was completed, the Turks engaged Clark to put his recommendations into effect. Although the Turkish government praised his work, it terminated Clark's contract in May, 1934. Gillespie reported that this action was "caused by the intrigues of the General Manager of the Monopolies," who apparently resented Clark's suggestions.[50]

In March, 1933, the Turks hired Matthew Van Siclen to study the gold mining industry and Sidney Paige as general mining adviser, and they worked in Turkey until their contracts expired in April, 1935. Apparently the Turks were not impressed with Paige and Van Siclen, since, as Ambassador Skinner reported, their search for oil and gold had been unsuccessful. Wallace Murray, Chief of the Near Eastern Division of the State Department, noted that they seemed "to have been rather forgotten by the Minister of National Economy and have therefore been left to face the natural hostility of subordinates in that Ministry." [51]

The Turkish need for a general economic survey was the basis for the most important and extensive work of American experts. With the aid of the State Department, the Turkish government in 1933 selected Walker D. Hines to head this mission. A well-known economic expert who directed the operation of United States railroads during World War I, Hines headed a law firm in New York. Associated with him in the Turkish proj-

[49] Sherrill to Stimson, November 1, 1932, DS 867.01A/76.

[50] Sherrill to Stimson, January 5, 1933, DS 867.01A/89; Skinner to Hull, November 10, 1933, DS 867.01A/126; Gillespie to Shaw, May 7, 1934, FDC Records, file 449.0; memo, Murray, May 19, 1934, DS 867.01A/132. See also the New York *Times*, March 19 and September 11, 1933. Clark headed a company of industrial and engineering consultants, and served previously with the United States Shipping Board. See the New York *Times*, May 5, 1933.

[51] Ahmed Mouhtar to Murray, March 29, 1933, DS 867.01A/112; Skinner to Hull, March 26, 1935, DS 867.01A/141; memo, Murray, May 19, 1934, DS 867.01A/132. Van Siclen previously worked for the Bureau of Mines and Paige for the Geological Survey. See the New York *Times*, May 5, 1933.

ect were his legal associates, Goldthwaite H. Dorr and H. Alexander Smith; O. F. Gardner, an agricultural expert; and Major Brehon B. Somervell, on loan from the United States Army Corps of Engineers. Preceded by Somervell and Gardner, Hines arrived in Turkey in June, 1933, to direct the project.[52] When Hines died in Europe in January, 1934, Dorr took over direction of the survey. Edwin W. Kemmerer of Princeton University, engaged to aid in completion of special reports on money and banking and to put the entire final report in order, went to Turkey in June, 1934.[53]

The Hines-Dorr-Kemmerer work in Turkey provided Vahan Cardashian with another opportunity to champion the cause of Armenia. He complained to Secretary Hull that personnel of the group were "prospecting on lands allotted to the Armenian Republic by arbitration of the President of the United States." Cardashian also charged that the American embassy in Istanbul was "an adjunct of the Turkish Foreign Office" and that "the so-called American experts, selected and recommended by the Department of State, and who are now prospecting on Armenian soil, are, under international law, trespassers and invaders." [54] Cardashian never overlooked an opportunity to argue for Armenia and to protest against friendly Turkish-American contacts.

The final 1,800-page report of the survey covered all phases of Turkish economic activity. Recognizing Turkish accomplishments after World War I, the report criticized Turkish customs and habits. Turkey's greatest need, according to the report, was greater efficiency in production, which would be facilitated by better transportation and communications systems, improvement of health, application of better techniques and practical knowledge, and a stable financial system. The emphasis in the report was on the need to modernize agriculture and transportation, rather than on extensive industrialization. Julian Gillespie, who was quite critical of the survey's conclusions, thought it was wrong to advocate increased agricultural output. He wrote Dorr that Turkey's greatest farm problem was

---

[52] Curti and Birr, *Prelude to Point Four*, p. 184; William Phillips to General Douglas A. MacArthur (Chief of Staff), April 11, 1933, DS 867.50A/14A (about Somervell).

[53] Phillips to Embassy (for Somervell from H. Alexander Smith), January 15, 1934, DS 867.50A/63A (report of Hines' death); Skinner to Hull, June 22, 1934, DS 867.50A/82; Curti and Birr, *Prelude to Point Four*, p. 184. Kemmerer had previously undertaken similar missions to the Philippines, Colombia, Chile, Ecuador, Bolivia, Peru, Poland, Germany, and South Africa.

[54] October 8, 1933, DS 867.50A/46.

143

"not to increase its agricultural production substantially but rather to assure that production and to maintain and improve wherever possible the quality and standards of the products which they produce." "The conservatism of the farmer and peasant" was one of the greatest obstacles to be overcome in Turkey, according to Gillespie.[55]

The Hines-Dorr-Kemmerer report, though not entirely implemented, was of substantial influence in Turkey. It was published, however, just as Benito Mussolini of Italy made ominous statements about his country's future destiny in Africa and the Middle East. The preparedness program then undertaken by Turkey required funds that otherwise would have been expended on internal economic development. At the same time Turkish leaders were influenced by the Soviet type of economic planning, which concentrated on a few economic areas at one time. The leaders of Turkey, a country with many economic and social conditions similar to those in the Soviet Union, were impressed because the Soviet program was progressing without foreign funds.[56] But when Dorr revisited Turkey in 1949 and 1950, he was told by various government officials that the report had been their "Bible," and both retiring President Ismet Inönü and Celal Bayar, the new president, told Dorr that the report had been very valuable.[57]

The Turkish government hired several other Americans during the 1930s. The American Friends of Turkey, organized in 1930 to promote Turkish-American friendship, cooperated with Turkish authorities in the early 1930s in support of the development of an experimental kindergarten and primary school in Ankara. Beryl Parker of New York University directed this project.[58] Stanley P. Clark of the University of Arizona worked for ten years at Adana in southern Turkey, where he conducted experiments to improve cotton production and quality. Dorr observed that Clark was "the most outstanding example of what a technical assistant can

[55] Skinner to Hull, March 26, 1934, DS 867.50A/76; Curti and Birr, *Prelude to Point Four*, pp. 184–185; memo, Gillespie to Shaw, May 7, 1934, FDC Records, file 449.0 (enclosure is copy of Gillespie to Dorr, May 4, 1934). See also the New York *Times*, July 15, 1934.

[56] Curti and Birr, *Prelude to Point Four*, p. 186; Cooke, *Challenge and Response in the Middle East*, p. 269.

[57] Curti and Birr, *Prelude to Point Four*, p. 186.

[58] American Friends of Turkey, Inc., *American Friends of Turkey* (New York, 1931), in Mark Lambert Bristol MSS (Manuscript Division, Library of Congress, Washington), Box 96 (a pamphlet explaining the origins and purposes of the group); Asa W. Jennings (executive director, American Friends of Turkey) to Murray, July 20, 1933, DS 867.42711/4; Shaw to Hull, April 26, 1933, DS 867.42711/1.

accomplish if he has the practical training and instincts, is willing to get into the life of the country, get his hands dirty and has the instinct for friendship and understanding of the people with whom he is working." [59] Edward D. Wright, a sanitation engineer employed in 1938 by the Ministry of Hygiene, made recommendations for the improvement of the Ankara sewerage system.[60] The Turks hired two other Americans, H. M. Kirk and Samuel H. Russell, to prospect for oil, but they met with little success.[61] Requests for other technicians, including a hydrographer, a highway engineer, a flood control expert, police instructors, and military aviation experts, were not filled in the United States for various reasons.[62]

Conclusions

Thus, the United States played an important role in Turkish economic development and administration during the interwar period, and especially in the 1930s. This special aspect of American cooperation with the new Turkey was of inestimable value as a stimulus to strengthening Turkish-American relationships. Because of the nature of the Kemalist revolution in Turkey, with its aims of economic modernization, expansion, and efficiency, it was natural for the Turks to turn for encouragement and aid to the United States, which they considered to be the personification of the West.

It was logical, also, for Turkey to be interested in American capital. Even though the whole world suffered from depression after 1929, some investment capital was available in the United States. If it could be lured to Turkey, it would come without any political strings attached. The Turks knew and emphasized the fact that the United States had no selfish political ambitions in the Middle East, whereas such countries as England,

[59] Skinner to Hull, June 3, 1935, DS 867.61A/15; Curti and Birr, *Prelude to Point Four*, p. 183, quoting letter, Dorr to Curti, October 23, 1951.
[60] Kelley to Hull, March 15, 1938, DS 867.124A/1.
[61] Shaw to Murray, March 30, 1936, DS 867.6363/152; Kelley to Hull, November 18, 1937, DS 867.6363/158; Frederick P. Latimer, Jr. (Consul, Istanbul), to Hull, February 9, 1938, DS 867.6363/159.
[62] H. Alexander Smith to Murray, March 5, 1934, DS 867.01A/127 (hydrographer); Skinner to Hull, April 5, 1934, DS 867.01A/129 (highway engineer); Turkish Embassy (Washington) to Department of State, November 9, 1936, DS 867.64A/1 (flood control expert); New York *Times*, March 14, 1939 (police); Turkish Embassy to Department of State, June 6, 1935, *Foreign Relations of the United States: Diplomatic Papers, 1935* (4 vols., 1952–1953), I, 1052; Murray to Münir Ertegün, June 24, 1935, *ibid.*, 1053; Ertegün to Hull, May 3, 1937, DS 867.20/70 (military aviation experts).

France, Germany, Italy, and the Soviet Union had spent many years interfering in and fighting over Turkey. American investors had to be cautious in establishing projects in Turkey because of Turkish nationalism and restrictive legislation. These and other factors help to explain why direct American investment in Turkey was not so extensive in monetary value as investment in other countries during the same era. But yet it was quite significant.

Perhaps the most valuable aspect of American participation in Turkey's economic development and administration was the work of the various technical experts and advisers. Although these individuals had difficulty because of harassing taxes, salary squabbles, and bureaucratic jealousy, they made important contributions and the Turkish government greatly appreciated their usually good work. The report of the Hines-Dorr-Kemmerer mission in 1933–1934 contributed much to Turkish economic planning and development. As in the case of private investors, Turkey called on these technical advisers in the belief that they would perform their duties without hidden political motives.

It cannot be stated that American business interests and technical assistants played a dominant part in Turkey's economic programs of the interwar period, but they certainly had considerable influence. The contributions made by these Americans were perhaps as important as the various treaties and agreements arranged during this period in cementing close Turco-American friendship. Quite significant, too, were the precedents set for assistance during the World War II and postwar periods. The rapid westernization of Turkey, forced by Kemal Atatürk and his government, was facilitated somewhat by politically disinterested American business investments and technical aid. The fact that American citizens, aided and encouraged by their government, were willing to play this role in Turkey's economic development and administration gave proof of their accommodation to Turkish nationalism.

146

✿ "Unnamed Christianity": The American Educational Effort

BEFORE World War I, American missionary educators provided the basis for one of the most important links between the United States and the Ottoman Empire and also played a prominent role in education within the Empire.[1] World War I, which found Turkey fighting with the Central Powers, of necessity led to some curtailment of American educational work, especially after the United States became associated with Turkey's enemies in April, 1917. Factors of more significance than World War I in explaining the problems of American educators in Turkey included the postwar disintegration of the Ottoman Empire and the Turkish nationalist movement, which emphasized secularism among its basic principles of operation.[2]

An obvious exemplification of the Turkish secularization movement was the intense effort to reform and control the educational system by cleansing it of all religious influences. The Turks wanted to expand and improve their system, but first priority went to secularization of the schools, a program which involved a large number of American educational institutions. Turkish fear of foreign political, economic, and cultural domination also affected the educational system, particularly foreign schools. Closing of many schools, imposition of crippling taxes, strict regulation of curricula and teaching personnel, and arbitrary inspections

---

[1] This chapter in slightly different form appeared as " 'Unnamed Christianity' in Turkey During the Atatürk Era," *Muslim World*, LV (January, 1965), 66–76 (pt. I), and *ibid.* (April, 1965), 101–111 (pt. II). For information on the work of American missionaries before World War I, see the first chapter above.

[2] See above, pp. 66–72.

147

were among the by-products of these basic attitudes. In spite of the hardships, the persons responsible for the operation of American educational institutions in Turkey resolved to continue their work after World War I. American educators adjusted admirably to Turkish nationalism, even though they became involved in many disputes requiring the services of American diplomatic representatives. In 1939, education continued to be one of the most significant Turco-American contacts, as it had been since the two countries first established formal diplomatic relations in 1830. During the Atatürk era, these American educators by their actions and attitudes contributed much to good Christian-Muslim relationships in an important part of the Islamic world.

Secularism, Educational Reform, and the Missionaries

World War I, the ten-year break in formal diplomatic relations between the United States and Turkey, and the nationalist revolution under Kemal Atatürk had profound effects on American educational work in Turkey. By the time Turkey and the United States re-established diplomatic relations in 1927, the American Board conducted classes for fourteen hundred students at eight primary and secondary schools and one institution of higher learning, International College in Izmir.[3] The two private American institutions, Robert College and Istanbul Woman's College, continued to operate.

However, given the Turkish attitude toward foreign schools and the multiplicity of restrictions imposed upon them, it is surprising that any American schools existed in Turkey in 1927. By this time the secularization program was well under way. Furthermore, the past work of American schools had been almost exclusively with minorities, mainly Greeks and Armenians. The Turks felt that the presence of these Christian minorities was an obstacle to national unity. Even though most of the Christian non-Turkish population was effectively removed after World War I, foreign schools were not cleared of all suspicion. The Turks wanted to prevent the growth of new Christian communities, which could result from continued Christian missionary work.[4]

---

[3] *The One Hundred and Seventeenth Annual Report of the American Board of Commissioners for Foreign Missions* [1927] (Boston, n.d.), pp. 63–77; Frank A. Ross, C. Luther Fry, and Elbridge Sibley, *The Near East and American Philanthropy* (New York, 1929), pp. 156–160. The eight schools were at Adana, Merzifoun, Izmir, Tarsus, Bursa, and three in Istanbul.

[4] Kenneth Scott Latourette, *A History of the Expansion of Christianity* (7 vols.,

The Turks were also aware of the role played by the missionaries in developing a hostile American public opinion toward Turkey. "If American opinion has been uninformed, misinformed and prejudiced," one observer wrote in 1929, "the missionaries are largely to blame. Interpreting history in terms of the advance of Christianity, they have given an inadequate, distorted, and occasionally grotesque picture of Moslems and Islam." [5] Although no proof exists that knowledge of the past activities of mission interests was an important factor in determining secular education policy, it must have influenced the Turks somewhat.

Turkish fear that the mission schools would be used to propagate foreign culture was another factor. The Turks believed that a student educated in a foreign school, especially if religious teaching was allowed, would be dominated by an alien culture. Foreign schools, if unregulated, would be hostile to Turkish nationalism and instruments of foreign political influence.[6] Ambassador Grew expressed the point well:

As for the question of religious teaching in the schools, I heard a remark the other day which it seems to me is very much in point. Somebody said, referring to our recent Presidential campaign in the United States, "It is therefore not the Catholic religion at all that is under attack, but the idea of the Catholic church as a foreign institution." If you alter the word "Catholic" to "Christian" you have in a nutshell the attitude of the Turks toward our American schools in Turkey. It is not religion but cultural nationalism that is the stumbling block. Christianizing to the Turk means the weaning of Turkish youth away from Turkish nationalism and all that the term implies.[7]

Grew later pointed out that the Turks felt "character should be formed not through religion but through the training of the mind plus the development of an intense nationalism." [8] A Turkish newspaper complained about "unnamed Christianity" in American schools. "By creating a com-

New York & London, 1937–1945), VII, 266; John Dewey, *Characters and Events: Popular Essays in Social and Political Philosophy*, ed. Joseph Ratner (2 vols., New York, 1929), I, 346–349.

[5] Edward Mead Earle, "American Missions in the Near East," *Foreign Affairs*, VII (April, 1929), 417. See also E. Alexander Powell, *The Struggle for Power in Moslem Asia* (New York & London, 1923), pp. 27–28.

[6] William Paton and M. M. Underhill, "A Survey of the Year 1929," *International Review of Missions*, XIX (January, 1930), 37; Dewey, *Characters and Events*, I, 328–329, 346–347.

[7] To Godfrey L. Cabot, January 19, 1929, Joseph C. Grew MSS (Houghton Library, Harvard University, Cambridge, Mass.), 1929, vol. 1.

[8] To Henry S. Coffin (President, Union Theological Seminary), November 16, 1930, *ibid.*, 1930, vol. 1.

plete Christian environment for the Turkish youth to live in, their aim is to instill in them gradually and unconsciously Christian ways and beliefs under the name of character-building, and so forth." The inner life in these schools, the article continued, did not reflect the true life of Turkish society.[9]

Believing that religion, particularly Christianity, did not mix with nationalism, the Atatürk government early prohibited any religious teaching in foreign as well as Turkish schools. Classrooms were to be free of religious symbols, teachers had to be approved by the government, and certain subjects were to be taught by Turkish teachers appointed by government educational authorities.[10] Faced with these restrictions, the missionaries of the American Board had to make the critical decision whether they should continue their work in Turkey. The decision should, it seemed, be based on the answer to this question asked by an American Board missionary, "Was it worth while to keep open schools in which the Bible could no longer be the backbone of the curriculum, as it originally was?" The missionaries decided this question in the affirmative; their existence would be justified, they felt, if they could maintain a Christian influence on education by personal example and friendly contact.[11] The missionaries were convinced that the Turkish people needed and wanted the American schools. As one American Board leader put it, "The Turks acted as if they expected the missionaries to remain. The number of pupils from Moslem families greatly increased. . . . It was evident from the patronage given that there was a desire and even a demand for the continuance of the schools."[12] The Board's annual report for 1924 pointed out that the Turks had witnessed the "great advance made by the Armenians and Greeks through their wide patronage of American institutions . . . and they covet this same opportunity for their own young men and

[9] Quoted in " 'Unnamed Christianity' in Turkey," *Missionary Review of the World*, XLI (June, 1928), 468–469.
[10] *The One Hundred and Fourteenth Annual Report of the American Board of Commissioners for Foreign Missions* [1924] (Boston, n.d.), pp. 67–68 (hereafter cited as *ABCFM Report, 1924*).
[11] Charles T. Riggs, "Turkey, the Treaties and the Missionaries," *Missionary Review of the World*, L (May, 1927), 345; Earle, "American Missions in the Near East," pp. 414–416; Lynn A. Scipio, *My Thirty Years in Turkey* (Rindge, N.H., 1955), pp. 212–213; Fred Field Goodsell, *You Shall Be My Witnesses* (Boston, 1959), pp. 244–245.
[12] James L. Barton, "Missionary Problems in Turkey," *International Review of Missions*, XVI (October, 1927), 489.

women."[13] Turkish parents who sent their children to American schools knew, of course, that the institutions had Christian affiliations, but they expected that laws against proselytizing would be obeyed. Obviously they did not want their children to become hostile to Turkish culture and traditions, but they recognized that the quality of instruction was superior to that in their own schools.[14]

The missionaries believed that through "unnamed Christianity" they would be able to mold the characters of their students, the majority of whom were Turks. "The Christian teacher . . . will impress upon his pupils those principles which lie at the very foundation of our Christian thinking and Christian living. The missionary will thus have opportunity to build Christian character into the lives of his Turkish pupils," the American Board reported in 1924.[15] Fourteen years later the same spirit prevailed: "A Christian atmosphere may be diffused even through a 'secular' school or hospital, and the Board is using all the opportunities these present. . . . Christians in Turkey today are trying to demonstrate through Christ-like work done in a Christ-like spirit, that the Christian possesses something of infinite worth; something, too, which Turkey needs, if the republic is to develop into a strong and noble state." [16] Thus, based on the conviction that they were wanted and needed and that they would be able to spread Christianity without open attempts to win converts, the American Board missionaries decided by 1923 to continue their work.

The Bursa Proselytizing Case, 1928

Even though it permitted Christian missionaries to carry on their educational activities, the Turkish government often made it clear that it would not tolerate direct proselytizing. The most obvious example of this attitude occurred in 1928, when the Turks abruptly closed the American Girls' Lycée at Bursa.[17] This incident defined clearly the basic conflict between the secularism of Turkish nationalism and religious teaching.

[13] *ABCFM Report, 1924*, pp. 71–72. See also *The One Hundred and Thirteenth Annual Report of the American Board of Commissioners for Foreign Missions* [1923] (Boston, n.d.), p. 53.
[14] Arnold J. Toynbee and Kenneth P. Kirkwood, *Turkey* (London, 1926), p. 250.
[15] *ABCFM Report, 1924*, p. 73.
[16] William Paton and M. M. Underhill, "A Survey of the Year 1937," *International Review of Missions*, XXVII (January, 1937), 52.
[17] The name of this city in northwestern Anatolia is variably spelled Bursa, Bru-

The charges against the Bursa school in January, 1928, involved the alleged conversion of three Muslim girls to Christianity. The girls, who became interested in Christianity while studying at Bursa, read the Bible and discussed it with three of their teachers, Lucille Day, Edith Sanderson, and Jeannie L. Jillson, principal of the school. Diaries in which the girls confided their thoughts fell into the hands of government authorities, who closed the school after an investigation.[18] The teachers, charged with violation of a law against religious proselytizing, were tried and convicted on April 30, 1928. Late in August, 1928, a court of appeals annulled the conviction because of procedural questions and ordered a new trial, which resulted in a second conviction. The highest Turkish tribunal, the Court of Cassation, upheld the decision on March 5, 1929. The penalties for the teachers, two of whom had already left Turkey, were three days' house imprisonment and fines of three lire each.[19] The light sentences proved that the Turks intended to demonstrate their determination to enforce the laws against religious instruction rather than to show vengeance against the three teachers involved.

The Turkish press expressed much hostility to American schools when the details of the Bursa incident became known.[20] An editorial in *Hayat*

sa, Broussa, and Brousa. Except as spelled otherwise in quotations, "Bursa" will be used. For comments on the significance of the Bursa incident, see Kemal H. Karpat, *Turkey's Politics: The Transition to a Multi-Party System* (Princeton, 1959), pp. 60–61.

[18] Diary, January 22, 1928, in Joseph C. Grew, *Turbulent Era: A Diplomatic Record of Forty Years, 1904–1945*, ed. Walter Johnson (2 vols., Boston, 1952), II, 755–756; Grew to Frank B. Kellogg, *Papers Relating to the Foreign Relations of the United States, 1928* (3 vols., Washington, 1942–1943), III, 964–965 (hereafter cited as *FR 1928*); Hoffman Philip (American Embassy, Teheran) to Kellogg, April 19, 1928, DS 367.1164 Brussa School Trial/38. Enclosed in this despatch is a copy of letter, Lucille Day to Dr. Hutchinson, Dean of the American School, Teheran, February 22, 1928, explaining the Bursa incident. See also John K. Birge to E. W. Riggs, January 26, 1928, American Board of Commissioners for Foreign Missions MSS (Houghton Library, Harvard University, Cambridge, Mass.), ABC 16.9.1, vol. 3, unnumbered (hereafter cited as ABCFM MSS). Mr. Luther Fowle, an American Board lay missionary in Turkey between 1914 and 1950, believed that at least one of the girls had an Armenian Christian mother. Letter, Fowle to Roger R. Trask, July 1, 1964.

[19] Grew to Kellogg, May 8, 1928, *FR 1928*, III, 974–975; Grew to Kellogg, August 30, 1928, *ibid.*, 980; Grew to Kellogg, September 27, 1928, *ibid.*; diary, March 6, 1929, Grew, *Turbulent Era*, II, 804–805.

[20] See Charles E. Allen (Consul, Istanbul), Review of the Turkish Press, January 12–25, 1928, DS 867.9111/209; Allen, Review of the Turkish Press, January 26–February 8, 1928, DS 867.9111/210; Royal R. Jordan (Vice-Consul, Istanbul), Review of the Turkish Press, February 23–March 7, 1928, DS 867.9111/212, for summaries of press comment.

magazine on February 2, 1928, entitled "The Christianizing Incident," raised some critical questions: "Why is there an American school in Brousa when there is not even one American family there? . . . It is well known that the duty of the school is to give education; the function of education is to innoculate the younger generation with the thoughts, feelings, desires, and ideals of the society *to which it belongs.* . . . In a word these schools are institutions which by their lessons, by their training turn Turkish youth away from the society to which they belong to another society and carry them forward toward a foreign ideal." [21] The Istanbul *Cümhuriyet* observed that religion was a "personal matter" and that "modern society condemns any attempt to infuse foreign religion into the consciences of the young. It is a terrible crime and the most shameful thing in the world, so society ought to prevent it." [22] Ambassador Grew deplored the press attacks on American institutions and worried about their effect on public opinion in the United States. He acknowledged that the Bursa school broke faith with the Turkish government and that the "action of the Turkish authorities cannot properly be resented." In a letter to a friend in the State Department, Grew wrote: "The school incident is bad, very bad. But they had it coming to them and it came." [23] Grew also was uneasy about the effect the affair would have on Robert College and Istanbul Woman's College, even though they had no religious connections. He reported to Secretary of State Kellogg that these institutions "deplore [the] situation owing to possible ultimate effects of the incident on all American educational institutions." [24]

Like Grew, the State Department was concerned about publicity in the United States hostile to Turkey. The Department warned the Turkish embassy in Washington that the incident at Bursa "furnishes the best kind of ammunition to Turkey's opponents in this country" and that the trial of the teachers "will do much to convince the American public of Turkey's still being fanatically Moslem." [25] Owing to the circumstances, Grew felt that formal diplomatic representations to the Turkish Foreign Office on the Bursa incident were unwarranted. Even before this affair he had recorded

[21] Translation in ABCFM MSS, ABC 16.9.1, vol. 4, no. 224.
[22] Quoted in "Turkey's Dayton Flare-up," *Literary Digest*, XCVII (May 19, 1928), 28.
[23] Grew to Kellogg, February 1, 1928, *FR 1928*, III, 967–968; Grew to G. Howland Shaw, February 1, 1928, Grew MSS, 1928, vol. 2.
[24] January 31, 1928, *FR 1928*, III, 965.
[25] Kellogg to Grew, February 14, 1928, *ibid.*, 972.

his attitude on the schools: "I don't want them [the Turkish government] to feel that every time I come to Angora it is for the purpose of asking for something, nor do I want them to feel that I am going to use my position to demand all sorts of rights for American scholastic and philanthropic institutions in opposition to their own wishes. If they don't want American schools and other institutions, it is not for us to cram them down their throats; the days of the capitulations are over." [26] Secretary of State Kellogg suggested informal talks with Turkish authorities about the Bursa events. When Grew met with Foreign Minister Tevfik Rüsdü Aras on February 7, 1928, he confined his remarks to pointing out "the unfortunate reaction" to the incident in the United States and "the harm that could be done to Turco-American relations if the drastic attitude of the Turkish authorities and Turkish press should be permitted to continue." Grew asked Aras to halt the press attack, suspend prosecution of the teachers, consider reopening the Bursa school, and state that the incident was "sporadic" and did not compromise other American institutions in Turkey. Except for dropping the charges against the teachers, the Foreign Minister promised to implement Grew's suggestions, and later, when he announced that the Bursa school could never resume its work, added that he would consider reopening other schools.[27] The Turkish government made concessions along these lines later in 1928 after Grew pointed out to Prime Minister Ismet Inönü that reopening some American schools as a beau geste would have a "favorable effect" and indicate that "the Turkish Government was holding no brief against the American schools as such but only against religious propaganda." [28]

Although Grew first thought the affair was "only one step in the ultimate closing of most of the American and other mission schools in this country," the Bursa problem did not initiate a movement to drive all American schools from Turkey. Grew felt that the abrupt action in Bursa was due partly to fundamental opposition to foreign schools by the Minister of Public Instruction, Nedjati Bey, whom he described as "a politician of the rougher sort with little culture and little claim to be regarded as an

---

[26] Diary, December 9, 1927, Grew, *Turbulent Era*, III, 748–749.

[27] Kellogg to Grew, February 1, 1928, *FR 1928*, III, 965–966; conversation, Grew and Tevfik Rüsdü Aras, February 7, 1928, Grew, *Turbulent Era*, II, 759–762; Grew to Kellogg, February 8, 1928, *FR 1928*, III, 970; Grew to Kellogg, February 12, 1928, *ibid.*, 971.

[28] Conversation, Grew and Ismet Inönü, February 21, 1928, Grew, *Turbulent Era*, II, 766–767; diary, August 20, 1928, *ibid.*, 789.

educationalist." [29] The Bursa affair did prove that cultural nationalism and secularism were extremely important parts of Turkish nationalism. Foreign schools could continue their work as long as they conformed to Turkish regulations and confined their teaching to secular subjects; the promotion of antinationalism through religious teaching would not be tolerated.[30]

Some American Board representatives felt that the Bursa incident had beneficial effects. Fred Field Goodsell, field secretary of the Board in Turkey, wrote that the event "may be a blessing in disguise. It may be the means of clarifying our position and helping us to estimate the real value of our educational work under present restrictions. I think more good than evil will come out of it." [31] "From the point of view of the missionaries themselves . . . ," the Board pointed out in its annual report in 1928, "this event has been one of helpfulness in establishing our cause among the Turks. . . . The whole influence of the Brousa incident has been to clarify the position of the American Board in Turkey and to make clear to the officials of the Turkish government our genuine purpose to be of service to their people." [32]

The conflict between Turkish nationalism and religious teaching, most clearly demonstrated at the time of the Bursa affair, never disappeared, but there were fluctuations in the Turkish attitude toward foreign schools. Grew noted in July, 1929, that there had been a "marked change for the better" in this attitude over the past year, a development ascribed partly to the death of Nedjati Bey, and to Turkish realization of the need for foreign schools until Turkey had adequate funds and teachers of its own. Grew recognized "a gradual but clearly perceptible diminution of the fanatical chauvinism" of the early years of the Turkish Republic: "In other words, the wind is clearly blowing in the direction of increased self-confidence, the inferiority complex is moderating, and proportionately with this development a new psychological outlook is created which is

[29] Grew to Kellogg, February 1, 1928, *FR 1928*, III, 969; Grew to Kellogg, May 8, 1928, Grew, *Turbulent Era*, II, 782–783.

[30] Grew to Kellogg, May 8, 1928, Grew, *Turbulent Era*, II, 780; Fowle (Treasurer, American Board Near East Mission) to Lucille Day, November 26, 1929, ABCFM MSS, ABC 16.5, vol. 27, no. 8; Arnold J. Toynbee, *Survey of International Affairs, 1928* (London, 1929), p. 209.

[31] To Mabel E. Emerson (American Board Secretary, Boston), February 8, 1928, ABCFM MSS, ABC 16.9.1, vol. 4, no. 223.

[32] *The One Hundred and Eighteenth Annual Report of the American Board of Commissioners for Foreign Missions* [1928] (Boston, n.d.), p. 69.

automatically reflected in a more tolerant attitude of the Government toward foreign educational and philanthropic institutions in Turkey." [33]

It is important to note that in their position on foreign schools the Turks seemed to distinguish between American educational institutions and those operated by European nations, particularly France, Germany, and Italy. These countries had a political interest in Turkey, whereas the United States did not, and their schools were less willing to comply with restrictions placed on their operation. Significantly, the Turkish government closed all French and Italian schools in April, 1924, when they refused to remove Roman Catholic symbols from their classrooms.[34] Also, American schools profited because the Turks were influenced by American educational methods, particularly the progressive ideas advocated by John Dewey. Furthermore, considerable emphasis was placed on the teaching of the English language in Turkish schools in the 1930s.[35]

As the time drew near for the expiration in August, 1931, of the establishment provisions of the Allied Lausanne Treaty of 1923, which protected European schools in Turkey, American diplomatic and educational officials expressed concern about the future of foreign schools. Rumors circulated that the Turkish government would take drastic action against the schools once it was free of the Lausanne restrictions.[36] There appears, however, to have been no perceptible change in Turkish policy toward American schools after August, 1931. The United States was able to conclude a treaty of establishment and sojourn in October, 1931, guaranteeing most-favored-nation treatment to American nationals residing and

[33] Diary, July 3–July 17, 1929, Grew, *Turbulent Era*, II, 811–813. The same ideas appear in Grew to Stimson, June 30, 1929, DS 367.1164/123.

[34] Toynbee, *Survey of International Affairs, 1925* (3 vols., London, 1927–1928), I, 79–80; Fowle to Mabel Emerson and Dr. Alden Clark, August 2, 1933, ABCFM MSS, ABC 16.5, vol. 27, no. 390A; Robert P. Skinner to Cordell Hull, January 14, 1936, DS 367.0064/8 (enclosure is a sixteen-page report by S. Walter Washington, Second Secretary of Embassy, entitled "Some of the Current Problems of Foreign Schools in Turkey [Other than American]").

[35] Fowle to Emerson and Clark, August 2, 1933, ABCFM MSS, ABC 16.5, vol. 27, no. 390A; Charles H. Sherrill to Henry L. Stimson, December 23, 1932, DS 367.1164 R54/84. The Turks were interested in educating youth to live a practical life in the modern world. Dewey's repudiation of formalized learning and his emphasis on adapting school programs to the child's needs along practical lines thus appealed to Turkish leaders.

[36] Circular letter, Fowle to American Board School Directors in Turkey, March 31, 1930, ABCFM MSS, ABC 16.5, vol. 11, no. 161; Caleb F. Gates to Mark L. Bristol, September 5, 1930, Mark Lambert Bristol MSS (Manuscript Division, Library of Congress, Washington), Box 92; Jefferson Patterson (Chargé d'Affaires) to Stimson, June 13, 1930, DS 367.0064/1.

working in Turkey.[37] The Turks would not have agreed to such a treaty if they planned any significant changes in the status of American schools.

Operating Problems of the Schools

The desire of the Turkish government to eliminate all religious influences in the schools accounted not only for various restrictions during the period up to 1939, but also explained Turkish procrastination on the question of reopening various American Board schools. When Ambassador Grew arrived in Turkey in the fall of 1927, his most pressing problem was the Board's campaign to reopen schools closed during the preceding decade. Turkish authorities had rejected the Board's petitions to reopen the schools in May, 1925, and March, 1927. Fred F. Goodsell, the field secretary of the Board in Istanbul, attributed the delay to Nedjati Bey.[38] Grew did not believe in unwarranted formal diplomatic intervention on behalf of the schools, but he supported the Board's application to resume operation of the schools at Sivas, Gaziantep, Caesarea, Talas, and Marash. After Grew pointed out to Foreign Minister Aras that the staffs were ready and waiting to begin work at Talas and Marash, Aras promised to support the Board's position in talks with Nedjati Bey.[39] The Foreign Minister later linked the question of reopening schools with the Turkish wish to purchase some buildings in Anatolia where there were no plans to resume operations. Although the Board sent a representative to Ankara to talk with Turkish officials about this proposition, no immediate action resulted on either problem.[40]

A few months later when the Bursa incident occurred, Grew suggested to Turkish officials that its adverse effects in the United States could be eliminated if they would permit the reopening of one or more American

[37] Text of the treaty, *Papers Relating to the Foreign Relations of the United States, 1931* (3 vols., Washington, 1946), II, 1042–1043. See below, pp. 194–200.

[38] Editor's note, Grew, *Turbulent Era*, II, 746–747, n. 18; diary, conversation, Grew and Goodsell, October 5, 1927, Grew MSS, 1927, vol. 1.

[39] Conversation, Grew and Aras, November 3, 1927, Grew, *Turbulent Era*, II, 746–747; aide-mémoire, Embassy to Turkish Foreign Office, November 3, 1927, *Papers Relating to the Foreign Relations of the United States, 1927* (3 vols., Washington, 1942), III, 809–810 (hereafter cited as *FR 1927*); Grew to Kellogg, November 5, 1927, *ibid.*, 804–805.

[40] Aras to Grew, November 13, 1927, *FR 1927*, 810; Grew to Kellogg, November 23, 1927, *ibid.*, 806–809; Grew to Aras, December 2, 1927, *ibid.*, 812. The American Board negotiated the sale of several of its Anatolian school properties to the Turkish government in 1933. See Sherrill to Hull, March 6, 1933, DS 367.1163/20.

schools. Thereupon, the government on February 26, 1928, authorized the reopening of the boys' school at Sivas and the addition of a vocational department to the school at Merzifoun.[41] Later Grew discovered that the concession was not really significant, since the Ministry of Public Instruction on its own initiative previously had requested a vocational department at Merzifoun. Also puzzling was the fact that the Ministry of Public Health held a lease on the school at Sivas until 1930, whereas the government had specified that it must be opened in September, 1928. Grew felt that Nedjati Bey was resorting to "Machiavellian tactics" and that his *"beau geste . . .* cost him nothing because it is incapable of fulfillment. . . . I haven't the slightest belief that Nedjati Bey intends to permit the reopening of any of our schools at all."[42] When Grew explained the Sivas situation to the Foreign Minister, Aras "gave every evidence of perturbation and said that he was entirely unaware of this situation." Aras fulfilled his promise to release the Sivas building or to reopen another American school in August, 1928, when the Ministry of Public Instruction announced that the institution at Talas could reopen if it would allow Turkish instructors to teach certain subjects, appoint a Turkish vice-principal, and comply with several other conditions. Ambassador Grew felt that the Talas concession was "a distinct victory in a long-pending issue." [43] This gesture served to satisfy Grew and the American Board representatives, but the Turks did not intend to make really significant concessions because the building at Talas was the only one permitted to reopen. Several American newspapers viewed the Talas action "as testifying to the Turkish Republic's appreciative attitude toward American educators, as well as to the ability of Ambassador Grew to create a closer Turkish-American understanding." [44] Incidentally, if the Turks had permitted other schools to resume instruction, the American Board probably would have closed them later, in view of the curtailment of its work arising from financial difficulties during the depression.

A troublesome problem for American educational institutions in Turkey was heavy taxation, which at times forced them to consider closing.

[41] Conversation, Grew and Inönü, February 21, 1928, Grew, *Turbulent Era,* II, 766; diary, February 26, 1928, *ibid.,* 767; New York *Times,* February 27, 1928.

[42] Diary, February 29, 1928, Grew, *Turbulent Era,* II, 769–771.

[43] Conversation, April 19, 1928, Grew MSS, 1928, vol. 3; diary, August 20, 1928, Grew, *Turbulent Era,* II, 789. The school finally reopened in the fall of 1928, after a further delay in issuing the permit. See diary, September 29, 1928, *ibid.,* 794–795.

[44] The item appears as quoted in the New York *Times,* August 23, 1928, and the New York *Sun,* August 23, 1928, clippings in Grew MSS, 1928, vol. 4.

Of the various taxes imposed by the Turkish government after 1927, the most irritating ones applied to inheritances, bequests, and buildings. The gift tax, enacted by the Grand National Assembly on April 3, 1926, provided for taxation of from 10 to 30 per cent on the transfer of property by inheritance, bequest, donation, or any other gift form. Apparently the legislation was to prevent evasion of inheritance taxes by persons who transferred their property to prospective heirs before death.[45] The Turkish government first applied the law to American educational institutions in 1927, when it assessed a tax of fifteen hundred liras against the American Collegiate Institute in Istanbul. The American Board paid part of the tax but appealed through various Turkish courts to the Council of State in Ankara. Before the Council made its final decision, Istanbul Woman's College was requested to pay £T109,000 in back taxes.[46]

The gift tax posed a serious problem for the schools because if actually collected it would consume a significant part of their income from sources in the United States. Representatives of the institutions stated emphatically that they could not continue their work if the Turks persisted in collecting the tax. Fred F. Goodsell noted that this "would inevitably cripple the service which the American Board seeks to render in Turkey. . . . We cannot ask even the best friends of Turkey to carry such a burden." [47] Grew explained this situation clearly to Turkish authorities and stressed the adverse effect the closing of the institutions would have on American public opinion and on Turkish-American relations in general.[48] The colleges and the American Board felt that they should be exempt from the tax, since funds received from the United States represented investment income of the colleges or direct subscriptions to the American Board rather than gifts or bequests. Financial support from the United States was simply money sent to pay the operating expenses of the institutions. Grew pointed out to Turkish officials another significant fact: that Turkish stu-

[45] Grew to Stimson, January 8, 1930, DS 367.1164/126; Fowle to Station Treasurers and Heads of Institutions in Turkey, May 5, 1930, ABCFM MSS, ABC 16.5, vol. 11, no. 162A.

[46] *Ibid.*; diary, April 2, 1930, Grew MSS, 1930, vol. 3.

[47] Goodsell, "Memorandum Regarding the Inheritance Tax Case," March 27, 1929, ABCFM MSS, ABC 16.9.1, vol. 4, no. 220; conversation, Grew and Aras, April 8, 1930, Grew, *Turbulent Era*, II, 852–854.

[48] Diary, conversation, Grew and Aras, March 21, 1929, Grew MSS, 1929, vol. 3; Grew to Aras, December 24, 1929, *Papers Relating to the Foreign Relations of the United States, 1930* (3 vols., Washington, 1945), III, 873–874 (hereafter cited as *FR 1930*).

dents benefited from reduced tuition rates because of financial support from the United States.[49]

When Grew learned about the tax on Istanbul Woman's College, he immediately discussed the problem with the Foreign Minister and Prime Minister İnönü. The Prime Minister, who explained that the Ministries of Finance and Public Instruction disagreed about whether the tax should apply, promised it would not be pressed until the Council of State made a final decision.[50] The Council held in July, 1930, that the tax should not be applicable to money received by the American Collegiate Institute in a current account from the American Board in the United States.[51] This decision favorable to American institutions set a precedent later applied to all the schools and colleges. One American Board missionary wrote: "It is a cause for devout thanksgiving that the highest authorities, when appealed to, have stood for justice and not for financial bleeding." Grew described the decision as "an immense satisfaction as it removes what was unquestionably my outstanding diplomatic problem and a problem which has caused a great deal of anxiety." He also thought that his representations to Ismet İnönü "turned the trick." [52]

The buildings tax, enacted in 1931, bothered the schools and colleges throughout the 1930s. In April, 1932, the Minister of Finance decided that American institutions were exempt since they "serve the cause of public instruction in Turkey," they "are not established with the aim of financial profit," and the buildings are not "rented or hired." [53] Luther Fowle of the American Board wrote: "Perhaps the most significant aspect of this situation is that the Ministry of Public Instruction officially and categorically goes on record as to the value which it places on our schools. . . . I find it very gratifying and believe that it marks another step in the development of mutually satisfactory relationships on a basis not of outside

[49] Grew to Stimson, January 8, 1930, DS 367.1164/126; Grew to Aras, December 24, 1929, *FR 1930*, III, 873.
[50] Conversation, Grew and Aras, April 8, 1930, Grew, *Turbulent Era*, II, 852–854; conversation, Grew and İnönü, April 9, 1930, *ibid.*, 854–855; Grew to Acting Secretary of State, April 17, 1930, *FR 1930*, III, 876–878.
[51] Grew to Stimson, July 25, 1930, *FR 1930*, III, 879.
[52] Charles T. Riggs to Mabel E. Emerson and Ernest W. Riggs (American Board Secretaries, Boston), July 14, 1930, ABCFM MSS, ABC 16.5, vol. 11, no. 7; diary, July 14, 1930, Grew, *Turbulent Era*, II, 858.
[53] Fowle to H. B. Belcher, Goodsell, and E. W. Riggs, April 12, 1932, ABCFM MSS, ABC 16.5, vol. 12, no. 487. See also Shaw to Stimson, April 19, 1932, DS 367.1164/172.

compulsion but a basis of cooperation and mutual confidence in a common endeavor for the well-being of the youth of Turkey." [54]

In 1934, however, because of the attempt of a non-American institution to benefit from the situation, Turkish authorities reopened the question and subsequently applied the tax to American schools and colleges,
with demands that back taxes be paid for all years beginning with 1931.
When pressed by Turkish officials, the American Collegiate Institute in
Izmir and Istanbul Woman's College appealed the decision but actually
made tax payments. In the case of the college, the Turks threatened se-
questration and sale of its property if the tax was not paid. [55] The problem
became acute late in 1936, when the highest Turkish court rejected the petition of the colleges for exemption from the tax. At this time Walter L.
Wright, Jr., president of both Robert College and Istanbul Woman's College, conferred with government officials, who told him that the Ministry
of Finance was not anxious to collect the tax, but that it would have to do
so unless some other arrangement could be made with the more insistent
Ministry of Public Instruction. [56]

The colleges considered the buildings tax situation critical. President
Wright complained that the absence of high United States diplomatic officials from Turkey at the time weakened the colleges' bargaining position. [57]
The State Department in Washington described the seriousness of the situation to Turkish Ambassador Münir Ertegün, a graduate of one of the
mission schools. If American educational institutions were forced to close,
Ertegün was told, the event "would not fail to have a widespread reper-
cussion in this country and might have an unfortunate effect upon the generally favorable public attitude in this country towards Turkey." [58] In
June, 1938, the Ministry of Public Instruction again decided that American schools and colleges would be exempt from the buildings tax because

[54] Fowle to Belcher, Goodsell, and Riggs, April 12, 1932, ABCFM MSS, ABC 16.5,
vol. 12, no. 487.

[55] H. H. Kreider to Station Treasurers, Near East Mission, March 24, 1938,
ibid., vol. 11, no. 185 (this circular letter summarizes the history of taxation of
American institutions in Turkey from before World War I to 1938); Fowle to School
Directors and Station Treasurers in Turkey, December 6, 1935, *ibid.*, no. 183.

[56] John V. A. MacMurray to Hull, December 29, 1936, DS 367.1164 R54/131
(reporting conversation with Walter L. Wright, Jr., November 15, 1936).

[57] Wright to MacMurray, February 14, 1938, DS 367.1164 R54/134. Counselor
of Embassy G. Howland Shaw left for an assignment in Washington in mid-1937,
and Ambassador MacMurray was serving temporarily in the Philippines.

[58] Memo of conversation, Wallace Murray (Chief, Near East Division) and
Münir Ertegün, March 2, 1938, DS 367.1164 R54/132.

they "serve public instruction." The exemptions officially applied to 1938 and after, but the Turkish government later decided not to collect taxes for previous years.[59]

It is especially significant that the Turkish government ultimately decided to exempt American educational institutions from both taxes. The exemptions proved that the attempted application of the taxes was not part of a concerted effort to drive all American schools from Turkey. Had this been the objective, the Turks could have forced the institutions to close by insisting upon payment. The Turkish desire to impose these taxes was rather an effort to raise badly needed revenue. When it became clear that the schools would close if the tax laws applied, the government backed down. The interest of American diplomatic officials in the cause of the schools and the adverse effect their closing would have had on Turkish-American relations were important factors in the final Turkish decision.

Restrictions other than taxes which the Turkish government imposed on American educational institutions also helped to curtail their work. Turkish officials made frequent inspections, sometimes quite arbitrary, to ensure that the schools complied with the various regulations. A rash of inspections occurred, for instance, after the incident at Bursa in 1928.[60] In 1931, government officials decreed that all Turkish pupils must attend Turkish schools through the primary grades, a step which resulted in the elimination of the lower grades where they existed in American Board schools.[61] The new regulation on primary grades came at a time when the American Board's financial condition became critical because of the depression; thus there was little protest about the new ruling. The Turkish government also regulated the hiring of teachers and the subjects they could teach. The American Board reported in 1926 that strict government rules about diplomas had temporarily prevented one of its teachers from acting as principal of the girls' school at Adana. The report also mentioned

[59] MacMurray to Hull, June 20, 1938, DS 367.1164 R54/138; MacMurray to Hull, September 3, 1938, DS 367.1164 R54/140; MacMurray to Hull, February 3, 1939, DS 367.1164 R54/142.

[60] Diary, February 14, 1928, Grew, *Turbulent Era*, II, 762–763; diary, conversation, Grew and Cass A. Reed (President, International College, Izmir), October 18, 1927, Grew MSS, 1927, vol. 1; *The One Hundred and Sixteenth Annual Report of the American Board of Commissioners for Foreign Missions* [1926] (Boston, n.d.), p. 79 (hereafter cited as *ABCFM Report, 1926*).

[61] Ethel W. Putney (American Board teacher, Istanbul) to Mabel Emerson, March 30, 1931, ABCFM MSS, ABC 16.5, vol. 15, no. 177.

the practice of assigning government-appointed Turkish teachers to teach certain subjects.[62] In August, 1931, the Ministry of Public Instruction expanded and formalized this procedure in an order specifying that history, geography, and civics must be taught in the Turkish language by Turkish teachers. This applied both to the American Board schools and the independent colleges. Grew, disturbed because this would put some American instructors out of work with little notice and necessitate the hasty hiring of Turkish teachers, was able to secure a year's delay in the application of the change to American institutions. A teacher who wrote sympathetically to the American Board pointed out that the rules were not dictated specifically against American schools, but "are rather signs of progress which makes it possible for them to give their children a more locally useful education. . . . Do pray that in their natural desire to control . . . foreign schools they may not throw away elements needed in the best education of their children." [63]

Although prohibition of religious teaching, imposition of taxes, curriculum requirements, and other restrictions were bothersome, the only American Board school actually closed by direct Turkish action was the Girls' Lycée at Bursa. By 1939, however, only three of the nine Board institutions existing in 1927, plus the school reopened at Talas, were still operating. With the exception of International College at Izmir, the schools closed because of financial difficulties. International College, when it closed in 1934, was no longer connected with the American Board, but was a member of the Near East College Association.[64] International College traditionally had more difficulty than Robert College and Istanbul Woman's College, partly because the college was located in the extremely nationalistic area of Izmir, where the final victory of the Turks over the Greeks had taken place in 1922. The student body of the college before World War I, as a matter of fact, was mainly recruited from the Greek community. The

[62] *ABCFM Report, 1926,* p. 79.
[63] Grew to Stimson, August 24, 1931, DS 367.1164/159; diary, August 23, 1931, Grew MSS, 1931, vol. 2; Ethel W. Putney, unaddressed, September 5, 1931, ABCFM MSS, ABC 16.5, vol. 15, no. 186.
[64] *The One Hundred and Twenty-First Annual Report of the American Board of Commissioners for Foreign Missions* [1931] (Boston, n.d.), p. 73. The Near East College Association, directed by Albert W. Staub, was incorporated in New York in 1928. It developed from an office established in 1920 to represent Robert College and the American University of Beirut. See Bayard Dodge, "The American University of Beirut, International College and Damascus College, 1910–1948," *Annual Report* (Beirut, 1948), pp. 11, 15 (hereafter cited as Dodge, *Annual Report, 1910–1948*).

inclusion of "international" in its title also disturbed many Turks because of their intense nationalistic feelings. Furthermore, the institution was plagued by administrative troubles, a faculty including many Turks who were not loyal to the college, and disciplinary problems.[65] The difficulties of Hunter Mead, an instructor at International College in 1931, illustrate the last point. Mead, after detecting several students cheating on an examination, allegedly "made remarks to his pupils disparaging to Turkish official honesty," causing the public prosecutor at Izmir to charge him with insulting the Turkish nation. The Turks wanted to avoid serious trouble and thus permitted Mead to leave Turkey unmolested, but the incident brought much unfavorable publicity to the college and contributed to its unpopularity among the Turks.[66]

Because of the difficulties at International College, President Cass A. Reed announced in June, 1934, that the board of trustees had decided to close the institution. The consul at Izmir reported that the press there "has observed the closing of International College with satisfaction, and has even been so petty as to seize the opportunity to hurl a few final insults at the benefactors." [67] In 1936, the trustees of International College accepted an invitation to move the college name and much of its program to Lebanon to affiliate with the American University of Beirut. At Beirut, the junior college, the French lycée course, the farm management course, and the preparatory school classes became the work of International College. Eventually a Turkish normal school purchased the Izmir campus.[68]

The financial difficulties which caused the closing of several American Board schools were due to decreasing support from the Congregational Church in the United States. One reason for this, according to Ernest W. Riggs, an American Board official, was the difficulty of convincing people that they should make contributions to schools giving Turkish students a purely secular education. Also critical were the effects of the post-1929 depression, which understandably forced the American Board to curtail

[65] Memo of conversation, Murray and Rev. William W. Patton (Member, International College Board of Trustees), September 18, 1934, DS 367.1164/212; Sherrill to Stimson, August 26, 1932, DS 367.1164/182; Skinner to Hull, June 14, 1934, DS 367.1164/205; Dodge, *Annual Report*, 1910–1948, pp. 14, 19.

[66] Grew to Stimson, January 23, 1931, DS 367.1164/138; Herbert S. Bursley (Consul, Izmir) to Stimson, January 29, 1931, DS 367.1164/144.

[67] Skinner to Hull, June 14, 1934, DS 367.1164/205; W. Perry George to Skinner, July 31, 1934, DS 367.1164/213.

[68] Dodge, *Annual Report*, 1910–1948, pp. 19–20; *The One Hundred and Twenty-Sixth Annual Report of the American Board of Commissioners for Foreign Missions* [1936] (Boston, n.d.), p. 20 (hereafter cited as *ABCFM Report, 1936*).

its work in Turkey as well as in other fields. American Board officials met in Hartford, Connecticut, in April, 1932, to consider the necessity of reducing the appropriation of the Turkish mission. A subsequent reduction caused the immediate closing of the Girls' School at Adana and the American Collegiate Institute in Istanbul. For the same reason the Board closed another school in Istanbul in 1933 and the Girls' School at Merzifoun in 1938.[69] By 1939 the only schools operated by the American Board were the American Academy for Girls, Istanbul; the American Collegiate Institute, Izmir; the American School for Boys, Talas; and the American College, Tarsus.[70]

Robert College and Istanbul Woman's College, partly because they had no religious affiliations, were more acceptable to the Turks than the mission schools. Fortunately for Robert College, an ill-advised plan to institute religious activities there did not materialize. When Henry Sloane Coffin, chairman of Robert College's Board of Trustees, visited Turkey in January, 1935, he intended to examine the possibility of introducing religious elements into the college program, as actually required by the college charter. Ambassador Skinner, worried about the purposes of Coffin's visit, wrote the Secretary of State that the Turks would never permit Robert College to make such changes in its program. Coffin apparently appreciated this fact, because he did not bring up the religious issue during his visit. His talks with Turkish officials, including Prime Minister Ismet Inönü, did indicate that the Turks valued the work of Robert College.[71]

One of the most critical problems of the colleges was unrelated to Turkish regulations. Ambassador Grew outlined the basic issue in July, 1930, in a despatch considering differences of opinion over administrative and educational policies in both colleges. Although the Turks wanted

[69] Memo of conversation, Murray and E. W. Riggs, July 29, 1931, DS 367.1164/157; circular letter, E. W. Riggs, unaddressed, April 6, 1932, ABCFM MSS, ABC 16.5, vol. 12, no. 381; Sherrill to Stimson, July 11, 1932, DS 367.1164/176; *The One Hundred and Twenty-Second Annual Report of the American Board of Commissioners for Foreign Missions* [1932] (Boston, n.d.), pp. 14–15; Goodsell, *You Shall Be My Witnesses*, pp. 227–231; New York *Times*, October 1, 1933; *The One Hundred and Twenty-Eighth Annual Report of the American Board of Commissioners for Foreign Missions* [1938] (Boston, n.d.), p. 11.

[70] *The Call for Colleagues, The One Hundred Twenty-Ninth Annual Report of the American Board of Commissioners for Foreign Missions, 1939* (Boston, n.d.), pp. 51–52.

[71] Skinner to Hull, December 11, 1934, DS 367.1164 R54/115; Skinner to Hull, January 23, 1935, DS 367.1164 R54/117. For comments on the colleges, see Robert L. Daniel, "The United States and the Turkish Republic Before World War II: The Cultural Dimension," *Middle East Journal*, XXI (Winter, 1967), 52–63.

practical programs, some college leaders were reluctant to give such an orientation to their work. Referring to Istanbul Woman's College, Grew explained that the Turks "are more interested in future Turkish house-wives than in future A.M.s and Ph.D.s." Grew deplored the lack of admin-istrative talent at the colleges, and expressed concern that if they did not develop "a positive program adapted to the needs of the Turkey of 1930 and a strong and energetic leadership," their future would be insecure.[72]

In 1932, Paul Monroe, Director of the International Institute at Teachers' College, Columbia University, became president of both Robert and Istanbul Woman's colleges. At Robert College he succeeded Caleb Frank Gates, who had served there as president since 1903.[73] Monroe ar-rived in Turkey with the objective of making the college programs more compatible with the Turks' own system of education. Ambassador Sher-rill reported that he found "the entire Ankara atmosphere changed toward our educational institutions since they have been informed of Professor Monroe's selection as President and also of my information given them about his plans fitting into the Turkish system." [74] In his search for a mis-sion for the institutions, Monroe developed the idea of transforming Rob-ert College into a Balkan educational center, which, he felt, would give it a special status with the Turks.[75] As Monroe explained it, "If the College could recover its old function as a cultural institute for the entire Balkan people and be recognized as an instrument of the Turkish people to gain the cultural leadership of the Balkan people, it would give us a new life and an assured future." When Monroe proposed the plan, the Turkish government showed no interest. Aras, the foreign minister, pointed out to Ambassador Skinner that the idea "might awaken sleeping national sus-ceptibilities" in Turkey and that "it was not yet a Turkish ideal to accom-plish a fusion or even federation of the [Balkan] States." [76]

Monroe had agreed to administer the colleges only temporarily. Thus in 1935 he was succeeded by Walter L. Wright, Jr., a historian at Prince-

[72] Grew to Stimson, July 28, 1930, DS 367.1164/134; Grew to Stimson, June 29, 1931, DS 367.1164/155.
[73] Albert W. Staub to Murray, June 9, 1932, DS 367.1164 R54/77. See Caleb Frank Gates, *Not to Me Only* (Princeton, 1940), for an account of the author's work in Turkey and at Robert College.
[74] To Stimson, November 1, 1932, DS 367.1164 R54/83.
[75] Skinner to Hull, January 15, 1934, DS 367.0064/7; Skinner to Murray, Feb-ruary 24, 1934, DS 124.671/122.
[76] Paul Monroe to Murray, April 3, 1934, DS 367.1164 R54/103; Skinner to Hull, March 26, 1934, DS 367.1164 R54/104.

ton University who had earlier been an instructor at the American University of Beirut and a trustee of Istanbul Woman's College. Wright, according to Ambassador John V. A. MacMurray, "made it clear that the purpose of the Colleges is to serve the new Turkey and he has spared no pains in seeking to bring the Colleges into contact with the life of the country." [77] There is no indication that the colleges experienced any serious difficulties with Turkish authorities other than the tax problems after the end of the Gates administration. Gates represented the old order among American educators in Turkey, whereas Monroe and Wright were more interested in adapting Robert College and Istanbul Woman's College to the aspirations of Turkish nationalism.

Conclusions

In 1939, the colleges and the four remaining schools of the American Board were operating satisfactorily. The Turkish government thought well enough of the school at Talas to support the education of fifty Turkish boys there in 1938. [78] The very fact that the Board schools were in existence in 1939 is proof that they had adjusted to Turkish nationalism. This adjustment did not come without hesitation, but the American institutions realized that they must either conform to Turkish policy or end their work. The events at Bursa in 1928 proved this. As for the missionaries, their decision was to rely on "unnamed Christianity" to propagate their faith. The two independent colleges found that their goal should be to offer to Turkish youth the type of education most fitted to the needs of the Republic of Turkey. The question whether American educators adjusted to Turkish nationalism, with its emphases on secularism, can be answered clearly in the affirmative.

It is more difficult to decide whether the determination to continue American educational work in Turkey was wise or produced fruitful results. The Turkish government proved in December, 1939, that it still demanded strict adherence to its laws when it closed the Young Men's Christian Association in Istanbul, along with its affiliates, a language and commercial school and a student hostel. The institutions were closed on the basis of a 1938 law requiring all associations operating in Turkey to

[77] Skinner to Hull, June 12, 1935, DS 367.1164 R54/126; MacMurray to Hull, July 10, 1936, DS 367.1164 R54/129.

[78] William Paton and M. M. Underhill, "A Survey of the Year 1938," *International Review of Missions*, XXVIII (January, 1939), 42.

have their headquarters there, a requirement with which the YMCA, of course, could not comply. Later the school and hostel reopened after they severed their connections with the YMCA. Although the Governor of Istanbul "made it clear that there was not the slightest feeling against the American institutions involved, or against American institutions in general," the Turkish action indicated that the position of American establishments was not yet absolutely guaranteed.[79]

The mission schools were filled to capacity in 1939 and had educated thousands of young Turks during the interwar period, but there was no increase in the number of Christians in Turkey. A foremost student of Christian missions, referring to the Middle East and Northern Africa, observed that on the eve of World War II "the outlook was sombre for a Christianity which was not well rooted in the soil but was dependent upon continuing infusions of life from Europe and America."[80] Another writer, however, concluded that the missionary work in Turkey "has produced a marked increase in mutual understanding. . . . With confidence on both sides growing stronger, the way has been prepared for an expanding influence."[81] The American Board optimistically reported in 1936 that it was rendering "a significant and far-reaching service. . . . Here is disinterested service in the name and in the spirit of Christ which can not fail to affect the life of the new Turkey." As late as 1953, the Board observed that its role in the Middle East "remains the essential one of representing the *Christian* West, of bringing the unique gift of Jesus Christ."[82]

The missionaries in the field sometimes questioned the immediate value of their work, but felt that the ultimate results would be significant. Luther Fowle, for instance, wrote in 1934: "I believe it is quite possible that one hundred years hence the apparently ineffective work which we are doing here in Turkey may prove to have been a larger contribution than the altogether admirable work carried on among refugee populations."[83] Whatever the case, the schools provided one of the few direct

[79] MacMurray to Hull, January 15, 1940, *Foreign Relations of the United States: Diplomatic Papers, 1940* (5 vols., Washington, 1955–1958), III, 990–994; MacMurray to Hull, March 27, 1940, *ibid.*, 996–998.

[80] Latourette, *A History of the Expansion of Christianity*, VII, 269, 272–273.

[81] James Thayer Addison, *The Christian Approach to the Moslem* (New York, 1942), p. 111.

[82] *ABCFM Report, 1936*, p. 10; *143rd Annual Report to the Churches, 1953* (Boston, 1954), p. 8.

[83] To E. W. Riggs (President, Anatolia College, Saloniki, Greece), January 11, 1934, ABCFM MSS, ABC 16.5, vol. 27, no. 409.

links between Americans and Turks, facilitating the spread of Western culture and ideals. American Christian educators, by remaining in Turkey during a highly nationalistic period in that country's history, made substantial contributions. Most important, they demonstrated the attitudes and methods necessary for satisfactory relations between Christianity and Islam.

✿ The Expansion of Friendship: Social, Cultural, and Philanthropic Activities

ALTHOUGH the settling of many specific diplomatic problems contributed greatly to the development of rapprochement between Turkey and the United States in the interwar period, social, cultural, and philanthropic activities also were extremely valuable. As already noted, the educational work of the missionaries, in part a philanthropic effort, was an important kind of interrelationship between Turks and Americans. The American Board of Commissioners for Foreign Missions also supported a medical program, which, together with two independent American hospitals, provided badly needed medical facilities in Turkey. Another outlet for American charity materialized when physical disaster struck. The American Red Cross, working through a sister organization in Turkey, extended aid on several occasions. A third evidence of American philanthropy was the substantial contribution to the relief of Russian refugees living in the Istanbul area. America's interest in Turkey, demonstrated through philanthropy, aided the increasing friendship between the two nations.

The only serious social problem complicating Turco-American relations in the interwar era was the illicit international traffic in narcotics. The United States was very much concerned about the smuggling of narcotics of Turkish origin through American ports. The combined pressure of world opinion and United States diplomats led to considerable progress in eliminating the problem.

Extensive cultural exchanges between the two countries were a useful means of expanding mutual friendship and understanding. American archaeologists working in Turkey, Turkish students in the United States, the

170

publication of American literature in Turkey, and the participation of American scholars in Turkish historical congresses were significant cultural contacts.

American diplomatic representatives in Turkey occasionally had to intervene in disputes resulting from these social, cultural and philanthropic activities, but they generally were carried on harmoniously. There were few clashes with Turkish nationalism, since the American citizens concerned demonstrated an ability to adjust to Turkish nationalism and a willingness to contribute to the domestic progress of the Turkish Republic.

American Medical Projects in Turkey

Exclusive of schools, the most important institutional work of Americans in Turkey was in hospitals and clinics. The American Board established several medical installations in Turkey before World War I. Nine hospitals existed in 1914, but several closed during the war period. By the mid-1920s, the Board still operated three, including the Azariah Smith Memorial Hospital at Gaziantep, established in 1884, the American Hospital at Adana, founded in 1909, and the American Hospital at Talas, which began its work in 1888. The Board also maintained several dispensaries which worked in cooperation with the hospitals. In 1926–1927, these medical institutions handled almost ten thousand new patients.[1] The most important American medical installation in Turkey, however, was the independent American Hospital in Istanbul, established in 1920 to provide medical service to Americans. Mark L. Bristol was a leader in founding the institution, which twenty years later was renamed the Admiral Bristol Hospital.[2]

Various restrictions resulting from Turkish nationalism complicated American medical work in Turkey. A suspicion of foreigners contributed to a desire to restrict the medical profession to native doctors. Both Admiral Bristol and Ambassador Grew recognized that the Turkish government's reluctance to license foreigners was the chief obstacle to American

---

[1] *The One Hundred and Seventeenth Annual Report of the American Board of Commissioners for Foreign Missions* [1927] (Boston, n.d.), pp. 4, 77–78 (hereafter cited as *ABCFM Report, 1927*). See also Robert L. Daniel, "The United States and the Turkish Republic Before World War II: The Cultural Dimension," *Middle East Journal*, XXI (Winter, 1967), 56.

[2] Lynn A. Scipio, *My Thirty Years in Turkey* (Rindge, N.H., 1955), pp. 188–189; radio address by Joseph C. Grew, June 12, 1930, in Joseph C. Grew, *Turbulent Era: A Diplomatic Record of Forty Years, 1904–1945*, ed. Walter Johnson (2 vols., Boston, 1952), II, 856–858.

medical work in Turkey. Bristol noted in 1924 that "hostility towards foreign doctors is a personal obsession" with some Turkish officials, and that American doctors waiting for permission to practice in Turkey were discouraged and were thinking of leaving.[3] According to the American Board, the Turkish government refused to license foreign doctors on the questionable grounds that there were too many native doctors. The American Board believed that the jealousy of doctors graduating from the Turkish medical school at Istanbul had influenced government regulations, which denied licenses to foreign doctors unless they had practiced in Turkey before World War I.[4] In 1927, mainly as a result of Bristol's work, the Turkish government licensed three American Board doctors, Dr. Lorrin Shepard, Dr. Albert W. Dewey, and Dr. Wilson F. Dodd; Dr. William L. Nute, another Board doctor, received a license in 1928. All except Shepard, for whom an exception was made, had begun their work before 1914.[5]

A law passed in April, 1928, provided that only Turkish citizens with a diploma from the University of Istanbul could practice medicine in Turkey, except for those foreign doctors who already had licenses.[6] The Turkish government jealously regulated the work of these foreign practitioners. In December, 1930, for instance, the Ministry of Hygiene appointed a Turkish doctor as surgeon of the American Hospital in Istanbul. The Ministry recognized Dr. Lorrin Shepard, the head doctor at the hospital, as a physician but not as a surgeon. Ambassador Grew, who felt that this "bolt from the blue . . . opens up a most serious prospect," believed that the hospital should discontinue its work "if the Ministry of Hygiene is going to arrogate to itself the right to dictate who shall be members of the staff." After Grew protested, the Ministry acknowledged Shepard as a surgeon and withdrew the Turkish doctor.[7]

[3] Mark L. Bristol to Charles Evans Hughes, September 27, 1923, DS 867.1281/11. See also Bristol to Hughes, March 7, 1924, DS 867.1281/16.
[4] *The One Hundred and Thirteenth Annual Report of the American Board of Commissioners for Foreign Missions* [1923] (Boston, n.d.), p. 54 (hereafter cited as *ABCFM Report, 1923*); *The One Hundred and Fourteenth Annual Report of the American Board of Commissioners for Foreign Missions* [1924] (Boston, n.d.), pp. 67–68 (hereafter cited as *ABCFM Report, 1924*).
[5] *ABCFM Report, 1927*, pp. 61–62; *The One Hundred and Eighteenth Annual Report of the American Board of Commissioners for Foreign Missions* [1928] (Boston, n.d.), p. 69 (hereafter cited as *ABCFM Report, 1928*); Sheldon L. Crosby (Chargé d'Affaires) to Frank B. Kellogg, August 22, 1927, DS 867.1281/20.
[6] Grew to Kellogg, April 6, 1928, DS 867.1281/22.
[7] Diary, December 16, 1930, Joseph C. Grew MSS (Houghton Library, Harvard

Because of Turkish restrictions and financial difficulties, the American Board curtailed its medical activities in the mid-1930s. By 1939 the only Board hospital in operation was the Azariah Smith Hospital at Gaziantep, but clinics were still open at Adana and Talas.[8] The American Hospital in Istanbul, although experiencing considerable financial difficulties of its own, made significant progress by 1939. This was due in part to the great interest the American colony in Istanbul, and especially Ambassador Grew, had taken in the hospital. When Grew arrived in Turkey in 1927, the Advisory Committee of Americans in Istanbul was thinking of closing the hospital because of insufficient funds, and in February, 1928, the Committee actually voted to begin liquidation on March 1. Grew wanted to preserve the hospital and took the initiative in an attempt to secure grants from the Rockefeller Foundation and the American Red Cross, which had contributed originally to the support of the institution. Neither of these organizations found it possible to aid the hospital at that time.[9] Grew did secure a donation of $6,000 from J. Pierpont Morgan when the latter visited Istanbul in April, 1928. This and other contributions from the American colony and various United States commercial interests in Turkey enabled the hospital to continue its work. In October, 1928, to cut expenses, the hospital facilities moved to another building which could be rented for less than the original quarters.[10]

In 1930, when the hospital faced another financial crisis, the Americans in Istanbul decided to conduct an appeal for support in the United States. On June 12, 1930, while Grew was on leave in the United States, he launched this campaign with a radio address explaining the work of the

University, Cambridge, Mass.), 1930, vol. 3; Grew to Bristol, January 25, 1931, *ibid.*, 1931, vol. 1. Dr. Shepard, an American Board doctor, was loaned to the private American Hospital in Istanbul but received part of his salary from the Board.

[8] *The One Hundred and Twenty-Fourth Annual Report of the American Board of Commissioners for Foreign Missions* [1934] (Boston, n.d.), pp. 5–6 (hereafter cited as *ABCFM Report, 1934*); *The Call for Colleagues, the One Hundred Twenty-Ninth Annual Report of the American Board of Commissioners for Foreign Missions, 1939* (Boston, n.d.), pp. 51–52 (hereafter cited as *ABCFM Report, 1939*). See above, pp. 164–165, for a discussion of the financial troubles of the American Board.

[9] Diary, October 7, 1927, Grew MSS, 1927, vol. 1; diary, February 22, 1928, *ibid.*, 1928, vol. 3; conversation, Grew and Ralph Collins (Near East representative, Rockefeller Foundation), November 19, 1927, *ibid.*, 1927, vol. 1; Grew to Judge Payne (American Red Cross), February 23, 1928, *ibid.*, 1928, vol. 3; diary, March 1, 1928, *ibid.*

[10] Grew to J. Pierpont Morgan, April 8, 1928, *ibid.*, 1928, vol. 2; Grew to Morgan, April 10, 1928, *ibid.*; New York *Times*, January 27, 1929; "The American Hospital of Constantinople," *Levant Trade Review*, XVI (October, 1928), 379.

American Hospital and its nurses training school. "Often have I come across the practical results of America's philanthropy," Grew said, "but in no country have I known of a more noble, helpful and effective institution than the American Hospital in Istanbul." [11] The money raised through this appeal, headed by Admiral Bristol, saw the hospital through its financial troubles. In 1938, hospital officials broke ground for a new building which was completed in 1939.[12]

Another notable example of American medical philanthropy in Turkey was the Schinasi Hospital. Morris Schinasi, who died in New York in September, 1928, had come to the United States from Manisa in Asia Minor about 1893. As a wholesale tobacco merchant and manufacturer of Turkish cigarettes, he amassed a fortune appraised at over $8,000,000 at the time of his death. His will provided $1,000,000 for the construction and maintenance of a hospital in Manisa, a city of about ten thousand persons a short distance northeast of Izmir. The hospital was to cost not more than $200,000, with the rest of the fund to be held in trust, its income available to the hospital. In May, 1930, Mrs. Schinasi and several Turkish officials laid the cornerstone for the building, which was finally dedicated on August 15, 1933. The Turkish Grand National Assembly cooperated by passing a law in December, 1931, donating the land for the hospital and admitting duty free its initial equipment and drugs. The law required that treatment should be free unless the income provided by Schinasi was not enough to support the forty-bed institution. In this event, fees could be charged for one-fifth of the beds in the hospital.[13]

The work of the American Board hospitals and clinics, the American Hospital in Istanbul, and the Schinasi Hospital was one aspect of the extensive contribution of American philanthropy in Turkey. These medical institutions had to comply with restrictions imposed upon them because

[11] Diary, January 13, 1930, Grew MSS, 1930, vol. 3; radio address, Grew, *Turbulent Era*, II, 856–858.

[12] Diary, June 28, 1931, Grew MSS, 1931, vol. 2; *The One Hundred and Twenty-Eighth Annual Report of the American Board of Commissioners for Foreign Missions* [1938] (Boston, n.d.), p. 12 (hereafter cited as *ABCFM Report, 1938*); *ABCFM Report, 1939*, p. 51; Scipio, *My Thirty Years in Turkey*, p. 189; Bristol to John V. A. MacMurray, December 13, 1937, in the John Van Antwerp MacMurray MSS (Princeton University Library, Princeton, N.J.), Box 164; MacMurray to Bristol, May 9, 1939, *ibid.*, Box 174.

[13] New York *Times*, September 11, 12, and 29, October 7, 1928, May 1 and 20, 1930; Grew to Henry L. Stimson, January 15, 1932, DS 367.1162 Schinasi Memorial/24; G. Howland Shaw to Cordell Hull, August 31, 1933, DS 367.1162 Schinasi Memorial/28.

174

of Turkish nationalism, but the services they rendered to the Turkish people, mostly without charge, were valuable and appreciated. Like the schools, Americans maintained these facilities because of their interest in Turkish welfare. The American Board, of course, hoped it would be able to demonstrate the goodness of Christianity through its hospitals and clinics. The Turkish government showed — for example, through its aid to the Schinasi Hospital — that it welcomed the services these institutions provided. The resulting interaction of Americans and Turks could not help but have a beneficial effect on Turkish-American relations.

The Narcotics Problem

The response of the Turkish government to United States pressures because of the narcotics problem led to similar results. The Turks in fact proved their sensitivity to world opinion in the 1930s by restrictions on the shipment of narcotics. Turkey, as one of the world's largest producers, was a key nation involved in efforts to solve this international problem. The United States played a very important role by pressuring Turkey to suppress the illicit narcotics traffic. The Turkish government hesitated to impose strict controls on the production and export of narcotics because they were an important source of income. An American newspaper reported in 1931, for instance, that the country's annual production of opium was about three hundred tons and provided employment for thousands of Turkish peasants.[14] During the conferences on the limitation of narcotics manufacture sponsored by the League of Nations in 1931 at Geneva, Turkey indicated its willingness to adhere to the planned convention if it was guaranteed a quota protecting it against severe economic loss.[15] Foreign ownership of the three major factories in Turkey complicated the task of effectively controlling narcotics production and export.[16]

Narcotics became an important issue in the diplomatic relations of the United States and Turkey during Ambassador Grew's term. Several seizures in New York of narcotics smuggled from Turkey in 1930 and 1931 provided the basis for strong representations to Turkish officials.[17] Grew

[14] New York *Times*, May 22, 1931.
[15] *Ibid.*, January 10 and 18, 1931; Charles E. Allen (Consul, Istanbul) to Stimson, January 28, 1931, DS 867.114 Narcotics/134.
[16] New York *Times*, January 18, 1931. See Allen to Stimson, October 11, 1929, DS 867.114 Narcotics/20, for information on the establishment of a French narcotics factory in Istanbul.
[17] Diary, December 17–23, 1930, Grew MSS, 1930, vol. 3; S. Lowman (Assistant

and Ahmed Mouhtar, the Turkish ambassador in Washington, pointed out to Foreign Minister Tevfik Rüsdü Aras that the seizures provoked very unfavorable publicity for Turkey in the United States. Mainly because of Grew's representations, the Turkish government in February, 1931, sealed the factories temporarily and placed strict controls on the manufacture and shipment of narcotics.[18] Because the clandestine shipments continued, Grew became more emphatic in his protests to the Foreign Minister. Grew felt that the narcotics seizures in New York made very effective impressions on Turkish officials. Before he left for Japan in 1932, Grew informed the Foreign Office that the narcotics problem was the "one unfortunate element which could exert an adverse effect" on the good relations of the United States and Turkey.[19]

Ambassador Sherrill was more successful than Grew in persuading the Turkish government to take strong steps to curtail the illicit narcotics trade. Sherrill, who had extraordinary access to President Kemal Atatürk as his biographer, took the narcotics problem directly to him. Sherrill wrote to Secretary of State Stimson about his intentions: "A man who wants to have his biography written in a foreign language for publication in a foreign country should be interested in clearing up one or two matters (such as the illicit drug trade) which might prejudice the public of that foreign country against him. It cannot be predicted how useful my efforts may be in this matter, but it certainly seems idle for me, thanks to this biography, to enjoy his favor unless I can turn that favor to the advantage of some American cause." [20]

Secretary of the Treasury) to Stimson, September 17, 1931, DS 867.114 Narcotics/300. From 1930 to 1933, the United States Consulate in Istanbul received information from an informant about illicit shipments of narcotics from Turkey to the United States. The informant received a regular salary from the United States Bureau of Narcotics for more than a year and bonuses when his information led to narcotics seizures. See Allen to Stimson, February 19, 1932, DS 867.114 Narcotics/514; Lowman to Stimson, March 21, 1932, DS 867.114 Narcotics/524; Stephen G. Gibbons (Assistant Secretary of the Treasury) to Hull, December 11, 1933, DS 867.114 Narcotics/960; Lowman to Stimson, January 5, 1933, DS 867.114 Narcotics/736.

[18] Grew to Stimson, December 23, 1930, DS 867.114 Narcotics/99; conversation, Grew and Tevfik Rüsdü Aras, January 11, 1931, Grew MSS, 1931, vol. 2; conversation, Grew and Aras, February 16, 1931, Grew, *Turbulent Era*, II, 883–885; New York *Times*, February 23, 1931.

[19] Grew to Stimson, November 3, 1931, DS 867.114 Narcotics/363; diary, November 17, 1931, Grew MSS, 1931, vol. 2; conversation, Grew and Shukri Kaya (Acting Minister for Foreign Affairs), February 29, 1932, Grew, *Turbulent Era*, II, 913–914.

[20] July 26, 1932, DS 867.114 Narcotics/635.

Sherrill's efforts yielded results late in December, 1932. Atatürk personally presided over a meeting of the Council of Ministers which decided that Turkey would adhere to the Hague Convention of 1912 and the Geneva Conventions of 1925 and 1931 for regulating the manufacture and sale of narcotics. The Council of Ministers also drafted legislation, later enacted, providing for limitation and supervision of the cultivation of drug-producing plants, permanently closing all private factories, and establishing a state monopoly on narcotics production and trade. Newspaper reports gave Ambassador Sherrill much of the credit for these steps. The New York *Times* in an editorial called Turkey's action "a Christmas gift to humanity" which obviously was not to the country's commercial advantage.[21]

The controls instituted by Turkey and the nation's adherence to the international conventions had a noticeable effect in the United States. A celebration in New York in July, 1934, marking the first anniversary of the effective date of the 1931 Geneva Convention, included the reading of a message from Secretary of State Hull, who congratulated Turkey on its enlightened narcotics control program. In March, 1935, Senator Joseph T. Robinson noted during a Senate speech that "under the guidance of President Kemal the Republic of Turkey has taken leadership in the world-wide warfare of humanity against the illicit narcotic-drug traffic." [22] Robinson's remarks of commendation for Turkey and Atatürk were far different from the accusations made eight years earlier, when the Senate rejected the Lausanne Treaty. The Turkish image in the United States had undergone a striking change.

American Archaeological Expeditions in Turkey

The extensive work of American archaeologists contributed greatly to the stature of the United States in Turkey. The Turkish government was quite willing to permit these projects, as the archaeologists themselves often pointed out. They faced only a few restrictions and rarely found it necessary to resort to diplomatic intervention. The archaeologists' con-

[21] Sherrill to Stimson, December 26, 1932, DS 867.114 Narcotics/731; Sherrill to Stimson, January 16, 1933, DS 867.114 Narcotics/777; Department of State, *Press Releases*, Weekly Issue No. 173 (January 21, 1933), p. 35; New York *Times*, January 15 and February 28, 1933 (source of the quotation); Shaw to Hull, June 13, 1933, DS 867.114 Narcotics/867.

[22] New York *Times*, July 10, 1934; *Congressional Record*, 74 Cong., 1 Sess., LXXIX, pt. 4, 4252.

tributions to the understanding of Turkish antiquity were significant and were so recognized by the Turkish authorities.

A major American archaeological expedition to Turkey began in 1926, under Hans H. von der Osten of the Oriental Institute of the University of Chicago. The original task of the expedition, mainly interested in the Hittite Empire, was the excavation of a large mound near the village of Alishar in Anatolia.[23] Later the project expanded over a large area of Asia Minor which, it was found, was the seat of the Hittite peoples. Von der Osten, a German citizen, experienced no difficulty in securing the complete cooperation of the Turkish government. In his reports and talks with United States embassy personnel he repeatedly emphasized that Turkish officials were very cordial and "did all that was in their power to facilitate our work."[24] The discoveries of the Oriental Institute, Grew reported in 1930, made possible the tracing of Anatolian history from the Stone Age. "It is my opinion," Grew wrote, "that this expedition and its members have added considerably to America's prestige in Turkey."[25]

The work of the University of Cincinnati at the site of ancient Troy from 1932 to 1938 was also extremely productive. After obtaining permission in 1931 to work at Troy, Carl W. Blegen directed the expedition during its seven seasons. The main goals of the project, designed to expand on the nineteenth-century work of Heinrich Schliemann and Wilhelm Dörpfeld, were to make new studies of the stratification at Troy and to search for prehistoric tombs and cemeteries. This expedition, like that of the Oriental Institute, received the complete cooperation of Turkish officials and United States embassy personnel.[26] In his final report on the

[23] See Erich F. Schmidt, *Anatolia Through the Ages: Discoveries at the Alishar Mound, 1927–29* ("Oriental Institute Communications No. 11," Chicago, 1931), for an account of the genesis of the project and the work at Alishar.

[24] H. H. von der Osten, *Explorations in Hittite Asia Minor, 1927–28* ("Oriental Institute Communications No. 6," Chicago, 1929), pp. 11–12; Mark L. Bristol, confidential diary, April 28, 1927, DS 867.00/1970. Although Turkish antiquity laws prohibited the export of archaeological discoveries, the Turkish government permitted von der Osten to take specimens of his finds from Turkey. See diary, December 11, 1927, Grew MSS, 1927, vol. 1; Grew to Stimson, October 6, 1930, DS 867.927/51.

[25] To Stimson, October 17, 1930, DS 867.927/52. For further information on the work of the Oriental Institute, see von der Osten, *Explorations in Hittite Asia Minor, 1929* ("Oriental Institute Communications No. 8," Chicago, 1930), and von der Osten, *Discoveries in Anatolia, 1930–31* ("Oriental Institute Communications No. 14," Chicago, 1933).

[26] Carl W. Blegen, "Excavations at Troy, 1932," *American Journal of Archaeology*, XXXVI (1932), 431–432, 451 (hereafter cited as *AJA*); Sherrill to Stimson,

project, Blegen wrote of its accomplishments: "New architectural monuments have been revealed for several periods, and with our formidable collections of pottery and miscellaneous objects of metal, stone, bone and terracotta, we have a fresh and voluminous set of human documents to illustrate the progressive evolution of culture and to fix a series of landmarks for the charting of otherwise unrecorded history." [27]

Americans conducted a third archaeological project in Turkey from 1934 to 1937 at Gözlü Kule on the edge of Tarsus. The sponsor was Bryn Mawr College, in cooperation with the Archaeological Institute of America, Haverford College, and the Fogg Museum of Harvard University. This expedition's discoveries added much to the knowledge of the biblical city of Tarsus. Hetty Goldman of Bryn Mawr, director of the project, emphasized in her reports the willingness of the Turkish government to aid the expedition's activities.[28]

Another important enterprise was the project on the mosaics of Hagia Sophia in Istanbul by Thomas Whittemore of the Byzantine Institute of America.[29] Although the Turkish government officially cooperated, Whittemore carried on his work with considerable difficulty. Given permission to undertake the uncovering and restoration of the mosaics in this ancient edifice in 1931, Whittemore hired two Italian mosaicists to aid him when he started the project in 1932. The Italian embassy in Turkey thereupon tried to take credit, intimating that the Italians rather than Whittemore directed the work. As a result, Whittemore hired English assistants in 1933.[30] Another problem for Whittemore was the unwelcome interference of Ambassador Sherrill. Because the mosaics depicted Christian scenes,

July 22, 1932, DS 867.927/72; MacMurray to Hull, July 13, 1938, DS 867.927/109; Blegen, "Excavations at Troy, 1935," *AJA*, XXXIX (1935), 586–587.

[27] "Excavations at Troy, 1938," *AJA*, XLIII (1939), 228.

[28] Hetty Goldman, "Preliminary Expedition to Cilicia, 1934, and Excavations at Gözlü Kule, Tarsus, 1935," *AJA*, XXXIX (1935), 526–549; Goldman, "Excavations at Gözlü Kule, Tarsus, 1936," *ibid.*, XLI (1937), 262–286; Goldman, "Excavations at Gözlü Kule, Tarsus, 1937," *ibid.*, XLII (1938), 30–54. According to Ann Perkins in *Background of the Middle East*, ed. Ernst Jackh (Ithaca, N.Y., 1952), p. 216, this expedition continued intermittently until 1949.

[29] Hagia Sophia, originally the Christian Church of the Divine Wisdom, was dedicated by the Emperor Justinian in A.D. 537. After the Ottoman conquest of Constantinople in 1453, it became a mosque. In 1935 the Turkish government transformed the building into a museum. See Martin Hürlimann, *Istanbul* (London, 1958), p. 50, and Robert Liddell, *Byzantium and Istanbul* (London, 1956), pp. 65–66.

[30] London *Times*, July 30, 1931; David Williamson (Second Secretary of Embassy) to Stimson, April 14, 1932, DS 867.927/63; Skinner to Hull, November 25, 1933, DS 867.927/82.

179

the Turkish press attacked the project as an evidence of religious propaganda. Sherrill told Turkish officials that if the attacks did not stop, he personally would halt the expenditure of American money for the work. Whittemore felt he should handle such matters himself, to avoid injecting political issues. Sherrill also wanted to be supplied with information about the mosaics for use in his book, but Whittemore refused to grant this request.[31] In 1938, Whittemore complained to Ambassador MacMurray about the accusations against him by a Turkish official who resented his work at St. Sophia. The official charged that Whittemore and the Turkish Director of Museums were removing mosaics from the building and smuggling them into the United States. The charges were unfounded, and the Turkish government did not take them seriously.[32]

American archaeologists were also active in the Sanjak of Alexandretta, in French-mandated Syria. Projects conducted by Princeton University and the Oriental Institute became an issue in Turkish-American relations in 1938 when Turkey, desiring to annex the area, started negotiations with the French over its future. The State Department asked for guarantees that the contracts of the two expeditions would be respected, no matter which country eventually controlled Alexandretta.[33] When Turkey and France signed a treaty on June 23, 1939, ceding the area to Turkey, the Turkish government guaranteed that the Princeton and Oriental Institute contracts would be honored. The Princeton agreement extended to 1943, the Oriental Institute's until 1941.[34]

Of the many Turco-American cultural activities, archaeological work was the most amiable and necessitated the least resort to diplomatic pressures and intervention. Unlike most other Americans who worked in Turkey, the archaeologists did not experience any substantial difficulty be-

[31] Memo of conversation, Wallace Murray and Thomas Whittemore, December 8, 1932, DS 867.927/77. See Charles H. Sherrill, *Mosaics in Italy, Palestine, Syria, Turkey and Greece* (London, 1933), *passim*.

[32] MacMurray to Paul H. Alling (Near East Division), November 1, 1938, DS 867.927/111 (enclosure no. 1, conversation, MacMurray and Whittemore, October 19, 1938).

[33] Hull to William C. Bullitt (United States Ambassador, France), June 14, 1938, *Foreign Relations of the United States: Diplomatic Papers, 1938* (5 vols., Washington, 1954–1956), II, 1036–1037 (hereafter cited as *FR 1938*); Sumner Welles (Acting Secretary of State) to Ely E. Palmer (Consul General, Beirut, Lebanon), June 3, 1938, *ibid.*, 1035; Welles to Edwin C. Wilson (Chargé d'Affaires, Paris), January 9, 1939, *Foreign Relations of the United States: Diplomatic Papers, 1939* (5 vols., Washington, 1955–1957), IV, 833–834 (hereafter cited as *FR 1939*).

[34] Robert F. Kelley (Chargé d'Affaires) to Hull, June 23, 1939, *FR 1939*, IV, 844–845. See below, pp. 234–236, for a discussion of the Alexandretta dispute.

cause of Turkish nationalism. Its efforts to advance these projects proved that the Turkish government welcomed them and appreciated their contributions to Turkish history and culture.

Other Cultural Relations

A few other cultural activities contributed to better understanding between Turkey and the United States. These included the sending of Turkish students to the United States, American participation in Turkish historical congresses, and the publication of American literature in Turkey. The effort of the American Friends of Turkey to bring Turkish students to the United States has already been noted.[35] The Turkish government, which strongly backed this program, expected its students to study in the United States and then return home to aid in the country's development. In 1931 the government announced plans to send four students to study cotton cultivation, viticulture, and agricultural meteorology. The State Department cooperated by providing information on colleges in the United States offering such courses of study. Later, students came to study education, mathematics, anthropology, and printing.[36] The importance the Turkish government placed on its student program was illustrated in July, 1933, by the appointment of Ragip Nureddin, former Director of Elementary Education in Turkey, as resident Inspector-General of Turkish students in the United States. "The Ministry of Public Instruction's appointment of an inspector of students . . . and the decision to send official students of that Ministry to carry on their studies in American educational institutions are events of importance in the development of American-Turkish relations," the United States embassy in Turkey reported. Ambassador Ahmed Mouhtar expressed similar sentiments in a talk with a State Department official.[37] When World War II broke out in Europe in 1939, Turkish students in Germany and France were called home, but later the Turkish goverment decided to send many of them to the United States to continue their education. The American consul in Istanbul reported in November, 1939, that the Institute for Mineral Re-

[35] See above, p. 88.
[36] A. Bedi (Counselor, Turkish Embassy, Washington) to Murray, March 17, 1931, DS 811.42767/30; Murray to A. Bedi, March 23, 1931, *ibid.*; Skinner to Hull, November 27, 1933, DS 811.42767/46; Charles E. Allen to Hull, April 24, 1934, DS 811.42767/50.
[37] Shaw to Hull, July 13, 1933, DS 811.42767/37; memo of conversation, Murray to Ahmed Mouhtar, July 20, 1933, DS 811.42767/38.

search in the Ministry of Economy planned to send forty-seven technical students to the United States for instruction.[38] Even before the war began, Turkey sent various students for technical training. In 1939, the United States Navy Department arranged for two Turkish naval officers to study naval construction engineering with a group of American officers at the Massachusetts Institute of Technology.[39]

Considerable intellectual ferment in Turkey during the Atatürk era stimulated additional cultural exchanges between Turkey and the United States. Turkish nationalism demanded the development of an historical thesis glorifying the Turkish people. As a result, Atatürk and his historical commission developed the idea that Anatolia was the cradle of civilization and that all races could trace their origins to the Turks. The Hittites of Anatolia and the original inhabitants of Greece and Egypt were from a Turkish race, according to the new ideas. The Turkish Historical Society produced a four-volume history tracing Turkish development from the dawn of civilization to modern times in accordance with this thesis.[40] United States scholars participated in periodic congresses sponsored by the Turkish Historical Society. At the 1937 congress several Americans, including Thomas Whittemore, Carl Blegen, and Walter L. Wright, Jr., presented papers. An exposition held in connection with the congress included a display from the United States.[41]

The American Board, noting Turkish interest in education and culture and recognizing an opportunity to propagate its ideas, carried on an extensive program through its publication department. In cooperation with several Turkish leaders, the American Board published *Muhit*, which by 1929 had the largest circulation of any monthly family magazine in Turkey, even though the Turkish press attacked it as a vehicle of foreign propaganda.[42] The American Board also maintained a reading room in

[38] Frederick P. Latimer, Jr., to Hull, November 9, 1939, DS 811.42767/141.

[39] Hull to Claude A. Swanson (Secretary of the Navy), April 11, 1939, DS 811.42767/119; Hull to Swanson, May 16, 1939, DS 811.42767/120.

[40] Donald E. Webster, *The Turkey of Atatürk: Social Process in the Turkish Transformation* (Philadelphia, 1939), pp. 240–243; Jefferson Patterson to Stimson, June 5, 1930, DS 867.41/1; Sherrill to Stimson, July 13, 1932, DS 867.41/10. The citation for the four-volume history is Türk Tarihi Tetkik Cemiyeti (Turkish History Research Society), *Tarih* I, II, III, IV (Istanbul, 1932–1934). See Kerim K. Key, "Trends in Turkish Historiography," in *Report on Current Research, Spring 1957: Survey of Current Research on the Middle East*, ed. John Hartley (Washington, 1957), pp. 39–46, for a brief summary of Turkish historical theses.

[41] Kelley to Hull, October 7, 1937, DS 867.41/26.

[42] *The One Hundred and Nineteenth Annual Report of the American Board of*

Istanbul and published religious leaflets and book translations in the Turk-ish language.[43] Other American literature and even comics circulated in Turkey, some in complete disregard of United States copyright regula-tions. A dispute arose in 1935 over the unauthorized printing of the comic strips "Mickey Mouse" and "Little Annie Rooney." The protests of King Features Syndicate were to no avail because there was no copyright con-vention between Turkey and the United States. The United States gave up the idea of concluding such a convention when it became clear that the Turkish government would insist on the exclusion of translations. Ambas-sador MacMurray thought that to insist on the sanctity of United States copyrights "would not merely stir up irritation without contributing towards practical results, but would tend to predispose the Turks towards those cultural influences which they find more readily available by reason of an undisputed accessibility through translations." [44] American publish-ers were not happy about the appropriation of their materials, but such publication in Turkey provided another link with the United States. The popularity of typically American comic strips such as those involved in the copyright case, though perhaps not the best examples of American litera-ture, was evidence of westernization in Turkey.

Relief Programs

The willingness of Americans to contribute to charitable causes pro-vided another basis for the expansion of friendship between Turkey and the United States. When physical disaster struck in Turkey, the American Red Cross usually helped the Turks with their relief programs, as it did other nations in similar circumstances. On four occasions between 1928 and 1939, the Red Cross, through its Turkish counterpart, the Red Cres-cent Society, made contributions to flood and earthquake relief. Severe earthquakes at Izmir beginning on March 31, 1928, and continuing for over two weeks resulted in numerous deaths and high property damage. President Coolidge's message of sympathy to President Atatürk received

Commissioners for Foreign Missions [1929] (Boston, n.d.), p. 190; William Paton and M. M. Underhill, "A Survey of the Year 1930," *International Review of Mis-sions*, XX (January, 1931), 40–41.

[43] Charles T. Riggs, "Turkey, the Treaties and the Missionaries," *Missionary Re-view of the World*, L (May, 1927), 348; *The One Hundred and Twenty-Seventh An-nual Report of the American Board of Commissioners for Foreign Missions* [1937] (Boston, n.d.), p. 8.

[44] Skinner to Hull, October 16, 1935, DS 867.544 King Features Syndicate/1; MacMurray to Hull, April 9, 1936, DS 867.544 King Features Syndicate/7.

wide publicity in the Turkish press.[45] The American Red Cross offered its aid to the Red Crescent and learned of the pressing need for tents to house victims of the earthquake. The Red Cross thereupon allocated $5,000 for the purchase of tents in Europe to be used in the Izmir area. Grew wrote the Secretary of State "that this generous and helpful action of the American Red Cross, in view of its highly favorable influence upon American-Turkish relations, is highly appreciated by the Embassy." Five American tobacco companies conducted a separate campaign among Americans in Izmir for relief funds.[46]

The Red Cross came to Izmir's aid again in October, 1930, when a flood took fifty lives and left thousands homeless. Upon the suggestion of Consul Herbert S. Bursley, the Red Cross sent $2,500 to the Red Crescent Society for the relief of the sufferers.[47] An additional $1,000 was sent in December, 1930, to aid the victims of another flood at Adana in south-central Turkey.[48] The Red Cross made its largest contribution for disaster relief late in December, 1939, when a severe earthquake which killed thousands of people occurred in east-central Anatolia. On this occasion the Red Cross sent $10,000 to the Red Crescent, and the United States embassy secured State Department permission to contribute $200 from embassy funds.[49]

The modest contributions made by the Red Cross to aid in disaster relief in Turkey went for the direct benefit of Turkish citizens. Private American citizens and charitable organizations contributed a much larger amount for the relief of a non-Turkish group of refugees residing in Istanbul. From 150,000 to 200,000 White Russians fled from Russia to Istan-

[45] John Corrigan, Jr. (Consul, Izmir) to Kellogg, March 31, 1928, DS 867.48 Smyrna/1; Corrigan to Kellogg, April 19, 1928, DS 867.48 Smyrna/20; Calvin Coolidge to Kemal Atatürk, April 2, 1928, DS 867.48 Smyrna/2; Grew to Kellogg, April 4, 1928, DS 867.48 Smyrna/4.
[46] Kellogg to Embassy, April 2, 1928, DS 867.48 Smyrna/5; Grew to Kellogg, April 6, 1928, DS 867.48 Smyrna/11; Ernest P. Bicknell (Vice-Chairman, Insular and Foreign Operations, American Red Cross) to Robert E. Olds (Undersecretary of State), April 7, 1928, DS 867.48 Smyrna/12; Grew to Kellogg, April 13, 1928, DS 867.48 Smyrna/18; Corrigan to Kellogg, April 5, 1928, DS 867.48 Smyrna/16.
[47] Herbert S. Bursley to Stimson, October 26, 1930, DS 867.48 Smyrna Flood/1; Stimson to Embassy, October 30, 1930, DS 867.48 Smyrna Flood/8.
[48] Bursley to Stimson, December 19, 1930, DS 867.48 Adana Flood/1; Stimson to Embassy, December 26, 1930, DS 867.48 Adana Flood/6.
[49] MacMurray to Hull, December 28, 1939, DS 867.48 Anatolia/4; MacMurray to Hull, December 29, 1939, DS 867.48 Anatolia/5; Hull to MacMurray, January 5, 1940, DS 867.48 Anatolia/5; Ernest J. Swift (Vice-Chairman, American Red Cross) to Hull, December 29, 1939, DS 867.48 Anatolia/15.

bul after their armies had been defeated by Bolshevik forces in the civil war following the revolution of November, 1917. During the early 1920s, the League of Nations and the International Labor Office worked to resettle these refugees, and American groups, including the Red Cross and the Laura Spelman Rockefeller Memorial, contributed about $200,000 for this work. Only a few thousand refugees remained in Istanbul by 1927, when the Turkish government decided that they would be expelled unless they became Turkish citizens.[50] The Turkish government, which maintained a cautious attitude in regard to the Soviet Union, wanted to remove the refugees because it believed they were engaged in propaganda against the Bolsheviks.[51]

The Turkish government set February 6, 1928, as the deadline for the evacuation of the remaining refugees. An American group headed by Anson Phelps Stokes, Canon of Washington Cathedral, raised $90,000 from private contributors in the United States to aid in the evacuation program.[52] After a request from Grew, the Turkish government agreed to extend the deadline to February, 1929. When the International Labor Office ended its involvement in the evacuation program in 1928, an "American Advisory Committee," composed of several Americans in Istanbul, including an embassy representative, was established to supervise the disbursement of the money raised in the United States.[53] The Turkish government did not carry out its threat to expel the Russians when the 1929 deadline arrived. The American Committee by 1930 had helped to evacuate about 1,750 refugees.[54]

[50] Fridtjof Nansen, "Rescuing Millions of War Victims from Disease and Starvation," *Current History*, XXX (July, 1929), 572 (Nansen was League of Nations High Commissioner for refugees in Europe); Bristol and Anson Phelps Stokes, "Confidential Memorandum Regarding the Changed Situation of Russian Refugees in Istanbul, Turkey, and the Appeal of the American Committee There," December 20, 1934, in the Mark Lambert Bristol MSS (Manuscript Division, Library of Congress, Washington), Box 112 (hereafter cited as Bristol and Stokes, "Confidential Memorandum").
[51] Grew to Kellogg, January 16, 1929, *Papers Relating to the Foreign Relations of the United States, 1928* (3 vols., Washington, 1942–1943), III, 985–987 (hereafter cited as *FR 1928*).
[52] *Christian Science Monitor* (Boston), January 5, 1928; Kellogg to Grew, January 7, 1928, *FR 1928*, III, 981; Bristol and Stokes, "Confidential Memorandum," Bristol MSS, Box 112. Bristol and Stokes state that $105,500 was raised, whereas the figure $90,000 is mentioned in State Department documents.
[53] Grew to Kellogg, January 12, 1928, *FR 1928*, III, 981–982; Grew to Kellogg, April 10, 1928, *ibid.*, 982–983.
[54] Bristol and Stokes, "Confidential Memorandum," Bristol MSS, Box 112; Grew to Kellogg, February 27, 1929, *FR 1928*, III, 987.

In 1934, the situation of the two thousand White Russians still living in Istanbul became critical with the passage of a new law restricting most occupations to Turkish citizens. The Turkish government indicated its willingness to naturalize most of the Russians if they could pay the required fees. Admiral Bristol and Canon Stokes late in 1934 launched another public appeal for $30,000 to pay the naturalization costs. Ambassador Skinner explained to Stokes that the Turkish government's intention to exclude from Turkey a few refugees suspected of anti-Soviet political activities complicated the situation.[55] Available information does not reveal whether this fund drive was successful or whether the Russian refugees remained in Turkey. The Red Cross, which Ambassador Skinner asked to aid in the project, was unable to do so at this time because of a lack of funds.[56] The response of American philanthropists to the problem from its inception until 1935, however, stimulated improved Turkish-American relations. Stokes wrote Bristol in December, 1934, that American contributions to the Russian refugees have removed "a heavy burden upon the Turkish Government," which should make it receptive to American hopes for naturalization of the Russians.[57]

Conclusions

The various social, cultural, and philanthropic activities discussed here were prominent factors in determining the nature of Turkish-American relations during the interwar period. These activities generally did not cause serious diplomatic controversies. United States diplomatic representatives provided the necessary liaison between Americans engaged in this work and the Turkish government. The thought foremost in the minds of these representatives was that through these projects Americans and Turks could come to know each other better. The unselfish subscription of American charity to disaster relief in Turkey, for instance, could not help but contribute to the expansion of Turkish-American friendship. The medical services provided by Americans, for the most part free of charge, had a similar effect. The contributions of American archaeologists to Turkish history and the knowledge of early civilizations enlightened all peoples, including the Turks.

[55] Bristol and Stokes, "Confidential Memorandum," Bristol MSS, Box 112; Skinner to Stokes, January 30, 1935, Bristol MSS, Box 112.
[56] Cary T. Grayson (Chairman, American Red Cross) to Skinner, April 13, 1935, Bristol MSS, Box 112.
[57] December 18, 1934, Bristol MSS, Box 112.

Social, Cultural, and Philanthropic Activities

The only significant diplomatic question arising from the contacts involved the international traffic in narcotics. Two United States ambassadors, Grew and Sherrill, exerted the diplomatic pressure which helped to persuade Turkey to curtail illicit narcotics shipments and to institute a rigid state system of drug production. The Turkish government took these steps with the knowledge that they would have a detrimental effect on the Turkish economy. Turkey, concerned about world opinion, responded intelligently when warned by United States diplomats of the adverse effect the continuance of narcotics smuggling would have on public opinion in the United States. Partly because of American influence, Turkey worked to alleviate this international problem. The reaction in the United States was very favorable to Turkey.

It is notable that individual Americans involved in cultural and philanthropic work in Turkey protested very little about regulations reflecting Turkish nationalism. The difficulty in licensing doctors somewhat restricted the American Board's medical work, but there is no evidence that the program would have been more extensive had this situation not existed. American archaeologists were willing to comply with Turkish regulations. Turkey's international situation complicated the status of the Russian refugees, yet the Turkish government permitted aid from the United States and finally exhibited willingness to allow most of them to become Turkish citizens.

As with many other aspects of Turkish-American relations before World War II, it is difficult to assess the precise contributions of these social, cultural, and philanthropic activities to the expansion of friendship between the two countries. But Turkish officials and United States diplomatic representatives occasionally indicated that they were very worthwhile. In any case, these activities, intangible though some of them were, appear to have contributed their share to the developing Turkish-American rapprochement in the interwar period.

✧ The Status of Citizens: Problems and Solutions

ASIDE from the broad task of applying general policy and handling questions of bilateral or international scope, a diplomat in the field must spend considerable time looking after the interests of the individual citizens of the nation he represents. A United States citizen residing and working in a foreign country normally is protected by various treaties and agreements providing certain privileges and immunities. American citizens in Turkey after World War I — educators, traders, archaeologists, technical experts, manufacturers, or tourists — unfortunately did not have all of these normal guarantees. The capitulations, long a shield behind which foreigners in Turkey hid, were gone, and no effective treaty existed between the United States and Turkey. The Lausanne Treaty of 1923, designed to fill the void created by World War I and subsequent events in Turkey, failed in the Senate early in 1927. Thus, when Joseph C. Grew went later in the same year as the first ambassador of the United States to the Republic of Turkey, one of his most pressing tasks was that of regularizing the establishment and residence rights of American citizens.

Grew and his successors faced three other questions relating to the status of citizens — nationality, extradition, and claims. Within seven years of Grew's arrival in Turkey, all but the nationality dispute had been eliminated. These settlements resulted from long negotiations, during which United States representatives had to accept the fact that give-and-take diplomacy was essential in dealing with the Turks. Turkish nationalism complicated the discussions and ultimately prevented the settlement of the citizenship issue. But the negotiated solutions of three of the four

188

outstanding questions involving the status of nationals contributed tremendously to rapprochement between Turkey and the United States. The two nations accepted compromise as a necessary ingredient in the peaceful settlement of their problems.

The Nationality Imbroglio

The question of nationality resulted from conflicting theories of citizenship. The governments of the Republic of Turkey and its predecessor, the Ottoman Empire, applied the theory of jus sanguinis, which denied to a Turk the right to renounce his citizenship and accept naturalization in another country without government permission. An Ottoman law of January 19, 1869, clearly stated this principle.[1] The United States, in contrast, adhered primarily to the principle of jus soli, which basically determined citizenship by place of birth but recognized the right of expatriation. Thus, Turkish subjects could acquire United States citizenship without their government's permission. The existence of the capitulations before 1914 complicated this situation because many Ottoman subjects, including thousands of Armenians, came to the United States, acquired citizenship, and then returned to their homeland where, as naturalized Americans, they were not subject to Ottoman law. Between 1900 and 1924 about seventy thousand such persons returned to Turkey from the United States.[2] The conflict between jus sanguinis and jus soli was almost unsolvable since each state established its policy through domestic legislation. The first principle favors countries of emigration, like Turkey, which for various reasons want to retain the allegiance of their nationals. The latter normally has been accepted by important centers of immigration such as the United States.[3]

The United States and Turkey tried to eliminate the naturalization

[1] Nasim Sousa, *The Capitulatory Régime of Turkey: Its History, Origin, and Nature* (Baltimore, 1933), p. 105; Fred K. Nielsen, *American-Turkish Claims Settlement under the Agreement of December 24, 1923, and Supplemental Agreements Between the United States and Turkey, Opinions and Report* (Washington, 1937), p. 55 (hereafter cited as Nielsen, *Claims Settlement*); Americus, "Some Phases of the Issues Between the United States and Turkey," *North American Review*, CLXXXII (May, 1906), 696–700.

[2] Leland J. Gordon, "The Turkish-American Controversy over Nationality," *American Journal of International Law*, XXV (October, 1931), 658; Nielsen, *Claims Settlement*, p. 691.

[3] See Charles de Visscher, *Theory and Reality in Public International Law* (Princeton, 1957), pp. 174–179, for a useful discussion of the laws of nationality.

problem by treaty in August, 1874, but because of ratification reservations by both countries the treaty never became effective.[4] Failure of the negotiators to agree resulted in the omission of naturalization provisions in the Turkish-American Lausanne Treaty of 1923. The State Department hoped that the problem could be settled before the Lausanne Treaty came before the Senate but, on the advice of Admiral Bristol it agreed to postpone negotiations. Bristol believed that such deliberations might delay Turkish action on the Lausanne Treaty and that it might be easier to achieve an accord after re-establishment of formal relations. Because the Lausanne Treaty appeared essential for the protection of American citizens in Turkey, Bristol urged immediate ratification. He also pointed out that the Senate would probably delay action if negotiations on naturalization were in progress. In any case, Bristol saw little possibility of reaching agreement in 1923–1924. The State Department was justified in its fear that the nationality issue would adversely affect Senate opinion on the Lausanne Treaty, for the absence of a solution to the problem was one of the bases for rejection of the treaty in January, 1927.[5]

The February, 1927, exchange of notes provided for negotiation of a naturalization convention within six months after consular, establishment, and residence conventions become effective. The Turks were not technically bound to accept a naturalization convention because the proposed consular pact never materialized before World War II.[6] But the State Department continued to hope that a naturalization agreement could be negotiated. In May, 1928, the Turkish government passed a new nationality law retaining the old principles. The law provided that "every child born in Turkey or abroad of a Turkish father or a Turkish mother is a Turkish citizen," and that any child born in Turkey, regardless of his parents' nationality, was a Turkish citizen, although he would have the privilege of adopting the nationality of his parents when he reached age eighteen. The

[4] Oscar S. Straus, *Under Four Administrations: From Cleveland to Taft* (Boston & New York, 1922), pp. 90–92.

[5] Mark L. Bristol to Charles Evans Hughes, August 24, 1923, *Papers Relating to the Foreign Relations of the United States, 1923* (2 vols., Washington, 1938), II, 1193 (hereafter cited as *FR 1923*); Hughes to Bristol, September 29, 1923, *ibid.*, 1193–1194; Bristol to Hughes, December 31, 1923, *ibid.*, 1196–1198; Hughes to Bristol, January 10, 1924, *ibid.*, 1198. See above, p. 43.

[6] Wallace Murray (Chief, Near East Division) to G. Howland Shaw (Counselor of Embassy), October 23, 1934, *Foreign Relations of the United States: Diplomatic Papers, 1934* (5 vols., Washington, 1950–1952), II, 983–984 (hereafter cited as *FR 1934*).

law also stated that permission of the Council of Ministers was necessary for expatriation.[7] Passage of this law made a naturalization agreement between Turkey and the United States less likely.

One of the basic reasons for the desire of the United States for a naturalization agreement was Turkey's refusal to permit the temporary return of former citizens to Turkey. Since the special privileges of the capitulations no longer existed, it was hard to understand why Turkey took this position. Foreign Minister Aras answered this question in 1934 when he told Ambassador Skinner that the Turkish government was worried that former Turks would use their American citizenship when they returned to Turkey to claim immunity for offenses committed before naturalization.[8]

The difficulties, either potential or real, of many naturalized Americans of Turkish origin who did return to Turkey emphasized the need for an agreement. As described above, Morris Schinasi, a naturalized American from Turkey who died in 1928, provided a bequest for the construction of a hospital at Manisa. When his wife, who had also been born in the Ottoman Empire, wanted to return to Turkey in 1929 to make arrangements for the hospital, she asked the State Department how she could avoid difficulties with Turkish authorities over her nationality. A State Department official advised her to approach the Turkish ambassador in Washington, using the proposed hospital as the basis for a guarantee that she would not be arrested because of her previous Turkish citizenship.[9] As it turned out, Mrs. Schinasi experienced no trouble when she went to Turkey.

The Turkish nationality law of 1928 caused difficulty for George Bitar, born in the United States of Turkish parents. When he visited Turkey in 1929, Turkish authorities seized his passport and tried him in an Istanbul court on the charge of using a foreign passport, because according to the 1928 law he was a Turkish citizen. Although the court acquitted him, the United States consulate had to exert pressure to persuade Turkish officials to return his passport. Had the Turks persisted, Bitar might have been subjected to such requirements as the payment of taxes and military

[7] Gordon, "The Turkish-American Controversy over Nationality," p. 668; Arnold J. Toynbee, *Survey of International Affairs, 1928* (London, 1929), pp. 196–197; New York *Times*, July 29, 1928; Charles E. Allen (Consul, Istanbul) to Frank B. Kellogg, February 21, 1929, DS 867.111 American Passports/12.

[8] Gordon, "The Turkish-American Controversy over Nationality," p. 668; Robert P. Skinner to Cordell Hull, March 12, 1934, DS 711.674/46.

[9] Memo of conversation, Murray, Mrs. Morris Schinasi, and her lawyer (unidentified), May 8, 1929, DS 367.1162 Schinasi Memorial/3.

service.[10] Bitar's experience illustrated the legal difficulties caused by the divergence of Turkish and American citizenship statutes.

The nationality question emerged as an issue of immediate importance in Turkish-American relations in 1937. According to the Allied Treaty of Lausanne (1923), natives of the French-mandated, former Ottoman areas of Syria and Lebanon could opt for Syrian or Lebanese citizenship. If they did not do so, the Turkish government could claim them as Turkish nationals. A Franco-Turkish exchange of notes on May 29, 1937, extended the period when these persons could exercise their citizenship option until May 29, 1938.[11] The agreement technically covered many naturalized United States citizens of Ottoman origin. If they opted for Syrian or Lebanese nationality, they could inherit property in the area, and the Turkish government would then recognize that they were no longer Turkish citizens. The State Department advised such persons not to exercise their option because adoption of a second nationality would be inconsistent with the oaths taken when they became American citizens. In other words, they would lose American citizenship if they chose Syrian or Lebanese nationality.[12]

The long negotiations between Turkey and the United States over the plight of the Syrians and Lebanese eventually broadened into the general question of a naturalization treaty. Syrians and Lebanese in the United States wanted to disavow their Turkish citizenship even though American law prevented them from exercising their option according to the Franco-Turkish agreement of May, 1937.[13] In February, 1938, the State Department presented a draft exchange of notes by which Turkey would renounce claims for the allegiance of all natives of the Ottoman territories lost by Turkey at Lausanne in 1923. The Turkish government indicated interest in the proposal, but wanted to study the status of property owned

[10] Allen to Kellogg, February 21, 1929, DS 867.111 American Passports/12; Allen to Henry L. Stimson, March 19, 1929, DS 867.111 American Passports/23; Allen to Stimson, May 8, 1929, DS 867.111 American Passports/43.

[11] Theodore Marriner (Consul-General, Beirut, Lebanon) to Hull, September 13, 1937, DS 390D.11/50.

[12] Memo, Paul H. Alling (Near East Division) to R. W. Flournoy (Legal Adviser, State Department), October 4, 1937, DS 390D.11/62; memo, Flournoy to Near East Division, November 9, 1937, DS 390D.11/78; Alling to John V. A. MacMurray, November 10, 1938, DS 390D.11/162.

[13] Alling to MacMurray, November 10, 1938, DS 390D.11/162; memo of conversation, Murray and Münir Ertegün, December 9, 1937, *Foreign Relations of the United States: Diplomatic Papers, 1938* (5 vols., Washington, 1954–1956), II, 1101–1103 (hereafter cited as *FR 1938*).

by the affected persons to make sure "that there would be in the future no controversial questions concerning property rights." [14] An issue in the discussions was whether the Turkish nationality law permitted a blanket abrogation of citizenship for the persons concerned. The Turkish government persisted in claiming the right to refuse admission to persons who had given up Turkish citizenship and to reject diplomatic claims of persons who were Turkish citizens when the claims arose. The United States agreed informally to these stipulations. [15]

The situation became more complicated in November, 1939, when the Turkish government submitted a treaty proposal diverging from the earlier American draft and including several points at variance with United States ideas on naturalization. [16] Early in 1940, the State Department expressed its preference for a simple exchange of notes, since "the negotiations of such a treaty would doubtless be difficult and prolonged, due to the divergence between the American and Turkish principles relating to nationality, and it would seem preferable to conclude the negotiations already undertaken before approaching the general treaty." The Department again agreed, however, not to support "a claim on behalf of a person who is a national of that country [Turkey] or who was a national of that country at the time the events out of which the claim arose took place" and that "nothing in the agreement shall be construed as affecting existing statutes of either country in relation to the immigration of aliens or the right of either country to enact such statutes." [17] Although Ambassador Mac-Murray discussed the proposed agreement with Turkish officials periodically during 1940 and 1941, the Turks took no further action on it. The pressing problems of World War II occupied most of the time of the Turk-

[14] George S. Messersmith to Robert F. Kelley, February 15, 1938, *FR 1938*, II, 1103–1105; Kelley to Hull, April 13, 1938, *ibid.*, 1105–1107; Kelley to Hull, April 2, 1938, DS 390D.11/136.

[15] Memo of conversation, Murray and Ertegün, June 1, 1938, (memo dated June 2, 1938), *FR 1938*, II, 1108–1109; memo of conversation, George V. Allen (Near East Division), Murray, and Ertegün, June 20, 1938, *ibid.*, 1109–1111; MacMurray to Hull, April 1, 1939, *Foreign Relations of the United States: Diplomatic Papers, 1939* (5 vols., Washington, 1955–1957), IV, 849 (hereafter cited as *FR 1939*); Kelley to Hull, June 17, 1939, *ibid.*, 852; Murray to MacMurray, September 12, 1939, *ibid.*, 856; R. Walton Moore (Counselor, State Department) to MacMurray, June 21, 1938, *FR 1938*, II, 1116–1119.

[16] MacMurray to Hull, November 23, 1939, *FR 1939*, IV, 857–860 (includes text of draft treaty); MacMurray to Hull, December 29, 1939, *ibid.*, 860–861.

[17] Hull to MacMurray, January 19, 1940, *Foreign Relations of the United States: Diplomatic Papers, 1940* (5 vols., Washington, 1955–1958), III, 1001–1003 (hereafter cited as *FR 1940*).

ish Foreign Office during this period.[18] The nationality question entered into the negotiations on claims and establishment and residence, since both problems involved the status of individuals. But the basic citizenship problem proved insolvable in a period when the two nations settled all other major diplomatic controversies.

The Treaty of Establishment and Residence, 1931

The question of the establishment and residence rights of American nationals in Turkey and Turkish nationals in the United States had been covered in the Turkish-American Treaty of Lausanne. Shortly after rejection of the treaty, an exchange of notes on February 17, 1927, provided for the future negotiation of an establishment and residence convention if the Treaty of Lausanne remained unratified. In the meantime, the appropriate provisions of the Lausanne Treaty would regulate the conditions of residence of the nationals of each country in the other's territory.[19] When it became clear that the Lausanne Treaty was dead, the Department of State decided to handle the various problems in separate treaties. The first settlement to result was the commercial treaty of October 1, 1929. On the day they signed this treaty, the Turks suggested to Ambassador Grew that a "brief convention of residence and establishment" be negotiated. The Turkish formula for the proposed convention read as follows: "With reference to the conditions of residence and establishment and judicial competence to which the citizens and companies of the two countries will be submitted, Turkey will accord to the United States of America and the United States of America will accord . . . [to Turkey] national treatment in cases where the respective laws of the two countries permit national treatment and in all other cases most-favored-nation treatment." Grew suggested that it might be possible to cover residence and establishment by a modus vivendi or an annex to the minutes of the session of October 1, 1929, if the State Department felt it wise not to send two treaties to the Senate at the same time. The State Department, however, was unwilling to take any action on establishment and residence until the Senate approved the commercial pact.[20]

[18] MacMurray to Hull, July 16, 1940, *ibid.*, 1007–1008; MacMurray to Hull, November 23, 1940, *ibid.*, 1008; MacMurray to Hull, April 22, 1941, DS 390D.11/207.
[19] See above, p. 50.
[20] Joseph C. Grew to Stimson, October 2, 1929, *Papers Relating to the Foreign Relations of the United States, 1930* (3 vols., Washington, 1945), III, 852 (hereafter

194

Grew favored the brief formula proposed by the Turks, because it would be simple to interpret in practice, would give the United States the benefits of similar conventions between Turkey and other powers, and would probably win Senate approval more quickly than a detailed treaty. Once the Senate approved the commercial agreement in February, 1930, Grew advocated the immediate negotiation of a residence and establishment treaty. Rather than postpone negotiation of the proposed accord, Grew felt, it would be better to deal with the Turks while they were in a receptive frame of mind and then, if necessary, delay submission of the pact to the Senate.[21] In mid-March, 1930, the State Department instructed Grew to inform the Turkish government "in strict confidence" that the United States would be ready to discuss a treaty of residence and establishment late in September, 1930, with the hope that the completed document could be presented to the Senate when it met the following December. This procedure would prove the sincerity of the United States and would "obviate the risk of organized opposition in the United States . . . which might develop were there to intervene a considerable period between the treaty's signature and its presentation to the Senate." [22]

During the interval before formal negotiations began on October 18, 1930, the United States explored the formula proposed by the Turks a year earlier. The Treaty Division of the State Department thought the inclusion of national treatment where permitted by domestic law would cause serious complications. Nothing in the formula prevented the Turks from passing legislation to withdraw national treatment in matters of establishment and residence, whereas the real purpose of such provisions was to guarantee specific rights during the lifetime of the treaty. The Treaty Division was aware that the Senate preferred "general provisions which do not tie the hands of the legislative body." Its hands would be tied if the treaty included pure national treatment. To the relief of the State Department, the Turkish delegation proposed omission of all mention of national treatment when formal talks actually began.[23]

cited as *FR 1930*); Stimson to Grew, October 21, 1929, *ibid.*, 853. "National treatment" meant that a country would guarantee the same privileges to nationals of its treaty partner that it extended to is own citizens.

[21] Grew to Murray, January 8, 1930, Joseph C. Grew MSS (Houghton Library, Harvard University, Cambridge, Mass.), 1930, vol. 2; Grew to Murray, February 26, 1930, DS 711.679 Residence and Establishment/13.

[22] Joseph P. Cotton (Acting Secretary of State) to Grew, March 17, 1930, *FR 1930*, III, 853.

[23] Unsigned memo, Near East Division, March 17, 1930, DS 711.679 Residence

The Treaty Division suggested the addition of the words "entry and sojourn" after "conditions of residence and establishment" in the Turkish formula to ensure that Turkish nationals would be accorded the same treatment as nationals of countries having active residence and establishment treaties with the United States before the passage of the restrictive Immigration Act of 1924.[24] Shortly before negotiations began, the Department decided that the words should not be included after all, since it realized that the granting of most-favored-nation treatment in entry and sojourn would entitle the Turks to the special privileges accorded to nations of the Western Hemisphere. Although nationals of these countries could enter the United States without quota restrictions, according to the Immigration Act of 1924, the Senate obviously would not approve any treaty giving this privilege to the Turks. With this in mind, the State Department instructed Grew to omit most-favored-nation treatment on entry and sojourn in discussions of the treaty.[25]

The State Department thought originally that the negotiations would be relatively short, but they lasted more than a year. The talks were timed "so that the interval between the signing of the treaty and its presentation to the Senate will be as short as possible in order to allow no time for the Turcophobes in this country to organize a campaign against ratification." [26] Technical questions caused considerable delay, but the crucial point became clear at the first meeting of the two treaty delegations. The Turks proposd an article stating that when the projected treaty became effective, "all previous treaties between Turkey and the United States of a similar nature would thereby terminate." Grew told the Turks that this provision was inadmissable since, as he noted in his diary, "it would unquestionably give valuable ammunition to Turkey's enemies in the United States, of which there were still plenty, and . . . it would undoubtedly wreck the treaty." [27] Grew was thinking of the Armenian-Americans, who

and Establishment/9; Grew to Stimson, October 19, 1930, *FR 1930*, III, 863; Stimson to Grew, October 21, 1930, DS 711.679 Residence and Establishment/40.

[24] Unsigned memo, "Treaty of Residence and Establishment with Turkey," August 29, 1930, DS 711.679 Residence and Establishment/19; W. R. Castle, Jr. (Acting Secretary of State) to Grew, August 30, 1930, *FR 1930*, III, 855–856; Murray to Grew, September 3, 1930, DS 711.679 Residence and Establishment/24.

[25] Memo, Murray, September 19, 1930, DS 711.679 Residence and Establishment/28; Cotton to Grew, September 22, 1930, *FR 1930*, III, 858–859; Stimson to Grew, October 3, 1930, *ibid.*, 862.

[26] Memo, Murray to Stimson, October 16, 1930, DS 711.679 Residence and Establishment/38.

[27] October 18, 1930, Grew MSS, 1930, vol. 3.

maintained that the treaty of 1830 and the capitulations were still effective. The State Department, as a matter of fact, up to this time had never recognized the death of the treaty of 1830. The Department, not agreeing with Grew, observed that "such a Turkish interpretation would be of great assistance to the United States Government eventually in the presentation of claims against Turkey, because it would prevent the Turks from claiming then that the American capitulatory rights in Turkey ended in 1914." Grew received instructions not to argue against the Turkish suggestion and was told to "bear in mind that the treaty of 1830 must be disposed of eventually." [28]

A revised Turkish formula of November 6, 1930, included a statement that "there exists between the two countries no provisions regulating the . . . conditions" of establishment and sojourn. The State Department did not accept the Turkish proposal because the February, 1927, exchange of notes did contain such provisions and, more important, because United States agreement might imply recognition that the capitulations had been legally abrogated in 1914. The Department was willing, however, to include a clause stating that the new treaty would supersede all former treaties. [29] Clearly the Turkish fears of the capitulations and the United States refusal to recognize their abrogation as of 1914 were the real obstacles to the success of the negotiations.

Grew felt a direct approach to Prime Minister Ismet İnönü would be helpful and asked permission to make the following statement to him:

That the Department is fully alive to the changes which have taken place in Turkey in recent years; that its sole desire is that the development of treaty relations between the two countries should proceed upon the basis of these changed conditions; that it was with such considerations in mind that the Department negotiated the exchange of notes of February 27 [17], 1927, and the commercial treaty of October [1], 1929, and has been prepared to negotiate arbitration and conciliation treaties as well as a treaty of establishment and residence; and finally that it is a matter of sincere regret to the Department that the anxiety of the Turkish Government with respect to the past should have on more than one occasion delayed the complete regularization of the treaty relations between the two countries. [30]

[28] Grew to Stimson, November 19, 1930, *FR 1930*, III, 868–869; Stimson to Grew, November 21, 1930, *ibid.*, 869–870.
[29] Grew to Stimson, November 6, 1930, *ibid.*, 864–865; Stimson to Grew, November 10, 1930, *ibid.*, 866.
[30] Grew to Stimson, November 25, 1930, *ibid.*, 871.

The Department authorized Grew to make the statement, with the beginning altered to read, "the Department is fully alive to the changes which have taken place in Turkey since the establishment of the Republic," since the reference to "recent years" might imply acceptance of the abrogation of the capitulations in 1914. Grew presented the revised statement orally to Inönü on November 27, 1930.[31]

Because of the controversy over the theoretical continuance in force of the treaty of 1830 and the disputed date for abolition of the capitulations, the two delegations did not agree on a treaty text until August 27, 1931. Then they initialed the treaty and formally signed it on October 28, 1931.[32] Article I, the essential part of the brief accord, provided for mutual most-favored-nation treatment in regard to establishment and residence, fiscal charges, and judicial competence. Furthermore, "nothing contained in this treaty shall be construed to affect existing statutes and regulations of either country in relation to the immigration of aliens or the right of either country to enact such statutes." [33] The framers included this statement to satisfy Turkish fears about former Ottoman subjects and American concern about the Immigration Act of 1924. To subdue Turkish apprehension about the capitulations and the treaty of 1830, Grew addressed to Foreign Minister Aras a letter reading in part: "The Government of the United States of America is fully alive to the changes which have taken place in Turkey. Its sole desire is that the development of the relations between the two countries should proceed upon the basis of these changed conditions." This was essentially what Grew had said to Inönü earlier. The Department of State considered the acceptance of this treaty as effectively terminating the 1830 agreement containing the capitulatory rights of the United States.[34]

After he signed the treaty, Grew noted in his diary: "It is a profound satisfaction to have our treaty relations with Turkey now pretty well established, provided the Senate ratifies this last one, and I can't see how it can

---

[31] Stimson to Grew, November 26, 1930, *ibid.*, 872; Grew to Stimson, November 28, 1930, *ibid.*, 872.

[32] Grew to Castle, July 10, 1931, *Papers Relating to the Foreign Relations of the United States, 1931* (3 vols., Washington, 1946), II, 1038–1040 (hereafter cited as *FR 1931*); Grew to Acting Secretary of State, August 28, 1931, *ibid.*, 1041; Grew to Stimson, October 28, 1931, *ibid.*

[33] Text of the treaty, *ibid.*, 1042–1043.

[34] Grew to Aras, October 28, 1931, *ibid.*, 1043; memo, Flournoy to Murray, March 18, 1933, DS 711.679 Residence and Establishment/133.

refuse to do so." [35] Wallace Murray's memorandum to a colleague shortly before the treaty went to the Senate indicated the State Department's fears about ratification: "I hope that the Senate's attention is engaged in more serious matters at this time than in browbeating the Turks, but I think we must be prepared for considerable antagonism to any new treaties with Turkey for some time to come. The point is to obtain action by the Senate on the present instrument before this perennial antagonism has time to consolidate in an endeavor to defeat the Treaty." [36] The only noticeable opposition to the treaty on the Senate floor came from a traditional opponent of Turkey, Senator King of Utah, who suggested that the settlement was one of a series designed to "circumvent" the defeat of the Lausanne Treaty. King's opposition delayed action for a few days, but the Senate eventually approved the treaty on May 3, 1932.[37] Vahan Cardashian, who usually complicated Turkish-American relations, did not protest against this treaty. Although there is no specific evidence to support the idea, probably Cardashian was silent because the treaty paved the way for the eventual settlement of the claims problem, a matter of vital interest to him because of his two large personal claims against the Turkish government. No other explanation seems reasonable since Cardashian missed few opportunities to protest against the improvement of United States relations with Turkey.[38]

Although the Turkish Grand National Assembly accepted the treaty on June 4, 1932, the United States delayed the exchange of ratifications. According to the notes of February, 1927, Turkey and the United States would begin negotiations on the claims problem no later than six months after the exchange of ratifications of a commercial treaty and a convention of establishment and residence. The Department thought in the spring of 1932 that it would be unable to get an appropriation for a claims commission; thus, it desired to hold up the effective date of the establishment and residence treaty.[39] By November, 1932, the Department was ready to

[35] October 28, 1931, Grew MSS, 1931, vol. 2.
[36] To James G. Rogers (Assistant Secretary of State), February 18, 1932, DS 711.679 Residence and Establishment/84.
[37] *Congressional Record*, 72 Cong., 1 Sess., LXXV, pt. 8, 9227–9228; *ibid.*, pt. 9, 9484. President Herbert C. Hoover sent the treaty to the Senate on February 25, 1932.
[38] See below, pp. 209–210, for information about Cardashian's claims.
[39] Charles H. Sherrill to Stimson, June 9, 1932, DS 711.679 Residence and Establishment/104 (about Turkish ratification); Stimson to Embassy, May 27, 1932, DS 711.679 Residence and Establishment/92.

exchange ratifications because it then foresaw the possibility of getting the appropriation and it also did not want to carry the treaty over to the incoming administration of Franklin D. Roosevelt. Turkey and the United States exchanged ratifications in Washington on February 15, 1933.[40]

The conclusion of the treaty of establishment and residence was a significant step in the regularization of Turkish-American relations. The treaty, by guaranteeing most-favored-nation treatment for Americans residing in Turkey, eliminated their previous informal status. The treaty solved many of the problems resulting from the wartime breach in diplomatic relations, and was a valuable companion to the 1929 treaty of commerce and navigation. Ambassador Grew again proved his success in negotiating with the Turks. The exchange of ratifications for the treaty made it possible for the two countries to proceed to settling the problem of claims. Slowly but surely the gap left by the rejected Treaty of Lausanne contracted.

Claims and the Agreement of 1934

The claims issue was the most important unresolved diplomatic issue between Turkey and the United States in 1933. Most of the claims had arisen between 1914 and 1922, during World War I and the subsequent Greek-Turkish conflict. The United States roughly categorized its claims as follows: (1) property taken without adequate compenastion by Turkish military or civilian officials; (2) unnecessary destruction of property, looting, and pillaging by military forces; (3) violation, either by civilian or military authorities, of personal rights, including imprisonment and bodily injury; and (4) failure of Turkish authorities to use due diligence in preventing injuries to person and property, and failure to punish persons responsible for such injuries.[41] Although the Turkish and United States delegates discussed the issue during the Lausanne conference in 1923, they made no progress toward a settlement. An instruction to the United States mission at Lausanne on August 8, 1923, emphasized the importance the State Department placed on the problem. Explaining the necessity of avoiding an impasse, the Department suggested the formation

---

[40] Stimson to Embassy, November 17, 1932, DS 711.679 Residence and Establishment/113; Stimson to Embassy, February 15, 1933, DS 711.679 Residence and Establishment/128; Department of State, *Press Releases*, Weekly Issue No. 177 (February 18, 1933), p. 121.

[41] Nielsen, *Claims Settlement*, pp. 22–23; Hull to Shaw, May 4, 1933, *FR 1934*, II, 898–899.

of a bilateral commission to settle the claims question. The State Department wanted a claims settlement before submission of the Lausanne Treaty to the Senate because, as it pointed out to Admiral Bristol, this problem and the naturalization question would materially affect Senate action on the treaty.[42] Bristol's talks with the Turks led to an exchange of notes on December 24, 1923, providing for a mixed claims commission to meet no later than six months after ratification of the Lausanne Treaty. Claims dossiers presented to the commission were to include documents establishing the origin of, nature of, and justification for each claim.[43]

In April, 1933, the Secretary of State instructed Chargé d'Affaires G. Howland Shaw in Turkey to remind the Turks that, now that the prerequisite treaties had been ratified, the commission of two representatives from each government should meet by August 15, 1933. The State Department at this time estimated the value of more than twenty-five hundred American claims at about $55,000,000. Suggesting a lump-sum payment as "the most practicable and least expensive means of settlement," the State Department stated its willingness to accept $5,000,000 in full satisfaction of the claims. The instruction to Shaw continued: "The American Government fully appreciates the financial situation in Turkey and is prepared to take this situation into full consideration in ariving at a settlement. It is confident that if the Turkish Government will approach the question in the same spirit of conciliation and good will which the United States proposes to exercise it will be possible to work out a solution which will be mutually fair and acceptable to both parties." [44] The State Department meanwhile proceeded to gather evidence from the claimants in anticipation of the meeting of the claims commission.[45]

During preliminary discussion before the commission met, Turkish officials showed interest in the lump-sum idea but wanted detailed information about the nature of the American claims, including the date of the

[42] Hughes to American Special Mission at Lausanne, *FR 1923*, II, 1172–1174; Hughes to Bristol, December 3, 1923, *ibid.*, 1183.

[43] Bristol to Hughes, January 4, 1924, *ibid.*, 1189–1191 (texts of notes exchanged between Bristol and Adnan Adivar, delegate of the Turkish Ministry for Foreign Affairs at Istanbul).

[44] Hull to Shaw, April 4, 1933, *FR 1934*, II, 894–898. See DS 467.11/554A for the original instruction including an enclosure, "Classification of Claims Against Turkey." This document lists various categories of claims and their value.

[45] See Green H. Hackworth (Legal Adviser, State Department) to Eugene Moss, February 10, 1933, DS 467.11/318. This is a mimeographed form letter, identical to those sent to all claimants, advising them to complete their claims immediately. Many of these letters are present in this file.

act or event causing each claim and the nature of the evidence submitted as proof. The United States was unwilling to submit such data because many of the claimants were naturalized Americans of Ottoman origin and also because the dossiers for some cases were not yet completed. The State Department felt that an examination of each individual claim would lead to interminable negotiations with the Turks.[46] In Shaw's opinion, the refusal of the United States to submit a detailed list of claims was "asking the Turkish Government to make an act of blind faith in us and in our statement that we have $55,000,000 worth of claims against them." Prime Minister Inönü complained to Shaw "that the United States was seeking to convert Turkey into a debtor country." [47] When the Turkish government formally agreed to the mixed claims commission, it made clear its refusal to consider claims from anyone except those with "non-contested American nationality." The Turks excluded, in other words, claims of persons who, according to Turkish law, were Ottoman subjects at the time the claims arose. Thus the Turks early injected the nationality problem into the discussions.[48]

The first meeting of the mixed claims commission was at Istanbul on August 15, 1933, with G. Howland Shaw as the chief United States delegate and Sevki Bey and Essat Bey as the Turkish members. At this meeting Shaw outlined the plan for a lump-sum settlement amounting to 10 per cent of the American claim for $55,000,000. It was expected that the Turks would present counterclaims against the United States, but they submitted none at this meeting or later.[49] The commission made little progress during the next six months because of differences of opinion over the amount of the settlement. In November, 1933, the Turks proposed $500,-000 as "a reasonable and acceptable solution for both parties." The

[46] Shaw to Hull, May 9, 1933, *FR 1934*, II, 899; Shaw to Hull, May 10, 1933, *ibid.*, 899–900; Hull to Embassy, May 20, 1933, DS 467.11/581; Hull to Shaw, May 27, 1933, *FR 1934*, II, 901.

[47] Shaw to Hull, May 11, 1933, DS 467.11/598 (enclosure no. 2, memo of conversation, Shaw and Inönü, May 9, 1933).

[48] Turkish Ministry for Foreign Affairs to American Embassy, June 27, 1933, *FR 1934*, II, 901–902. The State Department sent mimeographed letters to all claimants of Ottoman origin or their representatives informing them of the Turkish position on nationality, but made it clear that the United States did not agree with this interpretation. See, for example, Hackworth to Eugene Moss, August 2, 1933, DS 467.11/318.

[49] Shaw to Hull, August 16, 1933, DS 467.11/673; Shaw to Hull, August 17, 1933, DS 467.11/694 (enclosure no. 1, memo on proceedings of the August 15, 1933, meeting).

amount apparently originated in a meeting of the Turkish Council of Ministers which decided that this was the maximum Turkey could afford to pay. The Turks described the American claims as "based upon one-sided ideas of the interested parties, and . . . so exaggerated that even taking the ten percent of the total amount one would still be far above reality." [50] The State Department replied that it could not accept this figure, since it was "dealing with the rights of American nationals so that the question of compromising liability of Turkish Government involves, in this case, unlike the cases of European war debts, conflict between rights of individual American citizens and companies on one side and the economic convenience of Turkish Government on the other. Turkish Government should appreciate that, in such circumstances, there is not the latitude of possible action which obtains in matters of purely Governmental rights and obligations." [51]

Because the two delegations could not agree, the Department of State suggested a new procedure. In January, 1934, the Department sent Ambassador Skinner the text of a proposed protocol providing for the consideration of all claims on an individual basis. According to the plan, a majority of the committee of four would decide on each individual claim. In cases where no agreement emerged, each side would submit its position on the claim to an umpire who would make the decision.[52] The Turks submitted a counterproposal suggesting that the mixed commission should again try to agree on a lump-sum settlement. If this effort was unsuccessful, individual claims would be considered, with cases not decided in this way submitted to an arbitrator. The United States agreed to this procedure, but it did not accept the Turkish idea that the commission, when considering individual cases, would do so only for claims by American citizens of uncontested origin. The Turkish formula would have restricted the competency of the commission as originally formulated in the December, 1923, and February, 1927, agreements.[53]

[50] Robert P. Skinner to William Phillips (Acting Secretary of State), November 21, 1933, *FR 1934*, II, 902; "Turkish Counter Proposal for a Lump Sum Settlement of American Claims Against Turkey," n.d., *ibid.*, 903–905; John W. Connelly, Jr., minutes of the Claims Commission, September 20, 1934, in the Fred K. Nielsen MSS (Manuscript Division, Library of Congress, Washington), Box 15.

[51] Phillips to Skinner (for Shaw), December 8, 1933, *FR 1934*, II, 902–903; Skinner to Hull, January 8, 1934, DS 467.11/749 (enclosure no. 1, memo of conversation, Shaw and Sevki Bey, December 30, 1933).

[52] Phillips to Skinner, January 13, 1934, *FR 1934*, II, 906–909.

[53] Skinner to Hull, February 8, 1934, *ibid.*, 910; Hull to Skinner, February 10,

Because of the possibility that individual claims might have to be considered, the State Department thought that experts should constitute United States membership on the commission. Consequently, to head the delegation the Department appointed Fred K. Nielsen, an international lawyer who had served in various government positions, including Assistant Solicitor and Solicitor of the State Department and as a member in the 1920s of the American-Mexican International Claims Commission. Accompanying Nielsen to Turkey were Francis M. Anderson and John Maktos from the office of the legal adviser in the State Department. Later John W. Connelly, Jr., joined the commission.[54] The expenses involved in the assignment of experts necessitated a congressional appropriation which President Roosevelt requested in March, 1934. When the House of Representatives considered a joint resolution authorizing the appropriation, Representative Thomas L. Blanton of Texas voiced strong objections. In May, 1934, Blanton referred to the commission as "a $90,000 junket to Turkey." On June 4, the House passed the resolution although Blanton again claimed that the money would be wasted: "It is taking good money of the people . . . and putting it down a rat hole. It is like pouring water in a prairie-dog hole. . . . You will not get back even a soiled and broken tail feather out of Turkey." The Senate passed the resolution on June 14, 1934, and the President approved it four days later. The resolution specified that any expenditure from the money authorized should be charged against the amount subsequently received from Turkey in settlement of the claims. Congress allotted $75,000 rather than the suggested $90,000 for the work of the commission in a deficiency appropriation act passed on June 19, 1934.[55]

The second phase of the claims negotiations under Nielsen lasted several months. Nielsen, as his private papers reveal, was a contentious per-

1934, *ibid.*, 911; Skinner to Hull, March 11, 1934, *ibid.*, 911–912; Hull to Skinner, March 23, 1934, *ibid.*, 912–913.

[54] Hull to Franklin D. Roosevelt, February 2, 1934, DS 467.11/751 ½ (proposing appointment of Nielsen, Anderson, and Maktos); Wilbur J. Carr (Assistant Secretary of State) to Nielsen, February 13, 1934, DS 467.11/755D (Nielsen's commission); R. Walton Moore to John W. Connelly, Jr., August 27, 1934, DS 467.11/903A; E. Russell Lutz, "Claims Against Turkey," *American Journal of International Law*, XXVIII (April, 1934), 347.

[55] *Congressional Record*, 73 Cong., 2 Sess., LXXVIII, pt. 4, 4375, 4463; *ibid.*, pt. 6, 6656–6657; *ibid.*, pt. 8, 8213; *ibid.*, pt. 10, 10460–10462, 10467; *ibid.*, pt. 11, 11489; New York *Times*, June 5, 1934, Nielsen, *Claims Settlement*, p. 6; Carr to Representative William B. Oliver, February 2, 1935, DS 467.11/1004A.

son who had difficulties with the Turks, some of his American associates on the commission, United States embassy personnel, and State Department officials back in Washington. Some of his complaints seem justified, but his suspicions of various people appear on occasion to have clouded his judgment. Although Nielsen understood the reluctance of the Turks to agree to an expensive settlement, he privately criticized them bitterly and apparently disliked them personally. To a friend in the State Department Nielsen wrote: "I have been in many diplomatic games, and I flatter myself that I have been able pretty quickly to size up what schemers have in mind. But I am only still guessing somewhat vaguely what are the designs of Sevki Bey. I am impatient with the dilatory tactics." Earlier he told the same friend, "Anderson loves the Turks and Turkish things; the rest of us must refrain from expressing any opinions except on asbestos." [56]

Nielsen was also convinced that Ambassador Skinner opposed his work. According to Nielsen's account, Julian Gillespie told him "that he had no doubt that the Ambassador had the idea that I had come over to jam the claims of 2,000 Ottomans down the Ambassador's throat." After his arrival in Turkey Nielsen had trouble arranging an interview with Skinner and difficulty in getting secretarial assistance from the embassy and consulate.[57] Nielsen's disputes with State Department personnel caused him on several occasions to write confidentially to Secretary Hull. In a letter in May, 1934, in which he asked Hull to recall him to Washington for a conference, he wrote: ". . . I have an idea that there is good reason to suppose . . . that we might have made some progress, had some officials of the Department not been out of sympathy with every important thing that has been suggested from this end before and after I came." [58] After finishing his work, he wrote again to Hull: "In the settlement . . . attempts were made by wholesale lies and frauds to obtain a vast sum of money from an impoverished nation. . . . The lies and frauds . . . may be said to fall into two classes: (1) . . . dishonorable claimants. . . .

[56] Nielsen to Hackworth, April 19, 1934, Nielsen MSS, Box 14; Nielsen to Hackworth, March 6, 1934, *ibid.* Anderson and Nielsen did not get along; Anderson left Turkey in July, 1934, officially because of health problems, but also clearly because of his strained relations with Nielsen. See Nielsen to Hackworth, July 30, 1934, *ibid.*, Box 15.
[57] Nielsen, memo of interview with Julian Gillespie, n.d. [spring, 1934], *ibid.* (source of the quotation); Nielsen, memo of interview with Skinner and Mr. Coe (Third Secretary of Embassy), n.d. [1934], *ibid.*; Nielsen to Hull, June 12, 1934, *ibid.*, Box 15.
[58] Nielsen to Hull, May 14, 1934, *ibid.*, Box 14.

(2) Infinitely worse are the preposterous falsehoods emanating from the Department of State through men making use of such methods." [59]

In addition to these rather serious problems, the chief obstacles continued to be the amount of the settlement and the nationality issue. The claims commission made only a cursory examination of the dossiers submitted by the United States, since the Turks were most concerned about the nationality of the individuals involved, especially where dual citizenship existed. The Turks particularly feared that Greek-Americans would press their claims through both the United States and Greece by virtue of their dual citizenship. The United States delegates refused to eliminate the claims of such persons since they could not be influenced by the possible intervention of any other government, such as Greece. But Nielsen did receive assurances through the United States minister in Athens that the Greek government would not grant compensation to Greek citizens who were also United States citizens. The joint commission actually did not consider claims where nationality was clearly disputed. [60]

There were certain claims categories to which the Turks objected, including those arising from the burning of Izmir in 1922. The commission eventually disallowed most of the Izmir claims since no one had produced convincing evidence of responsibility for the disaster. [61] Commissioner Nielsen complained that many of the American claims for "fantastic and fabulous amounts," some of them "purely fictitious," delayed the settlement. The Turkish delegation objected strongly to the use by many of the claimants of standard affidavit forms on which witnesses with widely varying qualifications swore to identical facts. [62]

Although the United States commissioners periodically suggested to their Turkish counterparts that they proceed to a consideration of individual cases in detail, the proposals simply reflected concern about lack of progress in the negotiations. The lump-sum approach was preferred by the United States, even though the task of distributing any money obtained

[59] Nielsen to Hull, June 30, 1937, *ibid.*, Box 16.

[60] Nielsen to Lincoln MacVeagh (United States Minister, Athens), September 16, 1934, *ibid.*, Box 15; MacVeagh to Nielsen, September 19, 1934, *ibid.*; Nielsen, *Claims Settlement*, pp. 11–12.

[61] Unofficial English translation (from French) of a memo from the Turkish Commissioners, April 24, 1934, Nielsen MSS, Box 14; Nielsen, *Claims Settlement*, pp. 24–39; Skinner (from Nielsen) to Hull, June 11, 1934, DS 467.11/824.

[62] Nielsen, *Claims Settlement*, pp. 9, 11, 22; Nielsen to Hull, April 13, 1934, DS 467.11/803.

from Turkey to American claimants would be formidable.[63] The United States recognized that inability to pay a large sum was the main reason for Turkish delay as the commission worked in 1933 and 1934. Nielsen preferred an amount the Turks could pay rather than one on which they would obviously default. As Nielsen reported to Secretary Hull, "When poverty is pleaded here, it is natural to recall that since 1911 Turkey has engaged in four international wars, and has been defeated in all but one of them. There is not much left of the Ottoman Empire, either as regards territory, relatively speaking, or wealth in liquid form." [64]

By mid-August, 1934, the commissioners completed a summary examination of the claims. Nielsen again urged the Turks to make a lump-sum proposal. Nielsen explained his position to Secretary Hull: ". . . [the claims] nearly all appear fully as bad as I previously indicated, lacking relevant proofs and abounding in absurd form affidavits. . . . My hope, faintly entertained, is that the Turkish Government, pressed with the possibility of some kind of arbitration which they shun, may yield from obstinate attitude and make some reasonably satisfactory offer." [65]

A break in the negotiations came on September 19, 1934, when Sevki Bey proposed a lump-sum settlement of $1,000,000 in twelve annual installments. Sevki increased his offer to $1,200,000 after arguments by Nielsen. Nielsen described to Sevki his fears about what the American claimants might say if he accepted his offer. Sevki responded: "I am afraid of the Minister of Finance, just as His Excellency is afraid of all the claimants he mentions." [66]

Nielsen, referring to the "sorry financial situation" in Turkey and the "sordid character evidence in some American cases and extreme weakness in others," suggested to the State Department that he be authorized to press for interest on the deferred payments and a shorter term of payment. The Department pointed out that the Turkish offer was worth only $995,-400, if interest was calculated at three per cent for twelve years. The Department proposed a payment of $1,500,000, or interest added to the or-

[63] Memo, Nielsen to Turkish commissioners, May 3, 1934, Nielsen MSS, Box 14; R. Walton Moore to Nielsen, February 13, 1934, *ibid.*; Hull to Nielsen, July 13, 1934, *ibid.*, Box 15.

[64] Nielsen to Hull, April 13, 1934, DS 467.11/803.

[65] Allen (for Nielsen) to Hull, August 17, 1934, Nielsen MSS, Box 15 (source of the quotation); declarations verbales by Nielsen, August 14, 1934, *ibid.*

[66] Connelly, notes of meetings of Claims Commission, September 20 [19], 1934, *ibid.*

iginal offer. Nevertheless, Secretary Hull instructed Nielsen to accept the Turkish offer of $1,200,000 if the Turks presented no other solution.[67]

On September 28, 1934, the Turkish delegation, displeased with the United States demand for interest, raised their offer to $1,300,000 without interest, payable in thirteen annual installments. The United States accepted this proposal.[68] On October 13 the commissioners signed the final act of the American-Turkish Claims Commission, which explained the procedures used and the cases considered. Two lists of claims were attached, one of 573 which the commission found without legal basis, and a second of 325 discussed by the commission but not passed upon "by judicial methods to determine their standing under international law." [69] The actual claims agreement, signed on October 25, 1934, provided for the first of Turkey's annual installments of $100,000 to be paid on June 1, 1936. Article II of the agreement was very important: "The two Governments agree that, by the payment of the aforesaid sum, the Government of the Republic of Turkey will be released from liability with respect to all of the above-mentioned claims formulated against it and further agree that every claim embraced by the Agreement of December 24, 1923, shall be considered and treated as finally settled." [70] The commission designed this article to eliminate without question any further presentation of claims. Since the settlement was an executive agreement, it did not require the approval of the United States Senate. The agreement became fully effective when the Turkish Grand National Assembly ratified it on December 23, 1934. In commenting on the claims accord, the Istanbul paper, *La Turquie*, contrasted Turkey's willingness to pay its debts to the policy of other European countries which had defaulted. The Turkish-American agreement, the newspaper observed, "will bring the blush to those who wish to present us to the world as a people who seek to escape from their obligations," and "will make the Turks better known to the Americans." [71]

[67] Nielsen to Hull, September 20, 1934, *FR 1934*, II, 929–930; Nielsen to Hull, September 21, 1934, *ibid.*, 930–931; Hull to Howard Elting (Consul, Istanbul) (for Nielsen), September 22, 1934, *ibid.*, 931.

[68] Elting (from Nielsen) to Hull, September 28, 1934, *ibid.*, 932–933; Hull to Elting (for Nielsen), October 1, 1934, *ibid.*, 933.

[69] Nielsen, *Claims Settlement*, pp. 45–46. The original final act and annexes are in DS 467.11/942.

[70] Nielsen, *Claims Settlement*, pp. 47–48 (text of the agreement). The text is also in *FR 1934*, II, 933–934.

[71] Skinner to Hull, December 24, 1934, *FR 1934*, II, 935; Skinner to Hull, December 21, 1934, DS 467.11/985 (enclosure, English translation of the article, December 21, 1934).

208

In view of the lump-sum settlement, the United States government had to decide which of the claims would be honored and which disallowed. Fred K. Nielsen, after congressional authorization on March 22, 1935, established an office in Washington to do this.[72] Nielsen's final report in 1937 allowed only thirty-three claims, valued at $899,338.09, including principal and interest. The largest payments went to the American Board of Commissioners for Foreign Missions, amounting to $191,583.48, and to MacAndrews and Forbes Company, for $260,870.96. In accordance with the act of March 22, 1935, the expenses of the claims commission in Turkey and Nielsen's office in the United States, amounting to $70,891.06, were deducted on a proportional basis from the money due to the successful claimants. Nielsen eliminated most of the claims on the basis of false or insufficient evidence.[73]

There appears to have been little dissent in the United States against the terms of the claims agreement or the subsequent Nielsen awards. The Allied Turkish-American War Claims Association, representing about two hundred naturalized Americans of Ottoman origin, protested because the American-Turkish Commission did not consider their claims. The State Department pointed out that if the United States delegates had pressed these claims, no settlement would have been possible. It would have been unfair, the Department explained, to pay from the money received from Turkey claims which were not taken into consideration in arriving at a lump-sum settlement.[74] Only Vahan Cardashian's death on June 12, 1934, prevented him from opposing the settlement.[75] Cardashian had two claims against Turkey, one for $20,000 he maintained was due to him and a partner for legal services to the Turkish consulate-general in

[72] Carr to Representative William B. Oliver, February 2, 1935, DS 467.11/1004A; Nielsen, *Claims Settlement,* pp. 6–7.

[73] Nielsen, *Claims Settlement,* pp. 780–784 (list of successful claimants, with principal amounts, interest, and deductions for the expenses of the claims commission); Hull to Acting Secretary of the Treasury, August 19, 1937, DS 467.11/1106A; Hull to Henry Morgenthau, Jr. (Secretary of the Treasury), September 27, 1937, DS 467.11/1106B; S. Walter Washington (Chargé d'Affaires) to Numan Menemencioglu (Acting Turkish Minister for Foreign Affairs), September 23, 1937, *Foreign Relations of the United States: Diplomatic Papers, 1937* (5 vols., Washington, 1954), II, 957 (hereafter cited as *FR 1937*). See Nielsen, *Claims Agreement,* pp. 87–775, for opinions and digests of the claims considered. MacAndrews and Forbes Company was engaged in the Turkish licorice root export trade. See Nielsen's opinion of this claim, *ibid.,* pp. 87–128.

[74] Aleck Cootsis (Secretary, Allied Turkish-American War Claims Association) to Hull, April 25, 1936, DS 467.11/1045; Hackworth to Cootsis, May 9, 1936, *ibid.*

[75] New York *Times,* June 13, 1934.

New York and the Turkish embassy in Washington during the period 1909–1914. The other was for $150,000 plus interest which he spent on behalf of the Ottoman government for buildings at the Panama-Pacific International Exposition at San Francisco in 1915. Informal negotiations on Cardashian's claims between the Turkish government and United States embassy officials from 1931 through 1933 proved unsuccessful. Cardashian's attempts to sue Ambassador Ahmed Mouhtar in District of Columbia courts also failed.[76] His death removed a major obstacle to the improvement of Turco-American relations.

Nielsen's final decisions provided for the expenditure of $400,661.91 less than the total amount due from the Turks. Consequently, on Nielsen's recommendation, the United States informed the Turkish government that this sum would be deducted from the total, so that the last installment would be payable in 1944 instead of 1948. The State Department cautioned the embassy in Turkey to keep the reduction confidential, since unsuccessful claimants might protest. Nielsen looked upon the remission as necessary in view of the nature of some of the claims. He told Hull that this deed "would serve in a measure to salvage the honor of the United States so shamefully prostituted by the wholesale misrepresentations made to the Government of Turkey." Wallace Murray of the Near East Division felt that "the only straight-forward and honest action, under our good neighbor policy, is to relieve the Turkish Government of its obligation to pay any sum in excess of that required to meet the awards to bona fide claimants." [77] Murray recorded the reaction of Turkish Ambassador Münir Ertegün when he told him about the claims reduction: "The Ambassador was obviously deeply stirred on being informed of this offer. . . . With tears in his eyes he stated that he was at a loss to give adequate expression to his deep feeling of appreciation of the spirit of uprightness, moral integrity and generosity of our Government. 'This is,' he said, 'incomparably the happiest day of my whole career.' " The Turkish Foreign

[76] Vahan Cardashian to Robert Lansing, January 25, 1919, DS 467.11 C172/3; Cardashian to Stimson, May 10, 1929, DS 467.11 Cardashian, Vahan/1; Leo A. Rover (United States Attorney, D.C.) to Hackworth, November 1, 1929, DS 467.11 Cardashian, Vahan/15; Castle to Grew, August 7, 1931, DS 467.11 Cardashian, Vahan no. 2/3; Sherrill to Stimson, January 10, 1933, DS 467.11 Cardashian, Vahan no. 2/23; Shaw to Hull, June 6, 1933, DS 467.11 Cardashian, Vahan/162.

[77] Nielsen to Hull, June 30, 1937, Nielsen MSS, Box 16; Hugh R. Wilson (for Hull) to Washington, September 8, 1937, *FR 1937*, II, 954–955; Washington to Menemencioglu, September 23, 1937, *ibid.*, 957; Murray to Washington, September 8, 1937, DS 467.11/1116A.

Minister interpreted the act "as an affirmation of sympathy toward the Government of the Republic." [78]

The settlement of the claims problem removed the most serious controversy existing between the United States and Turkey. The Republic of Turkey proved its good faith in agreeing to a settlement involving an amount of money which appeared large to Turkey in view of its financial condition. In the negotiations both sides exhibited a spirit of compromise facilitating final agreement. The United States might have insisted on pressing all the claims presented to the State Department, no matter how dubious some of them were, but such a course would not only have conflicted with Turkish views on nationality but also would have involved an amount which the Turks could not have paid. To promote agreement, the Turkish government accepted a lump-sum settlement rather than a minute examination of each claim. The claims agreement of October, 1934, and the subsequent reduction in principal by the United States, testified to the success of the art of diplomacy in both countries as a means of bringing Turkey and the United States closer together.

The Extradition Treaty

Another problem, extradition, had been left hanging as a result of the rejection of the Lausanne Treaty in 1927. This question, like those of claims, establishment and residence, and naturalization, involved the status of citizens. The United States and Turkey were able to solve the extradition problem shortly before signature of the claims agreement in 1934.

In August, 1874, the two countries had actually signed an extradition treaty, proclaimed in May, 1875. Eleven years later the Turks made it clear that they considered this treaty dead because the unacceptable naturalization treaty of 1874 was so closely connected with it.[79] At Lausanne in 1923, the two delegations at first considered reviving the treaty of 1874 and including it with some changes in the Lausanne Treaty, but they subsequently discarded this plan in favor of a new treaty.[80] The Coolidge Ad-

[78] Memo of conversation, Murray and Ertegün, September 10, 1937, *FR 1937*, II, 955–956; Menemencioglu to Kelley (Chargé d'Affaires), October 15, 1937, *ibid.*, 957–958.

[79] Leland James Gordon, *American Relations with Turkey, 1830–1930: An Economic Interpretation* (Philadelphia, 1932), p. 208.

[80] Grew to Charles Evans Hughes, June 3, 1923, DS 211.67/-; Grew to Hughes, June 22, 1923, DS 211.67/2; Grew to Hughes, July 3, 1923, DS 211.67/3; Hughes to American Mission, Lausanne, July 6, 1923, DS 211.67/3.

ministration submitted to the Senate an extradition treaty signed on August 6, 1923, along with the other Lausanne settlements. The Senate ignored the extradition compact after rejecting the Lausanne Treaty in 1927. In 1930, the State Department, still hoping to secure Senate action on the pending extradition treaty, instructed Ambassador Grew to inquire whether the Turkish government would follow suit if the United States ratified it.[81] The Turkish Foreign Minister asked for some modifications to make the treaty conform to current Turkish standards. Specifically, he wanted to eliminate the enumeration of extraditable crimes because in recent Turkish treaties the penalty and not the offense determined whether extradition would be granted. The Turks also felt that the country from which extradition was requested should pay the expenses incurred by the arrest, detention, and transportation of the individual to its own frontier.[82]

Because these proposed modifications were not in accordance with American practice on extradition treaties, and because in reality the United States had rare occasion to ask for the extradition of anyone from Turkey, the State Department felt negotiations with the Turks at this time would not be worthwhile.[83] The catalyst reopening the question was the flight of Samuel Insull, the Chicago utilities magnate, to Europe in June, 1932.[84] After Insull took up residence in France, investigation of his collapsed financial empire led Cook County, Illinois, and Federal grand juries to indict him and several associates on embezzlement and mail fraud charges. After requests from Illinois, the State Department instructed the United States embassy in Paris to seek the provisional arrest of Insull. Wanting to avoid trial, Insull fled France with his wife, going first to Italy and then to Greece, which had no extradition treaty with the United States.[85] After Insull arrived in Greece, the United States government en-

[81] Cotton (for Hull) to Jefferson Patterson (Chargé d'Affaires), July 3, 1930, *FR 1934*, II, 935; conversation, Grew and Aras, October 18, 1930, Grew MSS, 1930, vol. 3.

[82] Conversation, Grew and Aras, October 18, 1930, Grew MSS, 1930, vol. 3; diary, November 10, 1930, *ibid.*; Grew to Stimson, December 3, 1930, DS 211.67/26.

[83] Memo, J. R. Baker (Solicitor's Office, State Department) to Hackworth, January 10, 1931, DS 211.67/27.

[84] See the Daily Reports of the Near East Division, October 11, 1932–May 17, 1934, inclusive, in DS 251.11 Insull, Samuel/637, for a convenient summary of the diplomatic aspects of the Insull case. For a detailed account see Roger R. Trask, "The Odyssey of Samuel Insull," *Mid-America*, XLVI (July, 1964), 204–215. Forrest McDonald, *Insull* (Chicago, 1962), is a sympathetic biography.

[85] Stimson to Embassy, Paris, October 7, 1932, DS 251.11 Insull, Samuel/2; Theodore Marriner, Paris, to Stimson, October 8, 1932, DS 251.11 Insull, Samuel/3;

deavored to complete extradition treaties with countries in the Middle East where Insull might take refuge. This led to the exchange of ratifications for a Greek-American treaty on November 1, 1932, and an instruction to Counselor of Embassy G. Howland Shaw in Turkey to sound out the Turks once again on the question of an extradition treaty.[86] After Shaw learned that the Turkish government had agreed to an enumeration of extraditable crimes in a recent treaty with Switzerland and was willing to consider the United States argument that the demanding government should pay all of the costs involved, the State Department instructed him to suggest the adoption of the 1923 treaty. The Turkish Foreign Minister promised Shaw he would submit it to the Grand National Assembly in November, 1933.[87] The United States Senate approved the treaty on February 5, 1934. Senator King of Utah took this opportunity again to suggest that the proposed pact was part of the rejected Lausanne Treaty and that its submission was an attempt to circumvent Senate action on that treaty. King's token opposition did not affect Senate opinion — the Senate recognized that favorable action was desirable because of the possibility that Insull might flee to Turkey.[88]

When Greek courts twice refused to extradite Insull, partly because the case became involved in domestic politics, the United States denounced the Greek-American extradition treaty. American pressures on the Greek government finally forced Insull to leave Athens in March, 1934.[89] He cruised in Mediterranean waters aboard a chartered Greek vessel, the *Maiotis*, for two weeks before it anchored off Istanbul on March

Fred E. Sterling (Acting Governor of Illinois) to Stimson, October 9, 1932, DS 251.11 Insull, Samuel/7; Francis X. Busch, *Guilty or Not Guilty?* (Indianapolis & New York, 1952), pp. 129–133; McDonald, *Insull*, pp. 312–313.

[86] Stimson to Leland B. Morris (Chargé d'Affaires, Athens), *Foreign Relations of the United States: Diplomatic Papers, 1933* (5 vols., Washington, 1949–1952), II, 554 (hereafter cited as *FR 1933*); Murray to Shaw, March 20, 1933, DS 211.67/30A.

[87] Shaw to Murray, April 17, 1933, *FR 1934*, II, 937–938; Hull to Shaw, May 6, 1933, *ibid.*, 938; Shaw to Hull, June 12, 1933, *ibid.*

[88] Hull to Skinner, February 9, 1934, *ibid.*, 939; *Congressional Record*, 73 Cong., 2 Sess., LXXVIII, pt. 2, 1846–1847, 1924–1925; New York *Times*, February 6, 1934.

[89] Morris to Stimson, December 28, 1932, *FR 1933*, II, 556; Lincoln MacVeagh (American Minister, Athens) to Hull, October 31, 1933, *ibid.*, 562; Hull to MacVeagh, November 4, 1933, DS 251.11 Insull, Samuel/198; MacVeagh to Hull, March 18, 1934, DS 251.11 Insull, Samuel/484. The Greek-American extradition treaty was renewed in November, 1937. See MacVeagh to Hull, November 29, 1937, DS 251.11 Insull, Samuel/676. See also Trask, "The Odyssey of Samuel Insull," pp. 205–211.

29, 1934, supposedly to take on supplies.[90] Even though no extradition treaty existed with the United States, the Turkish government in October, 1932, and January, 1934, had promised to prevent Insull from landing in Turkey if he should come there from Greece. The Turks detained the *Maiotis* at the request of the United States embassy.[91] Although Greece protested against the detention of the ship, the Turkish government brought Insull ashore on April 1, 1934, and formally arrested him the next day.[92] A Turkish court on April 2 decided, even though no treaty was in effect, that Insull could be extradited to the United States according to Article IX of the Turkish Penal Code, which permitted extradition if the person involved was accused of a "common crime." [93] Turkish officials subsequently released Insull to Burton Y. Berry, vice-consul at Istanbul, who brought him back to the United States and delivered him to federal officials in Chicago on May 8, 1934.[94]

In the midst of the turmoil over Insull, the Turkish Grand National Assembly ratified the extradition treaty of 1923, and the United States and Turkey exchanged ratifications in Ankara on June 18, 1934.[95] Thus, another outstanding question between Turkey and the United States had been settled. In this instance Turkey again demonstrated a spirit of compromise and cooperation, for it accepted principles normally not included in its extradition treaties. For the first time in the history of formal relations between the two nations, Turkey and the United States had an effective treaty. Samuel Insull's legal difficulties in the United States hastened the conclusion of a treaty which probably would have come during the period in any case.

[90] *Christian Science Monitor* (Boston), March 29, 1934.

[91] Shaw to Stimson, October 19, 1932, DS 251.11 Insull, Samuel/33; Skinner to Hull, January 11, 1934, DS 251.11 Insull, Samuel/315; Skinner to Hull, March 29, 1934, *FR 1934*, II, 577.

[92] Skinner to Hull, April 1, 1934, *FR 1934*, II, 579; Skinner to Hull, April 1, 1934, DS 251.11 Insull, Samuel/464; *Christian Science Monitor*, April 2, 1934; Washington *Post*, April 1 and 2, 1934.

[93] Skinner to Hull, March 30, 1934, *FR 1934*, II, 578; *Christian Science Monitor*, April 2 and 3, 1934; London *Times*, April 2, 1934; Skinner to Hull, April 2, 1934, *FR 1934*, II, 579.

[94] Hull to Homer S. Cummings (Attorney General), April 12, 1934, DS 251.11 Insull, Samuel/562; Department of State, *Press Releases*, Weekly Issue No. 236 (April 7, 1934), p. 187; *ibid.*, Weekly Issue No. 237 (April 14, 1934), p. 200; Burton Y. Berry to Hull, May 8, 1934, *FR 1934*, II, 583. Two federal trials and an Illinois trial in 1934 and 1935 resulted in Insull's acquittal. See McDonald, *Insull*, 319–333, and Busch, *Guilty or Not Guilty?*, pp. 135, 192–194.

[95] Washington *Post*, April 3, 1934; Skinner to Hull, June 28, 1934, DS 211.67/48.

Conclusions

By the end of 1934, the United States and Turkey, through patient negotiation and a willingness to compromise, had built a system of treaties and other agreements placing their relations on a sound and permanent basis. These relations, disrupted by World War I, became more cordial than they had ever been before. The special purpose of the establishment and residence treaty of 1931 was to guarantee the status of Americans residing in Turkey. With most-favored-nation treatment in regard to conditions of residence in Turkey, American citizens could feel more secure, and the United States government had a sound basis for any needed representations. This important treaty affected all Americans in Turkey, whether they were educators, doctors, businessmen, archaeologists, missionaries, technical experts, diplomats, or tourists. The treaty was equally important as an indication of the adjustment of the United States government to Turkish nationalism, for it accepted the end of the treaty of 1830 and the abrogation of the capitulations. Technically, from the point of view of the United States, the capitulations were still legal until the treaty went into effect. The establishment and residence treaty removed an old obstacle to harmony between Turkey and the United States.

The claims convention of 1934 was an important milestone, eliminating a twenty-year controversy. As long as the question remained unsettled, there was a substantial number of American citizens who, for material reasons, were hostile to Turkey, and they formed the core of the anti-Turkish group in the United States. Obviously those claimants who received no benefits from the settlement were not pleased, but it was clear that the agreement with Turkey was final and that their claims were without legal foundation. In the claims compromise, the Unted States accepted terms providing for the payment of a small percentage of the original claims filed with the State Department. The United States took this course not only because many of the claims were questionable but also because of Turkey's poor financial condition. Turkey quibbled about the amount of the payment, but the later disclosure that the settlement had been excessive confirmed the justice of her argument.

The most complicated question concerning the status of Turkish and American citizens as individuals proved insolvable, even though both sides desired a settlement. The basis for the nationality controversy was the two conflicting theories of citizenship, both recognized by international law. Turkey as a country of emigration wanted to retain the allegiance of its na-

215

tionals, whereas the United States as a country of immigration felt these individuals should have the right of expatriation and naturalization. Since neither side would sacrifice its position, no settlement was possible.

The establishment and residence treaty, the extradition treaty, and the claims convention solved most of the problems concerning the status of American citizens in Turkey and Turkish citizens in the United States. Together with the treaty of commerce of 1929, they went a long way toward completing the rapprochement of Turkey and the United States.

The United States, Turkey, and International Politics, 1923–1939

THE Ottoman Empire emerged from World War I as a decadent, defeated, and dying nation. Occupied in many areas by Allied forces, invaded by the Greeks, and deprived of much of its territory by the Treaty of Sèvres in 1920, the future of the embattled nation seemed one of domestic confusion and international obscurity. A savior appeared, however, in the person of Kemal Atatürk, who rallied the Turkish peasants of the interior to resist the Greek invaders. The fight ended in success with the expulsion of the Greeks through Izmir in September, 1922. The Lausanne conference confirmed the Kemalist victory with a treaty in July, 1923, recognizing Turkey as a sovereign and independent nation. Turkey alone among the defeated Central Powers was able to annul a treaty forced upon it by the vengeful European powers.[1]

Although Turkey was greatly reduced in size by 1923, its strategic geographical position assured it a role of continued importance in European and Middle Eastern affairs. Because it was generally satisfied with the Lausanne settlement, Turkey, in contrast with such nations as Germany, Italy, and the Soviet Union, was a nonrevisionist or "status quo" power during the period before World War II. This basic attitude tem-

[1] William Yale, *The Near East: A Modern History* (Ann Arbor, Mich., 1958), pp. 276–293; George Lenczowski, *The Middle East in World Affairs* (3rd ed., Ithaca, N.Y., 1962), pp. 98–110; Roderic H. Davison, "Turkish Diplomacy from Mudros to Lausanne," in Gordon A. Craig and Felix Gilbert, eds., *The Diplomats, 1919–1939* (Princeton, 1953), pp. 172–209; M. S. Anderson, *The Eastern Question 1774–1923: A Study in International Relations* (London, Melbourne, Toronto, & New York, 1966), pp. 353–387; Bernard Lewis, *The Emergence of Modern Turkey* (London, 1961), pp. 234–250.

217

pered the Turkish Republic's foreign policy, which included the maintenance of Turkish independence and territorial integrity and the permanent preservation of international peace.[2] Turkish leaders resented the Anglo-French role in Turkey's humiliation during World War I and the years immediately following the war, but this feeling diminished as the years passed. Although basically unsympathetic with communist ideology, Turkey maintained close formal relations with the Soviet Union because an unfriendly spirit between the two countries could have caused considerable trouble for Turkey.[3] During the two decades following World War I, Turkey also mended its fences with its Balkan neighbors, first with Greece in a treaty on October 30, 1930, and then with Yugoslavia, Rumania, and Greece in the Balkan Pact of February 9, 1934. The pact represented not only a desire for friendship among the Balkan nations but also a means of maintaining peace through containment of revisionist Italy.[4]

Although Turkey did not seek comprehensive revisions of the Lausanne settlement, it desired several specific readjustments. The first involved Turkey's claims to the oil-rich Mosul area in British-mandated Iraq. When the two nations failed to settle the controversy by bilateral negotiations at Lausanne and later, England referred the question to the League of Nations in 1924. After an international commission investigated, the League Council awarded the Mosul area to Iraq on December 16, 1925. Turkey protested that the decision was beyond the competence of the Council and soon concluded a close political alliance with the Soviet Union. In a treaty with England on June 5, 1926, however, Turkey gave up its claims to Mosul in return for a guarantee that 10 per cent of the royalties from Mosul oil would be paid to Turkey.[5] Much to Turkey's credit, a potentially dangerous problem had been settled peaceably by

[2] Lenczowski, *The Middle East in World Affairs*, pp. 128–129.

[3] *Ibid.*, pp. 129–130; Sir Reader Bullard, *Britain and the Middle East from the Earliest Times to 1950* (London, 1951), pp. 91–92; Lewis, *The Emergence of Modern Turkey*, pp. 278–280.

[4] Lenczowski, *The Middle East in World Affairs*, pp. 131–133. See also John W. Wheeler-Bennett, ed., assisted by Stephen A. Heald, *Documents on International Affairs, 1933* (London, 1934), pp. 408–409, for text of the Balkan Pact.

[5] Dankwart A. Rustow, "Foreign Policy of the Turkish Republic," in Roy C. Macridis, ed., *Foreign Policy in World Politics* (Englewood Cliffs, N.J., 1958), p. 299. Turkey later gave up its share of the oil royalties in return for a payment of £500,000 sterling. See John A. DeNovo, *American Interests and Policies in the Middle East, 1900–1939* (Minneapolis, 1963), pp. 191–199, for a discussion of the Mosul oil problem and the involvement of United States oil interests.

218

compromise. Turkey illustrated the spirit which it was to demonstrate frequently during the interwar period.

The other changes Turkey desired related to the Straits and the Alexandretta region of Syria. Both problems assumed importance as the European situation became tense during the 1930s. The rise of totalitarian governments, especially in Italy and Germany, contributed to the division of Europe into two camps, both competing for Turkey's friendship because of its strategic position. Since many European countries were eager for Turkish support, Turkey was able to satisfy its objectives concerning the Straits and Alexandretta. When Turkey made clear its interest in a revision of the Straits regime, which would affect United States privileges in the area, the two nations discussed the possibility of a Turkish-American Straits convention. The presence of American archaeologists in the Alexandretta region made the Turkish-French dispute over the area a diplomatic problem for the United States.

Significant points of similarity between its foreign policy and that of Turkey caused the United States to be sympathetic with Turkish views on the Straits, Alexandretta, and various other issues of international concern. To implement their common hope for the preservation of peace, Turkey and the United States tried to arrange arbitration and conciliation treaties to provide for the peaceful settlement of bilateral disputes. Furthermore, Turkey subscribed without qualification to the Kellogg-Briand Pact of 1928, an attempt to promote peace by outlawing war.

Although the foreign policy of the United States between the two world wars prevented deep involvement in the many international issues of the era, the isolationist impulse did not prevent the United States from maintaining close relations with countries like Turkey where a substantial number of Americans lived and worked. But the United States, in its dealings with Turkey as well as other nations, maintained formal neutrality when its interests were not directly affected. Hence, the only major issues of international scope affecting Turkish-American relations and stimulating diplomatic activity were the Kellogg-Briand Pact, the Straits question, and the Alexandretta dispute. The United States played a minor role in the European struggle for Turkish allegiance just before the outbreak of World War II. Thus the following discussion of international politics as they affected Turkish-American relations in the period 1923–1939 is restricted to the specific issues already introduced.

The Proposed Arbitration and Conciliation Treaties

In 1928 both Turkey and the United States expressed interest in the negotiation of bilateral arbitration and conciliation treaties. The United States had traditionally fostered such agreements, particularly during the terms of Secretaries of State Elihu Root (1905–1909) and William Jennings Bryan (1913–1915). Under Root, the United States signed twenty-five bilateral arbitration treaties, and Bryan concluded thirty conciliation treaties containing "cooling-off" clauses to provide the disputants time for serious consideration of controversies. Although these treaties were of little or no use, some people described them as significant contributions to the cause of peace.[6] Secretary Kellogg, "possibly to ease a guilty conscience" because the United States had not joined the League of Nations, revived the idea of arbitration and conciliation treaties. Kellogg and his successor, Henry L. Stimson, concluded many new arbitration and conciliation treaties between 1925 and 1933.[7] On March 23, 1928, Kellogg explained his program to Ambassador Grew in Turkey, suggesting that such treaties with Turkey "might furnish an effective commencement of treaty relations between the two Governments." Not only would they be more acceptable to the Senate than other treaties, but "they would give [the] Turkish Government the satisfaction of having formal treaty relations with the United States." Kellogg also thought that a demonstrated willingness to negotiate such treaties on the part of the United States might make easier Grew's current efforts to extend the modus vivendi of February, 1927.[8]

Grew believed the Turkish government "would welcome the moral effect of such a treaty." Even before Grew was ready to make the proposals, Tevfik Rüsdü Aras, the Turkish Foreign Minister, broached the subject to him. A week later, the State Department handed draft treaties to Turkish Ambassador Ahmed Mouhtar in Washington. Kellogg wrote to Mouhtar: "I feel that by adopting [such] treaties . . . we shall not only promote the friendly relations between the Peoples of our two countries, but also advance materially the cause of arbitration and the pacific settlement

[6] Julius W. Pratt, *A History of United States Foreign Policy* (New York, 1955), pp. 454–455.

[7] *Ibid.,* pp. 534–535.

[8] Frank B. Kellogg to Joseph C. Grew, March 23, 1928, *Papers Relating to the Foreign Relations of the United States, 1928* (3 vols., Washington, 1942–1943), III, 940 (hereafter cited as *FR 1928*).

of international disputes." [9] When he presented the treaties to Aras, Grew discovered a major obstacle to agreement — the Armenians. The Foreign Minister was willing to sign the treaties if they included clauses making it impossible for the United States ever to invoke them on behalf of the Armenians. Aras thought this could be accomplished by "some simple formula which would give no indication of its actual purport or purpose. It could be phrased in such a way as to avoid any possible offense to American public opinion or to the American Senate." [10] The State Department stated clearly that it would never agree to such a procedure but also that it would not invoke a treaty on behalf of citizens of a foreign country. Aras suggested specific changes in the treaty drafts, but later agreed to omit these changes.[11] At the same time he brought up another controversial point.

This additional difficulty involved the definition of "domestic jurisdiction." Aras told Grew in May, 1928, "that he understood that the United States Government held that each country should itself decide what questions touched its own sovereignty and honor and what questions should be regarded as within its domestic jurisdiction." Later the Foreign Minister said he would sign the treaties if they defined domestic jurisdiction as covering "questions involving sovereignty and . . . questions which international law leaves to the exclusive competence of States." [12] The Turkish government wanted domestic jurisdiction included in the treaties, but with a clear explanation of what the term meant. The Turks were not willing to have the treaties invoked in problems they considered purely internal, such as the question of Armenians in Turkey. The State Department

[9] Diary, March 24, 1928, Joseph C. Grew MSS (Houghton Library, Harvard University, Cambridge, Mass.), 1928, vol. 3; Grew to Kellogg, April 11, 1928, *FR 1928*, III, 942; Kellogg to Grew, April 19, 1928, *ibid.*, 945; Grew to Kellogg, April 20, 1928, *ibid.*, 945–946; Kellogg to Ahmed Mouhtar, April 19, 1928, DS 711.-6712A/12.

[10] Grew to Kellogg, April 20, 1928, *FR 1928*, III, 945–946; conversation, Grew and Tevfik Rüsdü Aras, April 19, 1928, Grew MSS, 1928, vol. 3.

[11] Kellogg to Grew, April 25, 1928, *FR 1928*, III, 946–947; Grew to Kellogg, June 24, 1928, *ibid.*, 947–948; conversation, Grew and Aras, May 19, 1928, Grew MSS, 1928, vol. 3.

[12] Conversation, Grew and Aras, May 19, 1928, Grew MSS, 1928, vol. 3; Grew to Kellogg, July 3, 1928, DS 711.6712A/24. "Domestic jurisdiction" actually was a distinctive feature of the Kellogg arbitration treaties with many countries. Robert H. Ferrell in *Peace in Their Time: The Origins of the Kellogg-Briand Pact* (New Haven, 1952), p. 134, writes: "The loophole of the Kellogg formula was the reservation of all questions of 'domestic jurisdiction,' and this loophole made American arbitration treaties continue to be of questionable value."

221

would not agree to alter the standard treaty text but informed the Turkish ambassador that it would reply in the affirmative to a letter inquiring whether the United States would accept Turkey's definition of domestic jurisdiction. The text of the letter later proposed by Ahmed Mouhtar went further than the State Department had in mind, so the treaty draft was shelved temporarily.[13]

Aras reopened the question in an aide-mémoire to Grew on January 10, 1929, when he alluded to the perennial obstacles to Turkish-American agreement, the treaty of 1830 and the capitulations. The Foreign Minister suggested the addition of a clause "to insure that the provisions of the treaty of arbitration shall not be applicable to disputes and litigations arising from events which originated previous to the putting into effect of the treaty." Grew observed in a despatch to Secretary Kellogg that, since the Turkish formula was so far from the American, the likelihood of arriving at a solution was remote. The "bugaboo of the Treaty of 1830 and the Capitulations" would have to be eliminated before agreement could be reached, Grew felt.[14] Because of these difficulties, the treaty negotiations ceased late in 1929. In 1932, after ratification of the treaty of establishment and residence, which effectively abrogated the treaty of 1830 and the capitulations, the Department of State considered reopening negotiations with the Turks provided they would accept the standard United States text for arbitration and conciliation treaties.[15] By this time, of course, relations between the two countries were on a firmer basis, and no harm resulted when nothing came of the State Department plans because the Turks would not accept the American formula. The possibility of the United States and Turkey going to war over any dispute was remote. Even though they did not agree on the proposed treaties, the negotiations of the two countries demonstrated their dedication to the idea behind them — the peaceful settlement of disputes. Only a minute difference in principle concerning domestic jurisdiction blocked the successful conclusion of the negotiations.

[13] Kellogg to Grew, August 16, 1929, *FR 1928*, III, 948–949; conversation, Grew and Aras, August 21, 1928, Grew MSS, 1928, vol. 3; Kellogg to Grew, October 9, 1928, *FR 1928*, III, 949–950.

[14] Grew to Kellogg, January 16, 1929, DS 711.6712A/31 (telegram); Grew to Kellogg, January 16, 1929, DS 711.6712A/32 (despatch).

[15] Wallace Murray (Chief, Near Eastern Division) to Grew, November 12, 1929, DS 711.6712A/33; Murray to Charles M. Barnes (Treaty Division), May 20, 1932, DS 711.6712A/47; Henry L. Stimson to Embassy, June 2, 1932, DS 711.-6712A/46.

The Kellogg-Briand Pact

Closely related to Secretary Kellogg's program for arbitration and conciliation treaties was the pact he helped design to outlaw war as an instrument of national policy. Influenced by American advocates of the outlawry of war, including Nicholas Murray Butler, President of Columbia University, and James Thomson Shotwell of the Carnegie Endowment for International Peace, French Foreign Minister Aristide Briand proposed a bilateral treaty to outlaw war between France and the United States. On April 6, 1927, Briand made this proposition, not through normal diplomatic channels, but directly to the American people through the press. Secretary Kellogg and his superior, President Calvin Coolidge, were cool toward Briand's plan at first because it was clear to them that it would be in effect a negative military alliance designed to complement the French security system. After long sparring with the United States, France eventually accepted Kellogg's clever counterproposal to make the treaty a multilateral pact. Although Briand did not welcome Kellogg's suggestion, the Foreign Minister's reputation as a "man of peace," demonstrated by his possession of the Nobel Peace Prize, made it impossible for him to spurn it categorically. The United States, France, Germany, England, Italy, Japan, and nine other nations signed the Kellogg-Briand Pact at the Salle de l'Horloge in Paris on August 27, 1928.[16] Utopian in purpose, the pact pledged the signatories, who "condemn recourse to war for the solution of international controversies, and renounce it as an instrument of national policy in their relations with one another," to settle all disputes by "pacific" means.[17]

Turkey showed considerable interest in the Paris negotiations preceding the signing of the antiwar pact.[18] The Turkish Foreign Minister in an interview in April, 1928, with Dorothy Ring, an Associated Press correspondent, expressed his opinion that the pact should include a clause providing that, if one power attacked another, all other signatories would remain neutral. Although Aras considered making this proposal to Kellogg through Ahmed Mouhtar in Washington, he consented not to do so when Grew explained that this would further complicate the very difficult negotiations taking place in Paris.[19] Shortly before signature of the pact, Grew,

[16] Ferrell, *Peace in Their Time*, pp. 66–72, 129, 140–146, 215–219.
[17] *Ibid.*, pp. 266–269 (text of the pact).
[18] See editor's note in Joseph C. Grew, *Turbulent Era: A Diplomatic Record of Forty Years, 1904–1945*, ed. Walter Johnson (2 vols., Boston, 1952), II, 796.
[19] Grew to Kellogg, April 25, 1928, DS 711.6712 Anti-War/3. The Turkish For-

always looking for ways to advance Turkish-American friendship, suggested to Kellogg that Turkey be included among the original signatories. This move not only would enhance United States prestige in Turkey but also "the moral effect of including the leading power of the near and middle East would be considerable in the eyes of the world." Grew also believed such a move would promote the westernization of Turkey and draw her further away from Soviet influence.[20] Kellogg rejected Grew's proposal as impractical since the addition of Turkey to the original signers would necessitate similar invitations to various other countries which had expressed interest. At the same time Kellogg outlined the provision in the pact for the adherence of nonoriginal signatories.[21]

On August 27, 1928, Grew advised the Turkish Foreign Minister of the signing of the pact and invited Turkey to adhere. Aras responded on September 6, making clear that Turkey intended to accept the document without reservation.[22] The Turkish press generally did not express as much enthusiasm for the pact as did its government. *La République* of Istanbul observed: "Just as we applaud actors in a theatre for their skill alone, without believing in the seriousness of their love and tears let us applaud for the sake of peace the political actors playing on the stage of peace for the nice things they are saying, without taking them seriously."[23]

The Turkish government resolved to be the first nation to ratify the pact after the United States. Aras explained to Grew on December 12, 1928, that he was placing the pact on the calendar of the Grand National Assembly daily and that the Assembly would ratify as soon as it received word that the United States Senate had acted favorably. Grew requested Kellogg to send him a "flash" telegram when the Senate acted.[24] The Senate gave its advice and consent on January 16, 1929, and the Turks followed suit three days later. Grew noted in his diary that Aras got "out of a sickbed especially to make the speech necessary to put it through and then . . . [returned] to bed immediately thereafter. It looks as if he did

eign Minister's suggestion certainly was not consistent with the collective security ideas of the League of Nations, which Turkey later joined in 1932.

[20] Grew to Kellogg, August 11, 1928, DS 711.6712 Anti-War/5.

[21] Kellogg to Grew, August 13, 1928, DS 711.6712 Anti-War/6.

[22] Aras to Grew, September 6, 1928, *FR 1928*, I, 195–196.

[23] August 23, 1928, clipping and translation in Grew to Kellogg, September 8, 1928, DS 711.6712 Anti-War/15. This despatch includes clippings and translations of similar articles from the Turkish press.

[24] Conversation, Grew and Aras, December 12, 1928, Grew MSS, 1928, vol. 3; Grew to Kellogg, December 12, 1928, DS 711.6712 Anti-War/32.

wish to be the first to ratify after the United States and I imagine that he has succeeded. . . . I feel rather proud that this promptness on the part of the Turkish Government . . may be due, in some small measure, to my various talks with the Minister on the side lines. . . ." [25] The Turks deposited their instrument of ratification in Washington with those of the other signatories on July 8, 1929, in time to join in the ceremony proclaiming the Kellogg-Briand Pact at the White House on July 24.[26]

As is well known, the Kellogg-Briand Pact in practice was almost worthless. Even Turkey contributed indirectly to its ineffectiveness. The pact's first test, which originated before its proclamation, was a Sino-Russian dispute over the Chinese Eastern Railway, a line in Manchuria controlled jointly by the two nations. President Chiang Kai-shek of China used the dispute to divert attention from his domestic governmental and party difficulties. Secretary of State Stimson invoked the Kellogg pact, first in July, 1929, and again late in November, when actual fighting on a small scale broke out in Manchuria.[27] On December 1, 1929, Stimson sent special instructions to the United States diplomatic representatives in countries which had ratified the Kellogg-Briand Pact. They were to ask the governments to which they were accredited to make a statement invoking the pact similar to one he had addressed to China and indirectly to the Soviet Union. The countries circularized included Turkey.[28] The Turkish government declined Stimson's request, ostensibly because of current Chinese-Soviet negotiations to settle the dispute. Grew reported, however, that "the Russian Ambassador at Angora had held the ear of the Turkish Minister for Foreign Affairs constantly and has convinced him that White Russians, serving with Chinese troops and inciting them, engineered the attacks in Manchuria." In reference to a statement on the situation by Aras in which he emphasized the Sino-Russian negotiations, Grew wrote: "The obviously biased, and in my view, unsatisfactory nature of this Turkish statement clearly is owing to the Foreign Minister's leanings toward

[25] January 20, 1929, Grew, *Turbulent Era*, II, 797–798.
[26] Stimson to Ahmed Mouhtar, July 8, 1929, DS 711.6712 Anti-War/53; Ferrell, *Peace in Their Time*, pp. 258–261.
[27] See Robert H. Ferrell, *American Diplomacy in the Great Depression: Hoover-Stimson Foreign Policy, 1929–1933* (New Haven, 1957), pp. 45–67, for a discussion of this problem.
[28] Stimson to Certain Diplomatic Representatives, December 1, 1929, *Papers Relating to the Foreign Relations of the United States, 1929* (3 vols., Washington, 1943–1944), II, 371–373 (hereafter cited as *FR 1929*).

Russia, perhaps based more on *viva* than love." [29] As a matter of fact, the Russians and Chinese did arrive at a negotiated settlement on December 22, 1929. Five days earlier, the Turks and Russians signed a protocol extending for two years their treaty of friendship and neutrality of December, 1925. The Turkish government, apparently concerned about the effect this might have on relations with the United States, assured Grew and the State Department that the protocol was not an alliance and "that no obstacle whatever exists to the development and the consolidation of Turco-American relations in every domain and that such development and consolidation is in no way whatever opposed by the recently signed protocol." [30] Although the Turks paid lip service to the Kellogg-Briand Pact in their reply to Stimson's request, they were much more concerned with the problem of their relations with the Soviet Union. They redeemed themselves during the involved Sino-Japanese dispute beginning at Mukden, Manchuria, on September 18, 1931. Following the lead of France, Great Britain, and Italy, the Turkish government sent notes to China and Japan calling attention to the principles to which they had subscribed in the Kellogg-Briand Pact. The combined pressures of the pact and the League of Nations, however, failed to resolve this trouble, which initiated a conflict between China and Japan lasting until 1945.[31]

The experience of the United States with Turkey in regard to the Kellogg-Briand Pact, initially at least, had a beneficial effect on the relations of the two countries. Turkey's eagerness to approve the pact was further evidence of its agreement with the United States on how to maintain international peace. Turkey, like other nations, had to minimize the pact's value when its national interest was at stake, as in the case of the Sino-Soviet dispute of 1929. Although idealistic in its outlook, Turkey had to be realistic in its application of the pact. Even though the Kellogg-Briand

[29] Grew to Stimson, December 5, 1929, *ibid.*, 390–391; Grew to Stimson, December 10, 1929, *ibid.*, 414–415; Department of State, *Press Releases*, Weekly Issue No. 11 (December 14, 1929), pp. 101–102.

[30] Ferrell, *American Diplomacy in the Great Depression*, p. 60; Grew to Stimson, December 20, 1929, *FR 1929*, III, 842–844; Francis White (for Stimson) to Grew, January 7, 1930, *ibid.*, 844–845. See also diary, January 31, 1930, Grew, *Turbulent Era*, II, 839–842, for Grew's opinion of the effect of the protocol on Turkish-American relations. Grew agreed with the Turkish view.

[31] Ferrell, *American Diplomacy in the Great Depression*, pp. 122–124, 141; Grew to Stimson, November 1, 1931, *Papers Relating to the Foreign Relations of the United States, 1931* (3 vols., Washington, 1946), III, 349 (hereafter cited as *FR 1931*). See Ferrell, *American Diplomacy in the Great Depression*, pp. 120–193, for a discussion of the events in Manchuria in the early 1930s.

treaty turned out to be a ridiculously ineffective instrument for the pacific settlement of disputes, Turkey should be given credit for accepting it in good faith.

The Montreux Convention, 1936

During the second decade of the Turkish Republic's existence, the European situation changed radically. Germany led in the repudiation of the Versailles diktat and creation of the climate leading to World War II. The altered situation affected Turkey in many ways, but, in contrast with the totalitarian powers of Europe and Asia, the governments of Kemal Atatürk and his successor, Ismet Inönü, sought security by peaceful means. In a sense, Turkey followed the spirit of the ill-fated Kellogg-Briand Pact.

As Europe tensed in the 1930s, Turkey became more concerned about its security. The country oriented its foreign policy toward peaceful relations with all nations, but Turkey could not ignore the threats of revisionist powers like Germany, with its *drang nach osten*, and Italy, which, according to Benito Mussolini, had "historic objectives . . . in Asia and Africa." Nor could Turkey disregard Mussolini's reference to the Mediterranean as "mare nostrum" or his possession of the Dodecanese Islands off Turkey's coast.[32] Especially because of its fear of Italy, Turkey began a rearmament program in the mid-1930s. The key to Turkey's security, of course, was the area of the Straits (the Dardanelles, the Sea of Marmara, and the Bosporus), which for centuries had been of great geopolitical importance to Europe and Asia. From the Treaty of Kuchuk Kainarji at the end of the Russo-Turkish War in 1774 to the armistice of Mudros in 1918, the Straits had been under nominal Ottoman control but were subject to various treaties and threats from European powers.[33] The twelfth of Woodrow Wilson's Fourteen Points advocated free navigation of the Straits for all nations under international guarantee. The abortive Treaty of Sèvres in 1920 demilitarized the area and established an international administrative commission, backed by the joint occupation of England,

[32] Lenczowski, *The Middle East in World Affairs*, pp. 132–133, 139–140; Arnold J. Toynbee, assisted by V. M. Boulter, *Survey of International Affairs, 1936* (London, 1937), p. 601.

[33] Toynbee, *Survey of International Affairs, 1936*, p. 587. See James T. Shotwell and Francis Deák, *Turkey at the Straits: A Short History* (New York, 1940), for a history of the Straits from ancient times through 1939. Anderson, *The Eastern Question, passim*, also discusses the historical background of the Straits issue.

France, and Italy.[34] A Straits convention, drawn up at Lausanne in 1923, established conditions for the passage of commercial and war vessels and aircraft, demilitarized the zone, and continued the International Commission originated at Sèvres. The commission, under the permanent presidency of Turkey, included members from all signatory nations of the Allied-Turkish Lausanne Treaty.[35]

Although accepting the Straits settlement of 1923, Turkey became increasingly dissatisfied with it in the 1930s when Mussolini began to make his thinly veiled threats concerning Turkish territory. Turkey's entrance into the League of Nations in July, 1932, not only ended the irregular situation in which a nonmember state headed a League instrument, the Straits Commission, but also provided a forum for the gradual clarification of Turkey's views about Straits revision.[36] Between 1933 and 1936, Foreign Minister Aras hinted regularly about Turkey's distaste for the existing Straits arrangement, but not until April 10, 1936, did Turkey initiate formal diplomatic discussions looking toward a change. Turkey chose an opportune moment to press for revision, a time when most of the European powers were likely to be receptive. Italy's successful aggression in Abyssinia (Ethiopia) confirmed the impotency of the League, and the Germans had just reoccupied the demilitarized Rhineland in complete disregard of the Treaty of Versailles and the Locarno treaties of 1925. The Turkish notes of April 10, 1936, to the Lausanne signatories, Yugoslavia, and the League pointed out that the European situation had changed greatly since 1923, thus necessitating a conference to consider revision of the Straits convention in the interest of Turkish freedom and security.[37] Some recipients of the note hesitated, but the eventual acceptance of all except Italy led to the convening of the suggested meeting at Montreux, Switzerland, on June 22, 1936. The Soviet Union, which never approved the 1923 convention, strongly backed Turkey. As a small naval power, the Soviet Union believed that the Straits should have been closed to all war-

---

[34] Toynbee, *Survey of International Affairs, 1936*, pp. 593–594.

[35] *Ibid.*, pp. 596–597; Anderson, *The Eastern Question*, pp. 372–373.

[36] Toynbee, *Survey of International Affairs, 1936*, pp. 599–600.

[37] *Ibid.*, pp. 600–604, 643; Prentiss B. Gilbert (Consul, Geneva, Switzerland) to Hull, April 17, 1935, *Foreign Relations of the United States: Diplomatic Papers, 1935* (4 vols., Washington, 1952–1953), I, 1026–1027 (hereafter cited as *FR 1935*); Skinner to Hull, April 30, 1935, *ibid.*, 1027; Stephen Heald, ed., in conjunction with John W. Wheeler-Bennett, *Documents on International Affairs, 1936* (London, 1937), pp. 645–648 (text of the Turkish notes of April 10, 1936); memo, Cordell Hull, April 11, 1936, *Foreign Relations of the United States: Diplomatic Papers, 1936* (5 vols., Washington, 1953–1954), III, 503–506 (hereafter cited as *FR 1936*).

ships at all times. Russia, of course, had a traditional interest in the Straits and now saw a chance to achieve a goal unattainable in 1923. Great Britain and France approved the Turkish request for completely opposite reasons. England, looking for allies in the Middle East, thought cooperation with Turkey would draw that country away from the Soviet Union. France, on the other hand, believed that increased Soviet influence in the Mediterranean area would enhance the value of the Franco-Soviet pact of 1935.[38]

The Turks emerged from the Montreux conference (June 22–July 20, 1936) with a new Straits convention which not only met their wishes but also represented a moral victory for the Turkish Republic. The convention established conditions for the operation of commercial and war vessels and aircraft in the Straits and regulated the size of fleets in the Black Sea. More important to Turkey than these provisions was the abolition of the International Commission and the transfer to the Turkish government of its powers, including the right to remilitarize the Straits area immediately. As soon as the delegates signed the Montreux convention, thirty thousand Turkish troops marched into the demilitarized zone, where the entire Turkish fleet greeted them along the coast. Ironically, the *Yavuz*, the reconditioned *Goeben* of 1914 fame, led the fleet.[39]

Turkey won a moral victory through the methods it employed to achieve its objectives in the Straits. Arnold Toynbee has expressed the point well:

The occasion took on an interest far greater than its subject-matter merited, because of the light which it threw on . . . the problem of peaceful change. . . . Advocates of treaty revision welcomed it because . . . it provided both a proof that the doctrine of *rebus sic stantibus* . . . had not lapsed into oblivion and a precedent for its future application. Opponents of treaty revision welcomed it because, coming at a time when a series of unilateral treaty repudiations . . . had seriously damaged the prestige of international law and all but undermined the Geneva system, it seemed to prove that there was at least one "ex-enemy" Power with a

---

[38] Toynbee, *Survey of International Affairs, 1936*, pp. 597–598, 607–611.

[39] *Ibid.*, 613–645 (description of the Montreux conference); Heald, *Documents on International Affairs, 1936*, pp. 648–667 (text of the Montreux convention); C. G. Fenwick, "The New Status of the Dardanelles," *American Journal of International Law*, XXX (October, 1936), 704–705 (analysis of the convention); MacMurray to Hull, July 22, 1936, *FR 1936*, III, 526. See also Gilbert to Hull, March 11, 1937, DS 767. 68119/1000, for enclosure no. 1, *Actes de la Conférence de Montreux, 22 Juin–20 Juillet 1936: Compte Rendu des Séances Plénières et Procès-Verbal des Débats du Comité Technique* (Paris, 1936).

dictator at the head of its Government which had not succumbed to the fascination of the *fait accompli* and still retained a proper respect for its international engagements.[40]

The application of pacific means for the settlement of the Straits question, in the spirit of the Kellogg-Briand Pact and the League of Nations, raised Turkey's prestige, particularly when contrasted with the behavior of Germany and Italy, whose reliance on unilateral revisionism was laying the groundwork for World War II.

Since the Straits were a problem also in Turkish-American relations, the developments just described were of interest to the United States. Although American vessels and aircraft did not make extensive use of the Straits, the United States desired a guarantee of equal rights in the area. Article X of the rejected Turkish-American Treaty of Lausanne would have regulated these matters. The clause of the 1927 exchange of notes making effective the essential provisions of the Lausanne Treaty pending the negotiation of new treaties and agreements settled the problem for a time.[41] But the negotiation of a treaty of establishment and residence paved the way for termination of the 1927 agreement. A State Department official pointed out in March, 1931, that though the Allied Straits convention of 1923 was applicable to the vessels of all nations, the United States technically could not legally invoke it if such a need arose. "Our rights . . . ," the official continued, "to freedom of passage . . . through the Straits will depend, after our treaty of establishment and residence . . . and a consular treaty become effective, solely upon the whim of the Powers which are parties to the Straits Convention." The solution suggested was the negotiation of a Turkish-American Straits convention.[42] Ambassador Grew advised against this course of action because the Turks "are still rather technical-minded and suspicious and it is never wise . . . to raise theoretical questions with them or suggest doubts to their minds unless there is a sound practical reason for so doing. I cannot see that in the present case that practical reason exists." The Navy Department, however, when asked for its opinion, submitted a report from the General Board advising the negotiation of "some formal agreement, treaty or exchange of notes" to regulate American rights in the Straits. The Gen-

[40] *Survey of International Affairs, 1936*, pp. 584–585. Fenwick, in "The New Status of the Dardanelles," p. 701, expresses similar views.

[41] Murray to Grew, November 18, 1930, DS 711.672 Straits/1.

[42] Memo, M. J. Holland to Murray, March 7, 1931, DS 711.672 Straits/10.

eral Board also felt that the United States should insist on its right to deal directly with the Turks rather than through the International Straits Commission.[43] Despite the suggestions of the General Board, no action occurred at this time.

In June, 1934, when an article appeared in the New York *Times* about Turkish hopes for revision of the Lausanne Straits convention, the State Department reopened the question. The Department instructed Ambassador Skinner to inquire discreetly about the rumor that the Turks would seek revision and also requested his judgment about the need for a Turkish-American Straits convention. Skinner assured the State Department that the Turkish government had no intention of raising the question formally at that time and advised against a special agreement, since the United States in effect had all the privileges of other powers in the Straits.[44]

The State Department did not drop the question because it wanted to negotiate a consular convention with Turkey and felt that a preliminary clarification of American rights in the Straits was necessary. Foreign Minister Aras subsequently told Skinner on two occasions that a Straits convention would be feasible if the United States "would assume the same responsibilities for the defense of the Straits as the Powers signatory of the Straits Convention." [45] It was, of course, out of the question, considering American foreign policy at the time, for the United States to undertake such a commitment. In September, 1935, the United States Navy restated its view favoring a Straits convention, but the State Department decided to leave the question suspended because of the Turkish desire that the United States accept responsibilities for the defense of the Straits.[46]

Shortly after the Turkish proposal of April 10, 1936, for a conference on revision of the Straits regime, Ambassador MacMurray talked with Foreign Minister Aras about United States rights in the Straits. MacMur-

---

[43] Grew to Murray, May 12, 1931, DS 711.672 Straits/3; W. R. Castle, Jr. (Undersecretary of State) to Secretary of the Navy, June 5, 1931, DS 711.672 Straits/5; Ernest L. Jahncke (Acting Secretary of the Navy) to Stimson, July 13, 1931, DS 711.672 Straits/6.

[44] William Phillips (for Hull) to Skinner, June 29, 1934, *Foreign Relations of the United States: Diplomatic Papers, 1934* (5 vols., Washington, 1950–1952), II, 973–974 (hereafter cited as *FR 1934*); Skinner to Hull, July 20, 1934, *ibid.*, 980–981.

[45] Murray to Shaw, October 23, 1934, *ibid.*, 983–984; Skinner to Hull, October 29, 1934, *ibid.*, 984–985; Skinner to Hull, June 26, 1935, *FR 1935*, I, 1030–1031.

[46] R. Walton Moore (for Hull) to Shaw, September 11, 1935, *FR 1935*, I, 1040–1041; Henry L. Roosevelt (Assistant Secretary of the Navy) to Hull, August 17, 1935, *ibid.*, 1041–1042.

ray reported after the conversation that there was no reason to believe Turkey would disturb the complete freedom of commercial navigation through the Straits even if it succeeded in eliminating the 1923 convention. MacMurray continued: "And in view particularly of the disposition of the Turkish Government, because of the 'favorable balance of trade' with the United States, to give American commerce the most favorable treatment, I am confident that we need feel no anxiety about the continued enjoyment by our shipping of the benefits of the regime." [47]

The United States sent no observers to the Montreux conference because it did not intend to become a party to any settlement reached there. The Navy Department concurred in this course of action, although it reaffirmed again its view of the need for a bilateral agreement with Turkey to safeguard American rights in the Straits.[48] During the conference the Turkish delegation made it clear that countries like the United States would continue to have equal privileges in the Straits even though they were not signatories of the Lausanne convention or the proposed new arrangement.[49] After examining the Montreux convention, the State Department felt that it was "essentially satisfactory from the American point of view." The Department also believed that the United States could legally invoke the Montreux convention, even though it was not a signatory, because Turkey had assumed full responsibility for controlling navigation through the Straits, including vessels from the United States. The Turkish Foreign Minister in November, 1936, again stated that his government guaranteed to all nations, signatory and nonsignatory, free commercial navigation of the Straits and all other privileges embodied in the convention.[50] This interpretation of the Montreux convention eliminated the need for a separate Turkish-American Straits agreement.

The United States never voiced any objections to Turkey's effort to strengthen its security system by a revision of the Straits regime. The only concern was that American rights should be safeguarded. If Turkey had taken unilateral action to overthrow the International Commission and remilitarize the zone without permission of the interested nations, the

[47] J. V. A. MacMurray to Hull, April 23, 1936, *FR 1936*, III, 512–514.
[48] *Ibid.*, 513–514; Hull to MacMurray, June 22, 1936, *ibid.*, 521–522.
[49] Gilbert to Hull, June 23, 1936, *ibid.*, 522; Shaw to Hull, June 26, 1936, DS 767.68119/927.
[50] Unsigned memo, "The Straits Convention of July 20, 1936, As It Affects American Interests," August 13, 1936, DS 767.68119/973; MacMurray to Hull, November 13, 1936, *FR 1936*, III, 528–529.

United States probably would have lodged a serious objection. Turkey's behavior in this instance, however, gave an example of how it would act as the European situation became more tense.

European Interest in Turkey in the 1930s

Between 1936 and 1939, a close alliance with Turkey became an important objective for several European nations. Thus England, France, Germany, and the Soviet Union tried to extend their influence in Turkey. Italy never really entered into this contest because Turkey feared Mussolini's ambitions even before his conquest of Abyssinia. American neutrality legislation, precluding any direct intervention by the United States in the various crises of the decade, actually encouraged the revisionist powers to take action since they were assured that no American arms would go to their opponents.[51] Although as a result of this neutrality legislation and isolationist attitudes the United States played an insignificant role in the European power struggle, it was sympathetic with status quo powers such as England and France. Turkey could not maintain the neutrality dictated by Congress for the United States, but it welcomed the principles of foreign policy pronounced by Secretary Hull and President Roosevelt. The Turks reacted favorably to Hull's statement of July 16, 1937, on the American position in regard to international problems. The United States, Hull pointed out, advocated the maintenance of peace, abstinence from the use of force in pursuit of national policy, the adjustment of international problems and the revision of treaties by peaceful negotiations, and the limitation and reduction of armaments. The United States also wished to promote world economic security and stability and the end of excessive barriers to international trade. The United States would "avoid entering into alliances or entangling commitments but we believe in cooperative effort by peaceful and practicable means," Hull concluded. The Turkish Minister for Foreign Affairs made it clear that his government was "entirely in accord" with the principles Hull had advocated, particularly the idea of consultation for the peaceful settlement of disputes.[52]

---

[51] Selig Adler, *The Isolationist Impulse: Its Twentieth Century Reaction* (New York, 1966), pp. 238–242.

[52] Statement by the Secretary of State, July 16, 1937, *Foreign Relations of the United States: Diplomatic Papers, 1937* (5 vols., Washington, 1954), I, 699–700 (hereafter cited as *FR 1937*); S. Walter Washington (Chargé d'Affaires) to Hull, July 29, 1937, *ibid.*, 726; memo of conversation, Washington and Aras, August 11,

Shortly before Hull made his pronouncement, Turkey entered into an agreement with three other Middle Eastern countries which, according to Hull, "clearly put into practice . . . the good neighbor policy as advocated by the United States and explained in detail in my statement of July 16th." The agreement was the Middle Eastern Pact, signed by Turkey, Iran, Iraq, and Afghanistan on July 8, 1937. The four nations designed the pact, providing for noninterference, nonaggression, consultation, and mutual guarantees of frontiers, to discourage interference by other powers, particularly Italy and the Soviet Union. Turkey's membership in both groups indirectly linked the Balkan and Middle Eastern pacts.[53] Although concerned about security when it agreed to the Middle Eastern Pact, Turkey put into operation the principles for the peaceful settlement of disputes which were also cornerstones of American foreign policy.

The Sanjak of Alexandretta

The contest among various European powers for Turkish allegiance enabled Turkey to arrange a peaceful solution to another problem resulting from the post–World War I settlement. The Sanjak of Alexandretta, the section of France's Syrian mandate immediately south of the Turkish border, before World War I had been part of the Turkish vilayet of Aleppo. Since about forty per cent of the Sanjak's population was Turkish speaking, the Turkish government was unwilling to renounce claims to the area as it did in regard to other territories detached after World War I. The Franklin-Bouillon agreement of October 20, 1921, resulted in the establishment of a special administrative regime for the Sanjak.[54] The conclusion of a Franco-Syrian treaty in September, 1936, envisioning the eventual independence of Syria, including Alexandretta, disturbed the Turkish government and prompted it to bring the question before the Council of the League of Nations. The discussions thus opened led to an agree-

1937, *ibid.*, 779–780; memo by the Turkish Minister for Foreign Affairs, August 20, 1937, *ibid.*, 797–798.

[53] Hull to Cornelius V. H. Engert (Chargé d'Affaires, Teheran, Iran), August 5, 1937, *ibid.*, 753–754 (similar telegram sent to United States Chargé d'Affaires in Turkey); Washington to Hull, August 11, 1937, *ibid.*, 770; Stephen Heald, ed., *Documents on International Affairs, 1937* (London, 1939), pp. 530–533 (includes text of the pact in French); Lenczowski, *The Middle East in World Affairs*, p. 184. This agreement was also known as the Saadabad Pact.

[54] Heald, *Documents on International Affairs, 1937*, p. 465; Toynbee, *Survey of International Affairs, 1936*, pp. 767–768.

ment on January 27, 1937, providing for the establishment of the Sanjak as a special political unit with a Statute and Fundamental Law (adopted on May 29, 1937) but in a customs and monetary union with Syria.[55]

Turkey, still dissatisfied, thought that the electoral laws and procedures adopted did not guarantee enough influence to the Turkish-speaking inhabitants. At this point the worsening European situation aided Turkey in securing a new and more favorable arrangement. By mid-1938, events in central Europe, where Germany was making ominous moves, preoccupied the French. France was not willing to quarrel with Turkey over an area which it would lose in any case when the Syrian mandate ended. Furthermore, Turkey's strategic position in the Straits area, which would dominate Franco-Soviet communications in the event of a war, influenced the French. Agreements on July 3–4, 1938, proclaimed the Sanjak a Franco-Turkish condominium to be policed by the troops of both nations. A new election in September, 1938, based on electoral lists compiled jointly by Turkey and France, resulted in a Turkish majority in the assembly of the Sanjak.[56] The assembly then declared the area an autonomous nation named the Republic of Hatay, after the Turkish name for the area. For all practical purposes, Turkey had taken over the controversial territory. Another agreement on June 23, 1939, recognized this fait accompli. France was willing to agree to the annexation of Hatay by Turkey in return for a Franco-Turkish Declaration of Mutual Assistance pledging both countries to proceed to the negotiation of a long-term mutual assistance pact.[57] Once again Turkey had achieved revision of a postwar arrangement by peaceful negotiation rather than by strictly unilateral action. Turkey's conduct in this case, however, was more questionable than the Straits matter because the settlement required a large group of non-Turkish peoples to live under Turkish rule. The French sacrificed the interests of this group in return for a strengthening of their defensive system.

The United States felt an immediate concern about the dispute over Alexandretta because of the potential threat to American archaeological expeditions in the area.[58] In June, 1938, the State Department sought as-

[55] Toynbee, *Survey of International Affairs, 1936*, pp. 759–783; Heald, *Documents on International Affairs, 1937*, pp. 484–485, 490–501 (texts of the January 27, 1937, and May 29, 1937, agreements).

[56] The new electoral lists showed a Turkish majority of sixty-three per cent. See Lenczowski, *The Middle East in World Affairs*, pp. 316–318.

[57] Arnold J. Toynbee et al., *Survey of International Affairs, 1938* (3 vols., London, New York, & Toronto, 1941–1953), I, 479–492.

[58] See above, p. 180, for previous discussion of this matter.

surances from France that the archaeological contracts of Princeton University and the Oriental Institute of the University of Chicago would be honored regardless of the final disposition of the area. The French Foreign Office promised Ambassador William C. Bullitt in Paris that the contracts would not be jeopardized.[59] In January, 1939, after establishment of the Republic of Hatay, rumors suggested that the Turkish-controlled local authorities there would abrogate the contracts, which called for a division of all discoveries. The French Foreign Office received pledges from Turkey at this time that the American contracts would be honored as written, so the United States made no direct diplomatic approaches to Turkey.[60] During the Franco-Turkish negotiations in 1939 for the declaration of mutual assistance and the cession of Hatay, the United States made clear its wish that American archaeological rights in Hatay should be guaranteed. Both the French and Turkish governments gave such assurances.[61] When it signed the Franco-Turkish treaty on June 23, 1939, the Turkish government guaranteed the contracts of Princeton University and the Oriental Institute.[62] Turkey suspended the application of its laws on antiquities in order to accommodate the work of American archaeologists in Hatay.

Turkey and the United States on the Eve of World War II

It was only indirectly in regard to the Alexandretta controversy that the United States entered into the feverish negotiations of several European countries for Turkish allegiance. The European negotiations bore fruit, particularly after the German coup in Czechoslovakia and the Italian move into Albania, both in the early spring of 1939. The Anglo-Turkish Declaration of May 12, 1939, and the Franco-Turkish Declaration of June 23, 1939, paved the way for a definitive Anglo-French-Turkish treaty on October 19, 1939. Great Britain and France promised to aid Turkey if it was attacked by any country, whereas Turkey promised to aid

[59] Hull to William C. Bullitt, June 14, 1938, *Foreign Relations of the United States: Diplomatic Papers, 1938* (5 vols., Washington, 1954–1956), II, 1036–1037 (hereafter cited as *FR 1938*); Bullitt to Hull, June 17, 1938, *ibid.*, 1037.

[60] Sumner Welles (Acting Secretary of State) to Edwin C. Wilson (Chargé d'Affaires, Paris), January 9, 1939, *Foreign Relations of the United States: Diplomatic Papers, 1939* (5 vols., Washington, 1955–1957), IV, 833–834; Wilson to Hull, January 10, 1939, *ibid.*, 834; Bullitt to Hull, February 8, 1939, *ibid.*, 835.

[61] MacMurray to Hull, May 15, 1939, *ibid.*, 838–839; Hull to Bullitt, June 5, 1939, *ibid.*, 841–842; Wilson to Hull, June 7, 1939, *ibid.*, 842–843; MacMurray to Hull, June 14, 1939, *ibid.*, 844.

[62] Robert F. Kelley (Chargé d'Affaires) to Hull, June 23, 1939, *ibid.*, 844–845.

them only if war occurred in the Mediterranean area.[63] The German government, disturbed by the Turkish negotiations with Great Britain and France, sent former chancellor Franz von Papen to Turkey as its ambassador, with the hope that he could influence Turkey's foreign policy and draw that country closer to Germany. Von Papen reported to his government after the Anglo-Turkish Declaration in May, 1939, that "Turkey has left her previous political line of strict neutrality and has allied herself with the British group of Powers. This step means a complete shift of the balance of power in the eastern Mediterranean." The subsequent toughening of the German attitude, including economic pressures, did not coerce Turkey into closer ties with Germany during 1939.[64]

There was considerable similarity between the Turkish and American positions at the beginning of World War II. Both countries sympathized with the cause of England and France, although Turkey had to pay much more immediate attention to the German attitude than did the United States. Both nations tried to be officially neutral in the conflict, but only Turkey succeeded in doing so throughout most of the war. Turkey's conduct contrasted with its action during World War I, when it fought on the side of the Central Powers. German influence in Turkey in 1939 was extensive, particularly in the economic dimension, since Germany for years had been Turkey's best customer. The difference in the Turkish attitude in 1914 as compared with 1939 can be explained partly by the fact that the German government was not so close to Turkish leaders in the latter

[63] See Arnold J. Toynbee and Margaret Carlyle, eds., *Documents on International Affairs, 1939–46* (2 vols., London, New York, & Toronto, 1951–1954), I, 202–204, for texts of the two declarations; Viscount Halifax (British Foreign Secretary) to Sir Hughe Knatchbull-Hugessen (British Ambassador to Turkey), April 13, 1939, in E. L. Woodward and Rohan Butler, eds., *Documents on British Foreign Policy, 1919–1939* (3rd series, 9 vols., London, 1949–1955), V, 179–181; Knatchbull-Hugessen to Halifax, May 12, 1939, *ibid.*, 537; Lenczowski, *The Middle East in World Affairs*, p. 137.

[64] Franz von Papen to State Secretary Weizsächer, May 20, 1939, Department of State, *Documents on German Foreign Policy, 1918–1945* (Series D, 10 vols., Washington, 1949–1957), VI, 544–546; memo by an official of the Foreign Minister's Secretariat (Schmidt), June 6, 1939, *ibid.*, 650; Lenczowski, *The Middle East in World Affairs*, p. 140. During World War II, Turkey maintained its neutrality while obligated by circumstances to deal with both groups of belligerents. Turkey broke diplomatic relations with Germany on August 2, 1944, but did not declare war against her until February 23, 1945, and then only to make possible Turkish attendance at the San Francisco conference on the United Nations. See Lenczowski, *The Middle East in World Affairs*, pp. 141–145. See also Rustow, "Foreign Policy of the Turkish Republic," pp. 295–306, for a concise analysis of Turkish foreign policy, 1923–1945.

year. But this alone does not account for Turkey's attempt to remain neutral from a conflict which eventually engulfed practically all other countries of the world.

It would be gratifying to be able to conclude that the United States played a leading role in influencing Turkish neutrality at the beginning of World War II. However, Turkey's national interest was the main determinant of its foreign policy. The leaders of the Turkish Republic in 1939 had not forgotten the lessons of World War I, which resulted in the humiliation and dismemberment of the Ottoman Empire. Nor did they want to sacrifice the great progress made in Turkey since that war. Turkey designed its foreign policy during the interwar period to preserve national independence and, in contrast with many other European nations, it did not work to shatter the post–World War I settlement. Turkey did want changes in the Straits regime and the Franco-Syrian control of Alexandretta, and was able to bring about these revisions by peaceful means. Circumstances were favorable to Turkey in both instances so that the powers involved were willing to listen to its pleas. Considering Turkey's general policy of friendship with all countries and of dedication to peace, it is doubtful whether Turkey would have taken violent unilateral action if it had not been able to achieve satisfactory settlements of the Straits and Alexandretta problems. Actually, Turkey's national interest demanded sympathy with the Allied cause at the beginning of World War II. Italy had long been a threat to Turkey's independence, and Germany was a strong Italian ally and a potential threat to Turkish security.

It is not possible to measure tangibly the influence of the United States on the role of the Turkish Republic in European and Middle Eastern affairs before World War II. But by its attempts to negotiate arbitration and conciliation treaties with the United States and, more significantly, by its unqualified acceptance of the idealistic Kellogg-Briand Pact, Turkey demonstrated its sympathy with American goals to promote world peace. The ties between Turkey and the United States provided through the work of American diplomats, educators, businessmen, technical advisers, doctors, and archaeologists in Turkey certainly contributed to increasing American influence. America's indirect role in determining Turkey's position in 1939 was to demonstrate the influence of the West.

Former Ambassador MacMurray has expressed his opinion of the influence of the United States and European countries in determining Turkey's position during World War II:

As to that, I do not believe that the United States had any influence. From the beginning, the Turks were sensitive to the menace of Nazism, and became aloof and suspicious of Germany, and correspondingly friendly and close to Great Britain; so that they were all along strongly sypathetic towards the Allied cause, even though reluctant to be drawn into the conflict. The British themselves, pragmatically estimating the risks of extending the area of hostilities, generally approved and encouraged this attitude of friendly neutrality. The United States . . . made no effort in Ankara or (so far as I know) in Washington, to influence the Turks in the matter, although of course making no secret of American sympathy with the Allies.[65]

Actually, Germany played a role similar to the one MacMurray has described for England; Ambassador von Papen's purpose during 1939 and 1940 was to keep Turkey neutral, to influence the country against close alliance with England and France.[66] Turkey's position in 1939 was determined mainly by the political situation in Europe and was only indirectly influenced by the United States.

It took a major world conflagration, World War II, to awaken the United States to its responsibilities as a world power. Plagued by strong isolationistic sentiment between the two world wars, the United States refused to join the League of Nations and did little to resist the rise of totalitarianism and the march of aggression in the 1930s. By holding aloof in the hope of avoiding a war, the United States contributed to its coming. Thus, American relations with Europe, with the exception of such projects as disarmament conferences and the Kellogg-Briand Pact, were restricted to areas which, it was felt, could not involve the United States in any future conflict. Similarly, this was true of the political relations of the United States and Turkey. The shock of World War II convinced most of the American people that they must assume a position of world leadership. After this war, the United States was willing to ally itself militarily with Turkey and many other countries. However, the groundwork for postwar United States interest in Turkey was laid between 1923 and 1939.

[65] MacMurray, Norfolk, Connecticut, letter to Roger R. Trask, September 8, 1958.
[66] Lenczowski, *The Middle East in World Affairs*, pp. 140–141.

✿ Conclusions

THE occasional comments by scholars touching on Turkish-American relations usually dismiss the years between the two world wars as of little consequence. "Until World War II," Lewis V. Thomas has written, "Turkey remained for most Americans a distant land." [1] According to another scholar, "the political approach of the United States toward the Middle East up to 1941 could be described as one of indifference, good will, and a conviction that the area was a British preserve where no major American interests were involved." [2] These judgments are generally accurate in the sense that the United States did not view Turkey as a critical nation in the interwar period. But in the United States during this period there were many people who would gladly have allowed most of the world to become a British preserve or the domain of any country as long as the United States was not disturbed economically or politically by such developments. Turkey remained remote for the average American, as did most areas outside the Western Hemisphere. The feeling of revulsion caused by the events of 1914–1918 and their aftermath contributed to the desire of many Americans to remain aloof from international politics between World War I and World War II.

Conditions of Turkish-American Relations

After the failure of Woodrow Wilson's efforts to involve the United States on a permanent basis in the settlement after World War I, neutrality

[1] Lewis V. Thomas and Richard N. Frye, *The United States and Turkey and Iran* (Cambridge, Mass., 1951), p. 143.
[2] George Lenczowski, *The Middle East in World Affairs* (3rd ed., Ithaca, N.Y., 1962), p. 671.

in international politics resumed its traditional role as a basic principle of interwar American foreign policy. United States relations with Turkey illustrate this point clearly. When Turkey pressed in the mid-1930s for a revision of the Straits regime and later on for acquisition of Alexandretta, the United States did not take sides. These political problems were chiefly the concern of Turkey and European nations. The sole task of the United States was to ensure the protection of its nonpolitical interests in the two areas. Similarly, the United States abstained as several European nations competed for Turkish allegiance in the late 1930s. Intervention in these events was beyond the scope of American foreign policy.

In addition to neutrality, another principle generally associated with American foreign policy during this period appears in Turkish-American relations. The United States tried to be a "good neighbor" of Turkey. The main objective of its Turkish policy was to cement friendly relations between the two countries. The United States, in contrast to various European nations, did not adopt a "big brother" attitude toward Turkey. As a matter of fact, as illustrated by frequent comments by Turkish officials, the political disinterestedness of the United States in Turkey was an ever-present factor promoting closer Turco-American relations.

International politics is only a part of international relations. The history of Turkish-American relations from 1919 to 1939 contradicts the view that Americans followed a rigidly isolationist code during these years. On the contrary, a detailed investigation of the economic and cultural links between the two countries indicated public and private Americans' growing interest in Turkey. Although somewhat reduced in numbers, missionary and lay educators, now catering to Turks rather than to Armenians, Greeks, and other minorities, remained an important group of Americans in Turkey. The volume of trade between the two countries increased slightly. United States companies and technicians participated in the development and administration of the Turkish economy. American archaeologists undertook several very significant projects, adding considerably to the knowledge of antiquity. The presence of these Americans in Turkey, backed by other people at home and with the concurrence and aid of their government, is evidence of the many American economic and cultural contacts with this dynamic republic in the Middle East.

The attitude of the Department of State toward Turkey raises additional questions about the validity of the isolationist label often placed loosely on United States foreign policy of the interwar period. The State

Department, at least from 1923 on, worked hard to regularize Turkish-American relations as a means of protecting and promoting economic and cultural ties with Turkey. There was no tangible reason, other than the presence of a few Americans in Turkey and limited commercial operations, for the Department to adopt this course of action. The elimination of all American connections with Turkey would not have affected vitally the prosperity or the national interest of the United States, and comparatively few Americans would have felt any concern over such a development. The end of Turkish-American trade and the work of the missionaries of the American Board would have been a calamity for persons directly concerned with these activities, but their termination would not have seriously jeopardized the larger national interest. Although American isolation from Turkey might have been feasible before World War II, the United States government gave no consideration to this course of action.

Foremost among the factors conditioning American relations with Turkey between 1914 and 1939 was nationalism, which complicated every problem between the two countries and affected all Americans living and working in Turkey. Nationalism was the lifeblood of the Turkish revolution and the ideological foundation upon which Kemal Atatürk based his program. Turkey, like the United States a century and a half earlier, fought for its independence and the right to control its own destiny. Historically, Americans revered the right of independence and self-determination, and thus they were inclined to be sympathetic with the Turks' desire to establish and maintain themselves as a nation.

Although the American people eventually sacrificed many of President Wilson's idealistic principles in order to flee from involvement in European politics, they generally accepted the movement led by Kemal Atatürk at face value, with a willingness to give the Turkish leaders a chance to prove themselves. United States policy toward Kemalist nationalism, therefore, was to accept it as a necessary counterpart of Turkish development. Americans could do this on realistic grounds as in the national interest of the United States, and on idealistic grounds as according self-determination to a majority of the Turkish people. Armenians and their supporters based their opposition to Atatürk's program on moral (or idealistic) grounds, saying that the long Turkish record of brutality against minorities disqualified the new Turks from international recognition. The Greeks and Armenians in Turkey, although Turkish nationals, were clearly a small minority. Obviously, the principle of self-determina-

242

tion could not be applied to two hostile groups occupying the same geographical area. The United States government, assessing the situation realistically, recognized that only by military force could the Turks be forced to permit the establishment of an independent Armenia.

The United States did not hesitate to protect its citizens when they were unduly harmed or restricted as the result of Turkish nationalism, but it made no attempt to resist that nationalism by force or by political intervention after World War I. United States policy toward Turkey, a necessary combination of realism and idealism, recognized the right of the Turks to govern themselves and chart their own development as long as they did not seriously harm American interests.

The American people, especially those directly concerned with developments in Turkey, clearly demonstrated their ability to adjust to Turkish nationalism. Except for the economic loss, it would have been much easier for American missionaries, for example, to end their work in Turkey in the face of the almost overwhelming obstacles after World War I. They decided, however, to comply with regulations dictated by Turkish nationism rather than lose the opportunity, however limited, to advertise the goodness of Christianity by personal example in their schools and medical facilities. Obviously, the missionaries preferred to combine religion with education and to make direct attempts at converting Muslims to Christianity but, realistically, they acknowledged that these courses of action were impossible. At times missionaries and other Americans in Turkey grumbled and asked for diplomatic protection, but generally they recognized and respected Turkish nationalism.

The "Terrible Turk" stereotype was another important conditioner of Turkish-American relations, both during and after World War I. This conception of the Turk, circulated widely in the United States in the late nineteenth and early twentieth centuries, impeded the State Department's postwar effort to resume regular relations with Turkey. The description had some historical validity when applied to Turkish treatment of the Armenians, but it was unfair to the Turks of the post-Lausanne period. Armenian-Americans and their supporters, in their fight for an Armenian home and their opposition to the Turkish-American Lausanne Treaty, continued to use the timeworn epithet. This unfortunate representation contributed strength to the opponents of the Lausanne Treaty and helped to defeat it in 1927. Led by the Armenian-American lawyer, Vahan Cardashian, the enemies of Turkey in the United States sought, with some success, to cloud the issues in Turkish-American relations by poisoning American public opinion. As the years passed, the futility of the Armenian cause and the splendid example being set in Turkey blurred the "unspeakable" Turk image in the United States. The efforts of United States diplomatic representatives, the State Department, and other interested individuals to publicize Turkish development, and the praise from Americans who worked or visited in Turkey, did much to improve public opinion in the United States. The American Friends of Turkey, through philanthropic work in Turkey and a publicity campaign in the United States, made an impressive contribution toward painting a more accurate picture of the new Turks. Fortunately, the old stereotype had almost disappeared by 1939. The Turkish people had shown their capacity to change, and the American people forgave past misdeeds when confronted with a vastly changed situation.

An element assisting greatly in cementing close Turkish-American relations was the generally high quality of United States diplomatic representation in Turkey. Admiral Mark L. Bristol's service as High Commissioner between 1919 and 1927 was meritorious and contributed to good relations between Turkey and the United States despite the lack of formal ties. The State Department recognized Turkey's importance by appointing, with only one exception, topflight career diplomats to posts in Turkey beginning in 1927. Ambassadors Joseph C. Grew, Robert P. Skinner, and John V. A. MacMurray were extremely competent men dedicated to the cause of close and cordial relations between Turkey and the United States. Their appointments came after long and distinguished careers in the foreign service had given them intimate knowledge of foreign societies and expertise in the art of diplomacy. As a result, they were able to lead in the elimination of outstanding problems. Ambassador Grew, whose nearly five years of service in Turkey (1927–1932) laid the groundwork for close cooperation between the two countries, deserves the largest measure of credit. A diplomat less skilled and understanding than Grew in these transitional years might have been disastrous for the long-range goals of America's Turkish policy.

Grew's immediate successor, Charles H. Sherrill, merits few accolades. With a limited diplomatic background and a somewhat naive conception of his duties, Sherrill suffers in comparison with other United States diplomats in Turkey during the interwar period. His unprofessional approach to diplomacy might have led to considerable embarrassment if he had remained at the post for any appreciable length of time. Grew, Skinner, and MacMurray were career diplomats; Sherrill was a political appointee. Certainly, the records of these four men suggest the superiority of career over nonprofessional diplomats.

The methods used to formulate and conduct the foreign policy of the United States were another set of factors affecting Turkish-American relations. Foreign policy in the United States is traditionally more difficult to create and implement than that of most other countries because of the nature of the American system of government. The concurrent roles of the legislative and executive branches and the force of public opinion all must be taken into consideration in shaping a foreign policy decision. The President and, at his direction, the Department of State are the major decision-makers, as they were in the case of Turkish-American relations. The President and his advisers made the decisions to sign the Lausanne Treaty in 1923 and the agreement of February, 1927. But, particularly in the case of the Lausanne Treaty, the influence of a minority of the American public coupled with political considerations caused the Senate to reject the treaty. As a result, the only way formal relations with Turkey could be established was through an executive agreement. Several years passed before most traces of the executive-legislative antagonism evident between 1923 and 1927 disappeared. A major consideration for the State Department in its dealings with Turkey after the rejection of the Lausanne Treaty was to avoid antagonizing the Senate. The Department and diplomats in the field, especially Ambassador Grew, spent much of their time cultivating a more favorable climate of opinion for Turkey in the United States. When the State Department presented Turkish treaties to the Senate, it did so quietly, with little advance publicity. The executive branch of the United States government found that the effective handling of relations with Turkey depended upon a sympathetic legislative branch. The course of Turkish-American relations, particularly until the mid-1930s, illustrated well the point that though the President and the members of the executive branch under him are in theory the decision-makers in American foreign policy, their decisions in many cases cannot be implemented without legislative concurrence.

Rapprochement

Rapprochement was the key development in the general relations of the Republic of Turkey and the United States during the interwar era. By

1939, the two countries were staunch friends, whereas at the close of World War I they had no formal diplomatic relations and the only treaty basis for the protection of American citizens in Turkey had been repudiated by the Ottoman government. In the short space of twenty years, a new and enlightened republican government had installed itself firmly in a Turkey vastly changed from the time of the Sultans. The government of Kemal Atatürk was a benevolent dictatorship; it designed its principles, policies, and programs to revitalize the Turkish people as a nation and restore them to a position of consequence on the international scene. The United States government recognized the sincerity of the Nationalist government in Turkey and endeavored to cultivate good relations with it. Not until the resumption of formal relations in 1927 did this program gain enough momentum to yield positive results. During the next thirteen years, a series of treaties and agreements on commerce, establishment and residence, claims, and extradition settled most of the major problems between Turkey and the United States. Only the complicated problem of nationality, founded on conflicting theories of citizenship, proved insolvable. Both countries met each other halfway to resolve their problems amicably. The process of compromise contributed much to friendship and understanding between the two nations. Neither government sacrificed basic principles by compromise, but both saw it as a necessary technique for completing the regularization of diplomatic relations.

Although the two countries used treaties and agreements to regularize their formal relations, the work of individual Americans contributed most to the rapprochement of the United States and Turkey. American diplomats, missionaries, doctors, traders, businessmen, archaeologists, and tourists provided the individual links so essential to understanding between the two nations. The services and assistance extended to the Turkish people by these Americans, most of them working in private capacities, did much to influence the course of Turkish-American relations. The two countries smoothed over their problems and built a solid basis for friendship without the assistance of foreign-aid programs like those of the World War II and postwar eras. Money did not lure Turkey along the paths of harmony with the United States. During the interwar period, not one cent of such aid went to Turkey from the United States government.

The groundwork for post–World War II cooperation between the United States and Turkey was laid during the interwar period. After World War II, both countries could look back to two decades of amicable

246

relations. The conviction that the Soviet Union was a threat made necessary the extension of aid to Turkey in 1947 through the Truman Doctrine. The United States extended similar aid to Germany and Japan, its major enemies during World War II, for the same reason. The Truman Doctrine was not a direct result of the friendship established by Turkey and the United States between 1919 and 1939, but the events of the interwar years certainly provided a logical basis for it. Turkish President Celal Bayar told his Parliament on November 1, 1958, that the relationship between Turkey and the United States "is based on mutual respect and confidence" and that "the bonds are even stronger than ever. This sincere cooperation will continue to be the pivot of our foreign policy." [3] Implicit in President Bayar's remarks was a suggestion of the longer-range significance of Turkish-American rapprochement between 1919 and 1939.

[3] Quoted in the New York *Times*, November 2, 1958.

Bibliography

✸ Bibliography

THIS list includes all items cited in the text and a few additional books and other materials which provide pertinent information.

I. BIBLIOGRAPHICAL AIDS

Bemis, Samuel F., and Grace G. Griffin, eds. *Guide to the Diplomatic History of the United States, 1775–1921*. Washington: Government Printing Office, 1935.

Birge, John Kingsley. *A Guide to Turkish Area Study*. Washington: Committee on Near Eastern Studies, American Council of Learned Societies, 1949.

Buck, Elizabeth H. "Materials in the National Archives Relating to the Middle East," *Reference Information Papers*, No. 44. Washington: National Archives, 1955.

DeNovo, John A. "American Relations with the Middle East: Some Unfinished Business," pp. 63–68, in George L. Anderson, ed., *Issues and Conflicts: Studies in Twentieth Century American Diplomacy*. Lawrence: University of Kansas Press, 1959.

Department of State, Division of Library and Reference Services. *Point Four, Near East and Africa: A Selected Bibliography of Studies on Economically Underdeveloped Countries*. Washington: Department of State, 1951.

Ettinghausen, Richard. *A Selected and Annotated Bibliography of Books and Periodicals in Western Languages Dealing with the Near and Middle East, with Special Emphasis on Medieval and Modern Times*. Washington: The Middle East Institute, 1954.

Library of Congress, Division of Bibliography. *Turkey: A Selected List of References*. Washington: Library of Congress, 1943.

II. SOURCES

A. MANUSCRIPTS

1. Private Papers

The American Board of Commissioners for Foreign Missions, Houghton Library, Harvard University, Cambridge, Mass.

William E. Borah, Manuscript Division, Library of Congress, Washington.

Mark Lambert Bristol, Manuscript Division, Library of Congress, Washington.

Calvin Coolidge, Manuscript Division, Library of Congress, Washington.

Joseph C. Grew, Houghton Library, Harvard University, Cambridge, Mass.

American Response to Turkish Nationalism and Reform

John Van Antwerp MacMurray, Princeton University Library, Princeton, N.J.
Fred K. Nielsen, Manuscript Division, Library of Congress, Washington.
Laurence A. Steinhardt, Manuscript Division, Library of Congress, Washington.

2. State Department Records

Files of documents cited in the text are listed below. Asterisks indicate the most valuable. The description assigned to the file by the State Department index bureau follows the file number.

Class 1, "Administration, United States Government":
File 123 G 861. Joseph C. Grew, ambassador to Turkey.
File 123 Sh 5. Charles H. Sherrill, American ambassador to Turkey.
File 123 Sh 22. G. Howland Shaw, F.S.O.
File 123 Sk 3. Robert P. Skinner, ambassador to Turkey.
File 123 M 221. John V. A. MacMurray, ambassador to Turkey.
File 124.671. American embassy to Turkey — quarters.
File 124.676. American embassy to Turkey — conduct of office.

Class 2, "Extradition":
*File 211.67. Extradition treaty between the United States and Turkey.
File 251.11 Insull, Samuel. Extradition to the United States of Samuel Insull on charges of larceny, embezzlement, and violation of the income tax.

Class 3, "Protection of Interests":
File 367.0064. Maintenance of schools in Turkey.
File 367.1162 Schinasi Memorial. Construction of a hospital in Turkey as a memorial to the late Mr. Schinasi and provided for in his will.
File 367.1163. American missions in Turkey.
*File 367.1164. American schools and colleges in Turkey.
File 367.1164 Brussa School Trial. Trial of American school teachers charged with the teaching of Christianity at the American School at Brussa, Turkey.
*File 367.1164 R54. Robert College, Constantinople, Turkey.
File 390D.11. Protection of American interests in Syria.

Class 4, "Claims":
*File 467.11. American claims against Turkey.
File 467.11 Cardashian, Vahan. Claims against Turkey of Vahan Cardashian and William S. Bennet for breach of concession contract.
File 467.11 Cardashian, Vahan no. 2. Claims against Turkey of Vahan Cardashian, American citizen, for legal services rendered that government.

Class 6, "Commerce":
*File 611.6731. Trade relations, tariff treaties, arrangements, etc., between Turkey and the United States.
File 611.674. Food and drug regulations of the United States affecting imports from Turkey.
File 611.674 Figs. Regulations affecting figs exported to the United States from Turkey.
File 667.0031. Tariff agreements, arrangements, etc., between Turkey and foreign countries, trade relations.
File 667.006. Other administrative measures affecting the import trade of Turkey.
File 667.113 Second Hand Clothing. Turkish tariff on secondhand clothing from the United States to Turkey.

File 667.116. Other administrative measures of Turkey affecting imports from the United States.

Class 7, "Political Relations of States":
File 701.6711. Diplomatic representation of Turkey in the United States.
File 711.67. Relations, treaties between the United States and Turkey.
*File 711.6712A. Arbitration treaties between the United States and Turkey.
File 711.6712 Anti-War. Treaty between the United States and Turkey for renunciation of war.
*File 711.672. Treaty of commerce and navigation between the United States and Turkey [Lausanne Treaty].
*File 711.672 (1929). Treaty of commerce and navigation between the United States and Turkey (1929).
File 711.672 Protests. Protests against the Lausanne Treaty between the United States and Turkey.
File 711.672 Straits. Treaty between the United States and Turkey providing for navigation of the Straits of the Dardanelles, the Sea of Marmara, and the Bosphorus.
File 711.674. Naturalization treaties between the United States and Turkey.
*File 711.679 Residence and Establishment. Treaty of residence and establishment − United States and Turkey.
File 767.68119. Termination of war between Turkey and Greece, including the Straits convention.

Class 8, "Internal Affairs of States":
File 811.4061 Musa Dagh. Motion picture entitled *Musa Dagh*.
File 811.42767. Attendance of Turkish students at schools in the United States.
File 811.43 American Friends of Turkey. American Friends of Turkey.
File 811.71567. Parcel post arrangement between the United States and Turkey.
File 860J.01. Government of Armenia.
*File 867.00. Political conditions in Turkey.
File 867.001 K31. Kemal − President of Turkish Republic.
File 867.001 Atatürk, Kemal. Kemal Atatürk, President of Turkey.
*File 867.01A. Foreign advisers − Turkey.
File 867.111 American Passports. Taking up of American passports of persons visiting Turkey by Turkish authorities.
*File 867.114 Narcotics. Traffic in narcotics in Turkey.
File 867.1281. Practice of medicine and surgery in Turkey.
File 867.20. Military affairs − army posts − fortifications − Turkey.
File 867.20111. Visit to Turkish military establishments by United States Army officers.
File 867.248 Martin Co., Glenn L. Proposed sale to Turkey of bombing planes by the Glenn L. Martin Company.
File 867.41. History − Turkey.
File 867.42711. Cultural relations. Exchange of professors and students. Attendance of American students at Turkish schools.
File 867.48 Adana Flood. Flood at Adana, Turkey, in December 1930.
File 867.48 Anatolia. Earthquake in Anatolia, Turkey.
File 867.48 Smyrna. Earthquake in Smyrna in 1928.
File 867.48 Smyrna Flood. Flood at Smyrna, Turkey, in October 1930.
File 867.50 Five Year Plan. Five Year construction and industrialization program − Turkey. [A few documents in this file are marked 867.50 Three Year Plan.]
*File 867.50A. Economic adviser − Turkey.
File 867.504. Labor − Turkey.

File 867.51. Financial affairs — Turkey.

File 867.51A. Financial adviser — Turkey.

File 867.51 A.O.B. Corp. Loan of $30,000,000 to Turkey by the American Oriental Bankers Corporation of New York.

File 867.51 Shukri Bey Mission. Visit of Turkish financial mission to the United States.

File 867.51 Turkish-American Investment Corporation. Loan to the Turkish government by the Turkish American Investment Corporation, an American concern, of ten million dollars.

File 867.51 UL2. Loan to Turkey by Ulen and Company.

File 867.5123. Income tax — Turkey.

File 867.5123 Standard Oil. Tax imposed on the profits of the Standard Oil can factories in Turkey.

*File 867.5151. Exchange — Turkey.

File 867.516. Banks and banking — Turkey.

File 867.543 Kolynos. Infringement in Turkey of the trademark "Kolynos."

File 867.544 King Features Syndicate. Protection of copyrights "Mickey Mouse" and "Little Annie Rooney."

File 867.602 OT 81. Chester concession in Turkey — Ottoman-American Development Company.

File 867.61A. Agricultural adviser — Turkey.

File 867.63. Mines — Mining — Turkey.

File 867.6352. Copper — Turkey.

File 867.6363. Petroleum — Turkey.

File 867.64A. Engineering advisers — Turkey.

File 867.77 Fox Corporation. Railroad concessions in Turkey — Fox Brothers International Corporation.

File 867.796 Curtiss. Aeroplane project of Curtiss Aeroplane Company in Turkey.

*File 867.9111. Turkish press review.

File 867.927. Anthropology — Ethnology — Archaeology — Turkey.

3. Bureau of Foreign and Domestic Commerce Archives

File 128X Istanbul. Foreign service — copies of reports — Istanbul.

File 252 Turkey. Leather — Turkey, 1923–1934.

File 254.1 Turkey. Rubber — Tires — Turkey.

File 272 Turkey. Metals — Turkey.

File 281 Turkey. Motion pictures — Turkey — 1924–1944.

File 449.0. Turkey — General, 1927–1943.

B. PRINTED SOURCES

1. Publications of the American Board of Commissioners for Foreign Missions

The One Hundred and Ninth Annual Report of the American Board of Commissioners for Foreign Missions [1919]. Boston: Published by the Board, n.d.

The One Hundred and Tenth Annual Report of the American Board of Commissioners for Foreign Missions [1920]. Boston: Published by the Board, n.d.

The One Hundred and Eleventh Annual Report of the American Board of Commissioners for Foreign Missions [1921]. Boston: Published by the Board, n.d.

The One Hundred and Twelfth Annual Report of the American Board of Commissioners for Foreign Missions [1922]. Boston: Published by the Board, n.d.

The One Hundred and Thirteenth Annual Report of the American Board of Commissioners for Foreign Missions [1923]. Boston: Published by the Board, n.d.

The One Hundred and Fourteenth Annual Report of the American Board of Commissioners for Foreign Missions [1924]. Boston: Published by the Board, n.d.

The One Hundred and Fifteenth Annual Report of the American Board of Commissioners for Foreign Missions [1925]. Boston: Published by the Board, n.d.

The One Hundred and Sixteenth Annual Report of the American Board of Commissioners for Foreign Missions [1926]. Boston: Published by the Board, n.d.

The One Hundred and Seventeenth Annual Report of the American Board of Commissioners for Foreign Missions [1927]. Boston: Published by the Board, n.d.

The One Hundred and Eighteenth Annual Report of the American Board of Commissioners for Foreign Missions [1928]. Boston: Published by the Board, n.d.

The One Hundred and Nineteenth Annual Report of the American Board of Commissioners for Foreign Missions [1929]. Boston: Published by the Board, n.d.

The One Hundred and Twentieth Annual Report of the American Board of Commissioners for Foreign Missions [1930]. Boston: Published by the Board, n.d.

The One Hundred and Twenty-First Annual Report of the American Board of Commissioners for Foreign Missions [1931]. Boston: Published by the Board, n.d.

The One Hundred and Twenty-Second Annual Report of the American Board of Commissioners for Foreign Missions [1932]. Boston: Published by the Board, n.d.

The One Hundred and Twenty-Third Annual Report of the American Board of Commissioners for Foreign Missions [1933]. Boston: Published by the Board, n.d.

The One Hundred and Twenty-Fourth Annual Report of the American Board of Commissioners for Foreign Missions [1934]. Boston: Published by the Board, n.d.

The One Hundred and Twenty-Fifth Annual Report of the American Board of Commissioners for Foreign Missions [1935]. Boston: Published by the Board, n.d.

The One Hundred and Twenty-Sixth Annual Report of the American Board of Commissioners for Foreign Missions [1936]. Boston: Published by the Board, n.d.

The One Hundred and Twenty-Seventh Annual Report of the American Board of Commissioners for Foreign Missions [1937]. Boston: Published by the Board, n.d.

The One Hundred and Twenty-Eighth Annual Report of the American Board of Commissioners for Foreign Missions [1938]. Boston: Published by the Board, n.d.

The Call for Colleagues, the One Hundred Twenty-Ninth Annual Report of the American Board of Commissioners for Foreign Missions, 1939. Boston: Published by the Board, n.d.

The American Board in War Time: Report of the 133rd Year of the Work of the American Board, Prepared by the Executive Vice-President with the Assistance of the Staff, 1943. Boston: American Board of Commissioners for Foreign Missions, n.d.

143rd Annual Report to the Churches, 1953. Boston: American Board of Commissioners for Foreign Missions, 1954.

146th Annual Report, Spring 1957. Boston: American Board of Commissioners for Foreign Missions, 1957.

2. Congressional Publications

Congressional Record containing the proceedings and debates of the United States Congress from the following sessions: 65 Cong., 1 Sess., LV; 69 Cong., 1 Sess., LXVII; 70 Cong., 1 Sess., LXIX; 71 Cong., 2 Sess., LXXII; 72 Cong., 1 Sess., LXXV; 73 Cong., 2 Sess., LXXVIII; and 74 Cong., 1 Sess., LXXIX. Washington: Government Printing Office, 1917, 1926, 1928, 1930, 1932, 1934, 1935.

Hearings Before the Special Committee Investigating the Munitions Industry, United States Senate, Pursuant to S. Res. 206, a Resolution to Make Certain Investigations Concerning the Manufacture and Sale of Arms and Other War Munitions. 12 vols., 40 pts. (73 and 74 Cong.). Washington: Government Printing Office, 1934–1943.

American Response to Turkish Nationalism and Reform

Journal of the Executive Proceedings of the Senate of the United States of America for the following sessions: 70 Cong., 1 Sess., LXXIV; 73 Cong., 2 Sess., LXXV. Washington: Government Printing Office, 1928, 1934.

3. Department of Commerce Publications

Bureau of Foreign and Domestic Commerce. *Commerce Reports.* Vols. 30–43. Washington: Government Printing Office, 1927–1940.

————. *Foreign Commerce and Navigation of the United States for the Calendar Year* [1914–1941]. Washington: Government Printing office, 1915–1944.

————. *Trade of the United States with Turkey in 1938.* Washington: Bureau of Foreign and Domestic Commerce, 1939.

Hodgson, James F., Gardner Richardson, and Julian E. Gillespie. *Trade Financing and Exchange in Egypt, Greece and Turkey.* Trade Information Bulletin No. 506. Washington: Government Printing Office [1927].

Ravndal, G. Bie. *Turkey: A Commercial and Industrial Handbook.* Trade Promotion Series No. 28. Washington: Government Printing Office, 1926.

4. Department of the Navy Publication

Beers, Henry P. *U.S. Naval Detachment in Turkish Waters, 1919–1924.* Administrative Reference Service Report No. 2. Washington: Office of Records Administration, Navy Department, 1943.

5. Department of State Publications

Miller, Hunter, ed. *Treaties and Other International Acts of the United States of America.* 6 vols. Washington: Government Printing Office, 1931–1942.

Moore, John Bassett. *A Digest of International Law.* 8 vols. Washington: Government Printing Office, 1906.

Nielsen, Fred K. *American-Turkish Claims Settlement, under the Agreement of December 24, 1923, and Supplemental Agreements Between the United States and Turkey, Opinions and Report.* Washington: Government Printing Office, 1937.

Papers Relating to the Foreign Relations of the United States (title through 1931); *Foreign Relations of the United States: Diplomatic Papers* (title beginning in 1932). The list below of volumes used includes the year covered, number of volumes if more than one, and publication date. All were published in Washington by the Government Printing Office.

1862 (1862)	The Lansing Papers, 1914–1920 (2
1865 (3 vols., 1866)	vols., 1939–1940)
1876 (1876)	1921 (2 vols., 1936)
1883 (1884)	1922 (2 vols., 1938)
1914 (1922)	1923 (2 vols. 1938)
1914, Supplement, the World War	1924 (2 vols., 1939)
(1928)	1925 (2 vols., 1940)
1915 (1924)	1926 (2 vols., 1941)
1916 (1925)	1927 (3 vols., 1942)
1917, Supplement 1, the World War	1928 (3 vols., 1942–1943)
(1931)	1929 (3 vols., 1943–1944)
1918 (1930)	1930 (3 vols., 1945)
1919 (2 vols., 1934)	1931 (3 vols., 1946)
1919, the Paris Peace Conference	1932 (5 vols., 1947–1948)
(13 vols., 1942–1947)	1933 (5 vols., 1949–1952)
1920 (3 vols., 1936)	1934 (5 vols., 1950–1952)

1935 (4 vols., 1952–1953)   1939 (5 vols., 1955–1957)
1936 (5 vols., 1953–1954)   1940 (5 vols., 1955–1958)
1937 (5 vols., 1954)   1941 (7 vols., 1959–1966)
1938 (5 vols., 1954–1956)   1944 (7 vols., 1965–1967)

Press Releases. Washington: Government Printing Office, 1929–1939.

Reciprocal Trade: Agreement and Supplementary Exchange of Notes Between the United States of America and Turkey. Executive Agreement Series No. 163. Washington: Government Printing Office, 1940.

Register of the Department of State Corrected to July 1, 1893. Washington: Government Printing Office, 1893.

Register of the Department of State, November 18, 1914. Washington: Government Printing Office, 1914.

Register of the Department of State, July 1, 1933. Washington: Government Printing Office, 1933.

Register of the Department of State, July 1, 1936. Washington: Government Printing Office, 1936.

Register of the Department of State, October 1, 1939. Washington: Government Printing Office, 1939.

6. United States Tariff Commission Publications

Extent of Equal Tariff Treatment in Foreign Countries. Report No. 119, 2nd Series. Washington: Government Printing Office, 1937.

Trade Agreement Between the United States and the Republic of Turkey: Digests of Trade Data with Respect to Products on Which Concessions Were Granted by the United States. Washington: n.p., 1939.

7. Documents of Foreign Governments

Bryce, Viscount. *The Treatment of Armenians in the Ottoman Empire, 1915–16: Documents Presented to Viscount Grey of Fallodon.* London: His Majesty's Stationery Office, 1916.

Heald, Stephen, ed., in conjunction with John W. Wheeler-Bennett. *Documents on International Affairs, 1936.* London: Oxford University Press, 1937.

Heald, Stephen, ed. *Documents on International Affairs, 1937.* London: Oxford University Press, 1939.

Hurewitz, J. C., ed. *Diplomacy in the Near and Middle East: A Documentary Record, 1535–1956.* 2 vols. Princeton: D. Van Nostrand Company, 1956.

Kemal, Mustapha. *A Speech Delivered by Ghazi Mustapha Kemal, President of the Turkish Republic, October 1927.* Leipzig: K. F. Koehler, 1929.

Toynbee, Arnold J., and Margaret Carlyle, eds. *Documents on International Affairs, 1939–1946.* 2 vols. London, New York, & Toronto: Oxford University Press, 1951–1954.

United States Department of State, Division of Publications. *Documents on German Foreign Policy, 1918–1945.* Series D, 10 vols. Washington: Government Printing Office, 1949–1957.

Wheeler-Bennett, John W., ed., assisted by Stephen A. Heald. *Documents on International Affairs, 1933.* London: Oxford University Press, 1934.

———. *Documents on International Affairs, 1934.* London: Oxford University Press, 1935.

Woodward, E. L., and Rohan Butler, eds. *Documents on British Foreign Policy, 1919–1939.* 3rd Series, 9 vols. London: His [Her] Majesty's Stationery Office, 1949–1955.

C. AUTOBIOGRAPHIES, MEMOIRS, AND PERSONAL ACCOUNTS

Cannon, James, Jr. *Bishop Cannon's Own Story: Life As I Have Seen It.* Ed. Richard L. Watson, Jr. Durham, N.C.: Duke University Press, 1955.

Child, Richard Washburn. *A Diplomat Looks at Europe.* New York: Duffield and Company, 1925.

Cox, Samuel S. *Diversions of a Diplomat in Turkey.* New York: Charles L. Webster and Company, 1887.

Djemal Pasha. *Memories of a Turkish Statesman, 1913–1919.* New York: George H. Doran Company, 1922.

Dodge, Bayard, "The American University of Beirut, International College and Damascus College, 1910–1948," *Annual Report.* Beirut: mimeographed, 1948.

Einstein, Lewis. *A Diplomat Looks Back.* Ed. Lawrence E. Gelfand. New Haven & London: Yale University Press, 1968.

Ekrem, Selma. *Unveiled: The Autobiography of a Turkish Girl.* New York: Ives Washburn, 1942 (originally published in 1930).

Gates, Caleb Frank. *Not to Me Only.* Princeton: Princeton University Press, 1940.

Gerard, James W. *My First Eighty-Three Years in America.* Garden City, N.Y.: Doubleday and Company, 1951.

Grew, Joseph C. *Turbulent Era: A Diplomatic Record of Forty Years, 1904–1945.* 2 vols. Ed. Walter Johnson. Boston: Houghton Mifflin Company, 1952.

Griscom, Lloyd C. *Diplomatically Speaking.* Boston: Little, Brown and Company, 1940.

Hamlin, Cyrus. *Among the Turks.* New York: R. Carter and Brothers, 1878.

———. *My Life and Times.* 5th ed. Boston & Chicago: The Pilgrim Press, 1912 (originally published in 1893).

Lansing, Robert. *The Peace Negotiations, a Personal Narrative.* Boston & New York: Houghton Mifflin Company, 1921.

Lloyd George, David. *Memoirs of the Peace Conference.* 2 vols. New Haven: Yale University Press, 1939.

Morgenthau, Henry. *All in a Lifetime.* Garden City, N.Y.: Doubleday, Page and Company, 1922.

———. *Ambassador Morgenthau's Story.* Garden City, N.Y.: Doubleday, Page and Company, 1918.

Patrick, Mary Mills. *A Bosporus Adventure: Istanbul (Constantinople) Woman's College, 1871–1924.* Stanford, Calif.: Stanford University Press, and London: Oxford University Press, 1934.

———. *Under Five Sultans.* New York & London: The Century Company, 1929.

Porter, David Dixon. *Memoir of Commodore David Porter of the United States Navy.* Albany, N.Y.: J. Munsell, 1875.

Ramsay, W. H. *Impressions of Turkey During Twelve Years' Wanderings.* New York: G. P. Putnam's Sons, 1897.

Scipio, Lynn A. *My Thirty Years in Turkey.* Rindge, N.H.: Richard R. Smith Publisher, 1955.

Straus, Oscar S. *Under Four Administrations: From Cleveland to Taft.* Boston & New York: Houghton Mifflin Company, 1922.

Washburn, George. *Fifty Years in Constantinople and Recollections of Robert College.* Boston & New York: Houghton Mifflin Company, 1909.

Weizmann, Chaim. *Trial and Error: The Autobiography of Chaim Weizmann.* New York: Harper and Brothers, 1949.

Wilson, Woodrow. *The Public Papers of Woodrow Wilson.* 6 vols. Ed. Ray Stannard Baker and William E. Dodd. New York & London: Harper and Brothers, 1925–1927.

Yalman, Ahmed Emin. *Turkey in My Time.* Norman: University of Oklahoma Press, 1956.

D. CONTEMPORARY PERIODICAL ARTICLES AND PAMPHLETS

The following list of contemporary articles and pamphlets provides information both on domestic developments in Turkey and on Turkish-American relations. Many of them are indicative of the tone of American public opinion toward the events they cover.

Aaronsohn, Alex. "The Powder Magazine of Europe – the Near East," *Annals, American Academy of Political and Social Science*, CVIII (July, 1923), 125–131.

[Adivar], A. Adnan. "Ten Years of Republic in Turkey," *Political Quarterly*, VI (April–June, 1935), 240–252.

[Adivar], Halidé Edib. "Dictatorship and Reforms in Turkey," *Yale Review*, XIX (September, 1929), 27–44.

————. "Home from the War," *Asia*, XXVIII (October, 1928), 782–789, 843–849.

————. "My Share in the Turkish Ordeal," *Asia*, XXVIII (June, 1928), 437–443, 509–515.

————. "Poor Turks, Poor Greeks, Poor World!" *Asia*, XXVIII (August, 1928), 638–645, 654–661.

————. "The Rising Star of Mustapha Kemal," *Asia*, XXVIII (July, 1928), 570–576, 588–592.

————. "A Woman Soldier at the Front," *Asia*, XXVIII (September, 1928), 700–707, 747–752.

Allen, Henry E. "Factors in Turkey's Cultural Transformation," *The Open Court*, XLVI (May, 1932), 331–342.

"An Ambassador to Turkey," *The Independent*, CXVIII (June 11, 1927), 599.

"The American Hospital of Constantinople," *Levant Trade Review*, XVI (October, 1928), 379–382.

Americus. "Some Phases of the Issues Between the United States and Turkey," *North American Review*, CLXXXII (May, 1906), 689–700.

"Another Chapter in Insull's Long Flight," *Literary Digest*, CXVII (April 14, 1934), 17.

Arnold, Marguerite. "Elegy for Atatürk," *New Republic*, XCVIII (May 3, 1939), 373–375.

"Arrival of Ambassador Grew," *Levant Trade Review*, XV (September, 1927), 371–373.

Bachman, Robert A. "The American Navy and the Turks," *The Outlook*, CXXXII (October 18, 1922), 288–289.

Baker, Robert L. "State Planning in Turkey," *Current History*, XXXVIII (July, 1933), 504–506.

Barton, James L. "Missionary Problems in Turkey," *International Review of Missions*, XVI (October, 1927), 481–494.

Birge, John Kingsley. "Turkey Between Two World Wars," *Foreign Policy Reports*, XX (November 1, 1944), 194–207.

————. "Twelve Years of the Turkish Republic," *Missionary Review of the World*, LVIII (March, 1935), 118–120.

Blaisdell, D. C. "American Investment in Turkey: A Forecast," *Levant Trade Review*, XV (December, 1927), 521–529.

Blegen, Carl W. "Excavations at Troy, 1932," *American Journal of Archaeology*, XXXVI (October–December, 1932), 431–451.

————. "Excavations at Troy, 1933," *American Journal of Archaeology*, XXXVIII (April–June, 1934), 223–248.

————. "Excavations at Troy, 1934," *American Journal of Archaeology*, XXXIX (January–March, 1935), 6–34.

————. "Excavations at Troy, 1935," *American Journal of Archaeology*, XXXIX (October–December, 1935), 550–587.

————. "Excavations at Troy, 1936," *American Journal of Archaeology*, XLI (January–March, 1937), 17–51.

————. "Excavations at Troy, 1937," *American Journal of Archaeology*, XLI (October–December, 1937), 553–597.

————. "Excavations at Troy, 1938," *American Journal of Archaeology*, XLIII (April–June, 1939), 204–228.

"Certificates of Origin for Turkey," *Levant Trade Review*, XVI (September, 1928), 342.

Chester, Arthur T. "History's Verdict on New Turkey's Rise to Power," *Current History*, XIX (October, 1923), 79–86.

Chester, Colby M. "Turkey Reinterpreted," *Current History*, XVI (September, 1922), 939–947.

Cleveland, C. O. "Kemal the Victorious," *Commonweal*, XXIX (November 25, 1938), 118–120.

A Committee of Trustees of Near East Relief. *Near East Relief Consummated — Near East Foundation Carries On*. N.p.: Near East Foundation, 1944.

"Constantinople Ford Assembly Plant," *Levant Trade Review*, XVII (February, 1929), 43–47.

Dennis, Alfred L. P. "The United States and the New Turkey," *North American Review*, CCXVII (June, 1923), 721–731.

"The Divorce of Islam and Turkey," *Literary Digest*, XCVII (May 5, 1928), 32.

Franck, Harry A. "Steer Clear of Turkey," *The Outlook*, CXLVII (November 2, 1927), 271–274.

Gates, Caleb F. "American Schools in the New Turkey," *Our World*, III (July, 1923), 86–88.

————. "The Departure of Admiral Bristol," *Levant Trade Review*, XV (May, 1927), 183–186.

————. "The Making of the Turkish Republic," *Current History*, XXXIV (April, 1931), 89–93.

————. "The New Turkey under Mustapha Kemal," *Current History*, XXXIV (June, 1931), 390–394.

Gilman, William. "Turkey with Western Dressing," *Current History*, XLIX (November, 1938), 37–39.

Goldman, Hetty. "Excavations at Gözlü Kule, Tarsus, 1936," *American Journal of Archaeology*, XLI (April–June, 1937), 262–286.

————. "Excavations at Gözlü Kule, Tarsus, 1937," *American Journal of Archaeology*, XLII (January–March, 1938), 30–54.

————. "Preliminary Expedition to Cilicia, 1934, and Excavations at Gözlü Kule, Tarsus, 1935," *American Journal of Archaeology*, XXXIX (October–December, 1935), 526–549.

Gordon, Leland J. "American Commercial Relations with Turkey," *Levant Trade Review*, XVI (May, 1928), 175–178.

————. "Emigration from Turkey to the U.S.," *Levant Trade Review*, XVI (November, 1928), 417–421.

Hart, Albert Bushnell. "Making Friends with Unrighteousness," *The New Armenia*, XVII (January–February, 1925), 9–10.

————. "Reservations as to the Near Eastern Question," *Annals*, American Academy of Political and Social Science, CVIII (July, 1923), 120–124.

Heck, Lewis. "Sidelights on Past Relations Between the United States and Turkey," *American Foreign Service Journal*, XVII (February, 1940), 61–63, 110–114.

Howard, Harry N. "The Reduction of Turkey from an Empire to a National State," *The Open Court*, XLVI (May, 1932), 291–305.

————. "Turkey Goes Industrial," *Current History*, XLV (October, 1936), 99–104.

———. "Turkey Goes to School," *Current History*, XLV (March, 1937), 85–89.
———. "Turkish Foreign Policy," *Asia*, XXXVIII (January, 1938), 29–31.
———. "Who Can Succeed Atatürk," *Asia*, XXXVIII (December, 1938), 715–716.
"Islam's New Caliph," *Literary Digest*, LXXV (December 16, 1922), 33–34.
Jewett, Frank. "Why We Did Not Declare War on Turkey," *Current History*, XIV (September, 1921), 989–991.
"Larger Leather Sales to Turkey," *Levant Trade Review*, XVI (July, 1928), 258–259.
Linke, Lilo. "Social Changes in Turkey," *International Affairs*, XVI (July–August, 1937), 540–563.
Lybyer, Albert Howe. "The Political Reconstruction of Turkey," *The Open Court*, XLVI (May, 1932), 306–319.
———. "Turkey's Adoption of the Arabic Alphabet," *Current History*, XXVIII (August, 1928), 880–881.
Merrill, Frederick T. "Twelve Years of the Turkish Republic," *Foreign Policy Reports*, XI (October 9, 1935), 190–200.
Morrison, Charles C. "Christianity's Handicap in Turkey," *Christian Century*, LII (July 10, 1935), 911–913.
———. "An Interim Mission," *Christian Century*, LII (July 24, 1935), 959–961.
———. "The Rebirth of a Nation," *Christian Century*, LII (June 12, 1935), 785–786.
———. "Religion in Turkey," *Christian Century*, LII (July 3, 1935), 880–881.
———. "Should Missionaries Remain in Turkey," *Christian Century*, LII (July 17, 1935), 935–937.
———. "Turkey's Dictator," *Christian Century*, LII (June 26, 1935), 847–849.
Morrison, S. A. "Religious Liberty in Turkey," *International Review of Missions*, XXIV (October, 1935), 441–459.
"Muddling Through with Turkey," *Literary Digest*, XCIII (April 9, 1927), 14.
Nansen, Fridtjof. "Rescuing Millions of War Victims from Disease and Starvation," *Current History*, XXX (July, 1929), 567–576.
"Now on Speaking Terms with Turkey," *Literary Digest*, XCIII (June 11, 1927), 13.
Paton, William, and M. M. Underhill. "The Missionary Significance of the Last Ten Years: A Survey," *International Review of Missions*, XXI (April, 1932), 153–244.
———. "A Survey of the Year 1929," *International Review of Missions*, XIX (January, 1930), 3–74.
———. "A Survey of the Year 1930," *International Review of Missions*, XX (January, 1931), 3–82.
———. "A Survey of the Year 1934," *International Review of Missions*, XXIV (January, 1935), 3–112.
———. "A Survey of the Year 1937," *International Review of Missions*, XXVII (January, 1938), 3–101.
———. "A Survey of the Year 1938," *International Review of Missions*, XXVIII (January, 1939), 3–94.
Powers, Fred Perry. "The Lausanne Treaty," *The New Armenia*, XVII (January–February, 1925), 3–4.
"Pride of Detroit in Constantinople," *Levant Trade Review*, XV (September, 1927), 375.
Riggs, Charles T. "Always Something New in Turkey," *Missionary Review of the World*, LVIII (September, 1935), 401–402.
———. "Religion in Turkey Today," *Missionary Review of the World*, LXI (July–August, 1938), 327–329.
———. "Turkey – Fifty Years Ago and Now," *Missionary Review of the World*, LI (January, 1928), 13–20.

261

————. "Turkey, the Treaties and the Missionaries," *Missionary Review of the World*, L (May, 1927), 343–348.

Riggs, H. H. "The Missionary Situation in Turkey," *International Review of Missions*, XXVII (April, 1938), 195–200.

Ringwood, O. K. D., and J. K. Birge. "American Interests in Turkey," *Foreign Policy Reports*, XX (November 1, 1944), 208.

"Shake Hands with Turkey," *The Independent*, CXVIII (January 15, 1927), 58–59.

Sherrill, Charles H. "My Interviews with the Gazi," *Asia*, XXXIV (March, 1934), 140–143.

Sprengling, Martin. "Modern Turkey," *The Open Court*, XLVI (May, 1932), 281–290.

Talbot, E. Guy. "The Turk Malignant," *The New Armenia*, XIX (July–September, 1927), 41.

Tashjian, James H., ed. "Life and Papers of Vahan Cardashian," *Armenian Review*, X (March, 1957), 3–15; (September, 1957), 103–128; (December, 1957), 99–112; XI (April, 1958), 62–72; (July, 1958), 115–127; (November, 1958), 131–142.

"Thus Far and No Farther," *The New Armenia*, XIX (April–June, 1927), 17–18.

"Treaty Relations Between the Turkish Republic and the United States," *Levant Trade Review*, XVI (April, 1928), 138.

"Turco-American Relations," *Current History*, XXXVIII (June, 1933), 379.

"Turkey and America," *The Living Age*, CCCXXXII (March 15, 1927), 491.

"Turkey's Dayton Flare-Up," *Literary Digest*, XCVII (May 19, 1928), 28–29.

"A Turkish Presidential Message of 400,000 Words," *Literary Digest*, XCV (November 19, 1927), 16–17.

"The Turkish Treaty — A Debate," *Forum*, LXXII (December, 1924), 734–745.

" 'Unnamed Christianity' in Turkey," *Missionary Review of the World*, XLI (June, 1928), 467–470.

Van Norman, Louis E. "Ten Years of the New Turkey — An Economic Retrospect," *The Open Court*, XLVI (May, 1932), 320–330.

Vrooman, Lee. "Issues in Missionary Education in the Near East," *International Review of Missions*, XXII (January, 1933), 50–62.

————. "The Place of Missions in the New Turkey," *International Review of Missions*, XVIII (July, 1929), 401–409.

A Western Woman Resident in Turkey. "Turkish Women as Pioneers," *International Review of Missions*, XVII (October, 1928), 645–654.

Wheeler, Everett P. *The Duty of the United States of America to American Citizens in Turkey*. New York, Chicago, & Toronto: Fleming H. Revell Company, 1896.

————. "The Power of the President to Protect American Citizens in Turkey and Their Work," *The Outlook,* CXXXII (November 1, 1922), 370.

"Why the Democrats Defeated the Turkish Treaty," *Literary Digest*, XCII (January 29, 1927), 10–11.

Willett, Herbert L., Jr. "Turkey Has Changed!" *Christian Century*, XLVIII (January 7, 1931), 14–16.

Wise, Stephen S. "Looking Ahead," *The New Armenia*, XIX (January–March, 1927), 2.

E. NEWSPAPERS

Christian Science Monitor (Boston). 1927–1939.

London *Times*. July 30, 1931, April 2, 1934, August 9, 1938 (Turkish Number).

New York *Times*. 1927–1939, November 2, 1958.

Washington *Post*. 1927–1939.

III. SECONDARY WORKS

A. BIOGRAPHIES

Armstrong, H. C. *Gray Wolf, An Intimate Study of a Dictator*. London: Arthur Barker, Ltd., 1932.

Brock, Ray. *Ghost on Horseback: The Incredible Atatürk*. New York: Duell, Sloan and Pearce; Boston: Little, Brown and Company, 1954.

Heinrichs, Waldo H., Jr. *American Ambassador: Joseph C. Grew and the Development of the United States Diplomatic Tradition*. Boston: Little, Brown and Company, 1966.

Jenkins, Hester Donaldson. *An Educational Ambassador to the Near East: The Story of Mary Mills Patrick and an American College in the Orient*. New York & Chicago: Fleming H. Revell Company, 1925.

Kinross, Lord. *Atatürk: A Biography of Mustafa Kemal, Father of Modern Turkey*. New York: William Morrow and Company, 1965.

McDonald, Forrest. *Insull*. Chicago: University of Chicago Press, 1962.

Mikusch, Dagobert von. *Mustapha Kemal: Between Europe and Asia*. Garden City, N.Y.: Doubleday, Doran and Company, 1931.

Sherrill, Charles H. *A Year's Embassy to Mustafa Kemal*. New York & London: Charles Scribner's Sons, 1934.

Wortham, Hugh E. *Mustapha Kemal of Turkey*. Boston: Little, Brown and Company, 1931.

B. WORKS ON TURKISH HISTORY AND DEVELOPMENT

[Adivar], Halidé Edib. *Turkey Faces West: A Turkish View of Recent Changes and Their Origin*. New Haven: Yale University Press, 1930.

Allen, Henry E. *The Turkish Transformation: A Study in Social and Religious Development*. Chicago: University of Chicago Press, 1935.

Anderson, M. S. *The Eastern Question 1774–1923: A Study in International Relations*. London, Melbourne, & Toronto: Macmillan and Company; New York: St. Martin's Press, 1966.

Berkes, Niyazi. *The Development of Secularism in Turkey*. Montreal: McGill University Press, 1964.

———, ed. *Turkish Nationalism and Western Civilization: Selected Essays of Ziya Gökalp*. New York: Columbia University Press, 1959.

Bisbee, Eleanor. *The New Turks: Pioneers of the Republic, 1920–1950*. Philadelphia: University of Pennsylvania Press, 1951.

Cardashian, Vahan. *The Ottoman Empire of the Twentieth Century*. Albany: J. B. Lyon Company, 1908.

Furniss, Edgar S., Jr. *A New State Faces a Difficult World — The Position of Turkey Today*. New Haven: Yale Literary Magazine, 1940.

Harris, George S. *The Origins of Communism in Turkey*. Stanford, Calif.: The Hoover Institution, 1967.

Heyd, Uriel. *Foundations of Turkish Nationalism: The Life and Teachings of Ziya Gökalp*. London: Lizac and Company, Ltd., and The Harvill Press, Ltd., 1950.

Howard, Harry N. *The Partition of Turkey: A Diplomatic History, 1913–1923*. Norman: University of Oklahoma Press, 1931.

Hürlimann, Martin. *Istanbul*. London: Thames and Hudson, 1958.

Jackh, Ernst. *The Rising Crescent: Turkey Yesterday, Today, and Tomorrow*. New York & Toronto: Farrar and Rinehart, Inc., 1944.

Karpat, Kemal H. *Turkey's Politics: The Transition to a Multi-Party System*. Princeton: Princeton University Press, 1959.

Kilic, Altemur. *Turkey and the World*. Washington: Public Affairs Press, 1959.

Kruger, Karl. *Kemalist Turkey and the Middle East*. London: George Allen and Unwin, Ltd., 1932.

Lewis, Bernard. *The Emergence of Modern Turkey*. London: Oxford University Press, 1961.

Lewis, G. L. *Turkey*. New York: Frederick A. Praeger, 1955.

Liddell, Robert. *Byzantium and Istanbul*. London: Jonathan Cape, 1956.

Marriott, J. A. R. *The Eastern Question: An Historical Study in European Diplomacy*. 4th ed. Oxford: Clarendon Press, 1940.

Mears, Eliot Grinnell, ed. *Modern Turkey*. New York: The Macmillan Company, 1924.

Miller, William. *The Ottoman Empire and Its Successors, 1801–1927, with an Appendix, 1927–1936*. 4th ed. Cambridge: University Press, 1936.

Orga, Irfan. *Phoenix Ascendant: The Rise of Modern Turkey*. London: R. Hale, 1958.

Paneth, Philip. *Turkey — Decadence and Rebirth*. London: Alliance Press, Ltd., 1943.

Price, M. Philips. *A History of Turkey from Empire to Republic*. London: George Allen and Unwin, Ltd., 1956.

Ramsaur, Ernest E., Jr. *The Young Turks: Prelude to the Revolution of 1908*. Princeton: Princeton University Press, 1957.

Robinson, Richard D. *The First Turkish Republic: A Case Study in National Development*. Cambridge, Mass.: Harvard University Press, 1963.

Schmidt, Erich F. *Anatolia Through the Ages: Discoveries at the Alishar Mound, 1927–1929*. Oriental Institute Communications No. 11. Chicago: University of Chicago Press, 1931.

Shotwell, James T., and Francis Deák. *Turkey at the Straits: A Short History*. New York: The Macmillan Company, 1940.

Sousa, Nasim. *The Capitulatory Régime of Turkey: Its History, Origin, and Nature*. Baltimore: The Johns Hopkins Press, 1933.

Tobin, Chester M. *Turkey, Key to the East*. New York: G. P. Putnam's Sons, 1944.

Toynbee, Arnold J., and Kenneth P. Kirkwood. *Turkey*. Vol. VI, *The Modern World: A Survey of Historical Forces*. London: Ernest Benn Limited, 1926.

Trumpener, Ulrich. *Germany and the Ottoman Empire, 1914–1918*. Princeton: Princeton University Press, 1968.

Vere-Hodge, Edward R. *Turkish Foreign Policy 1918–1948*. Ambilly-Annemasse: Imprimerie Franco-Suisse, 1950.

von der Osten, Hans Henning, with the collaboration of Richard A. Martin and John A. Morrison. *Discoveries in Anatolia, 1930–31*. Oriental Institute Communications No. 14. Chicago: University of Chicago Press, 1933.

von der Osten, Hans Henning. *Explorations in Hittite Asia Minor, 1927–28*. Oriental Institute Communications No. 6. Chicago: University of Chicago Press, 1929.

———. *Explorations in Hittite Asia Minor, 1929*. Oriental Institute Communications No. 8. Chicago: University of Chicago Press, 1930.

Ward, Barbara. *Turkey*. London, New York, & Toronto: Oxford University Press, 1942.

Ward, Robert E., and Dankwart A. Rustow, eds. *Political Modernization in Japan and Turkey*. Princeton: Princeton University Press, 1964.

Webster, Donald E. *The Turkey of Atatürk: Social Process in the Turkish Reformation*. Philadelphia: The American Academy of Political and Social Science, 1939.

[Yalman], Ahmed Emin. *Turkey in the World War*. New Haven: Yale University Press, 1930.

C. OTHER BOOKS

Addison, James Thayer. *The Christian Approach to the Moslem.* New York: Columbia University Press, 1942.

Adler, Selig. *The Isolationist Impulse: Its Twentieth Century Reaction.* New York: The Free Press, 1966.

Armajani, Yahya. *The Middle East, Past and Present.* Englewood Cliffs, N.J.: Prentice-Hall, 1969.

Arpee, Leon. *A History of Armenian Christianity from the Beginning to Our Own Time.* New York: The Armenian Missionary Association of America, Inc., 1946.

Atamian, Sarkis. *The Armenian Community: The Historical Development of a Social and Ideological Conflict.* New York: Philosophical Library, 1955.

Barton, James L. *Daybreak in Turkey.* Boston: The Pilgrim Press, 1908.

————. *Story of Near East Relief (1915–1930): An Interpretation.* New York: The Macmillan Company, 1930.

Bourne, K., and D. C. Watt, eds. *Studies in International History.* Hamden, Conn.: Archon Books, 1967.

Brown, Philip Marshall. *Foreigners in Turkey: Their Juridical Status.* Princeton: Princeton University Press, 1914.

Bullard, Sir Reader. *Britain and the Middle East from the Earliest Times to 1950.* London: Hutchinson's University Library, 1951.

Busch, Francis X. *Guilty or Not Guilty?* Indianapolis & New York: The Bobbs-Merrill Company, Inc., 1952.

Cooke, Hedley V. *Challenge and Response in the Middle East: The Quest for Prosperity, 1919–1951.* New York: Harper and Brothers, 1952.

Craig, Gordon A., and Felix Gilbert, eds. *The Diplomats, 1919–1939.* Princeton: Princeton University Press, 1953.

Curti, Merle E. *American Philanthropy Abroad: A History.* New Brunswick, N.J.: Rutgers University Press, 1963.

———— and Kendall Birr. *Prelude to Point Four: American Technical Missions Overseas, 1838–1938.* Madison: University of Wisconsin Press, 1954.

Daniel, Robert L. *American Philanthropy in the Near East, 1820–1960.* Athens: Ohio University Press, 1970.

Dennis, Alfred L. P. *Adventures in American Diplomacy, 1896–1906.* New York: E. P. Dutton and Company, 1928.

DeNovo, John A. *American Interests and Policies in the Middle East, 1900–1939.* Minneapolis: University of Minnesota Press, 1963.

Dewey, John. *Characters and Events: Popular Essays in Social and Political Philosophy.* 2 vols. Ed. Joseph Ratner. New York: Henry Holt and Company, 1929.

Eddy, David Brewer. *What Next in Turkey: Glimpses of the American Board's Work in the Near East.* Boston: The American Board, 1913.

Evans, Laurence. *United States Policy and the Partition of Turkey, 1914–1924.* Baltimore: The Johns Hopkins Press, 1965.

Ferrell, Robert H. *American Diplomacy in the Great Depression: Hoover-Stimson Foreign Policy, 1929–1933.* New Haven: Yale University Press, 1957.

————. *Peace in Their Time: The Origins of the Kellogg-Briand Pact.* New Haven: Yale University Press, 1952.

Field, James A., Jr. *America and the Mediterranean World, 1776–1882.* Princeton: Princeton University Press, 1969.

Finnie, David H. *Pioneers East: The Early American Experience in the Middle East.* Cambridge, Mass.: Harvard University Press, 1967.

Fisher, Sydney Nettleton. *The Middle East: A History.* New York: Oxford University Press, 1959.

Fisher, W. B. *The Middle East: A Physical, Social, and Regional Geography.* 3rd ed. London: Methuen and Company, Ltd., 1956.

Frye, Richard N., ed. *Islam and the West*. The Hague: Mouton and Company, 1957.

George, Alexander L., and Juliette L. George. *Woodrow Wilson and Colonel House: A Personality Study*. New York: The John Day Company, 1956.

Gibbons, Herbert Adams. *The Blackest Page of Modern History: Events in Armenia in 1915*. New York & London: G. P. Putnam's Sons, 1916.

Gidney, James B. *A Mandate for Armenia*. Kent, Oh.: Kent State University Press, 1967.

Goodsell, Fred Field. *They Lived Their Faith: An Almanac of Faith, Hope and Love*. Boston: American Board of Commissioners for Foreign Missions, 1961.

———. *You Shall Be My Witnesses*. Boston: American Board of Commissioners for Foreign Missions, 1959.

Gordon, Leland James. *American Relations with Turkey, 1830–1930: An Economic Interpretation*. Philadelphia: University of Pennsylvania Press, 1932.

Hoskins, Halford L. *The Middle East: Problem Area in World Politics*. New York: The Macmillan Company, 1954.

Hovannisian, Richard G. *Armenia on the Road to Independence, 1918*. Berkeley & Los Angeles: University of California Press, 1967.

Howard, Harry N. *The King-Crane Commission: An American Inquiry in the Middle East*. Beirut: Khayats, 1963.

Hurewitz, J. C. *Middle East Dilemmas: The Background of United States Policy*. New York: Harper and Brothers, 1953.

Jackh, Ernst, ed. *Background of the Middle East*. Ithaca, N.Y.: Cornell University Press, 1952.

Kohn, Hans. *Western Civilization in the Near East*. New York: Columbia University Press, 1936.

Latourette, Kenneth Scott. *A History of the Expansion of Christianity*. 7 vols. New York & London: Harper and Brothers, 1937–1945.

Lenczowski, George. *The Middle East in World Affairs*. 3rd ed. Ithaca, N.Y.: Cornell University Press, 1962.

Lerner, Daniel, with the collaboration of Lucille W. Pevsner. *The Passing of Traditional Society: Modernizing the Middle East*. Glencoe, Ill.: The Free Press, 1958.

Macridis, Roy C., ed. *Foreign Policy in World Politics*. Englewood Cliffs, N.J.: Prentice-Hall, Inc., 1958.

Missakian, J. *A Searchlight on the Armenian Question (1878–1950)*. Boston: Hairenik Publishing Company, 1950.

Papazian, Bertha S. *The Tragedy of Armenia: A Brief Study and Interpretation*. Boston & Chicago: The Pilgrim Press, 1918.

Pinkney, David H., and Theodore Ropp, eds. *A Festschrift for Frederick B. Artz*. Durham, N.C.: Duke University Press, 1964.

Powell, E. Alexander. *The Struggle for Power in Moslem Asia*. New York & London: The Century Company, 1923.

Pratt, Julius W. *A History of United States Foreign Policy*. New York: Prentice-Hall, Inc., 1955; 2nd ed., 1965.

Ross, Frank A., C. Luther Fry, and Elbridge Sibley. *The Near East and American Philanthropy*. New York: Columbia University Press, 1929.

Royal Institute of International Affairs. *The Middle East: A Political and Economic Survey*. 2nd ed. London & New York: Royal Institute of International Affairs, 1954.

Rustow, Dankwart A. *Politics and Westernization in the Near East*. Princeton: Center of International Studies, 1956 (a pamphlet).

Sherrill, Charles H. *Mosaics in Italy, Palestine, Syria, Turkey and Greece*. London: John Lane, 1933.

Speiser, Ephraim A. *The United States and the Near East*. Cambridge, Mass.: Harvard University Press, 1947.

266

Stein, Leonard. *The Balfour Declaration.* New York: Simon and Schuster, 1961.
Strong, William E. *The Story of the American Board: An Account of the First Hundred Years of the American Board of Commissioners for Foreign Missions.* Boston, New York, & Chicago: The Pilgrim Press, 1910.
Tashjian, James H. *The Armenians of the United States and Canada.* Boston: Hairenik Press, 1947.
Thomas, Lewis V., and Richard N. Frye. *The United States and Turkey and Iran.* Cambridge, Mass.: Harvard University Press, 1951.
Thornburg, Max W., Graham Spry, and George Soule. *Turkey: An Economic Appraisal.* New York: The Twentieth Century Fund, 1949.
Toynbee, Arnold J. *Survey of International Affairs, 1925.* 3 vols. London: Oxford University Press, 1927–1928.
———. *Survey of International Affairs, 1928.* London: Oxford University Press, 1929.
———, assisted by V. M. Boulter. *Survey of International Affairs, 1936.* London: Oxford University Press, 1937.
——— and R. G. D. Laffan. *Survey of International Affairs, 1938.* 3 vols. London, New York, & Toronto: Oxford University Press, 1941–1953.
de Visscher, Charles. *Theory and Reality in Public International Law.* Trans. by P. E. Corbett. Princeton: Princeton University Press, 1957.
Yale, William. *The Near East: A Modern History.* Ann Arbor: University of Michigan Press, 1958.
Young, T. Cuyler, ed. *Near Eastern Culture and Society: A Symposium on the Meeting of East and West.* Princeton: Princeton University Press, 1951.

D. THESES

Allison, Elizabeth E. "American Participation in the Turkish Settlement, 1918–1920." M.A. thesis, Pennsylvania State College, 1953.
Cook, Ralph E. "The United States and the Armenian Question, 1884–1924." Ph.D. thesis, Fletcher School of Law and Diplomacy, 1957.
Edwards, Rosaline de Gregorio. "Relations Between the United States and Turkey, 1893–1897." Ph.D. thesis, Fordham University, 1952.
Kazdal, Mustafa Nebil. "Trade Relations Between the United States and Turkey, 1919–1944." Ph.D. thesis, Indiana University, 1946.
Kerner, Howard J. "Turco-American Diplomatic Relations, 1860–1880." Ph.D. thesis, Georgetown University, 1948.
Morse, L. Lucile. "Relations Between the United States and the Ottoman Empire." Ph.D. thesis, Clark University, 1924.
Sachar, Howard M. "The United States and Turkey, 1914–1927: The Origins of Near Eastern Policy." Ph.D. thesis, Harvard University, 1953.
Wright, Walter L., Jr. "American Relations with Turkey to 1831." Ph.D. thesis, Princeton University, 1928.

E. JOURNAL ARTICLES

Allen, Henry E. "The Achievements of Atatürk," *Yale Review*, XXVIII (March, 1939), 542–557.
Angell, James B. "The Turkish Capitulations," *American Historical Review*, VI (January, 1901), 254–259.
Brown, Philip Marshall. "The Lausanne Treaty," *American Journal of International Law*, XXI (July, 1927), 503–505.
Bryson, Thomas A. "An American Mandate for Armenia: A Link in British Near Eastern Policy," *Armenian Review*, XXI (Summer, 1968), 23–41.

————. "Walter George Smith and the Armenian Question at the Paris Peace Conference, 1919," *Records of the American Catholic Historical Society of Philadelphia*, LXXXI (March, 1970), 3–26.

————. "Woodrow Wilson and the Armenian Mandate: A Reassessment," *Armenian Review*, XXI (Autumn, 1968), 10–29.

Cohen, Naomi W. "Ambassador Straus in Turkey, 1909–1910: A Note on Dollar Diplomacy," *Mississippi Valley Historical Review*, XLV (March, 1959), 632–642.

Daniel, Robert L. "The Armenian Question and American-Turkish Relations, 1914–1927," *Mississippi Valley Historical Review*, XLVI (September, 1959), 252–275.

————. "The United States and the Turkish Republic Before World War II: The Cultural Dimension," *Middle East Journal*, XXI (Winter, 1967), 52–63.

Davison, Roderic H. "The Armenian Crisis, 1912–1914," *American Historical Review*, LIII (April, 1948), 481–505.

————. "Middle East Nationalism: Lausanne Thirty Years After," *Middle East Journal*, VII (Summer, 1953), 324–348.

DeNovo, John A. "A Railroad for Turkey: The Chester Project, 1908–1913," *Business History Review*, XXXIII (Autumn, 1959), 300–329.

Earle, Edward Mead. "American Missions in the Near East," *Foreign Affairs*, VII (April, 1929), 398–417.

Fenwick, C. G. "The New Status of the Dardanelles," *American Journal of International Law*, XXX (October, 1936), 701–706.

Gordon, Leland J. "The Turkish-American Controversy over Nationality," *American Journal of International Law*, XXV (October, 1931), 658–669.

————. "Turkish-American Treaty Relations," *American Political Science Review*, XXII (August, 1928), 711–721.

Grabill, Joseph L. "Missionary Influence on American Relations with the Near East, 1914–1923," *Muslim World*, LVIII (1968), 43–56 (first installment), 141–154 (conclusion).

Grew, Joseph C. "The Peace Conference of Lausanne, 1922–1923," *Proceedings of the American Philosophical Society*, XCVIII (February, 1954), 1–10.

Hovannisian, Richard G. "The Allies and Armenia, 1915–18," *Journal of Contemporary History*, III (January, 1968), 145–168.

Howard, Harry N. "President Lincoln's Minister Resident to the Sublime Porte: Edward Joy Morris (1861–1870)," *Balkan Studies*, V (1964), 205–220.

————. "The United States and the Problem of the Turkish Straits: A Reference Article," *Middle East Journal*, I (January, 1947), 59–72.

————. "The United States and the Problem of the Turkish Straits: The Foundations of American Policy (1830–1914)," *Balkan Studies*, III (1962), 1–28.

————. "The United States and Turkey: American Policy in the Straits Question (1914–1963)," *Balkan Studies*, IV (1963), 225–250.

Kohn, Hans. "Ten Years of the Turkish Republic," *Foreign Affairs*, XII (October, 1933), 141–155.

Lutz, E. Russell. "Claims Against Turkey," *American Journal of International Law*, XXVIII (April, 1934), 346–349.

Lybyer, Albert Howe. "America's Missionary Record in Turkey," *Current History*, XIX (February, 1924), 802–810.

Thayer, Lucius E. "The Capitulations of the Ottoman Empire and the Question of Their Abrogation As It Affects the United States," *American Journal of International Law*, XVII (April, 1923), 207–233.

Trask, Roger R. "Joseph C. Grew and Turco-American Rapprochement, 1927–1932," in Sydney D. Brown, ed., *Studies on Asia, 1967* (Lincoln: University of Nebraska Press, 1967), pp. 139–170.

————. "The Odyssey of Samuel Insull," *Mid-America*, XLVI (July, 1964), 204–215.

————. "The 'Terrible Turk' and Turkish-American Relations in the Interwar Era," *Historian*, XXXIII (November, 1970), 40–53.

————. "The United States and Turkish Nationalism: Investments and Technical Aid During the Atatürk Era," *Business History Review*, XXXVIII (Spring, 1964), 58–77.

————. "'Unnamed Christianity' in Turkey During the Atatürk Era," *Muslim World*, LV (January, 1965), 66–76 (pt. I), 101–111 (pt. II).

Trumpener, Ulrich. "German Military Aid to Turkey in 1914: An Historical Re-Evaluation," *Journal of Modern History*, XXXII (June, 1960), 145–149.

————. "Liman von Sanders and the German-Ottoman Alliance," *Journal of Contemporary History*, I (1966), 179–192.

————. "Turkey's Entry into World War I: An Assessment of Responsibilities," *Journal of Modern History*, XXXIV (December, 1962), 369–380.

Wright, Walter L., Jr. "The Turkish Crescent Points East and West," *American Scholar*, VII (Summer, 1938), 259–267.

Yale, William. "Ambassador Henry Morgenthau's Special Mission of 1917," *World Politics*, I (April, 1949), 308–320.

Index

✵ Index

Abdul Hamid II: opposition to missionaries, 11; overthrown by Young Turks, 13

Abdul Mejid Effendi, 67

Adivar, Halidé Edib, 90

Admiral Bristol Hospital, *see* American Hospital (Istanbul)

Agreement of February, *1927*: negotiated and terms, 49–51; significance of, 51; Turkish reaction to, 51, 52; U.S. press reaction to, 52; and naturalization convention, 190; establishment and residence problem, 194

Agreements, secret, of World War I, 24

Alexandretta: archaeological work in, 180; dispute over, U.S. interest in, 234–236; Franco-Turkish agreement on, 235

Allied Turkish-American Claims Association, 209

American Board of Commissioners for Foreign Missions (ABCFM): begins work in Turkey, 4; extent of activity by *1914*, 9–10; indemnity, *1901*, 12; officials of support Lausanne Treaty, 41; opinions on Turkish reforms, 70–71; educational work in *1927*, 148; bases for continuing educational work, 150–151; reactions to Bursa case, 155; efforts to reopen schools, 157–158; opinion of gifts tax, 159; dropping of lower school grades, 162; cut in school work, 164–165; report on educational work in *1936*, 168; extent of medical work, 171; cuts medical work, 173; relation between medical work and Christianity, 175; brings

Turkish students to U.S., 181; publications program, 182–183; claims award, 209

American Chamber of Commerce for the Levant, 9

American Collegiate Institute (Istanbul), 159, 160

American Committee Opposed to the Lausanne Treaty: opposes Lausanne Treaty, 38; opposes February, *1927*, agreement, 53; opposes Grew appointment, 56

American Express Company, 131

American Friends of Turkey: organization and activities, 87–89; evaluation of, 89, mentioned, 244

American Hospital (Adana), 171

American Hospital (Istanbul): established, 171; financial problems, 173–174

American Hospital (Talas), 171

American Oriental Bankers Corporation, 134–135

American Red Cross: relief work in Turkey, 183–184, 185

American University of Beirut, 164

Anderson, Francis M.: on claims delegation, 204; relations with Nielsen, 205, 205n56

Arabic numerals, 68

Aras, Tevfik Rüsdü: reaction to defeat of Lausanne Treaty, 47; suggests treaty of amity, 49; and Mouhtar appointment, 62; Grew's opinion of, 71–72; accepts most-favored-nation formula, 109; interest in American loans, 132; and Bursa case, 154; and closed ABCFM schools, 157–158; goals of Robert College, 166; narcotics problem, 176; nationality question, 191; extradition question, 212; and proposed arbitration and conciliation treaties, 220–222; and Kellogg-Briand Pact, 224–225; desire to revise Straits Convention, 228; sets terms for Turkish-American Straits Convention, 231; reaction to Hull's foreign policy statement, 233

Arbitration Treaty: negotiations on, 220–222

Archaeology: American work in Turkey, 177–181

Armenia: King-Crane mandate proposal, 26; Harbord mandate proposal, 26–27; U.S. recognizes, 27; Wilson arbitrates boundary, 27–28; issue in defeat of Lausanne Treaty, 39–40, 43; and *1929* commercial treaty, 113–114

Armenia-America Society, 38

Armenian Relief Committee: founded, 21. *See also* Near East Relief

Armenian-American League of California, 117

Armenian-Americans: reaction to February, *1927*, agreement, 53–54; and nationality problem, 189; and establishment and residence negotiations, 196–197

Armenians: ABCFM *19*th-century work with, 10; persecution in late *19*th century, 11–12; World War I persecutions, 20–21; and "Terrible Turk" stereotype, 83; portrayed in Werfel's novel, 90–91; and American schools, 148; issue in arbitration treaty talks, 221

Atatürk, Kemal: leads nationalist movement, 28; reaction to defeat of Lausanne Treaty, 47; leads reform movement, 66; name bestowed on, 69; nature of dictatorship, 69; praises Boardman and Polando, 85; unfavorable publicity on, 91–92; death, 92; and Turkish nationalism, 128; mentioned, 217

Azariah Smith Memorial Hospital, 171, 173

Bainbridge, Commodore William, 5
Baksheesh, 72
"Balkan Clause," 119

Balkan Pact, 218

Barton, James L., 21

Bayar, Celal: seeks American advisers, 142; quoted on Turkish-American relations, 247

Bell, Charles E., 141

Berry, Burton Y., 214

Biddle, Commodore James, 5

Bitar, George, 191–192

Blacque Bey, 13

Blanton, Rep. Thomas L., 204

Blegen, Carl W.: archaeological work at Troy, 178–179; mentioned, 182

Boardman, Russell, 85

Borah, Senator William E., 113–114

Breslau, 18

Briand, Aristide, 223. *See also* Kellogg-Briand Pact

Bristol, Mark Lambert: appointed Senior Naval Officer, 28; appointed High Commissioner, 29; relations with Ravndal, 29; role at Lausanne, 31, 32–33; comments on Inönü, 31n42; opposes Lausanne negotiations, 34; supports Lausanne Treaty, 41; explanations to Turks on Lausanne Treaty defeat, 46, 48–49; suggests resubmission of Lausanne Treaty, 48; negotiates February, *1927*, agreement, 49–51; comments on Cardashian, 54; ends Turkish appointment, 59–60; efforts to improve Turkish image, 84; heads American Friends of Turkey, 88; founder of American Hospital, 171; and Turkish restrictions on American doctors, 172; heads hospital campaign, 174; and problem of White Russians, 186; and naturalization negotiations, 190; negotiates *1923* claims agreement, 201; service evaluated, 244

Bryan, William Jennings, 220

Bryn Mawr College, 179

Buildings tax, 160–162

Bullitt, William C., 236

Bursa case: discussed, 151–157; Turkish press reaction to, 152–153; causes school inspections, 162

Bursley, Herbert S., 184

Butler, Nicholas Murray, 223

Byzantine Institute of America, 179

Caliphate, 67
Cannon, James, 84
Capitulations: in Treaty of *1830*, 5–6;

abrogation of, 19; disagreement on at Lausanne, 30; attitudes of Americans in Turkey, 42; U.S. *1927* policy on, 48–49; and nationality problem, 189; and establishment and residence negotiations, 197; and arbitration and conciliation negotiations, 222; mentioned, 129

Cardashian, Vahan: dominates American Committee Opposed to the Lausanne Treaty, 38; asks for Lausanne hearing, 48; opposes February, *1927*, agreement, 52–53; opposes Grew selection, 56; opposes Mouhtar appointment, 61–62; opposes Skinner appointment, 77; opposes *1929* commercial treaty, 113–114; objects to Saracoglu mission, 133; reaction to Establishment and Residence Treaty, 199; claims against Turkey, 209–210; mentioned, 243

Carp, Bertha: remarks on Grew's arrival, 58–59

Chester, Admiral Colby M.: founds Ottoman-American Development Company, 14; trip to Turkey, 14; and *1923* concession, 130

Chester concession: efforts in *1909–1913* to secure, 14; issue in Senate Lausanne debate, 39, 40; granted and cancelled, 130; Grew's opinion of, 130

Child, Richard W., 31

Chrome, 104–105

Cincinnati, University of, 178–179

Citizenship, *see* Nationality

Civil War, U.S.: Turkish attitude during, 8–9

Claims, U.S.: origins, 23; *1923* agreement on, 35, 201; provided for in February, *1927*, agreement, 50; issue at Lausanne, 200–201; *1933* position of U.S. on, 201. *See also* Claims Agreement (*1934*)

Claims Agreement (*1934*): discussed, 200–211; negotiations, 202–208; signed and summarized, 208; refund to Turkey, 210–211

Clark, Stanley P., 144–145

Clark, Wallace, 142

Coffin, Henry Sloane, 165

Commerce, Treaty of (*1862*): summarized, 7–8; terminated, 8

Commerce and Navigation, Treaty of (*1830*): summarized, 5–7; secret article, 6–7; issue in establishment and residence talks, 197, 198; issue in arbitration and conciliation talks, 222

Commerce and Navigation, Treaty of (*1929*): discussed, 108–114; Grew's comments on negotiations for, 111; summarized, 112

Commercial policy, Turkish: description of, 95–98

Compensation system: instituted by Turkey, 98; revision of, 124

Conciliation Treaty: negotiations on, 220–222

Connelly, John W., Jr., 204

Copyrights, 183

Cotton, Joseph P., 113–114

Crane, Charles R., 25

Crosby, Sheldon L., 134

Cümhuriyet Halk Partisi, 66

Curtiss-Wright Corporation, 138–139

Davis, James B., 140

Day, Lucille, 152

Dewey, Dr. Albert W., 172

Dewey, John: studies Turkish education, 140; influence on Turkish education, 156

Diplomatic relations, Turkey and U.S.: severed, 21; restored, 50

Dodd, Dr. Wilson F., 172

"Domestic Jurisdiction," 221–222

Dorr, Goldthwaite H., 143–144

Eastern Question, 13–14

Eckford, Henry, 7, 140

Ekrem, Selma, 83

Elkus, Abram I.: *1917* severing of relations, 21; work with American Friends of Turkey, 89

Embassy, American: ambassadors' comments on, 80–82; physical problems, 80–82; site survey, 82

English language: teaching of in Turkish schools, 156

Episcopalian bishops, 38–39

Ertegün, Mehmet Münir: appointed ambassador, 90; and buildings tax question, 161; and claims refund, 210

Essat Bey, 202

Establishment and Residence Treaty (*1931*): Turks suggest talks on, 194; negotiated and significance, 194–200; summarized, 198; mentioned, 156–157

Etatism, 128

Evening Star (Washington), 18–19
Exchange control: initiated by Turkey, 97–98; related to Turkish-American trade, 102–104; and *1939* reciprocal trade agreement, 119–121; *1939–1940* complications, 122–125
Export-Import Bank, 134
Extradition Treaty (*1874*), 211
Extradition Treaty (*1923*), 211–212
Extradition Treaty (*1934*): provided for in February, *1927*, agreement, 50; background and negotiations, 211–214; Senate approval, 213; Turkish ratification, 214
Extradition Treaty, Greek-American, 213

Feis, Herbert, 116
Fez, 67
Figs: early import, 3; U.S. inspection of, 95–96; decline in purchases, 104
Fisk, Pliny, 4
Five Year Plan, Turkish: and U.S. technical experts, 140
Flanders, Ralph E., 100
Ford Motor Company, 137–138
Foreign Policy Association, 42
Foreign Service Personnel Board, 55, 57
Fourteen Points, 24, 227
Fowle, Luther: buildings tax question, 160–161; comments on ABCFM educational work, 168
Fox Brothers International Corporation, 135
Franklin-Bouillon Agreement, 234

Gates, Caleb F.: opinion of Atatürk government, 70; retires, 166
Gerard, James W.: opposes Lausanne Treaty, 38; opposes February, *1927*, agreement, 53; opposes Grew appointment, 56; opposes Mouhtar appointment, 61
Germany: *1914* influence in Turkey, 16, 18; *1939* influence in Turkey, 237–238
Giannini, A. P., 117
Gift tax, 159–160
Gillespie, Julian: opinion of Kemmerer report, 143–144; and claims negotiations, 205
Goeben, 18
Gökalp, Ziya, 128
Gözlü Kule, 179
Goldman, Hetty, 179

"Good Neighbor," 241
Goodsell, Fred F.: analysis of Bursa case, 155; attitude on gifts tax, 159; mentioned, 157
Greece: invades Turkey, 28; and Insull case, 212–213
Greek-Americans: claims against Turkey, 206
Greeks: and American schools, 148; problems of International College, 163
Grew, Joseph Clark: comments on Turkish role at Lausanne, 30; heads Lausanne delegation, 33; opinion of Lausanne Treaty, 35; explanations to Episcopal bishops, 39; opinion of Lausanne opponents, 40; reasons for support of Lausanne Treaty, 42–43; remarks on defeat of Lausanne Treaty, 44; relations with Kellogg, 54–55; appointment as ambassador, 54–59; personal reaction to Turkish appointment, 55; public reaction to his appointment, 55–56; concern about Mouhtar, 60–61, 61–62; comments on Atatürk reforms, 70; opinion of Aras, 71–72; comments on baksheesh, 72; diplomatic career before *1927*, 72–73; general objectives in Turkey, 73; embassy research, 73–74; Shaw's comments on, 74; efforts to dispel "Terrible Turk" image, 84, 85–86; reaction to Boardman-Polando flight, 85–86; urges talks on commercial treaty, 109; opinion on treaty negotiations, 110; concern about Senate action on *1929* treaty, 113; comments on schools and nationalism, 149; reactions to Bursa case, 153–155; problem of closed ABCFM schools, 157–158; reaction to gifts tax settlement, 160; and colleges' administrative and educational policies, 165–166; supports work of American Hospital, 173–174; and narcotics problem, 175–176; evaluation of archaeological work, 178; and problem of White Russians, 185; comments on Turkish formula for establishment and residence, 194–195; statement to İnönü, 197; on signature of establishment and residence treaty, 198–199; and arbitration and conciliation treaty negotiations, 220–222; and Turkish interest in Kellogg-Briand Pact, 223–

225; on Russian influence in Turkey, 225–226; advises against Straits talks, 230; service in Turkey evaluated, 244

Hagia Sophia, 179–180
Hamlin, Cyrus, 10
Harbord, James G., 26
Harbord Report, 26–27
Hart, Albert Bushnell, 83
Haskell, William N., 26
Hatay, Republic of, *see* Alexandretta
Heck, Lewis, 28
Hines, Walker D., 142–143
Hines-Dorr-Kemmerer Report: summarized and importance, 143–144
Hittites: and American archaeological work, 178; role in Turkish historical thesis, 182
Hoover, President Herbert C., 131
Hoover, William H., 87
House, Edward M.: comments on Morgenthau mission, 23; asks FDR to thank Sherrill, 76
Hull, Cordell: disapproves Flanders project, 100; applauds Turkish narcotics program, 177; complaints to, from Nielsen, 205–206; *1937* statement on U.S. foreign policy, 233

Inönü, Ismet: Grew's comments on, 31; Bristol's opinion of, 31*n*42; proposes talks with U.S. at Lausanne, 33; interest in American loans, 132; and gifts tax problem, 160; on work of Robert College, 165; complaints about U.S. claims, 202
"Inquiry," 24
Insull, Samuel: flight to Europe, 212–213; and extradition treaty question, 212–214; arrest in Turkey, 213–214; return to U.S., 214
International College, 163–164
International Labor Office, 185
Isolationism: role in Turkish-American relations, 241–242
Istanbul Woman's College: breaks with ABCFM, 11; and Bursa case, 153; and gifts tax, 159, 160; mentioned, 148
Italy: threats to Turkish security, 227
Izmir: Greeks expelled from, 28; nationalism in, 163; claims originating at disavowed, 206

Jennings, Asa K., 87

Jillson, Jeannie L., 152
Jus sanguinis, 189
Jus soli, 189

Kellogg, Frank B.: comments on Chester concession, 40; *1927* statement on Turkish policy, 50–51; attitude in *1928* on trade negotiations, 109; and arbitration and conciliation treaties, 220–221; initial reaction to Briand plan, 223
Kellogg-Briand Pact: negotiated and signed, 223; Turkish interest in, 223–226; role in Turkish-American relations, 223–227; initial uses and Turkish role, 225–226; effect on Turkish-American relations, 226–227
Kemmerer, Edwin W.: services desired by Turks, 140; work on Turkish economic survey, 143–144
King, Henry C., 25
King, Senator William H.: spokesman for Lausanne opponents, 39–40; asks for hearings on Lausanne Treaty, 48; opposes Grew's confirmation, 57–58; opposes establishment and residence treaty, 199; opposes extradition treaty, 213
King-Crane Commission: origins and conclusions, 25–26; report publication delayed, 26
Knox, Philander C.: dollar diplomacy and the Chester concession, 14

Labor policy, Turkish, 132
Lansing, Robert: argues against capitulations abrogation, 19–20; opposes U.S. mandates in Middle East, 25
Lausanne conference: key questions, 30; U.S. concerns at, 32; relations within U.S. delegation, 32–33; mentioned, 217
Lausanne, Treaty of (Allied-Turkish): general provisions, 31; expiration of establishment provisions, 156
Lausanne, Treaty of (U.S.-Turkish): initial talks, 33; signature and terms, 34–35; Grew's opinion of, 35; evaluation of, 36; submitted to Senate, 37, 37*n*1; opposition to, 37–40; support for, 40–43; reasons for defeat, 43–45; role of politics in defeat of, 44–45; reactions to defeat of, 45–47
Law, Turkish, 68

League of Nations: and Mosul controversy, 218; and Straits question, 228;
discusses Alexandretta problem, 234–
235
Leishman, John G. A., 12
Lindbergh, Evangeline, 86
Lloyd George, David, 25

MacAndrews and Forbes Company, 209
MacArthur, General Douglas, 102
MacMurray, John V. A.: appointed ambassador, 77–78; work in Turkey, 78–
79; opinion of Shaw, 79; comments
on Ankara, 80; comments on Istanbul
embassy, 81; and purposes of American colleges in Turkey, 167; comments
on copyright controversy, 183; and
naturalization negotiations, 193; discussions with Aras on Straits, 231–
232; comments on U.S. influence,
238–239
Maktos, John, 204
Mandates: recommendations at Versailles, 24; King-Crane recommendations, 25–26; Harbord recommendations, 26–27; Senate rejects San Remo
proposal, 27
Manning, William T., 38, 39
Mead, Hunter, 164
Menemencioglu, Numan, 210–211
Middle Eastern Pact, 234
Modus Vivendi (Commercial) of *1926*:
role in U.S. recognition of Turkey, 49;
extended, 50, 108–110
Monroe, Paul, 166
Monroe Doctrine, 13
Montreux convention: discussed, 227–
233; summarized, 229; State Department attitude on, 232
Morgan, J. Pierpont, 173
Morgenthau, Henry: interest in Turkish
neutrality, 18; reaction to abrogation
of capitulations, 19; reaction to Ar-
menian persecution, 20; secret mis-
sion, *1917*, 22–23
Morris, Edward Joy, 8–9
Most-favored-nation principle, 116
Mosul controversy, 218
Mouhtar, Ahmed: appointed ambassador, 60; opposition to appointment,
61–62; retires, 90; sued by Cardashian,
210; and arbitration and conciliation
treaties, 220–221; mentioned, 181
Murray, Wallace: and *1929* commercial

treaty, 113; remarks on establishment
and residence treaty, 199; on claims
refund, 210
Musa Dagh, 90–91

Name reform, 69
Narcotics, 175–177
National treatment, 194–195
Nationalism, Turkish: importance and
role in economic policy, 127–129; and
American schools, 149, 150; and Bursa
case, 151–157; adjustment of American schools to, 167–169; and medical
work, 171–175; historical thesis, 182;
and social, cultural, and philanthropic
activities, 187; influence in Turkish-
American relations, 242–243
Nationality: problem in Turkish-American relations, 189–194; Turkish law,
190–191; problems of Syrians and
Lebanese, 192–193
Naturalization Treaty: abortive talks,
35; factor in defeat of Lausanne
Treaty, 43; new negotiations proposed, 50; failure of negotiations,
192–193
Naturalization Treaty (*1874*), 189–
190
Navy, United States, 230–231
Near East College Association, 163,
163*n*64
Near East Relief: organized, initial activities, 21; role in developing "Terrible Turk" stereotype, 83
Nedjati Bey: Grew's remarks on, 154–
155; death, 155; and closed ABCFM
schools, 157, 158
Neutrality: principle in Turkish-American relations, 240–241
Neutrality Laws (U.S.), 233
Nielsen, Fred K.: appointed head of
claims delegation, 204; relations with
colleagues, 204–205; opinion of U.S.
claims, 205–206; comments on Turkish financial condition, 207; final reports on claims awards, 209; on refund
to Turkey, 210
Notes, Exchange of (February, *1927*),
see Agreement of February, *1927*
Nureddin, Ragip, 181
Nute, Dr. William L., 172
Nye, Senator Gerald P., 101–102

Offley, David: appointed consular com-

mercial agent, 4; merchant in Turkey, 4; treaty negotiator, 5
"Open Door," 32
Oriental Institute of Chicago, 178
Ottoman Public Debt: origins and post–World War I role, 130–131; bondholders protest against Saracoglu mission, 133
Ottoman-American Development Company: founding and early efforts, 14; *1923* concession, 130

Parcel post convention, 96
Parker, Beryl, 88, 144
Parsons, Levi, 4
Polando, John, 85
Porter, Commodore David D.: first minister to Turkey, 12; arranges Eckford hiring, 140

Quotas, trade: established by Turkey, 97; and reciprocal trade negotiations, 119

Raleigh, 101–102
Rapprochement: bases for, 92–93; analyzed, 245–247
Ravndal, G. Bie: appointed commissioner, 29; relations with Bristol, 29
Rearmament, Turkish: Skinner's interest in, 100–101; reasons for, 227
Reciprocal Trade Agreement (*1939*): discussed, 115–122; tariff reductions in, 121–122; reception in U.S., 122
Reciprocal Trade Agreements Act (*1934*): passed, 115; Turkish interest in, 115–116
Red Crescent Society, 183–184
Reed, Cass A., 164
Reed, Senator David A., 57–58
Republican People's Party· role in Turkish reform, 66
Rhind, Charles, 5
Rhodes, Foster, 7
Riggs, Ernest W., 164
Ring, Dorothy, 223
Robert, Christopher, 10–11
Robert College: founded, 10; and Bursa case, 153; and religious activities, 165; Monroe's plans for, 166; mentioned, 148
Robinson, Senator Joseph T., 177
Rockefeller, Laura Spelman, Memorial, 185

Root, Elihu, 220
Rugs, oriental: decline in U.S. purchases, 104; and reciprocal trade agreement, 118–119
Ryndam, 86–87

Saadabad Pact (Middle Eastern Pact), 234, 234n53
San Remo conference, 27
Sanderson, Edith, 152
Saracoglu, Sükrü, 132–133
Schinasi, Morris, 174
Schinasi, Mrs. Morris, 174, 191
Schinasi Hospital, 174
Scipio, Lynn A., 70
Secularization movement (Turkish): bases for, 68; and education, 147–151
Sevki Bey, 202, 207
Sèvres, Treaty of: signing and terms of, 27; and Straits administration, 227–228
Shaw, Gardiner Howland: comments on Grew's work, 74; service in Turkey, 79; work with American Friends of Turkey, 87; receives claims instructions, 201; heads claims delegation, 202; opinion of U.S. claims, 202; and extradition treaty, 213
Shepard, Dr. Lorrin, 172, 172n7
Sherrill, Charles H.: appointed ambassador, 75; work in Turkey, 75–76; efforts to dispel "Terrible Turk" stereotype, 84–85; efforts to expand trade, 98–99; and technical experts, 141; biography of Atatürk, 176; narcotics problem, 176–177; and Hagia Sophia mosaics, 179–180; service evaluated, 244–245
Shotwell, James T., 223
Skinner, Robert P.: appointed ambassador, 76–77; comments on Ankara and Istanbul, 80; urges new embassy, 81; concern over trade relations, 99; attitude on Flanders project, 100–101; interest in Turkish rearmament, 100–101; opinion on Turkey's credit, 131; and question of religious activities at Robert College, 165; relations with Nielsen, 205; and Straits question, 231
Smith, J. Lawrence, 140
Soviet Union: role at Montreux, 228–229
Standard Oil Company: issue in Senate debate on Lausanne Treaty, 39–40;

exchange difficulties, 98; tax troubles, 137

Steinhardt, Laurence A., 82

Stewart, William, 4

Stimson, Henry L.: concern about most-favored-nation formula, 110–111; invokes Kellogg-Briand Pact, 225

Stokes, Anson Phelps, 185, 186

Straits Convention of *1923* (Allied-Turkish), 228

Straits Convention (Turkish-American): proposed, 230–231

Straits question: discussed, 227–233. *See also* Montreux convention

Straus, Oscar S., 14

Students, Turkish: study in U.S., 181–182

Sultanate, 66–67

Swanson, Senator Claude A.: opposition to Lausanne Treaty, 44; opposition to Grew, 58; opposes commercial treaty, 113

Sweden, 23

Taft, President William Howard, 14

Taxes: problem for ABCFM schools, 158–162

Technical experts, American: work in Turkey, 139–145

"Terrible Turk" stereotype: related to *1894–1896* Armenian crisis, 12; role in defeat of Lausanne Treaty, 37; missionary contributions to, 41; factor in U.S. diplomacy and efforts to dispel, 82–92; Turkish efforts to eliminate, 89–92; role in Turkish-American relations, 243–244

Thomas, Lowell, 89

Tobacco: importance in trade, 104; and *1939* reciprocal trade agreement, 118

Topcioglu, Nazmi, 124

Toynbee, Arnold, 229–230

Trade, Turkish-American: products involved, late *19*th century, 9; resumed after World War I, 29–30; statistics

on volume, 105; statistics on imports and exports, 106–107

Trademarks, 95

Troy, 178–179

Truman Doctrine, 247

Turkish Historical Society, 182

Turkish-American Investment Corporation, 135–137

Turkish language: mandatory teaching in, 163

Tyson, Senator Lawrence D., 43–44

Ulen and Company, 134

"Unnamed Christianity": Turkish complaints about, 149–150; as educational objective, 151

Van Siclen, Matthew, 142

Von der Osten, Hans H., 178

Von Papen, Franz, 237, 239

Vorfeld, Robert H., 141

Weber Pasha, 18

Weizmann, Chaim, 22–23

Werfel, Franz, 90–91

Wheeler, Senator Burton K., 44

Wheeler, Everett D., 11–12

White Russians, 184–186

Whittemore, Thomas, 179–180, 182

Wilson, President Woodrow: reasons for not declaring war on Turkey, 22; attitude on Middle East mandates, 25; arbitrates Armenian boundary, 27–28

Women, Turkish, 68

Woodhouse, Henry, 130*n*9

Wright, Walter L., Jr.: and buildings tax, 161; heads colleges, 166–167; mentioned, 182

Yalman, Ahmed Emin: comments on Bristol, 59–60; efforts to purchase arms, 100; comments on reciprocal trade program, 115–116

YMCA, 167–168

"Young Turks," 13

Zionists, 22